SKILFUL SHEPHERDS

And David shepherded them with integrity of heart;
with skilful hands he led them
Psalm 78:72

Dedicated to my wife
DIANNE
who more than fulfils Proverbs 18:22 and 31:10

SKILFUL SHEPHERDS
An introduction to pastoral theology

by
Derek J. Tidball, B.A., B.D., Ph. D.
Minister of Mutley Baptist Church, Plymouth

Inter-Varsity Press

Inter-Varsity Press
38 De Montfort Street, Leicester LE1 7GP

© Derek Tidball 1986

First published 1986

British Library Cataloguing in Publication Data

Tidball, Derek
  Skilful shepherds: an introduction to pastoral
  theology.
  1. Pastoral theology
  I. Title
  253   BV4011

ISBN 0–85110–761–3

Typeset in Great Britain by
Input Typesetting Ltd, London SW19 8DR
Printed in Great Britain by
Billing & Sons Limited, Worcester.

Inter-Varsity Press is the publishing division of the Universities and Colleges Christian Fellowship (formerly the Inter-Varsity Fellowship), a student movement linking Christian Unions in universities and colleges throughout the United Kingdom and the Republic of Ireland, and a member movement of the International Fellowship of Evangelical Students. For information about local and national activities write to UCCF, 38 De Montfort Street, Leicester LE1 7GP.

Contents

Preface

After finishing the manuscript of this book I returned from teaching at the London Bible College to the pastoral ministry. So far I have not found it necessary to recant what I have written! I have written out of a concern that much of our pastoral practice is not sufficiently related to our theological study. The result is that our study of theology often seems irrelevant to the real task before us as ministers, while our ministry is the poorer because we are too busy to reflect more deeply on what we are doing. Theology which is removed from ministry and ministry which is purely pragmatic are both poor servants of the church and even worse masters.

This book is not intended as a complete textbook of pastoral theology. The pastor will find himself disappointed if he hopes to look up every sort of problem or situation he encounters and find the solution here. Even if it were possible to write such a book, I believe it would be out of date as soon as it was published. It is much more by way of a preface to pastoral theology and, if that title had not already been chosen for a seminal work in the field by Seward Hiltner, it might have been an appropriate title for this work. I have sought to provide some of the bones which the pastor himself can flesh out.

It is an evangelical introduction to pastoral theology, because I have sought to find my foundation in Scripture, and a conservative view of Scripture at that. In Part Two I have sought to ask two questions. Firstly, what does Scripture say about pastoral leadership, and secondly, in what ways is Scripture itself a pastoral theology? The works on the first of these questions are already, of course, legion. But the question could not be ignored in this book. The second question is much neglected, although the groundwork for it is already done in much recent biblical scholarship. I believe we have much to learn from the way in which the authors of Scripture themselves approached and answered pastoral issues.

Part Three is historical. I have sought to use church history as a rich quarry from which many valuable insights could be mined. If only the subject were usually taught in the belief that the figures of history were real flesh–and–blood people, rather than conveying the idea that they were all arid theological disputants! Even if church history is not a favourite of yours, I would plead that you look again at and learn from the experience and insight of the pastors of previous ages. I do not think you will be disappointed. The final chapter in this section seeks to bring the picture up to date and to survey recent discussion in pastoral theology. It is far from comprehensive, since that would have required a book in itself, but I have sought to illustrate what is of lasting importance from the contemporary debate.

Part Four is of a different style altogether. Whereas in Parts Two and Three I have tried to be measured and disciplined by scholarship, in Part Four I have allowed myself greater freedom. I have selected five issues that face the church at the present time and mused on them as embryonic illustrations of what I see as pastoral theology. Deliberately I have chosen to use or not to use the different disciplines which contribute to pastoral theology. So one chapter makes use of history, another of sociology, while a third distinguishes the boundaries between pastoral theology and pop psychology and so on. Whatever other ingredients these chapters may have, I trust they will demonstrate that pastoral theology has to do with the interface between experience and truth, the subjective and objective sides of faith, between practice and Scripture. Pastoral theology is the discipline which seeks to bridge the gap between the two.

Some may find the opening chapter somewhat of an academic start. If so, just pass over it and come back to it later if you want to. It is the logical place to start, since it seeks to look at what pastoral theology is and why it is necessary, given present trends. But some people are impatient with discussions of definitions and would rather get on with a discussion of the concrete issues and return to that, if at all, at the end. Fair enough.

I should like to thank those who have helped to write this book. A former colleague of mine at LBC commented that he was always amazed when authors thanked their students for what they had learnt from them, since all he had ever learnt from his students was patience! Suffice it to say that that colleague has now emigrated. I should like to thank my students who grappled with at least some of this material and who taught me more than patience. I was enabled to write much of the book while on sabbatical leave from LBC, for which I was grateful not only to the Board of Governors but also to my colleagues who took on extra work to cover for me, and to my secretary there, Marilyn Wagnell, who had to put up with extra pressures because of an absent Director of Studies. The editors at IVP have been a great help and encouragement. More than all I would like to thank my wife, to whom the work is dedicated. She learnt typing in order to assist me in my writing and was almost immediately made redundant by a word processor. But she will never be redundant as far as love and encouragement go.

My favourite picture of pastoral ministry, outside of Scripture, comes from Chrysostom. (Not again, I hear my students say!) He spoke of the way in which no unskilled person would ever be asked to pilot a merchant vessel through the obstacles into harbour, laden as it would be with valuable cargo. How much more foolish it is, he argued, to ask an unskilled person to pilot the church through difficult waters, laden as it is with cargo of eternal value. If that picture spoke to Chrysostom's own day, it speaks volumes to ours. My prayer is that, like David, we may shepherd the church with integrity of heart and lead them with skilful hands.

DEREK J. TIDBALL

Abbreviations

AB	*Anchor Bible*
A-NCL	*Ante-Nicene Christian Library*
Black's *NTC*	Black's *New Testament Commentaries*
BST	*Bible Speaks Today*
CC	Calvin's *Commentaries*, edited by D. W. and T. F. Torrance
CGTC	*Cambridge Greek Testament Commentaries*
ECW	*Early Christian Writings*, translated by M. Staniforth
EQ	*Evangelical Quarterly*
ICC	*International Critical Commentary*
Interp.	*Interpretation*
JBL	*Journal of Biblical Literature*
JPT	*Journal of Psychology and Theology*
LCC	*Library of Christian Classics*
LW	Luther's *Works*
NCB	*New Century Bible*
NICNT	*New International Commentary on the New Testament*
NICOT	*New International Commentary on the Old Testament*
NIDNTT	*New International Dictionary of New Testament Theology*, edited by C. Brown
NIGTC	*New International Greek Testament Commentary*
Nov.T	*Novum Testamentum*
NP-NF	*Nicene and Post-Nicene Fathers*
NTS	*New Testament Studies*
OTL	*Old Testament Library*
SNTS	Society for New Testament Studies
TDNT	*Theological Dictionary of the New Testament*, edited by G. Kittel
TNTC	*Tyndale New Testament Commentaries*
TOTC	*Tyndale Old Testament Commentaries*
WBC	*Word Biblical Commentary*

INITIAL ORIENTATION

1

What is pastoral theology?

Pastoral theology has something of the character of an octopus. Anyone wishing to grapple with it should be warned that initially he may well find himself in the predicament of a deep-sea diver who, all unwillingly, gets entangled with it. Although the concerns of pastoral theology are widely distributed it remains a rare delicacy on theological menus and is largely unencountered except by those who have plunged to the depths. Like the octopus, it leaves many puzzled as to its exact nature. It too can vary in size from the tiny and trivial to the massive and weighty; its arms seem to extend in eight directions at once and its colour changes from the moral and traditional to the complexion of an *avant-garde* science. No wonder it causes bewilderment!

THE URGENT NEED FOR PASTORAL THEOLOGY

For most of this century pastoral theology has been in the doldrums. At the start of the century it had largely degenerated from being a serious theological discipline to not much more than handy tips on 'how to' practise the ministry. The multitude of simple techniques were valuable as far as they went, but as society changed they became more and more unsatisfying and, in any case, they left the pastor theologically undernourished.

In the mid-twentieth century behavioural and social sciences seemed to mount a rescue bid by providing pastoral theology with the theoretical framework which had previously been missing. Whilst that attempted rescue was of some value it was not without complications and it took a heavy toll on the spiritual and theological elements of pastoral theology. Many questioned if in the end there was much that was distinctively different from a secular approach to the social sciences.

At long last, however, there are some signs of a revival.[1] It

[1] E.g., A. V. Campbell, *Rediscovering Pastoral Care*; T. C. Oden, *Pastoral Theology: Essentials*

is a revival which is urgently needed. The momentous changes of the twentieth century, especially since the Second World War, with all their consequences for the church have left many a pastor, who entered the ministry with a clear vision and high ideals, battered, confused and disorientated. Six factors have contributed to this disorientation.

Firstly, the pastoral role has been superseded. Most of what the clergyman, as the only educated person in a parish, traditionally used to do has long since been transferred to other professions. It is a long time since he has acted as an officer of the law, or of health, a teacher or a local government administrator. Much more recently the task of caring has been given into the hands of other professionals. The advent of the secular therapist and the explosion of the social services have been a profound threat to the minister who so often has been made to feel an amateur among professionals, with little to contribute to the problems of the real world. For this, and other reasons, Anthony Russell has concluded that, 'At all levels in the Church there is an awareness that the ministry is passing through not just a period of temporary uncertainty but a profound crisis.'[2] He is now in a marginal position in society with skills, expertise and perspectives which 'have no market value'.[3]

The response of some has been to seek to equip themselves with just the sort of professional expertise which has a market value and which would place them back in the mainstream of society – even to the extent of leaving the ministry in order to fulfil their ministries. It is easy to understand why, with inadequate pastoral theology, this should have appeared such an attractive option. In the long term, however, such an accommodation to modern society must prove counter-productive.[4]

Secondly, pastoral imagery is outdated. To see the minister as analogous to a shepherd made a great deal of sense in a world which was basically composed of rural communities. It provided a familiar picture which enabled so much about the

---

of Ministry; M. H. Taylor, *Learning to Care, Christian Reflection on Pastoral Practice*. (Full bibliographical details are given in the Bibliography, pp. 339 ff.)

[2] A. Russell, *The Clerical Profession*, p. 262.

[3] *Ibid.*, pp. 281f.; R. Towler and A. P. M. Coxon, *The Fate of the Anglican Clergy*, pp. 187–205.

[4] A. D. Gilbert, *The Making of Post-Christian Britain*, pp. 102–158.

minister's role and relationships to be spoken of in a condensed analogy. Today, however, we live in a world dominated by urban societies and technological world-views. Sheep and shepherds are unfamiliar sights and the details of the analogy no longer communicate. The change of social structure affects us more deeply than we recognize. It is not only that we are unfamiliar with farms and sheep; it is that we no longer think in such personal and natural terms. We impose a scientific and rational framework on our world and approach its problems no longer as great mysteries but as mere problems to be solved through technological advance. We can cope with a therapist, an analyst or a counsellor, but a pastor sounds quaint and old-fashioned.

Thirdly, the pastoral structures of the church are outmoded. In the days prior to the upheavals produced by the industrial revolution it seemed an adequate approach to divide England into a number of parishes and to ensure that through adequate staffing in each place the spiritual needs of the nation would be well met. That, at least, was the theory! In support it could be claimed that, whatever the reality of personal belief, most people would be found at church and virtually everyone was within its orbit. The industrial revolution imposed severe strains on the parochial system and subsequent shifts in population have made it even more problematic; so much so that Leslie Paul's researches into the inflexibility of the parochial system have led him to state emphatically that the parochial system is now entirely inappropriate.[5]

This conclusion that the present arrangement is inappropriate should not be reached on the ground of management studies alone. More significantly, the parochial system is inappropriate because it is built on the presupposition that the nation is a Christian nation and all that needs to happen is that the sheep need to be penned. But as the official statement of the National Evangelical Anglican Congress (1977) declared, 'We are keenly aware that the church is no longer a pastoral institution in a largely Christian country, but rather a minority in a missionary situation.'[6]

Free churches may have been exempt from the bureaucratic problems imposed by a parochial system but they have not

[5] L. Paul, *The Deployment and Payment of the Clergy* and *A Church by Daylight*.
[6] *The Nottingham Statement*, p. 6.

necessarily been exempt from a similar parochial mentality. Commenting over a century ago on nonconformists, the Congregational preacher R. W. Dale said that, 'The parable of the leaven contains their conception of the normal growth of the Christian church.'[7] The quiet influencing of family and friends, of those who were already within the church's sphere of influence was all that was sufficient for the spiritual well-being of the nation.

In practice this conception of steady growth led to no growth and many dissenting churches were insular ghettos until awakened by the Evangelical Revival. The same danger is still apparent. Today any pastoral theology, if it is to be adequate to meet the needs of the contemporary church, must take into account the missionary situation in which it exists and which renders the present pastoral structure of the church entirely inadequate. Pastoral theology must concern itself not only with the penning of existing sheep but with the birth of more sheep.

Fourthly, the pastoral office is under fire. The church itself is in the ferment of change. Quite apart from the emergence of new independent groups outside the mainline denominational structures, many within the denominational structures are also seeking different pastoral arrangements. The idea of a 'one-man-ministry' is being questioned. Many would say it was both unbiblical and responsible for a good deal of the stresses imposed on men in the ministry. There has therefore been a rediscovery of ministry as the activity of the whole body of the church and not just its leaders. In addition to this, more support for the pastor is being sought both within the local fellowship, often in terms of forming an eldership or similar body, and outside the local fellowship in terms of wider alliances and the revival of the idea of apostleship.

This ferment takes place against the background of a widespread questioning of institutional authority. The 1960s dispelled the idea that the possession of a title or office was sufficient to make others accept what you say without further questioning. Authority has now to be earned and verified by personal experience rather than by institutional labels.

Fifthly, the pastoral approach is considered old-fashioned. If pastoral theology may be loosely and provisionally defined as

---

[7] R. W. Dale, *The Evangelical Revival*, p. 14.

the application of Christian truth to pastoral situations, it raises the question of the status of truth. Recent critiques of our society have argued that the concept of truth is no longer significant. What is more important is not whether it *is* true but whether it *seems* to be true or *becomes* true for them. How easy it is to believe and whether it appears to work are the criteria on which people base belief. 'The question of whether the group's belief is actually true or not may never become an issue.'[8]

The church has by no means been unaffected by this attitude to truth. Among its members, as much as among the wider society, plausibility and pragmatism determine what is accepted. This has proved a disastrous road pastorally but many still eagerly follow it. One of the urgent tasks required of pastoral theology is to provide a better foundation for building lives and churches than this flimsy and fickle option.

Sixthly, pastoral boundaries are being blurred. This particular cause of disorientation is hard to grasp because it is expressed in so many diverse forms. It stems from the growing recognition that God is not confined to work only in and through the church and truth is not to be found exclusively within the church's boundaries. As creator, God is capable of working in his world and communicating truth outside the church. At first sight this seems to restore a biblical doctrine of creation to its proper place. But when taken to extremes it leads to a total blurring of distinctions between the church and the world; to statements such as 'the world must set the agenda for the church'; to a belief in anonymous Christians and a view that forms of secular liberation are synonymous with a Christian view of salvation.[9]

Within pastoral theology the same tendencies are apparent. J. A. Whyte, for example, wrote recently that, 'To confine the data of practical theology to the practice of the Church, or to the practices of religion, may still be unduly restrictive of its scope.'[10] If, he argued, what happened outside the church had any theological significance to it, as he believed it had, that too must become the subject-matter of pastoral theology. The old idea that the pastor is exclusively the servant of the elect, called out from the world, is therefore to be rejected.

[8] O. Guinness, *The Gravedigger File*, p. 35. Also P. L. Berger, B. Berger and H. Kellner, *The Homeless Mind*, pp. 62–67.

[9] For evangelical expositions and responses to these ideas see P. Cotterell, *The Eleventh Commandment*, pp. 9–16 and H. T. Hoekstra, *Evangelism in Eclipse*.

[10] J. A. Whyte, 'New Directions in Practical Theology', *Theology* 76 (1973), p. 235.

No attempt has been made here to explore fully the issues which have been raised. The point rather has been to highlight these as issues which have unsettled the ministry, for good or ill, with the result that there is an urgent need to provide new theological foundations for the pastoral task. A re-examination of pastoral theology which takes place against the background outlined needs to be high on our agendas.

HOW IS PASTORAL THEOLOGY TO BE DEFINED?

It is possible to know that something is needed without being able to define exactly what that something is. Pastoral theology is an elusive and complex discipline, but some attempt must be made to define it. Part of its elusiveness stems from the multitude of labels which exist in this area and which seem to be used without any agreement as to their exact meaning or relationship, such as, practical theology, pastoral theology, pastoralia, applied theology, a theology of pastoral care and pastoral counselling. Equally, part of the elusiveness of pastoral theology stems from the fact that so many sub-disciplines of practical theology are spoken of as if they are pastoral theology itself. To return to the octopus with which this chapter began, these would seem, to the present writer, to be the 'arms' of the creature but not its essential body. Five such arms may be identified.

The first arm is the study of church order. New Testament scholars and early church historians combine with practical theologians to examine the nature and form of the church. In particular much attention is given to a discussion of offices and the role of bishops, priests and deacons. The authority of the church over its members, relationships between one church and another, and the relationship between charismatic and institutional authority are all considered. T. M. Lindsay,[11] B. H. Streeter[12] and K. E. Kirk[13] have written works which by now have become classics in any discussion of this area. But much has been done recently to push the discussion back into the

[11] T. M. Lindsay, *The Church and the Ministry in the Early Centuries.*
[12] B. H. Streeter, *The Primitive Church: studied with special reference to the origins of the Christian Ministry.*
[13] K. E. Kirk, *The Apostolic Ministry.*

realms of New Testament scholarship[14] and to apply the insights of contemporary sociology to the discussion.[15] Such study is a necessary adjunct to pastoral theology but it does not itself constitute pastoral theology.

A second arm comes closer to the heart of pastoral theology. T. C. Oden has recently defined pastoral theology as 'that branch of Christian theology that deals with the office and functions of the pastor'.[16] Later he adds the 'gifts' of the pastor to his definition and that pastoral theology 'seeks to reflect upon the self-disclosure of God witnessed to by the Scripture, mediated through tradition, reflected upon by critical reasoning and embodied in personal and social experience'.[17] Oden's work is excellent. It fulfils his stated aims and provides a thorough foundation from Scripture and tradition for the practical operations of the pastoral ministry today. Its concerns are with ordination, leading worship, preaching, celebrating the sacraments, visitation, the sick, the poor and the dying. Nonetheless it is still lacking if it claims to be a full-orbed pastoral theology, firstly because it is so completely tied to the ordained ministry and secondly because it starts primarily from the function of the ministry. Both of these lead to a restricted form of pastoral theology which, if it is to be adequate, must cater for more than simply what the minister does and must include the wider pastoral dimension of the life of the church.

Oden's work has the merit of being built on substantial theological foundations. But in the past this arm of pastoral theology has often lacked these foundations and degenerated into a series of handy tips for ministers of the 'never visit a parishioner on a Monday morning because it's washing day' variety!

A third arm also focuses on the pastoral ministry but concentrates on the questions of management and leadership. Delegation, the management of change and conflict, planning for growth, communication, group dynamics and so on are all topics of vital concern and excellent insights have been offered

---

[14] *E.g.,* J. D. G. Dunn, *Unity and Diversity in the New Testament*, pp. 103–123; E. Käsemann, *Essays on New Testament Themes*; J. H. Schütz, *Paul and the Anatomy of Apostolic Authority*

[15] *E.g.,* L. Grollenberg *et al., Minister? Pastor? Prophet?*; B. Holmberg, *Paul and Power*; G. Theissen, *The Social Setting of Pauline Christianity*, pp. 27–54.

[16] Oden, *Pastoral Theology*, p. x

[17] *Ibid.*, p. 311.

which the church cannot afford to ignore.[18] Even so it must be insisted that these are not in themselves what we mean by pastoral theology. They are the insights of modern management sciences and, like some dresses, where they fit they do so by accident rather than design. Certainly a case can sometimes be made out for there being biblical precedents or even principles behind the insights. Moses, for example, learnt the principle of delegation (Ex. 18) through hard experience. But since the Bible is not a management textbook, and not intended to be in the modern sense, it is often a case of reading back into the text what is presumed to be there. Essential therefore as such investigation is, it is unwise to claim it to be the sole legitimate subject-matter of pastoral theology.

A fourth arm, which has held sway in recent years, is in danger of completely identifying pastoral theology with pastoral counselling. This image has been cultivated in some circles by the close relationship with psychology and other human sciences, all of which have the advantage of providing a professional apparatus for the pastor. Michael Taylor has given a number of reasons for objecting to this identification. Pastoral care is so often undertaken by lay folk and very rarely takes place in the hands of a trained specialist. It involves a whole range of skills, few of which could be correctly labelled as counselling, and pastoral care is as much interested in a person's strengths as his problems.[19] If that is true of pastoral care, it is even more so of pastoral theology. To make it a specialist problem-centred discipline is to be over-selective and not to share the balanced biblical perspective on the pastoral role.

A fifth arm more nearly equates pastoral theology with moral theology or Christian ethics. The tradition is represented by V. A. Demant and Martin Thornton. In his inaugural lecture to the University of Oxford in 1950 Demant was critical of much Christian ethics for losing its theological roots and devaluing the word 'Christian' by reducing its meaning to little more than 'well-being'. 'The uprush of darker forces' which the world then faced meant that, of all the claims on pastoral theology, the

[18] *E.g.*, T. W. Engstrom and E. R. Dayton, *The Art of Management for Christian Leaders*; E. Gibbs, *I Believe in Church Growth*; P. F. Rudge, *Management in the Church*; L. Schaller, *The Change Agent*.
[19] Taylor, *Learning to Care*, pp. 14–18.

construction of a moral foundation and the development of Christian spirituality were to be paramount. True, Demant wished to cast the net wider and to include, for example, apologetics, but this was to serve as the core of the discipline.[20]

Martin Thornton similarly wrote,

> We conclude from this that ascetical theology, with moral theology as its correlate, is the true core of pastoral practice, and in view of the extraordinary range of subjects which creep in under the head of pastoral theology, this needs stating very clearly and very firmly.[21]

Subsequently Thornton offered a more precise definition in which pastoral theology was an 'adaptation of doctrine by the pastor in the general oversight of the flock' and what he had previously stated to be the 'core of pastoral practice' was now labelled 'applied or ascetical theology'.[22] Even so his emphasis on spirituality as the central theme of the discipline remained evident.

It is clear, then, that there is no consensus on the essential nature of pastoral theology. It would help to dispel the confusion if the term 'practical theology' or 'applied theology' was reserved as an umbrella term to refer to all the areas mentioned above, plus others such as homiletics, which is often over-identified with pastoral theology.[23] All these areas where theology is applied can make equal claims on the title. Pastoral theology should not be used as an umbrella term but should also be reserved for one aspect of practical or applied theology – an aspect which, nonetheless, is right at the heart of applied theology.

In 1958 Seward Hiltner proposed what has become a classic definition of pastoral theology. He wrote,

> Pastoral theology is defined here as that branch or field of theological knowledge and inquiry that brings the shepherding perspective to bear upon all the operations and functions of the church and minister, and then draws

---

[20] V. A. Demant, *The Responsibility and Scope of Pastoral Theology Today*.

[21] M. Thornton, *Pastoral Theology: A Reorientation*, p. 6.

[22] M. Thornton, *The Function of Theology*, p. 37.

[23] E.g., W. G. T. Shedd, *Homiletics and Pastoral Theology*; E. Thurneysen, *A Theology of Pastoral Care*.

conclusions of a theological order from reflection on these observations.[24]

This definition has several merits. The essence of pastoral theology must not be a particular function of the ministry but a 'shepherding perspective' which affects one's perception of the whole pastoral task and the content in which that task is pursued. Secondly, as Hiltner himself observes, this definition ensures that pastoral theology is seen as a theology in its own right. What he does not stress, and what in practice he sometimes appears to have forgotten, is that the foundation of the discipline is therefore theology not contemporary social sciences.[25] Thirdly, it stresses the close interaction between theology and pastoral experience and the way in which experience must lead to theological reflection.

The definition is not however without problems. James Lapsley has criticized it for its perspectival approach, saying that such an approach implies that it is only a way of looking at something and that it lacks the integrity of a discipline which has its own data. Furthermore he points out that 'shepherding' has unfortunate overtones now of 'ruling' because of developments in Catholic theology[26] (and one might now add because of recent developments in some parts of the renewal movement too). However, these objections are not all that convincing. It is the lack of a pastoral perspective which is the precise problem of so much recent theology. To complain that it does not thereby become a serious academic discipline, in the sense in which Lapsley means, is to worship at the altar of academic pride at the expense of adequately training pastors for the real task. True, the word 'shepherding' is problematic, but even so its roots can be uncovered and it is not now so marred as to be incapable of further usefulness.

The more serious problem lies in making the 'operations and functions of the church and minister' the starting-point. The consequence of this is that it sits too loose to the theology to which it claims to be related. If one starts purely from this inductive position then it leads to a selective and inadequate theology. To observe and reflect on pastoral experience and

[24] S. Hiltner, *Preface to Pastoral Theology*, p. 20.
[25] See J. L. Adams and S. Hiltner, *Pastoral Care in the Liberal Churches*, pp. 111f.
[26] W. B. Oglesby Jnr (ed), *The New Shape of Pastoral Theology*, p. 43.

to draw theological conclusions from that alone will limit the observer to his own individual, subjective and narrow perspective. Without in any way losing the insistence upon the 'groundedness' of pastoral theology one must insist that the anchor point of theology itself must be much more significant than Hiltner admits. The basic problem with Hiltner's definition is that it opens the door to pastoral theology being so relativized that the pastor, in the end, loses his authority as one called of God. At best it leads to *ad hoc* theology.

Carl Kromminga has vigorously expressed the objection in these terms:

> The functional approach, however, limits the definition of the discipline exactly at its most crucial point, the *theological* level. The functional approach cannot define the nature of theology which is supposed to ask questions and get answers of a theological order from an inspection of ministerial operations . . . The first business of this area of study is not to examine the operations but to establish what the valid operations are in the light of the sources, standards and objectives of these operations. Only a clear view of the sole authority of Holy Scripture in theological science can save this area of theological study from historical relativism, for only Scripture can give an absolute norm for judging the validity of the empirically perceived ministerial functions.[27]

A recent example may illustrate the point. Michael Taylor's stimulating book, in which his sensitive pastoral abilities are evident, propounds a view of pastoral care in which 'a fixed notion of orthodoxy' is rejected. What makes pastoral care distinctively Christian, he claims, is that 'we have taken faith deliberately into account'.[28] It must be a faith which is informed by dialogue between the Christian and his Lord and with the Christian community. The Bible, as a very early and especially interesting collection of documents that bears witness to Jesus, is a useful resource in informing our decisions. But it is not different in kind from a number of other resources which are available.

---

[27] From the Introduction to S. Volbeda, *The Pastoral Genius of Preaching*, no pagination. See also R. S. Anderson (ed), *Theological Foundations for Ministry*, p. 7.
[28] Taylor, *Learning to Care*, p. 35.

Taylor does not dismiss doctrine as unimportant. Indeed he shows, in an imaginative way, how relevant doctrine is to numerous pastoral situations. But the question as to how to determine what is correct doctrine is left unresolved. He rejects all reference to any final arbiter which can tell us what is right and welcomes pluralism as a positive means of resolving our problems.[29] Besides doctrine, his approach is to reflect on stories which are often built around key words or images, such as T. S. Eliot's *Four Quartets*. This use of contemporary imagination may well illuminate a pastoral problem and lead to its resolution.[30] None of this enables us to know, however, whether our pastoral care is a fundamental and effective cure or whether it is just a placebo, a temporary palliative or even a dangerous drug which, whilst inducing pleasant sensations for the moment, leads to even worse problems in the long-term.

With Eduard Thurneysen, we would wish to conclude that the pastoral theology which must be practised is one in which 'the Word of God retains its self-sufficiency' and that it must stand over against man and be his teacher, resisting every attempt by man to avoid being its pupil, whatever form that resistance may take.[31]

Pastoral theology, then, properly relates to the interface between theology and Christian doctrine on the one hand, and pastoral experience and care on the other. As such it is found to be a discipline in tension. It is not theology in the abstract, but theology seen from the shepherding perspective. The shepherding perspective may well inform and question the theology but more fundamentally the theology will inform and question the work of the shepherd and that relationship must not be reversed. This will give the pastoral dimension of the life of the church a secure starting-point and will prevent it from going off at all sorts of tangents.

If this is accepted, a number of more precise questions follow as examples of the subject-matter of the discipline. What is the nature and goal of pastoral work? Do the Scriptures and theology give any insights into how that pastoral task is to be conducted? What insights are there into the relationship between objective Christian truth and subjective Christian experience; between doctrine and particular pastoral issues or

[29] *Ibid.*, pp. 42–58.   [30] *Ibid.*, pp. 59–72.
[31] Thurneysen, *Theology of Pastoral Care*, p. 31.

24

problems? These are the basic questions which will be addressed in the subsequent chapters of this book.

THE NEED FOR DOCTRINE

Frederic Greeves wrote in the opening paragraphs of his *Theology and the Cure of Souls* of a conviction that 'all men, both as "sheep" and as "shepherds" need Christian doctrine, to a far greater extent than is now commonly recognised', even though that was not all they needed.[32] Such a conviction is shared in this book. Christian doctrine is even more disregarded now than it was when Greeves wrote in 1960. So often we fail to see that there is any connection between what we practise and the truth we believe. Even if we believe such a connection exists we are not sure how to make it.

James Whyte gives an illuminating example of just this disconnectedness. He describes speaking at a ministers' fraternal on the subject of confirmation where the assembled ministers argued strongly for a high view of confirmation, claiming that the Holy Spirit was conferred on the confirmees by such a service. But later in their conversation they turned to confront the problem of how the youngsters confirmed by the church could be kept within its fellowship. The ministers concerned all experienced a high drop-out rate. One minister commented, 'I have a gymnasium, and they are not allowed to come and use the gymnasium unless they come to communion. I keep hold of them through that.' Whyte's perceptive reply was to say, 'Friends, you do not believe in the gift of the Holy Spirit in confirmation. You cannot believe in it, because your whole experience runs contrary to that belief. You believe in the power of the gymnasium but not in the power of the Holy Spirit.'[33]

The problem is a common one even if we would not speak of it in the context of the sacrament of confirmation or would use different means to hold people within the church circle. And the same guilty exposure of our failure to fit our experience with our doctrine could be made. Our evangelism, pastoral care and church relationships are often dictated by pragmatic reasonings at the expense of any doctrinal understanding.

The divorce we have created between theology and practice

[32] F. Greeves, *Theology and the Cure of Souls*, p. 1.
[33] Whyte, 'New Directions', p. 238.

has led to major problems within the church which few can handle and only some can contain. If there are divisions within a church, how are they to be settled? If the Christian leader is caught practising adultery, how is he to be treated? If people suffer, how is that to be interpreted? If keen believers find that their Christian work leads not to a spiritual carefreeness but to their feeling that they are burdened and exhausted, what have we to say? Who should exercise authority in the church? How do we handle the experience of severe doubts? These and a host of others are questions which we have for so long answered pragmatically rather than theologically. If we have gone beyond the pragmatic it has probably been to exhort people to hold on or try harder. There is a place for such exhortation, but we have resorted to it far more than the Bible does. It is often forgotten that before Romans 12:1–2 Paul spends eleven chapters laying the foundation on which the exhortation is based. Often we are so eager for the answers that we exhort people to build on much too flimsy a foundation or on none at all. Such an approach may lead to an unhealthy activism or to a pious moralism, but neither of these square with true Christian experience.[34]

No-one has more adequately expounded the vital relationship between Christian doctrine and experience than Dr Martyn Lloyd-Jones. When he preached on Ephesians 4:17 he concentrated on the 'therefore' and explained the relationship between doctrine and practice.[35] He rebuked those in his congregation who felt relieved because they had now come to the applied part of the epistle and could leave the doctrine behind. He demonstrated how even in this second half of the epistle, which we generally consider to be the less theological, Paul is never content to speak in merely practical terms. Even here each practical issue is an application of a spiritual truth. Thus in 4:17–24 certain standards of behaviour are required because we are entirely new creatures in Christ. In 5:3–17 certain patterns of behaviour are to be rejected because, as is stated in verses 1 and 2, we are children of God. 5:18–21 lays down the doctrinal principle about the control of Spirit out of which teaching regarding relationships arises in 5:22 – 6:9.

Paul is shown to be a careful teacher who never leaves

---

[34] See further, R. Lovelace, *Dynamics of Spiritual Life*, p. 214.

[35] D. M. Lloyd-Jones, *Darkness and Light*, pp. 11–24. The whole work is an outstanding example of good pastoral theology.

anything to chance and is not content simply to enunciate principles without applying them. 'The Christian life is not a mere general philosophy: it is that but it does not stop at that! It is a life to be lived, and it is a life to be lived in particular details.'[36] Not even the most practical of matters is dealt with except in the light of doctrine. The Christian life is not a set of codes of conduct, morals or ethics to which we must conform. Rather it is something which inevitably arises out of what we believe. Doctrine helps to provide us with the 'why'. Sadly so much preaching, teaching or pastoral care never tells us 'why', because it is too concerned with telling us 'how' or 'what'.

From this, Dr Lloyd-Jones argues that, 'Failure in the living of the Christian life, therefore, must ultimately result from a failure somewhere or other to understand the doctrine and the truth'.[37] His own pastoral experience led him to believe that the biggest failures in the Christian life were those who decried doctrine and boasted that they were practical men. There was nothing more fatal than to adopt such a position.

The implication for many in the ministry is that we so often aim at the wrong targets. We make direct appeals to the will of people, whereas the will needs to be approached indirectly through the mind and heart: 'You do not appeal to the will of people to make them holy; instead you get them to understand the doctrine. It is not a matter of decision, it is a matter of understanding.'[38] Such a view stands as a radical critique of our contemporary approach to pastoral theology and stresses, once more, the need for a reconsideration of the field. That such a critique is unfashionable in the present context where the emphasis is on the practical, the subjective and the human, should not deter us from trying to engage in a more biblical approach to pastoral theology. Indeed the poverty of so much Christian experience which has resulted from its absence should serve as a powerful incentive. There is an urgent need to recover confidence in Christian truth and its power to change lives.

[36] *Ibid.*, p. 17.   [37] *Ibid.*, p. 21.   [38] *Ibid.*, p. 22.

SUMMARY

We began by reviewing the dilemmas and unrest facing the ministry which would suggest that the time is ripe for further study in the area of pastoral theology. Both external circumstances and internal developments have left many pastors bewildered about their role and relationships. But if help is to be given we need to ask what pastoral theology is.

At this point we tried to provide an elementary map to enable people to get their bearings through the related disciplines and confusing terminology. We concluded that pastoral theology was not a comprehensive title for all sorts of practical applications of theology, but was the restricted discipline that lay at the heart of practical theology and dealt with the relationship between doctrine and practice in both the ministry itself and in the pastoral task generally. It was the shepherding perspective which, whilst it took full account of experience and the pastoral function, nonetheless had its roots in doctrine.

Recognizing that few Christians today believe doctrine to be of much consequence, an attempt was made to suggest that it was more vital than we often think. The divorce between our stated beliefs and our pastoral practice was exposed, and the failure of superficial pragmatism and shallow exhortation was pointed out. The undergrowth has been cleared and the ground is now prepared for a fresh approach to pastoral theology which takes the biblical relationship between doctrine and behaviour more seriously.

BIBLICAL FOUNDATIONS

2

The Old Testament

THE MINISTRY OF GOD

When Jacob reflected on his relationship with God at the end of his eventful life he spoke of 'the God who has been my Shepherd all my life to this day' (Gn. 48:15). This was quite a claim for a man who had known such mixed fortunes in life, even if much of the misfortune had been self-inflicted. Yet it was an affirmation about God to which not only Jacob but all the people of God in the Old Testament would gladly have assented.

It was rare for them to speak of God as 'the Shepherd'. Genesis 49:24; Psalms 23:1 and 80:1 are the only other direct references to him by this name; but the evidence that they saw God as their shepherd is to be found everywhere. Behind even the darkest and most bewildering experiences of their history was a God who called, led, pastured, healed and carried his people. This belief served as the foundation for all their praying (Ps. 28:9) and their hoping (Is. 40:11).

Conversely, it shed light on their own identity. Psalm 100:3 declares 'we are his people, the sheep of his pasture'. As such they were aware that they could be wayward and foolish (Is. 53:6); lost (Ps. 119:176 and Je. 50:6) and vulnerable (Ps. 44:22 and Je. 23:1). They could even be subject to the anger of the shepherd himself (Ps. 74:1), but when such anger came it was precisely because they were his sheep and normally subject to his protection (Ps. 78:52–53) that enabled them to profit from the experience.

The shepherding imagery in no way exhausts the extent of God's ministry to his people. To it we must add the picture of God as father, which is so touchingly portrayed in Hosea 11:1–11. Not only does God call his people to freedom (v. 1) but then he lavishes on them that anxious, proud and gentle love which is so characteristic of parents with a newly-arrived child. Looking with both apprehension and joy on Israel's first steps; showing affection; kissing his

31

wounds better; gently guiding him by using the reins of love and providing him with what he needed was all undertaken perfectly.

Yet built into this relationship was the risk, inherent in creation itself, that the father's love would meet no response because the relationship was not founded on coercion but on freedom. Like so many teenagers, Israel having experienced some freedom wanted yet more and then in rebellious independence went her own way. Unlike the human father who may well have run out of patience (v. 9), God's love was exasperated but not exhausted and the heartbreak of Israel's indifference was endured and overcome (v. 10–11). Such divine patience is a mark of the true pastoral heart.

God's love for his people was not of the sentimental and indulgent variety which permits anything. Although often mistaken for love it is a denial of true love, since it indicates that the parent has no real care either for the child or the consequences of his behaviour. Since God had made himself known as a holy God such an attitude would have been inconsistent with his nature. God's love is purposive love.[1] Part of his ministry towards Israel was, therefore, to discipline and judge them, as he had warned them he would, if they broke the terms of the covenant (Dt. 28:1–68). After numerous warnings about sin and punishments for it, the ultimate judgment came in the form of the exile (Ezk. 7:1–9) so that Israel would realize that this God was not to be trifled with. Even here God's love for Israel remained as firm as ever and the separation was never intended to be final (Is. 50:1). It would be a misunderstanding to think that God confined his judgment to Israel simply because of their special relationship. As the sovereign Lord of creation he had a perfect right to call all nations to account for their behaviour, not least as it was demonstrated towards Israel itself. Amos (1:3 – 2:5), Isaiah (13 – 21), Jeremiah (46 – 51) and Ezekiel (25 – 32), among others, leave us in no doubt about that.

The exile gave way to the second great act of the exodus and God's nature as a saviour once more became apparent to Israel. Ever since the first exodus from Egypt they had been convinced that 'surely God is my salvation' (Is. 12:2) and

[1] J. A. Wharton, 'Theology of Ministry in the Hebrew Scriptures', in E. E. Shelp and R. S. Sunderland (eds), *A Biblical Basis for Ministry*, p. 34.

that salvation was to be found in him alone (Ps. 62:2, 6). In times of relative peace this had meant that the Israelites could be free from fear and, trusting in God, could enjoy life and creation to the full. In times of personal or national calamity it meant that, after due repentance, they could confidently look to God for deliverance. The deliverance they were to experience after the exile was of such an order that it was to usher in a new age with consequences for even the cosmos itself (Is. 60 – 65). Such was the power of their saviour.

This understanding of salvation was consistent with the idea that from the beginning Israel had not deserved their special relationship with God (Dt. 7:7–8). God's choice of them had always been a result of his grace alone and his relationship with them had always been through the word of his promise. Right to the end God was to relate to his creation in the same way.

All subsequent understanding of ministry takes its starting-point from the ministry of God to his people. Human ministry can never be more than a pale and partial reflection of that divine ministry. God the shepherd defines the relationship and function of the pastor to his flock. The fatherhood of God speaks both of the patience required of love and of the pain involved when the risks do not seem to be paying dividends. It is a picture, too, of the gentleness required to teach another. The judgment of God reminds us that love must not be undiscerning; that the basic problem of man is sin, for which he has earned God's judgment, and that all men are ultimately accountable to their creator. Salvation speaks of the object of all our ministry: that people may increasingly experience the salvation which God offers in Christ until it is fully consummated at the end of the age. It equally warns the pastor that the only position from which he can minister to someone else is that of recognizing himself to be on the same level as that person, since he too stands in need of the grace of God and is only fit for the service of God because of that same grace.

To state that all ministry derives from the ministry of God is true but not unproblematic. The chief problem arises from the scope of the claim which has enabled scholars to build such diverse constructions upon it, as the recent writings of Ray

Anderson,[2] Walter Brueggemann[3] and James Wharton[4] illustrate.

Anderson, writing within a Barthian framework, stresses that God is a God of revelation and that all ministry must take that revelation as its starting-point rather than, as is so often the case, beginning with man and man's problems and desires. It follows that instead of reconciliation being the primary concern of the ministry it is to be seen as a reciprocal response to revelation. The ministry is essentially, therefore, a ministry of the word and that word is both a word of judgment and grace. Only as the pastor proclaims the actualities of God's revelation does it become possible for man to achieve his potential. Contemporary pastoral practice, which subordinates the actualities of God to the possibilities of man, is fundamentally adrift from its moorings. All of this was most sharply focused in Christ and is today accomplished through the Holy Spirit. Anderson's foundation for ministry is thoroughly trinitarian.

Brueggemann's approach is to select the covenant as the key issue in the revelation of God and then explore its implications for pastoral care. He uses covenant in a loose and metaphorical way rather than in the stricter way which is customary among Old Testament theologians. Man, he argues, can live freely only within the covenant, because only in this way is he able to deal with God to whom he is bound by his creation. The nature of God as a unique creator *ex nihilo*, who creates by his word and remains an active agent in creation, gives rise to our pastoral approach. To take just two examples from the several which Brueggemann gives: if God is an active God of creation man must respond to his world and its problems with hope, for despair is a covert form of atheism. And if God is a God who speaks, man must respond by listening rather than always desiring to speak himself.

The most thorough exposition of the ministry of God is to be found in an essay by James Wharton, in which he observes that ministry to others is both simultaneously ministry to God and a 'fragmentary participation' in God's own ministry. Many of Wharton's themes have already been touched on but four new

---

[2] R. S. Anderson, 'A Theology for Ministry', in *Theological Foundations For Ministry*, pp. 6–21.

[3] W. Brueggemann, 'Covenanting as Human Vocation', *Interp*. 33 (1979), pp. 115–129.

[4] Wharton, 'Theology of Ministry', pp. 17–71.

themes emerge.

Firstly, God is no therapist objectively engaging in sorting out Israel's problems, but one who is engaged in the 'the whole fabric of real relationships'. These involve confrontations, disappointments and separations as well as reunions, acts of mercy and the provision of comfort. Secondly, man becomes most fully and freely human when he engages in true worship. Man's sickness derives from his engagement in 'interim worship' or the worship of idols which God conspires to overthrow in order that man might be truly healthy. Thirdly, ministry to others arises for Israel from their own experience of being a 'stranger' in Egypt. As God reached out to them when they were aliens and strangers, so they must reject a cosy parochialism and reach out to other strangers with that same love. They must not do this for the ulterior motive of converting them, for the relationship must be free from coercion in the same way that God's love is for them.

Fourthly, Wharton comments on the nature of the ministry, wishing to cut it down to size. In doing so he illuminates one aspect of the ministry yet perhaps at the expense of other equally valid aspects such as its authority and accountability. High and holy calling though it is, Wharton argues that it is not the responsibility of the minister to achieve reconciliation nor to be responsible for another's piety. That is God's responsibility. The ministry's responsibility is simply the modest task of 'translating the covenant love of God into specific human attitudes and actions that affirm it in one's life'.[5] The pastor who puts himself above his fellows and has an over-grand conception of his responsibility will spend most of his ministry suffering from fatigue and seeing other people as a burden or a problem. The pastor should rather be liberated to realize that 'Ministry grounded in the love of God is, above all, sheer celebration of the God-given capacity to receive, share and express the love of God for me and the other'.[6]

God's relationship with Israel is therefore a rich mine, full not only of valuable insights but of essential resources for our own ministry, even if caution needs to be exercised so that it is exploited in a disciplined manner. Our ministry is only legitimate to the extent that it is derived from God's.

[5] *Ibid.*, p. 48.   [6] *Ibid.*, p. 70.

Early in Israel's history it became apparent that God intended to mediate his ministry through others who would lead and guide Israel (Nu. 27:16–17 and Dt. 18:14–20). Only when these leaders eventually proved a total failure did God announce that he would resume his ministry in an unmediated form (Ezk. 34:1–31). Before that occurred however there were a succession of men whose leadership was a gift from God to his people.[7]

THE LEADERSHIP OF MOSES

Old Testament scholars have long acknowledged the difficulty of categorizing Moses.[8] Yet all agree that he stands at the centre of Israel's formation as a nation and people of faith and that he stands head and shoulders above every other leader they had.[9] W. Eichrodt[10] has explained the difficulty of classifying Moses. He was neither a king nor the commander of an army, for though he determined the direction of the people's march he had no prowess in war and made no provision for a son to succeed him. He directed the worship of the people of God, but he neither had the status of a priest nor did he ever offer sacrifices. He gave laws and administered justice, but was so much more than a judge since he mediated a new understanding of God. In one way he was a prophet – perhaps the greatest of the prophets (Dt. 18:15) – and yet he is clearly distinguished from them and placed in direct touch with God himself (Ex. 33:11 and Nu. 12:8). To speak of him as a seer or wonder-worker is simply inadequate.

The attempt to impose some classification on Moses is futile for, as Deuteronomy 34:10–12 indicates, there had never been his like before or since. The nature of his greatness lay in the combination of the excellent gifts he possessed. For all that, Moses is not totally removed from the level of other human leaders and he serves as a paradigm for all subsequent leadership. As Trent Butler has said, 'All leadership in Israel occurs in the shadow of Moses. He . . . died, but his example and teaching stand before every successor. The Israelite leader must

[7] W. Zimmerli, *Old Testament Theology in Outline*, p. 81.

[8] D. M. Beegle, *Moses, The Servant of Yahweh* p. 348; G. von Rad, *Old Testament Theology*, pp. 289–296 and Zimmerli, *OT Theology*, p. 82.

[9] For a recent summary of the view of Old Testament scholars as to the historicity of Moses see C. Brown and H. Seebuss, 'Moses', *NIDNTT*, vol. 2, pp. 635–643.

[10] W. Eichrodt, *Theology of the Old Testament*, vol. 1, pp. 289–291.

be an official, a minister of Moses.'[11] So what can be said about his leadership which has enduring significance?

Von Rad has commented that one source presents Moses as nothing more than 'an inspired shepherd whom Jahweh used to make known his will'.[12] True though that is, he was a shepherd uniquely prepared and called by God to undertake his task. His remarkable deliverance from the anger of Pharaoh at birth and his subsequent upbringing in the Egyptian royal household put him in a position second to none as a potential candidate to be tte deliverer of Israel. Paradoxically, however, he had to unlearn as much as he had learnt in Egypt if he was to be useful to God. Having tried to secure justice for the Israelites by his own methods (Ex. 2:11–15) he was forced to flee the country. What must have appeared to him and others at the time as a tragic mistake, leading to an enormous waste of potential, was used in the purposes of God to enable him to reject the life-style of Egypt (Heb. 11:24–26) in favour of the greater realities God had in store for him.

Forty years in the Midian desert was to be a harsh training school, but it was necessary that he should graduate in patience before attempting to lead Israel through the wilderness. When the time was ripe, on what began as a routine day for Moses, God broke in, made himself known and rescued Moses from obscurity. This encounter with God was essential if Moses was ever to be anything other than a shepherd. Equally significant was Moses' response to it. The impetuous activism of previous years was gone and Moses was prepared to worship and recognize his own unworthiness. J. O. Sanders has observed that, like the younger Moses, 'Most of us find it much easier to don our shoes in busy activity than to doff them in humble worship. We are more prone to turn our face to the limelight than to hide it in conscious unworthiness.'[13] His response proved him ready, in spite of all his objections, to be the instrument of God. A comparison of verses 8 and 10 in Exodus 3 shows that from now on God and Moses were going to work in co-operation. There was to be no either/or mentality – either God or Moses – but God was to deliver his people through Moses.

---

[11] T. C. Butler, *Joshua*, p. 13.

[12] Von Rad assesses the Moses narrative according to the different sources which he believes contribute to it. This view he attributes to J, *Theology*, p. 292.

[13] J. O. Sanders, *Men from God's School*, p. 63.

God's revelation of himself to Moses at the burning bush was to be the first of many encounters between them which were to become the hallmark of Moses' leadership. The secrets of his success lay quite simply, first in the conviction that God had called him and secondly that he kept in personal face-to-face relationship with God.[14] Although denied the ultimate sight of God's face (Ex. 33:23) no other man had been in such close contact with God (Ex. 33:11 and Nu. 12:6–8). It was the time Moses spent in the presence of God which authenticated his leadership (Ex. 34:29–35).

P. T. Forsyth tellingly remarked, 'If within us we find nothing over us, we succumb to what is around us.'[15] The Israelites more than once would have capitulated to what was around them (*e.g.* Ex. 14:11–12; 17:2–7; 32:1–35 and Nu. 11:4 – 14:45). Egypt, in retrospect, appeared so much more attractive than an unseen and unexperienced promised land. But Moses, the man of faith, was faithfully in touch with what was above and kept the people from falling into unbelief. He prevented the temporal from obliterating the eternal and the actual from obliterating the promise.

As a leader Moses was not called to be original or creative, but simply a faithful messenger of God (Dt. 5:23–27). It was his task to make known the covenant stipulations as God had revealed them to him and this he did in all their moral, religious and social detail. National and daily life was brought into conformity with the demands of God who, through Moses as mediator, had made his will known. It was in this way that Moses was able to build the nation and that they became a people of faith.

As a direct result of his intimate relationship with God, Moses is presented as a man of intercession. Whether it was pleading on behalf of sinful individuals, as in the case of Aaron and Miriam in Numbers 12:13, or for the nation as a whole, as in Exodus 32:31–32 and Numbers 14:13–19, or whether it was in facing another crisis in the nation, as in Numbers 11:11–15 or 16:22, there was always an urgency and a boldness about his praying. His faith was so unqualified that he was able to experience many remarkable and immediate answers to his requests. Like Charles Bridges, he must have suspected that 'we shall

---

[14] Beegle, *Moses*, p. 346.
[15] P. T. Forsyth, *Positive Preaching and the Modern Mind*, p. 47.

find that our most successful efforts for our people were the hours – not when we were speaking to them from God, but when we were speaking for them to God'.[16] Moses stood before God as the representative of the people and before the people as the representative of God.

Moses was the prototype for the leaders who were to follow him in yet another respect. He was the leader who called his people to decision. The challenge as to whether or not the people would choose to follow the Lord by keeping the terms of the covenant was constantly set before them, but it was never clearer than when the covenant was renewed at the end of Moses' life. After setting before them the blessings of obedience and the curses of disobedience he concluded, 'I have set before you life and death, blessings and curses. Now choose life . . .' (Dt. 30:19). His was no 'take-it-or-leave-it' attitude. He was possessed by a desire to persuade the people to do that which was right. From Joshua onwards (Jos. 24:14–24) his true successors have followed in his footsteps and have always challenged people to choose between life and death.

Given the enormous range of Moses' responsibility it was inevitable that before long the strain would begin to show and he would be unable to cope. The account, in Exodus 18, which records how the situation was resolved exposes two false expectations which are often encountered among Christian workers. The first is that a Christian leader ought to be able to cope with a task of superhuman proportions. The second is that he should be able to expect that the answer to all his problems will be handed down to him directly from Sinai.

No doubt it was all under the providential control of God, but Moses found his answer in an apparently casual way from Jethro who advised 'from his world of experience, that Moses share the burden of administering justice with men of judgment and integrity within the community according to their natural abilities . . .'.[17] Moses then proceeded, without any embarrassment, to adopt this secular wisdom concerning management in order to enhance the quality of his spiritual leadership. Few pastors claim to enjoy administration, although they are required to spend a good deal of their time engaged in it. Perhaps the church today needs modern Jethros in order to

---

[16] C. Bridges, *The Christian Ministry*, p. 149.
[17] B. S. Childs, *Exodus*, p. 335.

learn how to off-load the burdens of administration so that the primary tasks to which the pastor is called do not suffer.

The character of Moses is no less enigmatic than his office. On the credit side, he must have been a remarkable man to achieve all that he did and persuade the Israelites to co-operate with him as much as they did. He merited the reputation of being a 'friend of God' (Ex. 33:11), and of being the most humble man on earth (Nu. 12:3), whose strength never failed him (Dt. 34:7).

On the debit side, he must have been one of the most reluctant prophets of all time (Ex. 3:11 – 4:17), who dragged his feet and even elicited an accommodation out of God (4:14–16). But in the end he spoke for God in spite of himself. The narrow line between self-distrust which ensures that faith is fully placed in God and self-distrust which can engender spiritual paralysis was not crossed. Equally on the debit side we read of Moses as a volatile character who could be complaining and depressed in prayer (Ex. 17:4 and Nu. 11:10–15); precipitant in action; fearsome to encounter (Ex. 32:27–29 and Nu. 16:28–34) and even lacking in faith (Nu. 20:1–13). Like any other man he 'ran the gamut of human experiences: from the shining face of Yahweh's presence to the despair of doubt and resignation'.[18] His humanity and limitations serve as a great encouragement to lesser mortals whom God has called to leadership. But they do more than that. They ensure that 'the leading role in the whole story is Yahweh's. Moses was a gifted man, but it was only by Yahweh's grace that he lived to exercise those gifts'.[19] God will not share his glory with any man, no matter how great that man might be.

It must be noted, finally, that Moses was a prophet who pointed forward. In Deuteronomy 18:15 he declared, 'The Lord your God will raise up for you a prophet like me from among your own brothers. You must listen to him.' Often the New Testament portrays the work of Jesus as the founder of the new covenant in opposition to the covenant of Moses (*e.g.* Jn. 1:17; 2 Cor. 3:1–18). Yet it is also true that, when prophecy drew to a close in Judaism, Moses' statement was interpreted as a prediction of the Messiah and the New Testament writers certainly understood it in that light (*e.g.* Jn. 1:21, 45; 6:14; 7:40;

---

[18] Beegle, *Moses*, p. 348.   [19] *Ibid.*, pp. 347f.

Acts 3:22). Jesus there stands in continuity with Moses and not simply in contrast.[20] The greatest of all the prophets of the Old Testament, therefore, is ultimately nothing more than a signpost to Jesus.

THE PASTORS OF ISRAEL

After the death of Joshua, no settled leadership was available to guide Israel through the tumultuous years that followed. Leadership emerged in the form of the sporadic eruptions of judges who had no permanent place in the management of the nation.[21] Whether their style simply harmonized with the restless character of the times or whether it was in part responsible for it is hard to determine. But the nation was threatened with disintegration because, in the absence of leadership, 'everyone did as he saw fit' (Jdg. 17:6 and 21:25). Israel eventually sought leadership in the monarchy, but in addition to that three other groups were to emerge as the pastors of Israel – priests, prophets and wise men (Je. 18:18).

Before assessing their role, however, we should note John McNeill's wise reminder that both before and after these three groups were prominent, Israel laid great emphasis on the pastoral duties of parents.[22] The importance of parents in providing spiritual education for their children is stressed several times in the book of Deuteronomy (4:9; 6:7, 20; 11:19; 31:13 and 32:46). The responsibility of passing on the faith was firmly set in the context of the family and parents were not permitted to abdicate this in favour of a specialist teacher of religion. Deuteronomy 6:7 shows how religious conversation was to take place throughout the day and wherever they were. It was to affect every sphere of life without compartmentalization. Only by this means would the passing on of the tradition be safeguarded.

The teaching of the parents was to be personal, not academic, and was to arise out of their own experience of God. They had seen the revelation, judgment and deliverance of God in a way denied to their children (Dt. 11:2–7). To forget such experiences

---

[20] *Cf.* P. C. Craigie, *The Book of Deuteronomy*, pp. 263f.; J. A. Thompson, *Deuteronomy*, pp. 212f.

[21] Zimmerli, *OT Theology*, pp. 83–86.

[22] J. T. McNeill, *A History of the Cure of Souls*, p. 2. For a wider discussion of the role of the parents see H. W. Wolff, *Anthropology of the Old Testament*, pp. 178–184.

was spiritually suicidal (Dt. 8:1–20). Their teaching was also to arise from their understanding of God's revelation – again a privilege which was special to them (Dt. 5:3) – and they were, therefore, to urge obedience to his law. Parents, it may be argued, were the primary guardians of the faith of Israel.

By the time of Jeremiah, however, it was to the priest that the people looked for 'the teaching of the law'. Their function is presented by some Old Testament scholars as narrow and institutionalized by comparison with the prophet, but that is to belie the complexity of the situation.[23] They were essentially the means of access to the understanding of the divine will. Right from the start they had been charged with the responsibility of discerning God's will (Dt. 33:8), but that task had developed along particular lines. The divine will was seen as enshrined in the sacred tradition and established in the law. Consequently their task was seen as applying the law, in the whole range of its concerns, to the lives of the people (*e.g.* Ezk. 44:23 and Hg. 2:11–13).

Furthermore, they executed their task from the standpoint of the cult, in the belief that 'outward form is not a matter of indifference to the inner concerns of religion, but effectively mediates the presence of God'.[24] They became therefore the practitioners and keepers of the cult. Their daily duties consisted of offering sacrifices (Dt. 33:10), pronouncing blessings (Nu. 6:22–27) and maintaining moral, physical and social purity. The significance of their task is highlighted even more by an insight into the nature of the God whom they served. He was of 'awe-inspiring unapproachableness' and his majesty and holiness distanced him from the world. With a God of such transcendence it was clear why it was crucial to approach him in precisely the right way and to know his will in minute particulars.

It is all too easy to erect a series of false contrasts between the priests and the prophets.[25] Samuel, the man who dominated the transition from the chaos of the judges to the rule of the monarchy, served as a judge, priest and prophet, suggesting that the offices were not necessarily contradictory. The basic distinction between priest and prophet is not to be seen in terms of cult versus anti-cult, nor institution versus charisma, but in

---

[23] Eichrodt, *Theology of OT*, pp. 402–436 and Zimmerli, *OT Theology*, pp. 93–99.

[24] Eichrodt, *Theology of OT*, p. 404.

[25] On the contrast see *ibid.*, pp. 416–418 and 433–436.

their contrasting emphases on the law and the word. From the early days of prophecy around the time of Samuel through to the great writing prophets such as Jeremiah or Ezekiel, the hearing and the proclamation of God's word for the present situation was their concern. It is significant that Samuel, who is referred to in the New Testament only as a prophet, began his service for God at a time when 'the word of the Lord was rare' and was immediately taught by Eli to adopt the typical prophetic attitude of 'Speak, Lord, for your servant is listening' (1 Sa. 3:1–10).

The word of the Lord came to the prophets as men who were called of God individually rather than being qualified for office by heredity. For the most part it came through audition in a clear and unmistakable way, although visions were not unknown and more ecstatic methods were evident in the earlier days of prophecy. They had a much more dynamic conception of God than the priests and presented him as speaking, on a much wider ethical and moral platform, a word which addressed specific present or future historical situations. Their spontaneity often brought them into conflict with more static perceptions of the tradition.

It was a mark of the prophet that he never went beyond the word given (Dt. 18:20 and 1 Ki. 20:13–14) to announce his own programme, neither could he omit a word from what he had heard (Je. 26:2). But given the freedom which they exhibited there was wide scope for the growth of false prophets. So tests were devised by which false prophets could be identified (Dt. 13:1–4; 18:21–22 and Je. 23:14, 22). Even so it was impossible to ensure that the purity of this pastoral group would never be violated.

The third group of pastors have an altogether different character.[26] The objective of the wise men was to provide down-to-earth counsel about the ordinary affairs of life, not least as a means of training the young. They had no place for the grand affairs of nations which occupied the prophets, neither did they appeal to the emotions as the prophets did. Their approach was to consider, with steady logic, the truth which was hidden within human nature and creation in order to discover the regularities which could form the basis of their lives and

---

[26] McNeill, *Cure of Souls*, pp. 5–11; G. von Rad, *Wisdom in Israel*; Zimmerli, *OT Theology*, pp. 107f. and 155–166.

counsel. Their thinking was not stimulated by immediate divine revelation and there seems sometimes to be scant reference to God. They were rather motivated by humanity. They were men in search of themselves.[27] They worked on the assumption that creation would reveal truth and behind all the 'artful pleasure in originality',[28] the clever use of pictures and metaphors and the inventive use of comparisons and contrasts, lay a mundane purpose.

The exact profile of the group of wise men is obscure. Solomon is obviously the wise man *par excellence* (1 Ki. 3:1–15) but only a few others are actually named (1 Ki. 4:31; Pr. 30:1 and 31:1). We know that Solomon's father had the advice of wise men at his court (1 Ch. 27:32–33) and we know too that their widespread existence was known to Jeremiah (Je. 8:8–9 and 9:23). But we know them most through the extensive legacy they have left in the wisdom writings of the Old Testament which cover such an enormous scope from the mundane to the profound. Von Rad's thorough study of these writings identifies their themes as follows: correct social behaviour, the essentials of coping with reality, the doctrine of the proper time, wisdom's self-revelation in creation, a polemic against idols, the basis of trust, the problem of suffering and the purpose of life.[29]

The quest for knowledge in these writings is never a dispassionate search for intellectual understanding, since that would yield nothing. The writings, for all their apparent absence of reference to God, show that it is only a commitment to him which will reveal truth as there can be no reality except that which he controls. The key to all, which is repeated in one form or another five times over, is that 'the fear of the Lord is the beginning of knowledge' (Pr. 1:7).[30]

Pastoral leadership in Israel, then, never took the form of a monolithic and static structure. It was always varied and over time it was modified and continued to be so even into the later period when Judaism was to emerge.[31] In taking care of his people, God mediated his love through different channels which all had their distinctive contributions to make with their

---

[27] Von Rad, *Wisdom*, p. 309.   [28] Zimmerli, *OT Theology*, p. 157.

[29] Von Rad, *Wisdom*, pp. 74–96 and 113–239, see also D. Kidner, *Wisdom to live by*.

[30] Proverbs 1:7 is paralleled by Job 28:28; Psalm 111:10; Proverbs 9:10 and 15:33. *Cf.* Ecclesiastes 12:13–14. See von Rad, *Wisdom*, pp. 64–66.

[31] McNeill, *Cure of Souls*, pp. 11–16.

different emphases on law, word and wisdom, and who, because of their distinctive limitations, needed and complemented each other.

THE ANALOGY OF THE SHEPHERD

Underlying all the specific forms of leadership in Israel lay, in Thomas Oden's words,[32] the 'pivotal analogy' of the shepherd. It is important to examine this analogy carefully if a full understanding of the nature of biblical pastoral leadership is to be gained. The trouble with such a familiar picture is that either, on the one hand, its meaning is assumed which leads to a superficial understanding or, on the other hand, it provides productive soil for fruitful imaginations which give the analogy some depth but at the expense of its original meaning.

The shepherd was a natural figure to choose for a people whose roots lay in nomadic life and whose greatest leaders, Moses (Is. 63:11) and David (Ps. 78:70–72), had been shepherds. Elsewhere in the ancient world 'the shepherd' was widely used as a title for deities and kings. To rule was to pasture the people. This predominantly pagan use may well explain why there seems to be a reluctance on the part of the Old Testament writers to apply the term either to God or their human leaders even though it is fully recognized that they fulfilled the functions of the shepherd.[33]

The wider background makes it plain that the shepherd was essentially a leader and that in order to accomplish his task he needed authority. The authority of the true pastor of Israel was different in style from that of the despots and pagan rulers of other nations, hence the desire not to over-identify the two by using the same titles too glibly. Nonetheless the shepherd did possess real authority. Even in Psalm 23, the most gentle and consoling of psalms, the shepherd is said to have a rod, the symbol of his authority, with which he would discipline his sheep and examine them for disease as well as defend and protect them. The rod was the equivalent of the king's staff. The basis for his authority lay not in his office but in his competence and that in turn was determined, since his sheep

[32] Oden, *Pastoral Theology*, p. 49.
[33] E. Beyreuther, 'Shepherd', *NIDNTT*, vol. 3, pp. 564–569 and J. Jeremias, *'poimēn'*, *TDNT*, vol. 6, pp. 485–502.

were unable to communicate with him, by his ability to engage in acute empathy. The shepherd's work, therefore, demanded a subtle blend of authority and care. Both must be present, but perhaps it is significant that in the Old Testament the picture of the shepherd occurs most in Psalms and the prophets of the exile where the theme of consolation rather than rule is uppermost.

In denouncing the false shepherds of Israel, in Ezekiel 34, God unfolds the true nature of the shepherds' responsibilities. The false shepherds had exploited the people and instead of feeding them had fed on them (vv. 2, 3, 5 and 10). They had also failed to demonstrate any of the requisite pastoral qualities (v. 4). Worst of all they had scattered the flock, not by permitting the flock to drift through indifference and neglect, but through an abuse of power which had frightened and terrified the sheep. In the light of this dramatic failure God announces that he himself will assume direct responsibility for the shepherding of Israel (vv. 11–16). Later in the chapter the task is committed to 'my servant David' (vv. 23–24) who is rightly interpreted as a messianic figure.[34] But what is the task which God undertakes?

A threefold task is detailed within an overall framework, with each of the first two of the specific tasks being present in a dual aspect. The overall framework assumes that the shepherd's responsibility is to feed the sheep, protect them, ensure that they have good quality pasture and keep them integrated as a flock. The administration of the flock must be conducted with scrupulous fairness and justice.

Within that framework God says 'I will search for the lost and bring back the strays. I will bind up the injured and strengthen the weak, but the sleek and the strong I will destroy' (v. 16). Searching for the lost and bringing back the strays are almost certainly complementary expressions rather than descriptions of different tasks, as also are the next two phrases. It is tempting to translate the last sentence, as in the RSV, as 'the fat and the strong I will watch over', and many have done so, since that would direct attention to the importance of

---

[34] J. B. Taylor comments: 'Every new paragraph of this chapter opens out the analogy still further. If the chapter is taken as a whole it will appear full of inconsistencies, but if each section is taken separately it will be obvious that new ideas are being added all along.' *Ezekiel*, p. 222.

ensuring that the healthy members of the flock were well fed and encouraged to develop, and that not all the shepherd's time can be spent on the problem characters. But almost certainly the textual evidence is against it and in favour of the harsher translation.[35]

None the less, Martin Bucer's exposition of the pastoral task conforms to the teaching of these verses. He saw the responsibilities of the ministry as:

(1) To draw to Christ those who are alienated.
(2) To lead back those who have been drawn away.
(3) To secure amendment of life for those who fall into sin.
(4) To strengthen weak and silly Christians.
(5) To preserve Christians who are whole and strong and urge them forward to the good.[36]

Ezekiel 34 presents God's unchanging manifesto for the ministry and serves as an impressive and appealing call to all who are shepherds to fulfil their obligations and consider their priorities in evangelism, restoration, teaching, encouraging and feeding; all of which are aspects of the shepherd's role.

Recently, Alastair Campbell has drawn attention to an often neglected aspect of the life of the shepherd.[37] No-one could undertake the occupation in Israel without being quickly made aware that it required courage. Long dry summers would demand that the shepherd be constantly and tirelessly engaged in searching for new pastures. His journeys would often take him a long way from home and entail many lonely nights on exposed hills. When seeking the higher plains for summer pasture the shepherd would need to go through the cool valleys which, whilst they provided some shelter from the scorching sun, would nevertheless remain 'valleys of shadow' and would not be free from danger or anxiety. David was certainly aware from his own experience of the extent of those dangers and of the courage needed to be a shepherd (1 Sa. 17:34–37). Campbell has remarked that 'His unsettled and dangerous life makes (the shepherd) a slightly ambiguous figure – more perhaps like the cowboy of the "Wild West" than the modern shepherd in a

---

[35] *Ibid.*, p. 221. *Cf.* W. Eichrodt, *Ezekiel*, pp. 471f.
[36] M. Bucer, *Martini Bucer Opera Omnia Series 1: Deutsche Schriften*, vol. 7, pp. 67–245.
[37] A. V. Campbell, *Rediscovering Pastoral Care*, pp. 26–36.

settled farming community'.[38]

Whatever the truth of that remark, it is right to stress that the work of the shepherd involved as much toughness as tenderness, as much courage as comfort. The shepherd today must still be a man of courage, for that is what it takes to enter the darkness of another man's lostness and pain, to share with him his bewilderment, his anguish and suffering. Those who are not prepared for such vulnerability, but are concerned for their own comfort, will never be true shepherds.

The aspect of the shepherd's suffering is heightened in the Old Testament as the figure of the messianic shepherd, alluded to in Ezekiel 34:23–24, is developed by Zechariah. There the good shepherd is rejected (11:7–11) and a worthless shepherd is followed instead (11:15–17). The good shepherd is struck (13:7) and pierced (12:10 is usually linked with 13:7).[39] By his representative death the people's fortunes are turned and salvation dawns (13:1–9). The shepherd has to be prepared to pay the ultimate price in caring for his sheep.

Perhaps the most surprising reference to the shepherd in the whole of the Old Testament is in Isaiah 44:28, where God says of Cyrus, 'He is my shepherd'. For God to have attributed this title to a pagan king so deliberately would have sent shock waves through the people of Israel sufficient to be registered on the Richter scale! This appellation of Cyrus not only illustrates the complexity of the analogy, but once more points to the sovereign freedom of God in deciding how his pastoral care for his people will be undertaken, since God himself had, only a few chapters before, been presented as the one who would tend his flock like a shepherd, and carry the lambs in his arms (Is. 40:11). The ways of God should not be limited to the self-imposed structures of man. As the sovereign Lord of the nations he can use whoever he will. His concern for his sheep overrides all other concerns and moves him, when their interests demand it, to be disconcerting to human expectations.

Authority, care, courage and death are the principal characteristics of the shepherd motif, which stands, too, as a striking reminder of the sovereignty of God over all peoples.

---

[38] *Ibid.*, p. 27.
[39] For a careful exegesis of these difficult passages see J. G. Baldwin, *Haggai, Zechariah, Malachi*, pp. 179–182.

THE EXAMPLE OF ISAIAH 40 – 66

The prophecy of Isaiah 40 – 66 can fairly claim to be pastoral theology *par excellence*. After recurring cycles of success and failure the tragedy of the exile took place and it looked as if all was lost for Israel. Into the gloom which descended God sent Isaiah with a message of comfort. 'Without him', as C. R. North has said, 'it is difficult to see how Israel could have recovered herself or even survived the disaster of the exile.'[40]

Isaiah 40 – 66 reaches new heights in its revelation of God, and Isaiah, whether he realized it or not, is more far-sighted than any of the prophets. The problem of how to express such unsurpassed thought was resolved for him by the use of sublime poetry. Yet Isaiah was not engaged in an exercise in academic theology, nor did he wish to make an original contribution to the cultural and literary circles of his day. He spoke and wrote in response to urgent pastoral needs.

The most obvious problem facing the exiles was their lack of freedom. In spite of the fact that they were forced to labour on the splendid building projects of Babylon, the conditions of the exile, to begin with at least, were relatively humane and tolerable; more like those of liberal internment than a concentration camp. The people of Israel grew in numbers during these years and were able to carry on some life of their own as well as make a contribution to the political life of Babylon. Even so they were still not free. Their homeland, separated from them by a three-month journey, lay in ruins and their heritage was in tatters. Like many today they had a desire for a theology of liberation.

The physical separation of the exile gave birth to attitudes of mind which were just as problematic as the exile itself. They felt the shame and suffering of the exile deeply and many allowed depression to descend on them like a thick cloud. In the words of George Adam Smith, 'Throughout the exile the true Jew lived inwardly. He was an inhabitant not so much of a foreign prison as of his own broken heart.'[41]

At a deeper level still the exile was the cause of a profound spiritual crisis. The numerous aspects of the crisis can be fairly summarized in three groups. Firstly, there was the need to provide an explanation for the exile. Why had God permitted

---

[40] C. R. North, *The Second Isaiah*, p. 28.
[41] G. A. Smith, *The Book of Isaiah*, vol. 2, p. 63.

it to happen? How was it to be understood in the light of his election of Israel and his promise to secure the throne of David? Had God abandoned them? Secondly, there was the problem of how to worship God in exile, no doubt most keenly felt by the priests. Worship depended on the temple and on observing the niceties of the cult, but neither of these was now accessible. How then was the worship of God to be conducted in an alien culture?

The third group of questions were the most profound of all. The experience of the exile caused some to be deeply sceptical and many to have at least passing doubts. Where was their God? Marduk and the other gods of the Babylonians seemed to be present everywhere. Moreover in the light of the turn of political events they seemed to be the ones who possessed and exercised real power in the world. So, even if God was still alive, was he able to act on behalf of his people and would he do so even if he could? The exile raised questions about the plausibility of their faith in the most serious of ways.

Isaiah's answer to these problems was theological. It need not have been so. Isaiah could have adopted a political solution and either incited revolution, which would have been pointless, or tried to negotiate a release from captivity with the authorities. Alternatively he could have adopted a psychological approach. The people were depressed and by unfolding the causes of that depression which lay buried in their psyches they could be freed from it and enabled to face the reality of their lot. Once they accepted that it was unlikely to change they could at least begin to function freely and fulfil their presently untapped potential. There again, he could have answered in the manner of a social worker and tried to secure better conditions for the exiles. Isaiah, however, preaches some sermons – an approach just as likely to meet initially with derision in his day as much as in ours. The basic problem, as he saw it, was simply that they had a wrong conception of God.

The style which Isaiah adopted was one best calculated to win a hearing. There was little condemnation or denunciation in his messages, even of Babylon, except in chapter 47. Yet he is not indifferent to the awfulness of sin and squarely puts the blame for the exile on the shoulders of the people (50:1). His message is as uncompromising in its attitude towards sin as that of Amos or Micah but it is announced in a different tone of voice. In this connection the comments of George Adam Smith on chapter 58 are worth recording:

> Perhaps no subject more readily provokes to satire and sneers than the subject of this chapter, – the union of formal religion and unlovely life. And yet in this chapter there is not a sneer from first to last. The speaker suppresses the temptation to use his nasal tones, and utters, not as the satirist, but as the prophet. For his purpose is not to sport with the people's hypocrisy, but to sweep them out of it. Before he has done, his urgent speech, that has not lingered to sneer nor exhausted itself in screaming, passes forth to spend its unchecked impetus upon final promise and gospel. It is a wise lesson from a master preacher, and half of the fruitlessness of modern preaching is due to the neglect of it. The pulpit tempts men to be either too bold or too timid about sin; either to whisper or to scold; to euphemise or to exaggerate; to be conventional or hysterical. But two things are necessary, – the facts must be stated, and the whole manhood of the preacher, and not only his scorn or only his anger or only an official temper, brought to bear upon it.[42]

Certainly Isaiah can sneer at the idols of Babylon (41:5–7 and 44:9–20) and persist in disputation with the severity of a modern lawyer cross-questioning a defiant witness (41:1–4, 21–29; 43:22–23 and 45:20–21). He never minimizes the seriousness of Israel's sin, nor their responsibility for it, but his words are chosen to invite not to indict, to woo not to wound.

The people are invited to look once more at their God. Isaiah portrays him in chapter 40, in words which are not so much an argument as a sacrament,[43] as the supreme creator of the universe, sovereign over men, over governments and over the planets which were the object of worship in Babylon. As the sovereign Lord of history he not only knows in advance what will take place but freely determines that it shall (46:8–13). The exile was, therefore, no accident but all within the plan of God as his way of punishing them for their sin. Even more, having delivered them into captivity, it is within his sovereign power

---

[42] *Ibid.*, p. 417.   [43] *Ibid.*, p. 90.

to arrange for them to be released and to fix the rise and fall of empires as a means of doing so. Cyrus, so confident of his own powers, is nothing more than an instrument in the hand of Yahweh (44:8 – 45:7). Israel needs to hear that he alone is God and apart from him there is no other.

For all the greatness of this God whom Isaiah presents so sublimely, he is also presented in the most tender and personal terms to Israel. He was their lover (43:4), their mother (49:15) and their husband (54:5), and it was inconceivable that he would have abandoned them. He had both the power to act on their behalf and the will to do so. It was impossible to prove the existence or nature of this God, but he was not as inaccessible as the people believed (45:15). Isaiah repeatedly invites them to consider the evidence for the truth of his claims (*e.g.* 48:1–11) and to recall to mind their past experiences as a means of evaluating them (46:9). So God is shown not only to be gracious and tender by nature, but to be patient and sympathetic to the need for his people to work through the after-effects of the shock administered by the exile with its consequences for their relationship.

Such bold claims were all very well, but Israel needed even more. So Isaiah proceeds to proclaim the implications of the existence of this God. He will do a 'new thing' (43:19) and restore his people to Israel (49:8–26). To describe the wonder of this event Isaiah takes the familiar picture of the exodus from Egypt, intensifies it and projects it into the future (43:16–21).[44] The exodus will not only lead to a Zion of unimagined splendour (60:1 – 61:11) but will be cosmic in its significance (65:17–25).

In a nutshell, the message from God was 'my salvation is on the way' (51:5). It was not a salvation which was to be accomplished simply through the rise of Cyrus. It was to be achieved through the death of the servant, whose identity in Isaiah is ambiguous, but whom Christians have justifiably interpreted as Jesus, not least because of the way in which Jesus consciously adopts the role himself.[45] His role was vital in ensuring that the original cause of the exile – the sin of the people – was fully dealt with without compromise to the holi-

[44] W. Zimmerli, *Man and his Hope in the Old Testament*, p. 126.
[45] See C. Kruse, *New Testament Foundations of Ministry*, pp. 34–45. C. Westermann argues that the identity of the servant is deliberately ambiguous, *Isaiah 40–66*, p. 93.

ness of God (52:13 – 53:12).[46] It was by his words that the people were to be healed. There was therefore no room for glib political triumphalism in Israel, but what it did entail was a deep repentance on their part for their sin – both past and that which was still being committed in exile (chapters 58 and 59).

The experience of the restored people was to be diametrically opposite to what they were experiencing in exile. They would have a new status, a new beauty and a new name, and instead of being the servants of other nations and subject to their scorn they would be served by them and receive their allegiance (52:1–12; 60:1–22; 61:4–7). In the new Jerusalem, however, they would not be able simply to continue their previous life-style. New patterns of behaviour were expected and new members would be counted as fellow citizens (56:1–8). This people would be a missionary people not because they sent out missionaries to evangelize other nations but because, by exhibiting salvation at work among themselves, they would become the object of wonder and many would come to enquire and find it for themselves (42:6; 44:5; 45:14 and 60:3).

There was little that Israel could do to bring this deliverance to pass. Two things were necessary, however: a genuine repentance and a renewed faith. Isaiah works to enable both to be a genuine expression of the people's inner convictions rather than an external act imposed on them by others. All his strategy is committed to that end. What he does therefore is to paint pictures of faith and encourage the people to include themselves in them. He encourages them to get out of the valleys and to cast off the despondency, to remove the obstacles in their line of sight and level the mountains. It was time to 'prepare the way for the Lord' (40:3); to hear, look and see (42:18); to awake and clothe themselves with strength (52:1) and to 'arise, shine, for your light has come' (60:1). Only as they did this would the slogan 'Your God reigns' cease to be a pious irrelevancy and become a meaningful reality.

---

[46] Isaiah 40 – 66 refers to Yahweh as 'the Holy One of Israel' thirteen times. W. S. La Sor comments, 'If the punishment of the nation was because of uncleaness, which is a violation of Yahweh's holiness, then the restoration of the nation must require some kind of cleansing, which is involved in salvation and redemption. To present the indictment of uncleaness without the remedy of divine salvation would be of little help, and to speak of salvation or redemption without making clear the reason for such divine activity – as in much present-day preaching – would verge on nonsense,' W. S. La Sor, D. A. Hubbard and F. W. Bush (eds), *Old Testament Survey*, p. 383.

SUMMARY

The Old Testament lays essential foundations for any understanding of pastoral theology. All ministry begins with the ministry of God. From his ministry all others are derived.

The humanity of Moses, the archetype of all subsequent servants of God, demonstrates that no ministry is based on anything but God's grace. His leadership speaks of the importance of the call of God and the necessity of keeping in close contact with him. It exemplifies, too, that the task of ministry is to make known the word of God and to point to his eternal demands even in a context where such faith is out of step with the prevailing climate. It frees us from the bondage that says that no help for our responsibilities can be found from any secular source, whilst ensuring that we never stray from the anchor of God's revelation.

Parents were shown to have an enduring place in the pastoral structure of Israel. In addition, later developments in the pastoral leadership of Israel demonstrate that no one strand can serve as a comprehensive guide. Priests with their emphasis on God's holy law, prophets with their emphasis on God's dynamic word and wise men with their emphasis on practical wisdom all have their place and serve to complement each other and to make up for each other's deficiencies.

The image of the shepherd is the underlying paradigm of ministry. This single image contains within it references to the authority, tender care, specific tasks, courage and sacrifice required of the pastor.

Lastly, we looked at Isaiah as an example of a pastoral theologian at work, dealing with the problems of the people in exile. He demonstrates how it is possible to provide theological answers to weighty problems and exemplifies the manner which is best calculated to have the desired effect.

3

The Synoptic Gospels and Acts

New Testament pastoral theology consists of the interweaving of two strands. An explicit strand deals with the nature and constitution of the church and speaks directly about its ministry. It is both conspicuous and unsystematic in character and it is not surprising, therefore, that scholars have usually been intrigued and occupied with this strand of pastoral theology. The explicit strand does not, however, stand alone. It is accompanied by an implicit strand which has been comparatively neglected. Implicitly, the New Testament documents are pastoral documents. They are theology called forth by the pastoral situation of the church and theology shaped to speak to particular pastoral situations.

Both form criticism and redaction criticism were, in part, concerned to discover the real life situations which lay behind the Gospels. Their conclusions were often excessive and had disturbing consequences for the authority of the Bible.[1] But to argue that the New Testament was written as a pastoral response to the needs of the churches rather than as an unrelated abstract theology need not cast doubt on its validity as revealed truth. It may simply indicate that this was the way the Holy Spirit chose to cause truth to be mediated and recorded rather than in theoretical textbook form. Nor does it lock them into a particular time zone. His inspiration could easily ensure that it contained all that was sufficient for the churches to which it was originally addressed and those yet to come. In any case, an examination of those pastoral needs suggests that many of the pastoral situations which the writers had in mind have persisted down the centuries.

The neglect of this simple fact has had a detrimental effect both on theology and on pastoral ministry. In theology, it has led to the erection of false and irrelevant debates. In the current

---

[1] D. A. Carson, 'Redaction Criticism: On the Legitimacy and Illegitimacy of a Literary Tool', in D. A. Carson and J. D. Woodbridge (eds), *Scripture and Truth*, pp. 119–142; S. S. Smalley, 'Redaction Criticism', in I. H. Marshall (ed), *New Testament Interpretation*, pp. 181–195.

debate regarding unity and diversity in the New Testament, for example, Donald Carson has recently pointed out that 'the diversity in the New Testament very often reflects diverse pastoral concerns, with no implications whatsoever of a different credal structure' as some have supposed.[2] Because most pastors are taught within an academic theological context, many have been blinded to the pastoral strategies and pastoral value of the New Testament. In the ministry they have faced a different set of problems from those faced in the theological college and so dispensed with the theory they were taught as irrelevant. Having been taught no better, they have failed to appreciate the pastoral value of much doctrine and have not seen that the pastoral strategies within the New Testament could enrich their own ministries. Pastoral ministry, therefore, has often been divorced from its theological anchor and it has been the poorer for it.

It would be absurd to claim that the New Testament is exclusively a pastoral document. Clearly it is not. It has evangelistic, missiological, apologetic, ethical, socio-political, purely theological and even polemical dimensions as well. Our survey of the New Testament will show that the consistency of pastoral theology is uneven because of these diverse interests. But the pastoral dimension is a legitimate and distinct dimension none the less.

Our approach will be to examine both these strands in the New Testament books, but, consistent with the belief that many of the books are pastoral theology rather than merely about pastoral theology, the emphasis will fall on the implicit strand.

THE GOSPEL OF MATTHEW

Scholarly interest in Matthew's Gospel has recently been revived and scholarly opinion is in a state of flux with many questions concerning the Gospel unanswered.[3] But much recent study has concentrated on the pastoral perspective which is to be seen in Matthew. Some years ago, Massaux argued, with good justification, that Matthew was the most popular

---

[2] D. A. Carson, 'Unity and Diversity in the New Testament: The Possibility of Systematic Theology', in *Scripture and Truth*, pp. 65–95, especially pp. 86–89.
[3] G. N. Stanton (ed), *The Interpretation of Matthew*, pp. 1–19.

Gospel in the early church and was normative for its understanding of the Christian life.[4] The exposure of Matthew's pastoral interest has served to illuminate Massaux's claim even more.

That Matthew's Gospel has a pastoral purpose is self-evident. He alone, of the Gospel writers, uses the word church (16:18 and 18:17) and he alone speaks openly about church discipline (18:15–20). In addition, Ralph Martin[5] has referred to four other clues which draw attention to Matthew as a pastor, clues which are particularly discernible when Matthew's handling of the gospel story is compared with Mark's.

Firstly, Matthew has a didactic interest. The inclusion of blocks of teaching by Jesus (5:1 – 7:29; 10:5–42; 13:1–52; 18:1–35 and 23:1 – 25:46) shows a very real concern for instruction in the Christian community. It is not only the content of the teaching which demonstrates this but its style. It is written in a compressed form which would be both suitable to enable young converts to grasp and remember it or for pastors and teachers to use it as their own textbook. Details, recorded by Mark, which do not serve this end are omitted by Matthew.

Secondly, when Matthew does expand Mark's material he does so with a pastoral intention. Martin illustrates this from the way in which Matthew tells the story of Peter's attempt to walk on the water to Jesus (14:22–31; cf. Mk. 6:45–52). Mark makes no reference to Peter and his lack of faith, whereas Matthew clearly intends to teach that when a man is in distress he should not lack faith but look to Jesus.

This feature of Matthew's Gospel has been explored more fully by David Hill,[6] who in turn draws on the work of Heinz Joachim Held,[7] in relation to the way in which Matthew narrates the miracles of Jesus. Hill believes that the miracles are not important for Matthew for their own sakes but primarily for their value as instruments of instruction for the church. They have, he suggests, three interrelated themes: the need for and the nature of faith (8:5–13; 9:18–26

[4] E. Massaux, *Influence de l'évangile de Saint Matthieu sur la Literature Chrétienne avant Saint Irenée*.

[5] R. P. Martin, *New Testament Foundations*, vol. 1, pp. 229–231.

[6] D. Hill, *The Gospel of Matthew*, pp. 62f.

[7] H. J. Held, 'Matthew as Interpreter of the Miracle Stories', in G. Bornkamm, G. Barth and H. J. Held (eds), *Tradition and Interpretation in Matthew*, pp. 165–299.

and 15:21–28), discipleship (8:23–27; 14:13–21, 22–33 and 17:14–21) and the authority and person of Christ (8:16–17, 28–34 and 9:2–7).

Martin's third clue is that the twelve are characterized as a school of disciples who are making progress in their faith and growing towards maturity as they receive instruction from their master. In Mark, progress is often impossible because they are characterized as confused and faithless, but Matthew has improved their image and they no longer fail to understand.[8] Martin cites Matthew 11:28–30 and 23:8–10, to which we might add 13:12, as examples. Furthermore, the disciples are seen as potential teachers themselves (*e.g.* 13:52) although Luz's view that the disciples do not so much represent the leadership of the church as the Christian community as a whole should be noted.[9] Matthew's concern is not to define the office of the leader but to ensure that the church is a community of mutual instructors and eager learners.

Fourthly, Martin notes the way in which Matthew has shaped the teaching of Jesus. When compared with Mark, he has often simplified it and concentrated on the didactic points. Matthew's retelling of Jesus' meeting with the rich young ruler (19:16–30) is examined as a case in point. The changes suggest that 'Matthew's concern is to rebuke the moral laxity in a church which is facing temptation to ethical indifference'.[10]

The detection of this pastoral seam has shed further light on the Jewish-Gentile tensions which occur in Matthew. For a long time it has been debated whether Matthew was pro- or anti-Jewish or pro- or anti-Gentile and there appeared to be much to be said on both sides. The pastoral emphasis, however, has led to a fairly widespread agreement that Matthew is writing for a church that was composed of both Jews and Gentiles and which was sadly divided.[11] He writes, therefore, to clarify the nature of Christian discipleship particularly in relation to the Jewish traditions from which Christianity emerged and in relation to the validity of mission to the Gentiles.

In his recent commentary on Matthew, R. H. Gundry has

[8] For a fuller discussion see G. Barth, 'Matthew's understanding of the Law', *ibid.*, pp. 106–110 and 118–121; and the qualification of U. Luz, 'The Disciples in the Gospel according to Matthew', in Stanton (ed), *Interpretation of Matthew*, pp. 102f.

[9] Luz, *ibid.*, pp. 110f.   [10] Martin, *Foundations*, vol. 1, pp. 230f.

[11] Hill, *Matthew*, p. 49 and W. G. Thompson, *Matthew's Advice to a Divided Community*.

given a slightly different emphasis to these divisions. Whilst not disagreeing that the Jewish-Gentile split was central to the division, he has spoken in terms of the church being a mixed church in a more specific sense.[12] The problems of the church arose not only because of differing religious backgrounds but more generally because as a growing church it was experiencing an influx of new converts, not all of whom would have fully understood the gospel or have been genuine in their faith (13:24–30, 36–43, 47–50; 25:1–46). The division was not only between Jewish and Gentile converts but between true and false disciples. Gundry's wider interpretation enables us to make more sense of the inclusion of some topics in Matthew's syllabus. The divided and mixed nature of the church, then, determines Matthew's agenda.

Matthew's pastoral method is to remind the church of the clear teaching of Jesus on the relevant issues. From first to last Jesus is portrayed as having commanding authority (see especially 16:16 and 28:18) and his true disciples are cast in the role of followers or learners (4:22; 8:22–23; 10:38; 11:29 and 24:32). The true test of learning was obedience (13:13–15; 21:28–32 and 28:20).

Discipleship, then, was obedience to Jesus Christ – a Jesus who came as the Jewish Messiah in fulfilment of the Old Testament prophecies. The twelve fulfilment passages, the sermon on the mount, the issue of divorce (19:1–12), the question of the temple tax (17:24–27), the expectation of persecution from the Jews, the attack on the Pharisees in chapter 23 and numerous other references throughout would have served the purpose of defining the relationship between Christianity and Judaism, both so that the apologetic task of defending the faith to Jews could be clarified and so that internal tensions could be resolved.

One of the biggest single issues that the church faced was its uncertainty over the law. Jewish members were naturally more prone to emphasize its significance whilst it is clearly implied that Gentile members had antinomian tendencies. To answer this Jesus is presented as a teacher of righteousness, almost the giver of a new law, although that may be a misleading description of his intention. External legalism is definitely rejected

---

[12] R. H. Gundry, *Matthew. A Commentary on his Literary and Theological Art*, p. 5.

(*e.g.* 5:21–6:18; 15:1–11),[13] but the law is not therefore of no consequence. He came to fulfil it, not to abolish it, and to call his disciples to a greater righteousness (5:17–20). The demand to reject accommodation with pagan society and to cultivate righteousness in the concrete affairs of life is evident from beginning to end. Those who taught moral laxity were false prophets (7:15–23). All genuine disciples of Jesus could be known by their commitment to the goal of perfection (5:48 and 19:21).

Another issue which Matthew addresses is the need to confess Jesus publicly. With the growth of the church it is not surprising if the cutting edge of evangelism was being blunted, but Matthew holds no comfort for those who believe in secret discipleship or introverted fellowship (5:13–16; 10:32–33; 26:69–75). The fear of witnessing to Christ was aggravated by the threat of persecution – a threat which was likely only to increase as the end of the age drew near (24:9–10) – but to be true to Jesus the disciples were called upon to suffer with endurance (10:16–31). Failure to be faithful was none other than a failure of faith to which Matthew constantly draws attention (6:30; 8:26; 14:31; 16:8; and 28:17). On the other hand, prayer and fasting could give the necessary courage to remain faithful (6:16–18 and 26:36–46).

As well as talking about the nature of discipleship Matthew talks much about the community of the disciples. For him, it is first and foremost a brotherhood, not an institution (5:21–26, 47; 18:15–17, 35; 23:8; 25:40 and 28:10). It is a brotherhood where there is to be special care provided for the weak and vulnerable 'little ones' (18:2–14, especially v. 10; 21:14–16). The strong and the self-sufficient either do not need the attention or would not heed it if it was offered to them (9:12–13).

At first sight Matthew appears to speak of the ecclesiastical hierarchy which was to lead the church. This is especially so in Matthew 16:16–19, where Peter is given the keys of the kingdom and apparently spoken of as the rock on which Christ would

---

[13] Gundry's comment on the legalism which Matthew's approach threatens is worth noting, 'These emphases pose the danger of legalism and need balancing by the doctrine of the indwelling Spirit, through whose life and power alone Jesus' disciples can fulfill the righteous requirement of the law (Rom. 8:1–4). But it is good to have Matthew's emphases without that balance; for in some situations to introduce the doctrine of the Spirit quickly is to dull the edge of the demands made on Jesus' disciples. They might fail to feel the pain caused by the sharp edge of those demands. Only when that pain is felt will the Spirit's enablement amount to more than a comfortable sanctification open to the incursion of antinomianism.' *Ibid.*, pp. 9f.

build his unconquerable church. Most scholars agree, however, that it is wrong to see these verses as establishing the authority of Peter or his successors. Peter is seen throughout as a representative disciple and that must govern our exegesis of these verses.[14] Furthermore, leaders consistently stand as representatives for the whole community.[15] Peter stands as the representative of all who are open to receive God's revelation and to confess Jesus as the Christ. This is why Peter is the rock. There is, therefore, no basis for believing in the primacy of Peter in any hierarchy.

It must be asked, however, whether the keys of the kingdom and the responsibility of binding and loosing on earth (16:19) do not give Peter personal authority in the church. Again, if Peter is here referred to in his representative capacity, and Matthew 18:18 where the same authority is given to the whole church shows that he is, there is no need to assume this to be so. Moreover, it is questionable whether the granting of the keys and the binding and loosing injunction are intended to convey personal authority in any case. Keys are a means of entry. The scribes and Pharisees had thrown away the key to prevent others from entering (23:13; *cf.* Lk. 11:52) but the announcement of the gospel by Christ's disciples would throw the door open once more. Peter was to be the first to admit people through his preaching at Pentecost and – as far as Gentiles were concerned – to the household of Cornelius. Binding and loosing must be seen in the same way. That is to say they must be seen, not as a personal right belonging to members of a hierarchy, but as the consequence of their preaching of forgiveness through Christ and of the reception which that message met.[16]

To be sure, Matthew is aware of the role of teachers, wise men and prophets (23:34) within the church, but such functions are not restricted to the few.[17] The spirit of leadership is his more prominent concern. Four times (10:24–25; 18:2–9; 20:25–28 and 23:7–12) he returns to this matter to emphasize that true

---

[14] O. Cullmann, *Peter: Disciple, Apostle, Martyr*; see also Gundry, *Matthew*, p. 9 and p. 334; D. Guthrie, *New Testament Theology*, pp. 710–715.

[15] Luz, in Stanton, *Interpretation of Matthew*, p. 110 and Thompson, *Matthew's Advice*, p. 84, etc.

[16] Guthrie, *NT Theology*, pp. 713–715 and Thompson, *Matthew's Advice*, pp. 201f.

[17] E. Schillebeeckx, *Ministry*, seems to reach strangely contradictory conclusions regarding Matthew's church leaders, pp. 20–24.

leaders in the church follow the pattern of Christ and take the path of self-humiliation and service, caring not for their own status but for the needs of the most insignificant members of their flocks.

The brotherhood is presented as a disciplined community in Matthew 18:15–20. The arrangement of the chapter as a whole is no accident and the location of these particular verses is something like meat in a sandwich. The verses are prefaced by the parable of the lost sheep (18:10–13), which stresses the responsibility of the community actively to seek a weak brother who has strayed. They are followed by the parable of the unmerciful servant (vv. 21–35), which lays upon Christians the obligation to forgive to a totally unreasonable extent. Only if both sides of the sandwich are observed can the discipline of verses 15–20 be truly exercised.

Matthew 18:15–20 is more properly to be understood as providing the guide-lines for reconciling a brother rather than disciplining a brother. Verse 14, which speaks of God's desire that none should be lost, should be seen not only as concluding the previous paragraph but providing the springboard for the next. An individual disciple should attempt to win back his straying brother by approaching him privately and exposing his fault in such a manner as to cause him to abandon it. If that fails he should take one or two witnesses who should also encourage his repentance and reconciliation. Only if that fails should the matter be brought to the wider church whose involvement, it was hoped, would lend further authority to the attempts to persuade the wayward brother to be reconciled. If the straying brother is still unmoved, 'redemptive excommunication' should be applied.[18]

Here is neither a magisterial system of church discipline nor any rationale for the establishment of church courts. Still less does it provide any encouragement for the exercise of authoritarian leadership within the church and the advent of petty dictators. Here is a brotherhood relating to each other as a close community with the aim of reconciling those who are breaking away. Only if all attempts to reconcile have failed is discipline to be exercised. The church so often swings from one extreme to the other. It either exercises little concern over its straying

[18] Thompson, *Matthew's Advice*, p. 201.

members and becomes lax in a way which is foreign to the spirit of Matthew or it exercises too tight a control and loses sight of the objective of discipline. The need to exercise carefully balanced discipline, which both reconciles the straying and keeps the church free from compromise, is one to which the whole church needs to be committed. It is precisely because such great skill is required of those who exercise discipline that it is too important to be left to the leaders alone.[19]

A final characteristic of the community of disciples in Matthew is that it is a missionary community. Matthew 10:5–15 establishes the disciples as a missionary group and gives the priority in their missionary activity to the Jews. Matthew 28:19–20 reaffirms their missionary character but universalizes the scope of the mission, consistent with the earlier universalistic notes within the Gospel (*e.g.* 8:11; 21:43; 24:14 and 26:13). Just as the individual disciple cannot be a true disciple if he is afraid to acknowledge Jesus before men, so the community cannot be a true community of disciples unless it too acknowledges Jesus before the nations.

Matthew's essential method is to take the discourses of Jesus and use them to address the problems of the church of his day. He has no need to twist or invent history to do this, as some suggest.[20] The teaching of Christ who called Matthew to follow him is sufficient for the needs of the expanding church of a later day. What is more, Matthew's Gospel has a timeless quality about it, for as Gundry has written,

Wherever the church has grown large and mixed, wherever the the church is polarized between the extremes of latitudinarianism and sectarianism, wherever the church feels drawn to accommodation with forces that oppose the gospel, wherever the church loses its vision of worldwide evangelism, wherever the church lapses into smug religiosity with its attendant vices of ostentation, hypocrisy, and haughty disdain for its underprivileged and correspondingly zealous

[19] For a recent thorough discussion of church discipline, to which the phrase 'redemptive excommunication' is owed, see M. Jeschke, *Discipling the Brother*.

[20] Paul Achtemeier seems to overstate the case for the pastoral intention of the Gospels and is unnecessarily defensive about their value as historical records in 'Resources for the Pastoral Ministry in the Synoptic Gospels', in E. E. Shelp and R. Sunderland (eds), *A Biblical Basis for Ministry*, pp. 152f.

members – there the Gospel of Matthew speaks with power and pertinence.[21]

THE GOSPEL OF MARK

Mark's Gospel is much less obviously concerned with pastoral theology than Matthew's, even though it has many relevant themes in common with Matthew. The conciseness of its portrait of Jesus and its brisk style make it amply suited as an evangelistic tract and so it is.[22] But that is not its sole purpose. As with the other Gospels, there is a wide diversity of opinion as to its precise origin, purpose and destination,[23] but among the plethora of voices certain ideas are both common and enduring.

William Lane represents many in stating that Mark's Gospel is 'a pastoral response' to the critical situation of the Gentile Christians in Rome who were facing persecution and martyrdom and who had been forced underground to an existence in the catacombs during the reign of Nero.[24] If this is so, in what ways does Mark provide pastoral support for them?

Like Matthew, Mark conveys some of his pastoral message through the teaching of Jesus. The disciples, in particular, often lack faith and understanding and so provide their master with an opportunity for careful instruction. But the discourses of Jesus do not provide Mark, as they did Matthew, with his main pastoral method. For that, Mark turns to the example of Jesus.

Mark does not provide the church in Rome with any cheap encouragement. As Ralph Martin has put it, 'He provides no props for a weak faith and extends no crutch on which persecuted believers may lean.'[25] To pretend that there are easy answers or that sudden deliverance is around the corner is not only cruelly deceptive but contrary to the very constitution of Christian discipleship. The answer does not lie in the avoidance of suffering in this world but in enduring, as Christ did, so that one might be vindicated and receive a reward in the next world (10:29–31 and 13:16–27).

---

[21] Gundry, *Matthew*, p. 10.

[22] D. Guthrie, *New Testament Introduction*, pp. 57f.

[23] R. P. Martin, *Mark – Evangelist and Theologian*, provides a survey of the main views.

[24] W. L. Lane, *The Gospel of Mark*, p. 15. See also E. Best, *Mark: The Gospel as Story*, pp. 51–54; C. E. B. Cranfield, *The Gospel according to Mark*, p. 15; Guthrie, *NT Introduction*, pp. 59–63; and Martin, *Foundations*, vol. 1, pp. 214–216.

[25] Martin, *Mark*, p. 219.

Suffering Christians were to be encouraged by the complete identity there was between their experience and that of their Lord.[26] He had suffered in his personal life (1:12–13; 3:20–35 and 6:1–6) and been betrayed by a close companion (3:19). He was in continuous conflict with both Jewish and Roman authorities. His own disciples deserted him (14:41–52, 66–72) while he endured the shameful process of martyrdom without being spared a single indignity. Discipleship was costly, but that was no more than the life of Jesus predicted. It was also exactly what his plain teaching had foretold (8:31; 10:30, 38–40; 13:9–13).

Some, doubtless, were inclined to dismiss such teaching with the comment that it was all right for Jesus because he was more than a man. Mark, therefore, stresses the humanity of Jesus throughout his Gospel and makes frequent use of the title 'Son of Man'[27] in an attempt both to encourage suffering Christians and to combat a false and dangerous heresy that devalued the humanity of Jesus. Theologically, an overstress on the divinity of Christ at the expense of his humanity is erroneous; pastorally it is disastrous. A Christ who was exempt from the feelings of humanity could provide no incentive to others to share with him in suffering. Only a Christ who was truly human and who could feel as men felt when they experienced suffering could be a comfort to those enduring persecution for his sake.

If this were the whole picture it might be unrelentingly grim. But Mark also invites them to endure because the Christ whom they serve was not only the humiliated 'Son of Man' but the 'Son of God' – a man of tremendous power and authority. A central theme of Mark's Gospel is that of Christ in conflict. The conflicts, in which he continually engaged, were occasions when his authority and power were displayed. Apart from the human authorities who were opposed to God (*e.g.* 2:24; 3:6, etc.) Jesus is shown to battle against all the Satanically-inspired forces which destroy men. Thus, in 4:35 – 5:43, he encounters nature, demons, disease and death and liberates men and women from the imprisoning effect they all have. There can be no neutrality in this battle against evil (9:38–41). Equally, there need be no neutrality, for Christ is always victorious, even

---

[26] This interpretation owes much to Lane, *Gospel of Mark*, pp. 15f.

[27] On Mark's stress on the humanity of Jesus see Guthrie, *NT Introduction*, pp. 55–57 and Martin, *Foundations*, vol. 1, p. 220.

when his opponents think they have him trapped.

Although Howard Kee's suggestion[28] that Mark's Gospel was compiled as a handbook for itinerant preachers is almost certainly to be rejected, it does serve to draw attention to the value of the Gospel as an instructional guide for Christian workers as well as a pastoral theology for a suffering church. The essence of discipleship is captured by Mark in his account of the appointment of the twelve (3:13–19). Two dimensions are crucial. Firstly, the disciples are chosen to be companions of and apprentices to Jesus. Secondly, they are appointed to be sent out as his representatives and to continue his mission (see also 6:6–13).[29] With this in mind, it is possible to identify a number of other features of the true apostle of Jesus.

Jesus' own understanding of ministry, which is formative for that of his disciples, is spoken of in 1:35–39, where he is shown to have a sense of mission from which he will not deviate. He does not amble through life meeting whatever comes and merely reacting to it. He refuses to be side-tracked into becoming a sensational miracle worker. He exercises control over his own life and ministry so that it conforms to the calling of God. His priority is neither to respond to the immense needs of the sick nor to respond to the pressure of his well-meaning but misguided disciples. He has come as a preacher of the kingdom of God and as one who can demonstrate the in-breaking of that kingdom. Equally he has come to die (8:31). Those who have learnt from him will want to exercise the same sense of purpose in their own ministries.

As well as sharing his sense of purpose, Jesus expects his disciples to share his authority and power. Such a conclusion is inescapable from Mark's Gospel. Jesus says that his disciples were to have authority to drive out demons (3:15) and later they are shown to be exercising it (6:13). 9:38–41 shows that such authority was available more widely and was not to be limited to the apostles alone. In addition, the longer ending of Mark continues to underline the point (16:15–18). Ministry is expected to change people's life situations in definite ways but not simply for their personal comfort. It is a display of the victory of God over Satan which was such an essential dimension of the ministry of Jesus. It is in this context that the theme of faith

---

[28] H. C. Kee, *Community of the New Age*, *passim*.

[29] Kruse, *NT Foundations for Ministry*, pp. 32f.

rightly fits (2:5; 4:40; 6:6; 11:22; 16:14). In Mark the disciples leave much to be desired. They continually lack understanding and equally lack faith in Jesus. Jesus challenges them to trust him. Faith is not to be thought of as the power of positive thinking. It is rather an active recognition of the authority of God. The lack of faith would be a great hindrance to their mission.

With such exciting prospects before them it is not surprising that they should have suffered from oversized egos. Jesus, therefore, spends as much time teaching them about the other side of the ministry. They are called to follow in the footsteps of the suffering servant (10:35–45, especially v. 45).[30] They must reject any notions of status (9:33–37) or reward (10:28–31) in this life. They must be content even to do without the accepted minimum means of security if they are to be his messengers (6:8–9). The most they can hope for is that all these will be obtained in the after-life. In this life, their path is to be one of suffering and serving and they are for ever destined to be alienated from the wider social context in which they live.

This is by no means a comprehensive theology of Mark. It is simply intended to point out certain key pastoral perspectives which are inherent in Mark. The suffering church is invited to meditate on the Lord who endured the same experience. The same invitation to look at Christ is issued to Christian leaders so that they also can imitate his sense of purpose, his power and his servanthood.

LUKE – ACTS

Picking one's way through the multitude of suggestions about the purposes Luke had in writing his two-volume work[31] is rather like trying to pick one's way through a Dutch tulip field in spring without stepping on any of the flowers. The field is both crowded and colourful. A recent trend, however, has tended to emphasize Luke's writing as a pastoral enterprise[32] and ironically, even those who are less than enthusiastic about such an approach have themselves unwittingly concluded that

---

[30] *Ibid.*, pp. 41–45.

[31] Throughout this discussion Luke and Acts will be treated as a single work.

[32] P. S. Minear, 'Dear Theo (The Kerygmatic Intention and claim of the Book of Acts)', *Interp.* 27 (1973), pp. 131–150; S. G. Wilson, *The Gentiles and the Gentile Mission in Luke-Acts* and Martin, *Foundations*, vol. 1, p. 249.

Luke–Acts is to a great extent pastoral in intention.[33]

Before proceeding to expound Luke's pastoral approach it may be wise to clarify three possible misconceptions. Firstly, to argue that Luke wrote in response to pastoral needs in the church of his day is not to claim that this was his only purpose in writing. It is unwise therefore to assume that one will find deep and hidden pastoral problems lying behind every nuance of his writings. Even if it were agreed that he was primarily concerned with pastoral matters, there would still be room for Luke to have other objectives in view. Many have thought, with good reason, that he is also concerned to write evangelistically for a Gentile audience. Still others see something of a missiological textbook in his writings. Although crude apologetic motives are no longer credited to Luke, some apologetic themes are evident. There are equally some theological concerns which he wishes to express even if some of the claims made by earlier scholars in this direction are no longer tenable.[34]

Secondly, the claim that Luke is writing pastorally should not be taken to mean that he is unreliable as a historian. Luke's historical trustworthiness has been the subject of much debate for a long time, but to concede that he has a pastoral intention is not to provide those who wish to question his reliability with another argument in their favour. Although Luke would have clearly selected his material and, to some extent, shaped its expression, to meet his pastoral ends it does not mean that he had to invent or fabricate his material. He himself emphasizes in his preface (Lk. 1:1–4) that his concern was to present a reliable account of the life of Jesus and the birth of the church and he stresses the role played by eye-witnesses in putting together his account (Acts 2:32; 3:15; 5:32; 10:39–40; 13:30–31 and 22:15). Anything less reliable would not have rendered Theophilus' faith more certain, as Luke aimed to do. There is a good deal of evidence to suggest that he succeeded in being historically trustworthy.[35]

Thirdly, to argue that Luke wrote pastorally is not to argue that his writing is merely practical and therefore untheological. Robert Maddox seems to fear that this is where the emphasis

---

[33] R. Maddox, *The Purpose of Luke-Acts*, p. 2.

[34] *Ibid.*, *passim*; Martin, *Foundations* vol. 1, pp. 244–50 and Minear, 'Dear Theo', p. 132.

[35] For a justification of Luke as a historian see I. H. Marshall, *Luke – Historian and Theologian*; *cf.*, Wilson, *Gentile Mission in Luke-Acts*, pp. 255–267.

on pastoral motivation might lead.[36] But the fear is based on a false assumption. It is a misleading dichotomy to oppose the practical and the theological. Maddox's fear means that, in the end, he fails to see that his own solution to the question of Luke's purpose is nothing short of saying that he intended to write a pastoral theology. Even S. G. Wilson, who is one of the leading exponents of Luke's pastoral purpose, wrongly over-states the contrast between Paul and Luke and claims that, in comparison with Paul, Luke is no theologian.[37] The assumption which underlies these views is that theology is very restricted in its nature. True, there are differences between Luke and Paul. Luke is far less of a systematician or dogmatician. But he is no less of a theologian for all that. It is simply that, as Paul Minear has put it, 'Qua theologian he was closer to the modern preacher-teacher-counsellor than to the graduate school exegete or dogmatician.'[38] To be practical is not to be untheological. To be a good pastor demands that one is both practical and theological.

Reading much of the New Testament today is like listening to one side of a telephone conversation. We can only infer what is being said at the other end from what is being said at our end. Similarly, assessing what questions Luke is answering, whether spoken or unspoken, can only be inferred from the themes which he addresses. Certainty, therefore, cannot be claimed, but a fair degree of understanding may well be reached.

What is more tantalizing with Luke-Acts is that we do not know who is on the other end of the telephone. We know he is called Theophilus and that he is almost certainly a Gentile, probably of some social standing. It is possible that he was a believer who, although committed to Christ, now faced a complex set of questions as to the validity of his faith. Possibly his Christian experience did not match up to the claims he had heard made for the gospel when he first believed. We can equally assume that Theophilus is not alone but that he is a representative of a whole host of Christian believers who were facing, and possibly voicing, the same questions.[39] The ques-

---

[36] Maddox, *Purpose of Luke-Acts*, p. 2.
[37] Wilson, *Gentile Mission in Luke-Acts*, p. 255.   [38] Minear, 'Dear Theo', p. 149.
[39] For the difficulties in identifying Theophilus see Martin, *Foundations*, vol. 1, pp. 245f.

tions provide Luke with his pastoral agenda.

One easily identifiable theme sought to answer the question, 'Where does the Christian church fit in the overall purposes of God?' This general question was prompted by a number of supplementary questions, such as, 'Where had the church come from and where did its roots lie?' To answer this Luke sets out to write an 'orderly account' (Lk. 1:3) which demonstrates how the church is the proper outcome of the ministry of Jesus Christ. The gospel story is incomplete without the church story.[40] Conversely, the church story makes no sense apart from the gospel story. He takes, therefore, a much broader chronological sweep than do the other Gospel writers, and narrates developments from the birth of John the Baptist to the ministry of Paul. Acts may well be thought to focus on the church or be a 'Gospel of the Spirit', but in Luke's understanding it is the record of the continuing ministry of Jesus himself (Acts 1:1; 9:5; 16:7; 22:18 and 23:11).

Luke's intention should not be reduced to this alone, for he goes on to answer the awkward question of how the church now related to Judaism. There were plenty of uncomfortable incidents which made it imperative that this question be answered. Luke sets about giving them an answer. On the one hand the Christian church finds its origin in the Jewish heritage and is the fulfilment of their hopes of redemption. This can be particularly seen in the birth narratives in Luke 1:5 – 2:52. Everything in the Jewish heritage should have prepared them for the gospel of Jesus and Luke demonstrates how many, particularly of the Pharisees, accept this to be so (*e.g.*. Lk. 13:31; Acts 5:34; 15:5 and 23:6–10). On the other hand the Jews, as a whole, reject Jesus and his message. Jerusalem increasingly dominates Luke's Gospel, from 9:31 onwards, as the place where Jesus must go to die (9:51, 53; 13:33–34; 18:31–34). And Stephen's attack on the Temple, law and the people (Acts 7:1–53) and the discussions about the place of the law (*e.g.* Lk. 11:37–54 and Acts 15:1–35) show how much Christianity is to be distinguished from Judaism.[41]

But the greatest evidence of this concern to understand the identity of the church lies in the major discussion of the legit-

[40] Maddox, *Purpose of Luke-Acts*, p. 10 and pp. 183–186.
[41] *Ibid.*, pp. 30–65. See also E. E. Ellis, *The Gospel of Luke*, pp. 16–18.

imacy of the mission to Gentiles.[42] Should Gentiles be actively evangelized and added to the church? The apostles, after all, had not taken the initiative in seeking their conversion to begin with and Peter is shown to have been reluctant to make the break (Acts 10). None the less, once the break has been made and Paul has been commissioned by Christ to be an apostle to the Gentiles (Acts 9:15), the Gentile mission increasingly dominates the scene. God's unfolding plan for his church was that it should spread from Galilee to Jerusalem and then through 'all Judea and Samaria, and to the ends of the earth' (Acts 1:8).[43]

The canvas is even broader, in that Luke paints the picture of the church against the background of world history (Lk. 3:1–2) and in relation to contemporary political authority. The church is shown to be politically non-subversive (Lk. 20:25 and 23:1–25). Paul's missions meet with favour from Roman authorities and are commended by them as legitimate (Acts 13:4–12; 18:14–16; 19:35–41; 26:31–32). Given Luke's grand perspective, it is remarkable that he gives such a prominent place to individuals, and especially to women, children and the socially deprived in his writing.[44] The purposes of God can be painted on an immense canvas, for he is the 'Sovereign Lord' (Lk. 2:29 and Acts 4:24). But his purposes are worked out through, and his salvation is available to, very surprising and very ordinary people. Here is no story of an impersonal grand political force at work which moves at the expense of the needs of ordinary people. Rather than neglecting them, they are the chief recipients of the grace of God.

Yet another cause of unrest in the church was the delay in the return of Christ. The argument that Luke wrote precisely in order to address the embarrassment caused by the delay[45] is no longer considered to be acceptable in an unmodified form. The principal objection being that Luke does not seem to have removed the return of Christ to some distant unspecified time, as some proponents of the theory suggested, but continues to speak of it as a sudden and impending event. What Luke's emphasis on eschatology adds is that the coming of Jesus

---

42 Maddox, *Purpose of Luke-Acts*, p. 184 and Wilson, *Gentile Mission in Luke-Acts, passim.*
43 K. Barth, *Church Dogmatics*, iv, Part 2, pp. 641–660.
44 L. Morris, *Luke*, pp. 40–42.
45 H. Conzelmann, *The Theology of Luke*, pp. 95–136.

and the founding of the church have already fulfilled eschatological hopes in part (Lk. 4:17–21; 17:21; Acts 2:14–39, etc.).[46] Their present role, therefore, is not insignificant and there is no encouragement for the church to be monastically withdrawn from or pietistically inactive in the world, whilst waiting for their full salvation to come. *Now* is the day of salvation; the last days have dawned. They are an eschatological people and should play their part in the end times to the full.

The people who were first called Christians at Antioch may well have been wondering about their self-identity and confused by the changing nature of their movement, but Luke assures them that they conform exactly to God's plan for them, for the Jews and for the world.

As well as asking 'where do we fit?' Theophilus and others were almost certainly asking for some explanations regarding events which may have shaken their confidence in the church. This eschatological people seemed to be far from perfect – a point worth remembering when we are constantly urged to return to the New Testament church! Internally they were composed of people who were still prepared to lie (Acts 5:1–10), they discriminated against Hellenistic widows (6:1–6), they attracted people for the wrong motives (8:9–24), they lacked the faith to believe that God really could change people (9:26), they were led by apostles who were less than clear-sighted about their mission (10:9–17) and they faced internal disputes about the true nature of their message (15:1–29) and quarrels among their leaders (15:36–41). Externally they met with opposition, suffering and poverty.

Luke does not present a romantic picture of the early church, but he counters the doubts of his readers by showing how every time a crisis was faced and the church's condition seemed hopeless, it was followed by a new advance.[47] What triggered the new advance was not confidence in the church and its people but confidence in the word of God. When the word was preached the people discovered that 'nothing is impossible with God' (Lk. 1:37) and they could be amazed once more at the greatness of God (Lk. 9:43). The remarkable events which Luke records occurred against all odds and showed that the word of

---

[46] Maddox, *Purpose of Luke-Acts*, pp. 100–158.
[47] Minear, 'Dear Theo', pp. 136–139.

God would triumph (Acts 6:7; 12:24; 13:49; 19:10, 20 and 28:31). What was needed was for the church to be strengthened (Lk. 22:32 and Acts 18:23), for their little faith to be exercised (Lk. 17:5) and for the word to be preached with boldness (Acts 4:29, 31; 8:4). Part of Luke's answer to the growing uncertainty about faith is to show that the doubts and questions his readers face can be silenced by their gaining a truer picture of God at work.

Luke's method throughout is simply to recount the narrative of the ministry of Jesus and the growth of the church and let it speak for itself. He does not draw out explicit lessons, nor explicitly hold up examples. In teaching Christian virtues, for example, he tells of Barnabas with his generosity, of Philip and his passion for evangelism, of Paul and his joy in suffering[48] and presents them as models to be followed. But he does so in an unobtrusive manner so that the convictions are carried within the narrative itself. Theophilus and his contemporaries would not miss their lessons.

The Acts of the Apostles gives much insight into the life of the early church, particularly in its summary statements in 2:42–47 and 4:32–37. From it we can learn something of the importance of baptism, of worship and of fellowship, as well as of mission and miracle. But it is surprising how little we can learn about its organization, and those who have detected 'early catholicism' in Luke's portrait seem to be reading much into Luke's account.[49]

Clearly it is not intended to be a textbook for church order. No one picture of church government is presented. In Acts 1 the replacement for Judas is chosen by lot, in Acts 6 the 'deacons' are chosen by the people, in Acts 11 Barnabas is delegated by the apostles, in Acts 13 Paul and Barnabas are singled out through prayer, in Acts 14 elders are appointed by Paul and Barnabas and in Acts 15 James presides over the church at Jerusalem in conformity to Jewish tradition as the older brother of the Lord. Prophets, too, play a crucial, if varying role, in Acts as one of the Lord's instruments in the

---

[48] Martin, *Foundations*, vol. 1, p. 248, writes, 'The parallels between Jesus and Paul may have been constructed for a pastoral purpose. By showing how a model Christian's life conforms to that of his Lord, Luke could effectively demonstrate to his congregation the way a Christian should live.' See also Minear, 'Dear Theo', p. 139.

[49] For a recent exposition of the idea of 'early catholicism' see J. D. G. Dunn, *Unity and Diversity in the New Testament*, pp. 341–366. For contrary views see Maddox, *Purpose of Luke-Acts*, p. 185 and Morris, *Luke*, pp. 39f.

church.[50] Nor is there any trace of sacramentalism or rampant institutionalism. The church is a free, spontaneous body, consisting of personal relationships rather than highly organized structures, living and adapting as God moves them into new territory and novel situations.

Luke does, however, give an insight into the inner dynamics of Christian leadership in his account of Paul's speech to the Ephesian elders in Acts 20:17–36, where Paul, coming to the end of his free ministry, is portrayed as an exemplary Christian leader. Every detail of the speech is rich in significance for the pastor. Its message speaks of seven dimensions of the pastoral life.

Firstly, it speaks of the relationship between a pastor and his people. Paul's deep concern for them is shown by the tears he shed on their behalf (v. 19). But their concern and love is reciprocal as is seen by their response to his news (vv. 37–38).

Secondly, the speech has much to say about the character of pastoral work. The lives of leaders should be open to scrutiny and be capable of withstanding close examination. They should be of such a quality as to be fit to serve as an example to others in the church (v. 35). Paul is evidently confident from his repeated use of 'you know . . .' (vv. 18, 20) that his life would pass these tests. This not only sets a high standard for any ministry, but underlines what a privileged position the pastor enjoys, if the flock are to look to him as the example. The other side of the coin, however, is that the minister is no more than a servant of God and as such has nothing to boast about, but rather should exhibit humility (v. 19). This inner humility is accompanied by an outward humiliation, for the true pastoral life is never far from the experience of suffering (vv. 19, 23–24). Ultimately the pastor's life on this earth is of no consequence in itself (see also Phil. 1:15–26). What matters is his service to the flock.

With this in mind the pastor, thirdly, needs to be alert to the special temptations of the ministry. Paul mentions the temptation to curry favour with the congregation by watering down the message (vv. 20, 27), the temptation to be inconsistent and to be one thing in public and another in private (v. 20) and the temptation to be in the job for what can be got out of it (vv.

[50] E. E. Ellis, 'The Role of the Christian Prophet in Acts', in W. W. Gasque and R. P. Martin (eds), *Apostolic History and the Gospel*, pp. 55–67.

33–35). Few pastors today gain much financially from being in the ministry, but that sometimes intensifies the temptation to covet which Paul so roundly exposes here. These temptations, to fear, to professionalism and to greed, perhaps together with the sexual threats of our own day, remain potent traps for ministers and have been the ruin of more than one.

Fourthly, Paul speaks of the message of the ministry. It is at one and the same time a command (to repent and believe, v. 21), a testimony (personally witnessing to God's grace, v. 24), an announcement (of God's reign, v. 25) and an exposition (of the will of God, v. 27). It is evident that it is thoroughly God-centred and not man-centred.

Fifthly, there is much about pastoral obligations in these verses. The pastor has an obligation to the whole word of God (v. 27) for the whole flock of God (v. 28). He can neither select his message nor his sheep. Both are given to him and he must be faithful to his commission. Consequently, he can neither harp on his favourite themes or hobby-horses – a peril which has been suffered by many a congregation – nor ignore those parts of God's will, contained in Scripture, which prove difficult or unpopular. Similarly, he dare not give excessive attention to some members of the flock – perhaps those with whom he is most comfortable – at the expense of others who are less responsive or less flattering. The difficult, the prickly, the unresponsive, the reactionary and the feeble are just as much his responsibility as others. To remind oneself of the cost involved in making them members of the church (v. 28b) is to dismiss instantly any temptation to selective pastoral care.

The fulfilment of these pastoral obligations depends on the pastor keeping himself in a constant state of spiritual fitness (v. 28) and on the related ability to be alert to potential danger (vv. 28–31). As in medicine so in the church: prevention is better than cure. The true pastor warns his flock and prepares them for encroaching danger, even when others are unaware of its existence. The dangers referred to certainly include heresy but are not confined to false doctrine alone. The threats may well derive from moral deviation or sociological opposition as much as theological error.[51]

---

[51] Although Minear overstates his case that the threats Paul refers to are not doctrinal he does have a valid point in arguing that they may come from other areas of the church's life and context as well, 'Dear Theo', p. 148.

The sixth dimension concerns the sharing of ministry. Paul's evangelistic mission was never content with the conversion of individuals. It aimed at the founding of churches and Paul was careful to ensure that these had local leadership before he left (Acts 14:23). He strengthened them in any way he could (Acts 18:23), but leadership was really delegated into their hands. With the impending developments in Paul's ministry he recognized when he met the elders from Ephesus that leadership was finally and fully being handed over to them.[52] Two things should be noted. It seems everywhere to have been a plurality of leadership, never a one-man-ministry, which was exercised in the early church. And, whatever means of appointment placed them in the leadership role, they were commissioned to fulfil it by the Holy Spirit (v. 28) just as surely as the apostle Paul was commissioned by the Lord himself. The fact that they had a delegated authority from Paul did not mean that they were less worthy of their service than he himself was.

Lastly, Paul calls attention to the Holy Spirit. Throughout his work Luke has emphasized the role of the Holy Spirit and it is not surprising to find three references to him in this short address.[53] Paul's own ministry is shown to be totally directed by the Spirit and to be in daily touch with the Spirit (vv. 22–23). It is the Spirit who energizes his work. Similarly it is the Spirit who has commissioned the local leaders of the church and without such a commissioning they are simply unable to minister (v. 28).

Although not part of the address itself, it is significant that Luke records them praying together as soon as Paul had finished speaking. Prayer, too, is one of the recurring themes of Luke's writings.[54] Maybe, like Samuel at the end of his ministry (1 Sa. 12:23), Paul recognizes that although his active work on their behalf will from now on be limited, there is still much he can accomplish through prayer and to fail to exercise that privilege would be tantamount to sin. Acts demonstrates the vital necessity and tremendous power available to the church which prays.

[52] E. Schillebeeckx, *Ministry*, pp. 32f.
[53] Morris, *Luke*, pp. 44–46 and Kruse, *NT Foundations of Ministry*, pp. 67–69.
[54] Morris, *Luke*, p. 46.

SUMMARY

The Gospels are not just historical, theological and evangelistic documents; they are pastoral as well. Behind them lie the needs of the churches. Although it is not possible to be precise about the situations being addressed, it is possible to discern something of their problems from the way the Gospels are written.

We can say that each Gospel responds to those needs by looking afresh at the life, teaching, death, resurrection and, in Luke's case, the continuing ministry of Jesus. Each Gospel does so in a particular way. For Matthew the emphasis falls on the teaching of Jesus; for Mark it is the example of Jesus; whilst Luke is content to narrate the events, of which he can be so sure, and let them speak for themselves. What is important is that each pastoral need was related back to the original gospel. No short cuts were taken in providing the answers and no shallow exhortations were offered. The needs of the church could only be met through a deep understanding of their Lord.

With Kruse,[55] we can conclude that three recurring themes concerning future ministry are that subsequent church leaders would be a continuation of the ministry of Jesus, that they would adopt his servant attitude and share in the authority of his Spirit. But the Gospels are far richer than that, and to restrict what they have to say to these three themes is limiting and does not do justice to the distinctive nuances which each Gospel contains. Both as examples of pastoral theology and in what they say about the theology of pastoring they continue to speak volumes to the church.

---

[55] Kruse, *NT Foundations of Ministry*, pp. 13–70.

4

The writings of John

JOHN'S GOSPEL AS A PASTORAL DOCUMENT

John's self-declared aim in writing was 'that you may believe that Jesus is the Christ, the Son of God, and that believing you may have life in his name' (20:31). From this statement it is usually assumed that his purpose was evangelistic. The verse may, however, be translated 'that you may go on believing that Jesus is the Christ, the Son of God . . .' and there is much textual evidence in favour of doing so.[1] If this were so it would suggest that John's purpose was not so much evangelistic as pastoral. It is unwise to erect too grand a theory on such a debatable point and it is in any case quite unnecessary to choose between the two. John's object was to stimulate faith, whether it was the virgin faith of unbelievers or the continuing faith of believers. We may say, though, that it should not be ignored that John's Gospel is a pastoral document as well as an evangelistic tract, and that such a view enables us to make better sense of the profundity of its teaching than if it were meant to be merely an initial introduction to Christian belief.

In order to ascertain with any precision the way in which John's Gospel functions as a pastoral theology we would need to be able to determine accurately the readership John had in mind and their situation. That very question has provided New Testament scholars with a happy hunting-ground for a long time and cannot easily be resolved, even though it is possible to dismiss a number of the proposals.[2] We must be content then with outlining some features of the readership on which there would be general agreement.

Probably written towards the end of the first century, the

---

[1] C. K. Barrett, *The Gospel According to St John*, p. 479; R. E. Brown, *The Gospel According to John*, vol. ii, p. 1056; Dunn, *Unity and Diversity*, p. 26; S. Smalley, *John: Evangelist and Interpreter*, pp. 143f.

[2] Guthrie, *NT Introduction*, pp. 271–282 and Smalley, *John*, pp. 122–149. More recently attention has turned to the Johannine circle which is believed to have issued the document, on which see D. A. Carson, 'Recent literature on the fourth gospel: some reflections', *Themelios* 9 (1983), pp. 8–18.

Gospel was addressed to Christians who had witnessed the rapid growth of their movement and now faced the resulting problems. They also faced the passing of the generation who knew Jesus and had served as the original witnesses.[3] The environment in which they lived was hostile to their faith and some of that hostility emanated, in particular, from the synagogues.[4] Moreover we can be fairly sure that John's readers were divided among themselves owing to their different views on the nature of Jesus Christ. In Smalley's view, the Jews may have felt Jesus to be something less than divine and the Gentiles found him something less than human. This led to friction which needed to be overcome.[5]

How does John address that situation? His answer is primarily Christological. To begin with, due to their divided views of Christ, neither side had fully appreciated the wonder of the word made flesh (1:14). For the benefit of Jewish believers the divinity of Jesus is stressed from the prologue onwards. The divine consciousness of Jesus is displayed in his claim to have a unique relationship with God his Father (5:9–23; 6:46; 8:14–29, 40, 54; 10:15, 17; 20:17, etc.) and in the 'I am' sayings (6:35; 8:12; 10:7, 11; 11:25; 14:6 and 15:1).[6] But John's presentation of Christ is not one-sided and he equally portrays him as fully human. He is a man who can thirst (4:6–7), be subject to the life and love of a typical family (2:12; 7:3–5 and 19:25–26), be sad and angry in the presence of death (11:33, 35) and shrink from pain (12:27). Pilate's declaration, 'Here is the man!' (19:5; cf. 8:40) is not without significance for John.[7]

It is only when this theological basis has been established that John exhorts the believers to love one another and to be united (13:34; 15:12 and 17:21–23). The exhortation without the revelation of the dual nature of Jesus would have been a futile plea.

The problem of maintaining belief in the face of the death of the apostles and a delayed parousia is met in two ways. Firstly, the reliability of the original witness is stressed. Belief is based on that which was seen (1:14). True sight alone –

---

[3] J. M. Boice, *Witness and Revelation in the Gospel of John*, pp. 36–38.

[4] W. A. Meeks, 'The Man from Heaven in Johannine Sectarianism', *JBL* 91 (1972), pp. 44–72.

[5] Smalley, *John*, p. 147.

[6] G. E. Ladd, *A Theology of the New Testament*, pp. 237–251.

[7] *Ibid.*, pp. 251–253.

a desire to see miracles as acts of power but not as signs pointing beyond themselves to the word made flesh – is condemned (4:48; 6:26 and 12:37). But *the seen* is the proper basis on which faith is to be built and comprehension of the real identity of Jesus is to be grasped. Thomas' plea after the resurrection is, therefore, not to be condemned as asking for anything illegitimate, but to be understood to be asking for that which was the proper basis for apostleship, consistent with the revelation the other apostles had received (20:24–29). Those who accepted this apostolic witness without seeing for themselves would henceforth, says Jesus, receive blessing.[8]

In addition to the reliability of the eyewitnesses' testimony which formed the foundation of their faith, the wavering Christians could derive encouragement from the fact that they themselves could rely on the continuing witness of the Holy Spirit (14:15–19, 26; 16:5–16). The paraclete, the *alter ego* of Jesus, would ensure that later Christians were no further removed from the ministry of Jesus than were the earlier Christians. He would dwell within them as Christ dwelt with the original eyewitnesses.[9]

John also addresses himself to the hostility experienced by his readers. In doing so he draws sharp boundaries around the church and distinguishes it starkly from the world (15:18–19; 16:33 and 17:14–17) and even from the Jews (8:44; 9:41).[10] They no longer belonged to the world or to Judaism and could not expect to receive a welcome there. The hostility was just as Jesus had predicted it would be. But the pastoral encouragement came not only from the fact that Jesus had warned them of the opposition in advance, but that in meeting it they were identifying with their Lord. Jesus, too, was rejected both by the world and the Jews (1:10–11) in spite of his love for them (3:16) and they were not to expect better treatment than their master. They were to keep in mind, therefore, that the world hated him first (15:18). Even more, they were not to face persecution with grim resignation but in the confidence that Jesus had overcome the world (16:33).

John 15 exhorts the believers to 'abide' or 'remain' in Christ

---

[8] G. L. Phillips, 'Faith and vision in the fourth gospel', in F. L. Cross (ed), *Studies in the Fourth Gospel*, pp. 83–96 and Boice, *Witness and Revelation*, pp. 145–151.
[9] Brown, *John*, vol. ii, p. 1142.   [10] Barrett, *John*, p. 47 and p. 139.

and, given the growing uncertainty of faith, the point of that exhortation can now be seen. Once more it must be stressed that the exhortation was only issued in the context of a Gospel which gave many reasons as to why the believer should continue in Christ and many clues as to how he could survive. It was not a foundationless exhortation of the 'hold on though I don't know why' variety.

C. K. Barrett has contrasted John with Paul as a pastor.[11] Paul's writings, he argues, arose because of particular pastoral concerns in his churches and he gives very definite pastoral guidance. John, on the other hand, gives only general commands without any attempt at application. Certainly there is a difference but it ought not to be overstressed. John's method and style clearly differ from Paul's but, for all that, he is no less a pastoral theologian. He takes the great concerns of the church of his day and brings Christian truth, particularly regarding Jesus Christ, to bear on them. In doing so he is true to his own eyewitness experience of Jesus. He has no need to invent a Christ to suit his needs, but only to speak of the Christ whom he knew. So John proves to be both a sensitive pastor and a great evangelist.

MINISTRY AND COMMUNITY IN JOHN'S GOSPEL

John's Gospel says nothing explicit about the ministry or the church and some hold it to be supremely the gospel of individualism. C. F. D. Moule, for example, wrote, 'This is the gospel, *par excellence*, of the approach of the single soul to God: this is the part of the scripture to which one turns first when trying to direct an enquirer to his own personal appreciation of salvation.'[12]

The emphasis indisputably falls on the individual's relationship with God, as the many encounters between Jesus and individuals show. It has been pointed out that the climax of the signs is the resurrection of one individual, that there is a stress on the individual believer dwelling in Christ and that even the pictures of the shepherd and his flock or the vine and its branches, which undoubtedly do have corporate significance, do

---

[11] *Ibid.*, p. 47.
[12] C. F. D. Moule, 'The Individualism of the Fourth Gospel' in *Essays in New Testament Interpretation*, p. 104.

not deal with the relationship between sheep and sheep or branch and branch. If the accent falls on the individual, however, it does not fall on the individual in isolation from others and it simply is not possible, from John, to construct any theology of individual discipleship, at the expense of the church. The only way to fulfil the command to obey Christ is to 'love one another' (13:34). The corporate aspects of discipleship are never far from the surface.

It may be, as R. E. Brown believes, that ecclesiology is presupposed by the Gospel.[13] Even if that were agreed it would form an insecure basis for the construction of a doctrine or structure of the ministry. The most that John provides in relation to this is some insight into the role of the twelve. Yet even here, in comparison with the Synoptic Gospels, there is little to offer. John makes it clear that Jesus chose them (15:16) and that they were slow to perceive who Jesus was (14:9) and fickle in their discipleship (16:32). They are not described as a separate group nor do they seem to have particular ministries, and still less offices, within the church. If they are significant, it is because they are representative of the whole church in the receipt and fulfilment of a commission from the risen Lord. Or, in the case of the beloved disciple, his significance lies in the example he sets in his close relationship with his Lord.[14]

The essence of John's view of the disciples is that they are given the important responsibility of being 'witnesses' with a commission to spread the news of what they have seen and heard (15:27; 17:18, 20 and 20:21).[15] But this is not a ministry to be confined to the apostles. It is incumbent on all believers and, to paraphrase William Temple, all that we have here is a focalization of a function of the whole church and all its members.[16] The later church can claim to be apostolic only to the extent, then, that it believes the same truth about Jesus and engages in propagating it.

The question of whether there is any reference in John to the sacraments is even more vexed. Some see sacramental allusions frequently and others see no references at all.[17] On balance, the

---

[13] Brown, *John*, vol. i, pp. cv–cxi.

[14] Dunn, *Unity and Diversity*, pp. 118f. and Barrett, *John*, pp. 80f.

[15] Boice, *Witness and Revelation*, pp. 114–123.

[16] W. Temple, *Readings in St John's Gospel*, p. 159.

[17] O. Cullmann, *Early Christian Worship*, ch 2. For a discussion see Brown, *John*, vol. i, pp. cxi–cxiv and Dunn, *Unity and Diversity*, pp. 168–171.

absence of any direct reference seems to suggest that John cannot be concerned to advocate sacramentalism. His silence, combined with what may be implicit correction to a wrong stress on sacramentalism, suggests that his major concern was not the sacramental life of the Christian church but the furthering of the work of the life-giving Spirit in the life of the individual believer.[18] But none of this must be misunderstood as implying that there is nothing in the Gospel of John to further our understanding of the pastoral task.

THE EXAMPLE AND TEACHING OF JESUS

As we have seen, John's teaching is thoroughly Christocentric. So it is not surprising to discover much of value in the example and teaching of Jesus regarding pastoral ministry. On one occasion Jesus explicitly stated that his action was to serve the disciples as an example (13:15) and the concept may legitimately be extended to present Jesus as an example of a skilled counsellor, a wise teacher and a faithful intercessor.

Granted that there is little in the ministry of Jesus which closely parallels a modern professional counselling ministry,[19] the Gospels are still rich records of how Jesus dealt with the needs of people.[20] This is especially true of John's Gospel which, consistent with its personal perspective, displays Jesus' skill in the art of ministering to individuals, as chapters 3–5 exemplify. To begin with, Jesus approaches Nicodemus, the Samaritan woman and the man at the pool of Bethesda in very different ways, and the way in which he expresses the salvation he has to offer is shaped to meet the particular needs of that individual. To the respectable Pharisee Jesus seems almost curt, cutting off his polite exchanges and anticipating his real question before he has chance to express it (3:3). Jesus' message to this man is as uncompromisingly simple as it is uncompromisingly demanding. Nicodemus, who had demanded so much of others and had so much to offer, was now being told of God's demand on him and that he had nothing to offer unless he were born again.

[18] Ladd, *Theology of NT*, pp. 283–285 and Guthrie, *NT Theology*, pp. 726–730.
[19] Taylor, *Learning to Care*, pp. 94f.
[20] D. Carlson, 'Jesus' Style of Relating. The Search for a Biblical View of Counselling', *JPT* 4 (1976), pp. 181–192.

How different it was when Jesus spoke to a woman who had craved fulfilment all her life and looked for it in married and sexual relationships without ever being satisfied. He knew her greatest need was the need for fulfilment and he was able to provide it (4:13–14). From the moment he requests a drink from her, thus demonstrating his freedom from all the inhibitions of social convention, he gently draws her out. He refuses to be side-tracked into academic disputes since his concern is personal; though he does not avoid the issue raised, in case silence be read as assent, in a single sentence he pronounces the truth of the matter (4:19–24). Equally noticeable is the fact that he offers no cheap grace. He does not offer what even he cannot give, for there is no way to receive the water of the Spirit until sin has been confessed. Yet he is not there to condemn; in all probability the poor woman was riddled with self-condemnation. His ministry was not to condemn but to give life (3:17) and it was life in its fullness that she received through his revelation of himself as the Messiah (4:26).

The encounter with the man at the pool of Bethesda reveals yet another insight into his dealing with people. Although undoubtedly the incident is recorded by John for other purposes, it is significant that when Jesus came to meet the need of this man, which he was able to do instantly, he delayed long enough to get to the man's innermost thoughts. The prolonged physical disability from which the man was suffering had taken its toll on his mental attitudes and he lay there at the pool apparently full of pity, blaming others for not coming to his aid as quickly as they should have done (5:7). The self-pity, as so often, seemed to disguise the man's contentment with his sickness, for Jesus perceptively asks, 'Do you want to get well?' (5:6). It is not unknown for those who come for counselling to derive masochistic pleasure from their problems and whilst professing, on the one hand, a desire to be free from them, they manifest, on the other, an ability to avoid taking steps which will enable them to be released. The need of this man was for a wholeness of body and attitude, and this Jesus delighted to give.

A second respect in which Jesus serves as an example to pastors lies in his portrayal as a wise teacher. Again and again he uses the misunderstandings of his disciples or of the crowd to serve as a launching-pad for the careful exposition of some new truth, as in 6:34–51 or 14:5–7. Furthermore, he is even seen to anticipate his disciples' questions and voice them on their behalf when they are too reticent to do so themselves (16:19–24). Similarly he displays his understanding of their limitations by not teaching them more than they are able to bear at once (16:12). The wise teacher lets his pupils set the pace but not in an apathetic way; he lets them set the pace where he has provided them with every incentive to learn.

The third respect in which he serves as an example is to be found in his 'high priestly prayer' in chapter 17. Here John affords a unique glimpse of the Son in conversation with the Father, which surely makes any reader feel that he has entered the holy of holies. It is not our intention to deal with the content of the prayer in any detail, except to remark on the complete identification of interest which is revealed between Father and Son and the way in which the protection of the disciples and their preservation in holiness is uppermost in the thoughts of Jesus. Although he was shortly to gain complete victory over the world, the world was still to remain a battlefield for his immediate disciples and those who would follow. So prayer was vital. John here shows an earthly example of Jesus' continuing ministry as the advocate in heaven (1 Jn. 2:1; *cf.* Heb. 7:24–25). Faithfulness in intercession remains a mark of the true disciple of Jesus.

The most notable feature of the teaching of Jesus which is relevant to pastoral ministry is found in the parable of the Model Shepherd (10:1–21). Although its main teaching is clear, it is notoriously difficult in structure and detail.[21] R. E. Brown helpfully views it as a parable (vv. 1–6) which is then developed through allegories on the gate (vv. 7–10), the shepherd (vv. 11–18) and the sheep (vv. 26–30),[22] although many other approaches have been suggested. It is clear that Jesus brings to a climax the wealth of imagery in the Old Testament regarding the shepherd and especially what is found in Ezekiel 34 and Isaiah 53.[23] At the same time he adds new depth and a new dimension to the motif.

Four elements of the parable should be noted. Firstly, the

---

[21] L. Morris, *Commentary on the Gospel of John*, p. 499.

[22] Brown, *John*, vol. i, p. 390.

[23] For further details see B. Lindars, *The Gospel of John*, pp. 352f. and Brown, *John*, vol. i, pp. 392–398.

parable warns of false shepherds. The warning was familiar enough in the Old Testament, but in more recent days shepherds had acquired a reputation as thieves and they were considered so dishonest that it was forbidden to buy from them or even use them as a witness in court.[24] Jesus' use of the picture of the shepherd as a means of presenting himself was therefore an act of tremendous grace and his emphasis on himself as the 'good' shepherd even more necessary.

The false shepherds have been interpreted in many ways. In essence they are men who serve their own interests instead of the interests of the sheep. So the spectrum of false shepherds is wide, including those who deceive the sheep into thinking that they themselves are the Messiah, those who serve in a partisan manner, those who pretend that the way into the fold is other than it is and those who take up pastoral work because of the power or status which they will derive from it.[25] As Calvin commented, 'This warning has been very useful in every age (for) . . . There is no plague more destructive to the church than when wolves go about under the mask of shepherds.'[26]

Secondly, the parable illustrates the close relationship between the flock and the true shepherd. He knows them individually (v. 3) and leads them safely (v. 4), whilst they have complete trust in him because they recognize his voice. His intimate knowledge of the sheep and their perfect security while under his care are again emphasized in verses 14 and 27–29. No-one can expect to lead God's people unless this relationship is formed first. The pastor needs intimate knowledge of his people and they need to feel confident in his leadership and to be able to trust that he will not lead them into any danger. To this, Temple pertinently adds, 'whether we seem to his sheep their shepherds or strangers will depend on whether they recognise our voice as His . . .'.[27]

The third aspect of the parable worthy of note is the universalistic emphasis of verse 16. The flock is not confined to the Jews and can never be permitted to indulge in self-centredness. As with Jesus, the true shepherd must always be extending his care beyond the boundaries of any particular fold so that others

---

[24] J. Jeremias, *'poimēn'*, *TDNT*, vol. 6, pp. 489f.

[25] Temple, *Readings in St John*, pp. 159f.

[26] J. Calvin, *St John 1–10*, edited by D. W. Torrance and T. F. Torrance, p. 258.

[27] Temple, *Readings in St John*, p. 386.

outside can be incorporated into it. It is impossible, biblically speaking, to compartmentalize pastoral work from the continuing task of evangelism. The shepherd has duties both to his present flock and to those yet to be united to it.

Fourthly, we come to the heart of the matter. The new element in the teaching of Jesus on the Model Shepherd is that he lays down his life for the sheep (v. 11). The good shepherd is not only prepared to face danger in defending his sheep (v. 12) but actually pays the ultimate price of his own life on their account. Only in this way do the sheep experience life to the full (v. 10). Jesus here combines the figure of the messianic shepherd with that of the suffering servant. The true model for pastors must be to keep both in mind. Here in a nutshell is the essence of all John's understanding of pastoring. Ministry is self-giving sacrifice.[28]

That same stress is to be found in the other great passage which is relevant to pastoral ministry – the washing of the disciples' feet – in John 13:1–17. Here, in acted form, the whole drama of the incarnation is portrayed as the close parallels between these verses and Paul's exposition of the incarnation in Philippians 2:6–11 suggest. On this occasion Jesus explicitly relates his action to the behaviour required of his disciples (v. 15). The incarnation, then, serves as the pattern for ministry, in addition to the model of the cross implicit in the parable of the Model Shepherd. Both have in common that they demand a voluntary abandoning of one's rights in the service of others.

This amazing act on the part of Jesus was no exercise in conveying the abstract truth of the incarnation. Still less did Jesus intend to institute a new ritual. It was an exercise intended to define once and for all the only legitimate style of leadership which those who claim to act on his behalf can adopt. John was stating dramatically what Luke 22:26 had stated explicitly. In washing the disciples' feet, Jesus was voluntarily and humbly adopting the role of the servant and, since 'no servant is greater than his master, nor is a messenger greater than the one who sent him' (v. 16), his followers, too, needed to adopt the same attitudes of humility. As Hans Küng has written,

It is not law or power, knowledge or dignity but service which

[28] D. M. Smith, 'Theology and Ministry in John', in Shelp and Sunderland, *A Biblical Basis for Ministry*, p. 226.

is the basis of discipleship. The model for the disciples in their following of Christ is therefore not the secular ruler and not the learned scribe, nor even the priest who stands above his people, the only valid model is that of a man who serves tables.[29]

There can be no ministry to people from above but only from below. There can be no ministry from a position of superiority but only from a position of servanthood.

After the resurrection the idea of commission becomes evident. In John 20:21 Jesus issues a general commission to his disciples in words reminiscent of those he had already used in conversation with his father (17:18). Three points are apparent in this commission.

The first point is that their mission was to continue the mission of Jesus and not to engage in anything new. Moreover, the form of the commission makes it clear that the ministry of Jesus was to serve as the model for their own. The second point derives from the context. Jesus immediately bestows on them the Holy Spirit, without whom their mission would have been impossible. It was already clear from his earlier teaching that without this gift they would be impotent (14:1–16:16), but that with it they would be able to do even greater works than those of Jesus himself (14:12). Thirdly, a point is made about their authority (20:23). Their authority rests on possessing the commission and possessing the gift; without those they could have no authority, whatever their office. This problematic verse cannot be seen as investing individuals with the personal right to forgive or to refuse to forgive sins. Nor do they set up an authoritative structure. They are words addressed to the whole church who, in the power of the Spirit and armed with the gospel of Christ, can announce his forgiveness and equally declare where and how it will not be found.[30] The commission, then, goes hand in hand with the equipment necessary to fulfil it, both in terms of the gift of the Spirit and the authority of the risen Christ.

Much of the teaching of John on pastoral issues is encapsulated in Peter's restoration to service (21:15–23). Jesus delicately handles a bruised individual who, for all his enthusiasm,

---

[29] H. Küng, *The Church*, p. 392.
[30] Lindars, *Gospel of John*, p. 613 and Morris, *Commentary on John*, pp. 847–850.

must have felt disqualified from service since his denial. The irreducible test is simply of Peter's love for Jesus. The individual relationship with the chief shepherd is what matters and it matters to the exclusion of curiosity about the future of others (vv. 20–23). If the love is there it is sufficient to overcome the failures and enable rehabilitation to take place. If reinstatement takes place the task is clear: a flock is in need of the tender care of a shepherd – the model for which was none other than Jesus himself.

It is difficult to read notions about the primacy of Peter in these verses as some would do.[31] Peter stands as a representative witness in whom all the love, forgiveness and calling of God is focused. But the call to serve with sacrificial love is a call, for John, to all who are witnesses to Christ.

THE LETTERS OF JOHN

By the time John wrote his first letter the problems alluded to in his Gospel had surfaced more fully. Heretical views on the person of Christ were having severe pastoral repercussions. They were now not only threatening the unity of the church but also causing great confusion regarding the nature of Christian experience and creating havoc in regard to moral standards. Consequently, with these urgent needs in mind, John writes a trenchant letter which is pastoral rather than polemical in character.[32] His letter is a model of pastoral instruction – 'a masterpiece in the art of edification'.[33]

Throughout this and his other two letters John is careful to define his relationship with his readers so that they may appreciate his motivation for instructing them. They are his 'dear children' (2:1, 12, 13, 18, etc. and 3 Jn. 4) and 'dear friends' (2:7; 3:2, 21, etc. and 3 Jn. 1, 2, 5, etc.). John is about to build on the affection and tenderness which is already established in his relationships with them. Furthermore, this helps us to understand his concern for his own joy (1:4; 2 Jn. 12 and 3 Jn. 4), for the joy of any father is inextricably bound up with the

---

[31] For a detailed discussion of these verses see Brown, *John*, vol. ii, pp. 1110–1117; J. Calvin, *St John 11–21 and First John*, p. 220 and Morris, *Commentary on John*, pp. 869–877.
[32] Ladd, *Theology of NT*, p. 611. A. E. Brooke comments, 'He is a pastor first, an orthodox theologian, only afterwards' in *The Johannine Epistles*, p. xxx. See pp. xxvii–xxx.
[33] G. G. Findlay, *Fellowship in Life Eternal*, p. 59.

welfare of his children.[34]

The method of his teaching is repetitive. He had no desire to be original in his teaching but only to remind them of what they already knew (2:21; *cf.* 2:7–8 and 2 Jn. 5). They did not need to learn new things; they only needed to understand more fully what they knew already. Accordingly, John carefully goes over the same ground more than once in his first letter leading some to detect a circular structure in his writing.[35]

Findlay remarked, 'Under the placid surface of St. John's nature there lay a slumbering passion, a brooding ambition, that blazed on occasion with startling vehemence.'[36] It is evident in his letters. And yet the method of his teaching is almost wholly positive. In spite of his concern to counteract the false teachers, he only rarely attacks them directly. His approach is essentially to make a positive statement of the truth.

The fundamental cause of disturbance was the teaching of some that Christ did not really come in the flesh but only appeared to be fully human. Those who taught this considered themselves to have arrived at the true understanding of the faith and looked down on those who had not yet received enlightenment as inferior. Their devaluing of the humanity of Christ had a number of moral consequences. They believed, on the one hand, that all that was material was evil. Yet, on the other hand, they lived in the realm of the Spirit and, having themselves gained freedom from the flesh through enlightenment, they had reached a state of perfection. Such a view led, in turn, to ethical indifference and antinomianism.[37]

The presence of the false teachers had caused some to doubt the validity of their conversion and to be perplexed about their Christian experience.[38] What were they to make of sin in their lives? Was it an indication that they had not truly arrived or were they foolish to pay any attention to it at all? What of their relationship to the world? And how were they to treat those with whom they seemed spiritually incompatible?

John's answer is to begin by establishing the veracity of the doctrine they were taught (1:1–3). The only basis for any

[34] J. R. W. Stott, *The Epistles of John*, p. 219.
[35] I. H. Marshall, *The Epistles of John*, pp. 22–26 and Stott, *Epistles of John*, p. 55.
[36] Findlay, *Fellowship in Life Eternal*, p. 51.   [37] Ladd, *Theology of NT*, pp. 609–611.
[38] For a discussion of the theme of Christian experience in 1 John see R. E. O. White, *An Open Letter to Evangelicals*, pp. 157–169.

confidence they could have in their standing before God was one that came from knowing the truth, not one that was built on the miserably unsure foundation of their own subjective experience. Patiently, therefore, he goes over the truth about the nature of Christ, warning them to be on the lookout for antichrists (2:18–27) and to be discriminating about whose teaching they accept (4:1–3).

From that basis John is able to turn to their more immediate pastoral questions. The continuing presence of sin in the believer must be admitted, since only by doing so could God's answer to it become effective. It was simply untrue to claim perfection (1:8–2:2). It was also a false lead as forgiveness, not perfection, was the foundation of the Christian life from which all else followed. But sin no longer dominated as once it did. Hence anyone who claimed to be a true Christian but who did not usually exhibit behaviour characteristic of the truth itself was to be suspect (3:9–10 and 5:18). In determining who was a true Christian this moral test could be added to the test of belief.

Early in his letter John hints at his understanding of darkness (1:5–7). The false teacher taught the necessity of escaping from this dark material world to the light of 'gnosis', yet for John the character of darkness was not material but moral, or rather, immoral. To hate your brother was, to him, to be in darkness (2:9, 11). True, the world was not to be accepted uncritically (2:15–17) since it was fundamentally in opposition to God. But what Johns means by the world is not its material form but the system of humanity organized contrary to God.

The believer who was frustrated by his slow spiritual progress or frustrated by the limitations imposed by living on this earth, 'everyman's own feeling', as Calvin pointed out,[39] was encouraged by the vision John had of the future (3:2). What they had experienced of God's grace so far was nothing in comparison with that which they would experience. With John Newton they could say, 'I am not what I ought to be; I am not what I would like to be; I am not what I hope to be. But I am not what I was: and by the grace of God I am what I am.'[40]

In the meantime the believer had laid upon him the continuing obligation to love. There could be no short cut to super-spirituality which would exempt him from this

---

[39] Calvin, *John 11–21 and First John*, p. 266.
[40] Quoted in David Watson, *In Search of God*, p. 101.

uncomfortable requirement. John's teaching on love is aimed at avoiding two opposite mistakes. On the one hand, he repeatedly refers to the commandment and, so that there can be no mistaking it, spells out in practical terms what it means. Like all good teachers he does not leave his readers puzzled about the specific application of a general principle; he illustrates the general principle with at least some specific applications (3:17 and 4:19). On the other hand, he spells out the meaning of love in such a way that none can feel he has fulfilled his obligation by the mere practice of a few acts of charity. Love is firmly rooted both on earth and in heaven. For 'God is love' (4:16) and ultimately we can derive our true understanding of love only from the self-giving of Jesus (3:16). As in the Gospel, therefore, love means sacrificing oneself in the interests of others, whether it be in the ultimate sacrifice of one's life or in the many lesser sacrifices one is more usually required to make.

It is clear, from the number of times John refers to the verb 'to know', that John's overriding desire is that his children should be settled in their faith and assured in their experience that they belong to God.[41] In achieving this end he is careful not to neglect the needs of even the most timid of his children. Doubtless there would have been at least one who, having applied to himself all the tests that John had given, remained uncertain of his relationship with God. To such, John has a specially tender word to say. To pacify those whose hearts beat loud in self-condemnation, John assures them that they can leave their lives safely in the care of God (3:19–20). Astonishingly, he is the God who knows all that there is to know about us and has therefore even more reason to condemn us. And yet in his grace this God who is also love does not condemn but rather accepts. If that does not set the troubled heart at rest, nothing can.

There is only one category of person for whom John holds out no hope and that is the man whose sin is mortal (5:16), by which he has in mind the man who refuses to repent and deliberately rejects the truth.[42] John is not seeking to establish a league table of sin, merely to make the point that it is useless to pray for such a man, whereas for the most part prayer provides the believer with a tremendous pastoral resource that

---

[41] John mentions 'to know' thirty-two times in the letter.
[42] Stott, *Epistles of John*, pp. 186–191.

is available to him even when all other strategies may be closed.

The first letter of John is a model of pastoral instruction. It is written with gentle strength. Whilst fully appreciating the dilemmas of his readers, John is uncompromising in his answers. But the toughness of the reply is couched in terms which ensure a hearing and that it can be understood. The problems of which it speaks remain problems even today and still raise uncertainty and doubts in the minds of many believers.[43] The letter remains therefore an essential tool for the use of any pastor.

REVELATION

Those who use Revelation as a means of predicting the details of future political events, as if it were a Christian version of Old Moore's Almanac, seem to ignore both its original purpose and the nature of its literary genre. Although the style John adopted is so totally different from that to be found in his Gospel or letters, Revelation continues to show John to have been an excellent pastor.

The book itself gives a great deal of information regarding the churches of Asia to whom it is addressed. And assuming, as is common, that it was written during the reign of Domitian, even more can be known of their situation. The passing of time had meant that the churches had lost some of their pristine spiritual fitness and were now in a state of marked spiritual deterioration.

Associated with this were four other problems. Firstly they had experienced sporadic persecution from which, although it was less than they had known in the past, they had not emerged with flying colours. Moreover, it was nothing in comparison with the storm which was about to break and for which they needed to be prepared. Secondly their relationship with Judaism continued to be a source of serious irritation. The Jews claimed to be the true children of God and persistently undermined the claims of the Christians to be the true Israel. Thirdly, there was the infiltration of false teaching. Fourthly, there was growing pressure to compromise with the pagan society in which they lived. Was it necessary, after all, they

---

[43] R. Macaulay and J. Barrs, *Christianity with a Human Face*, pp. 28–58.

questioned, to be so nonconformist in their attitudes to civil ceremonies and pagan social customs?[44]

John's purposes, therefore, were to arrest spiritual decline and produce holiness, to encourage faithfulness and prevent lapses. His answer is to introduce his readers to another dimension of reality, other, that is, than the reality of their earthly circumstances of which they were all too aware. Accordingly, he draws back the curtain which hides the reality of heaven and gives them a glimpse of the true situation. What they were seeing on earth was only a part of the picture, but they had mistaken it for the whole with the result that they had been deterred from making the spiritual progress expected of them.

John faced two problems in conveying that answer to the churches. The first was the problem of expressing such tremendous truth about heavenly realities in earthly language. The second was how to write about the precarious and doomed nature of earthly political powers without being manifestly seditious. Both of these were overcome by expressing reality in symbolic form. As far as the human authorities were concerned John adopted a method akin to a political cartoon,[45] so that its meaning was evident to those who needed to see it but a puzzle to others who were not in the know. What to us is so often a mysterious method of communication would to the original readers, in their context, have communicated well. It is inconceivable that John's prophecy would have been obscure, since it was meant to be an encouragement to the churches.

Consistent with his previous writings, John's pastoral theology in Revelation is thoroughly Christological, although his Christology is now different in its emphasis. Whereas before he focused on the earthly life of Christ and drew out the implications of his dual nature, here he focuses on the risen and exalted Christ. Previously his teaching had looked back to Christ who had come in the flesh; now it looks forward to the Christ who will come in judgment. His approach is still Christological but with an eschatological complexion. In essence, he invites the flagging believer to take a long cool look at the exalted Jesus.

---

[44] F. F. Bruce, 'The Revelation of John', in G. C. D. Howley (ed), *A New Testament Commentary*, p. 637 and J. Sweet, *Revelation*, pp. 27–35.
[45] G. R. Beasley-Murray, *The Book of Revelation*, pp. 16f. and G. B. Caird, *A Commentary on the Revelation of St. John the Divine*, pp. 60f.

The prophecy opens with a description of the Christ whom John perceived in a vision (1:9–18). While behind the locked door of a prison on Patmos he sees through an open door into heaven and the sight completely alters his perspective on the suffering church. Every detail of the vision he saw stressed that his Lord was not subject to the passing nature of this world, nor was his power transient. Here was one who, though he was from eternity, maintained a sharp and perceptive authority. His permanence was guaranteed by his having defeated death and his jurisdiction extended over hell itself. If he had genuine faith in this Lord, the believer need not fear the earthly power who must have appeared closer to hand.[46]

The vision of Christ alone changes into a vision of Christ addressing the seven churches of Asia (2:1 – 3:22). Christ is not only the sovereign power at the centre of the cosmos but also Lord of the church. As such he displays acute knowledge of their situation and commanding authority over their affairs. The symmetry of the letters has often been noted and it is there that the clue to their pastoral cogency lies. Each letter begins by being addressed to a particular church. This is followed by one aspect of the previous vision of Christ being selected for special mention on the basis of the message which will follow. Thus, to the church at Ephesus, which is going to be warned that it will cease to be a church unless it mends its ways, Christ is revealed as the one who holds the seven stars in his hand and who walks among the seven lampstands (2:1), the latter being a symbol of the churches themselves. To Smyrna, for whom he has nothing but encouragement to hold on in a difficult situation, he reveals himself as the one who outlasted the worst that the powers of evil could throw at him (2:8). And so on.

This unveiling of Christ is followed by a word of encouragement. Their Lord is not unmindful of how much there is to approve in their lives, except in the cases of Sardis and Laodicea where there is nothing to commend. Indeed, he demonstrates a detailed knowledge of their achievements. They will not be able to argue that he did not understand them when he came to criticize. He is aware of the full picture and his evaluation is both accurate and sympathetic. The commendations also serve as an encouragement to continue in good works, to persist in

[46] For details of the interpretation of this vision see Beasley-Murray, *Revelation*, pp. 66–68 or R. H. Mounce, *The Book of Revelation*, pp. 77–81.

the truth or, more specifically, to persist in the belief that they are the true heirs of Israel (2:9; 3:8–9).

The commendation is followed, except in the cases of Smyrna and Philadelphia, with rebuke. The rebukes can be stern but, to John, they are another assurance of God's love (3:19). The judgment refers to specific failings and is not of the kind that leaves church members wondering if and how it applies to them. Similarly, with the judgment goes a prescription for action; they are not left floundering and asking, 'what next, Lord?' The recommended action falls roughly into one of two camps. It is either a call to repent or it is a call to have faith.[47] Both of these are essential requirements at the beginning of the Christian life, but John shows that they cannot thereafter be dispensed with. Repentance is a change of mind which leads to an amendment of life and the church frequently finds itself in the position of needing to exercise it (2:5, 16; 3:3 and 19). At Sardis, as elsewhere, it is necessary to preface the repentance by inviting the church to wake up and remember what they had received (3:2) or else it will not take place.[48] Faith is required in the sense of being faithful (2:10, 13) and reflects a quality to be found in Christ himself (1:5; 3:14 and 19:11).

On two occasions the letters contain threats (2:5 and 2:16), but the dominant tactic of persuasion is not to threaten but to promise. Every letter concludes with a promise, even that to recalcitrant Laodicea which ends with not one, but two notes of promise. God, the church is told, is longing to be invited back into its fellowship and will eagerly return if only it will open the door. They need have no fear that he has abandoned them (3:20). What is more, if they do repent, they will join with the exalted Christ and share his throne with him (3:21). The techniques of persuasion in our modern pulpits might prove more effective than they generally are if the biblical balance between promise and threat, of seven to two, were redis-covered. Too often it has been reversed with the consequence that results contrary to those desired are achieved.

The vision of Christ broadens once more to take in a view of his place at the centre of heavenly worship (5:1–14) and it goes on broadening until his place in the unfolding drama of history

---

[47] Guthrie, *NT Theology*, p. 601.
[48] The importance of remembering has already been pointed out in reference to Deuteronomy. See pp. 41f.

has been surveyed. Throughout the difficult chapters on the conflict between God and evil there is never any attempt to underestimate the horror and pain of what Satan can do in a world organized against God. Nevertheless the prophecy is clearly intended to encourage the belief that God will triumph over evil. The din of battle is constantly interrupted by a flashback to heaven where those who know the outcome are shown to be celebrating the victory of God (7:9–17; 11:15–18; 12:10–12; 14:1–5; 15:1–4 and 19:1–9). In addition the true identity of the lamb is unmasked and he is shown to be another deliverer like Moses (15:3), a powerful warrior (17:14), a confident bridegroom (19:6–9), a faithful judge (19:11–16), a restored creator (21:22–23) and an enthroned king (22:1, 3).

It is only once this truth about Christ has been fully grasped that there is any value in exhorting the afflicted believers to be faithful or to be holy.[49] Without such a revelation any exhortation would have proved too shallow and would have failed to provide a basis for a troubled people to remain resolute in their faith.

The book of Revelation says little in any explicit way about the structure of the church's life in John's day. References to leadership are almost entirely absent. The accent falls on all believers being kings and priests (1:6; 5:10 and 20:6). Although there is a significant place given to prophets, of whom John counts himself one (22:9; *cf.* 10:7; 16:6; 18:20, 24 and 22:6). But, as Dunn has commented, this does not so much inform us about particular offices within the church as it does that the character of the church was prophetic through and through.[50]

The other insight into the corporate life of the early church which one might draw from Revelation concerns worship. Here again any insight can be gained only by inference and, although the prominence of worship in Revelation may indicate its prominence in the early church, it is precarious to deduce dogmatic conclusions about the liturgy of the early church from this book.[51] It is better to rejoice at the way in which the great hymns of Revelation have continued to enrich Christian worship down the centuries. These omissions should not be surprising, as it must be remembered that Revelation first

---

[49] Rev. 18:4–8 may well be an oblique appeal to the churches of John's day.
[50] Dunn, *Unity and Diversity*, pp. 120f. and Guthrie, *NT Theology*, p. 786.
[51] Guthrie, *NT Theology*, pp. 786f.

and foremost *is* pastoral theology and is not *about* pastoral theology.

SUMMARY

John's greatest contribution to the early church was made through his writings where he is seen to be a skilful pastor.[52] Although the method he adopts to convey his teaching varies widely from the explicit teaching of his letters, through the less pastorally overt teaching of the Gospel, to the coded teaching of Revelation, there are certain features which are constant. All his pastoral theology revolves around Christology. The solution to the problems faced by the church and the incentive to greater progress lie in an all-sufficient Christ. A failure to look at him and to appreciate him in all his fullness lies at the root of the problems facing the churches to which John wrote. The problems increase and the progress slows as the believers fail to abide in him.

John also writes a consistently balanced pastoral theology. He never fails to correct but he never forgets to encourage. In fact, the negative is always firmly couched in the context of the positive as one would expect from a man whose ultimate idea of God was that 'God is love'.

He displays no interest in any structure of Christian service. His only interest in that regard was to insist that all service was a witness to Christ and a continuation of his love; a humble love which was defined by self-giving and self-sacrifice.[53] He insists that pastors must be shepherds and servants, not superstars. The church, to be true to her master, was to be a church of martyrs and Christian leaders were to be marked by self-giving.

[52] Findlay, *Fellowship in Life Eternal*, p. 49.
[53] 'Witness' and 'martyr' derive from the same Greek word, namely, *martyrion*.

5

The apostle Paul

It is surprising how little attention has been directed to the apostle Paul as a pastor. The last full-length study of his pastoral work was written by W. E. Chadwick in 1907.[1] There have been a number of short articles since which have discussed the matter further,[2] but a thoroughgoing study is long overdue. The reasons for this neglect are difficult to determine, but they probably stem from an over-emphasis on Paul as a theologian, by the scholars, and as a missionary, by the practitioners. The latter undue stress is even seen in Graham Leonard's recent book on pastoral theology, where he begins by stating that Paul saw 'pastoral theology as a regrettable necessity' and an interruption to his primary task of preaching the gospel.[3] Surely this was not the case.

Paul's commitment to the preaching of the gospel entailed a continuing commitment to those churches which were founded as a result. To be accurate, we must argue that Paul saw both the original proclamation of the gospel and its continuing proclamation in the church as one and the same process and both as manifestations of the activity of God (1 Cor. 3:1–9). Wherever he planted the seed of faith, he was concerned about its cultivation.[4] Because his converts became partners with him in the gospel his ongoing relationship with them brought him much joy (Phil. 1:3–11). On occasions they ceased to be a joy and became, instead, a burden, but when that happened it was because they had failed to appreciate the truth of the gospel to the full. His pastoral approach was simply to proclaim the gospel to them once more although, this time, more thoroughly (*e.g.* 2 Cor. 5:16–21). This he accepted as his daily responsibility and, even though it could be a burden (2 Cor. 11:28), it was one

---

[1] W. E. Chadwick, *The Pastoral Teaching of St Paul. His Ministerial Ideals.*

[2] V. P. Furnish, 'Theology and Ministry in the Pauline Letters', in E. E. Shelp and R. Sunderland (eds), *A Biblical Basis for Ministry*, pp. 101–144; S. M. Gilmour, 'Pastoral Care in the New Testament Church', *NTS* 10 (1964), pp. 393–398 and D. R. Hall, 'Pauline Church Discipline', *Tyndale Bulletin* 20 (1969), pp. 3–26.

[3] G. Leonard, *God Alive: Priorities in Pastoral Theology*, p. 1.

[4] Furnish, 'Ministry', pp. 102f. and 111 and J. H. Schütz, *Paul and the Anatomy of Apostolic Authority*, pp. 182 and 225.

he gladly bore; it was simply another reflection of his complete commitment to the gospel. Pastoral work is simply bringing to full flower the bud of the gospel.

All Paul's writings, even Romans,[5] were written in response to pastoral needs, although not always in response to specific pastoral problems. They demonstrate more explicitly than any other part of Scripture the connection between Christian living and Christian truth. They are writings which, like modern day bridge-builders, begin construction on two sides of a gulf – the side of experience and the side of theology – and span the gap to meet in the middle. Where they meet, however, is not a hit-or-miss affair, nor is it subject to negotiation with both sides having equal weight in determining the destination. The meeting-place is determined by the construction coming from the theological side, for the gospel which had been revealed to Paul was non-negotiable (Gal. 1:6–12). Thus even though we can say with C. K. Barrett that the practical questions 'had a catalytic effect in pushing forward (Paul's theological) developments that might otherwise have taken place more slowly',[6] it is not right to say that Paul's theology was a mere reaction to the questions raised or a mere invention mothered by the necessity of the situation in the churches.

AIMS AND OBJECTIVES

Paul defines the aim of his ministry in Colossians 1:28 as, 'that we may present every man mature in Christ' (RSV). The clauses either side of the aim demonstrate Paul's total determination to work for its fulfilment and his willingness to adopt varying methods to achieve it. He was not content to win converts. He desired to produce Christians who were able to stand on their own feet and who would not remain spiritual babies, but progress to becoming mature spiritual adults. Such men would be 'complete' and 'self-sufficient in the Spirit',[7] no longer unhealthily dependent on him or other Christian workers and no longer, for whatever reason, unstable in their discipleship.

---

[5] Leonard, *God Alive*, p. 2.

[6] C. K. Barrett, *The First Epistle to the Corinthians*, p. 17. Quoted by I. H. Marshall, 'Pauline Theology in 1 and 2 Thessalonians', in M. D. Hooker and S. G. Wilson (eds), *Paul and Paulinism*, p. 182, with approval, in reference to Paul's writing of the Thessalonian letters.

[7] R. Banks, *Paul's Idea of Community*, p. 176.

A similar aim appears in Ephesians 4:13. There it is even more clear what the measure of maturity is to be. It is none other than Christ himself. Any lesser standard by which to measure growth is inadequate and any lesser goal is unworthy. The same idea of maturity is evident in verse 12 as in Colossians, for the congregation are not to be passive recipients of the apostle's ministry but actively prepared for service themselves. This is the test of any special ministry given to the church; how effective is it in making every church member a servant and evangelist in his own environment? But a new element is added here. The context of Ephesians 4:13 insists, too, that progress towards maturity is not an individual matter. The individual can make progress only in the fellowship of the church. But Paul means more than that. He has a concern for a congregational development towards maturity; the church as a corporate body must also make progress. The body of Christ must be built up 'until we all reach unity in the faith and in the knowledge of the Son of God and become mature . . .'[8] And it must be an ever-increasing body making inroads into Satan's territory and winning converts from his control (Eph. 4:16).

The metaphor of 'building up' is frequent in Paul (Rom. 15:2; 1 Cor. 14:12; Eph. 2:22; 4:29; Col. 2:7 and 1 Thes. 5:11) and often refers to the mutual building up in which believers must engage. At the same time he sees it as a particular responsibility for the Christian leader to bend all his power, energy and influence to that end (Rom. 15:20; 1 Cor. 3:1–15; 2 Cor. 10:8 and 13:10). That is the purpose of any authority he possesses.[9]

Translating these aims into more tangible objectives, it means that Paul would seek to teach truth, promote holiness, encourage unity and sustain faithfulness. He taught truth so that all the spiritual and ethical implications of the gospel could be understood. But positive teaching was often impossible without engaging in combating heresy and exposing it for the lie that it was. Four recurring heresies added to the gospel – legalism, asceticism, pneumaticism and gnosticism; whilst one – libertinism – subtracted from it.[10] Teaching was not an end in itself but was aimed at cultivating personal, corporate and social

---

[8] See M. Griffiths, *Cinderella with Amnesia*, p. 31.
[9] H. Ridderbos, *Paul. An Outline of his Theology*, pp. 429–438 and Schütz, *Anatomy*, pp. 224f.
[10] R. Longenecker, *The Ministry and Message of Paul*, pp. 107–109.

holiness. One particular threat to corporate holiness was division and Paul spent much time resisting it and advancing the cause of unity. Internal strife often combined with external opposition to produce disillusionment, so much of Paul's pastoral energy was devoted to countering unfaithfulness with the clear aim of producing mature loyalty to Christ.

MOTIVES AND INCENTIVES

2 Corinthians exposes the inner heart and tensions of the ministry and shows that the minister of the gospel is called to share in the sufferings of his Lord. With immense aims (the fulfilment of which often proved elusive), with converts who often proved unresponsive and with life often proving harsh (2 Cor. 6:4–10; 11:23–29), Paul must have had some powerful motives and incentives to sustain his ministry. What were they?

Paul was a man who lived under a sense of obligation (Rom. 1:14; 1 Cor. 9:16). He had no choice in the matter. His compulsion to preach, and therefore to pastor, was inescapable, since it was inextricably bound up with his conversion (Acts 26:12–19). He was motivated, not simply by the commission he had received, but by the even more profound sense of amazement and gratitude that God's grace had been made available to him (1 Tim. 1:12–14). Although he could never discharge the debt, his conversion left him with an unquenchable thirst to do so. What is more, Paul's own conversion provided him with an overwhelming belief in the power of the gospel (Rom. 1:16). If God could save him, he could save anyone. How could he know of such a gospel and not make sure that others knew of it too? Without such an experience of God's grace Paul would never have begun, let alone survived, his work in the churches.

From his conversion onwards the motivating force in all Paul did was a desire to please God (Rom. 15:16; 2 Cor. 5:9; Gal. 1:10 and 1 Thes. 2:4). Although this desire should be the general aim of every Christian (Col. 1:10; 1 Thes. 4:1 and 2 Tim. 2:4), Paul particularly relates it to his ministry and shows it to be the determining factor in his conduct.

In addition to the consciousness of his past conversion and the urgency of his present desire Paul was motivated by his future prospects. He was conscious that his work would one day be subject to inspection (1 Cor. 3:11–15) and his life subject

102

to judgment (2 Cor. 5:10–11). But even though this gave Paul
a proper sense of seriousness about his life, it was not, for him,
a terrifying or crippling thought. Rather he looked forward to it
confidently in the belief that he would be able to boast that he
had won a number of prizes on that day. His converts were to
be his joy and crown when Christ returned (Phil. 4:1; 1 Thes.
2:19). Howard Marshall resolves any fears we might have that
Paul is being inconsistent in this talk about boasting with the
comment that, 'it may be taken for granted that Paul is not
looking forward here to any sort of proud display of his apostolic achievements before the Lord Jesus, but is rather thinking
of the joyful exultation which he will be able to feel when
the work which God has done through him (1 C. 15:10) is
recognized'.[11]

The same passage which speaks of the incentive of Christ's
judgment balances the thought with the motive of Christ's love
(2 Cor. 5:14). Love can be as compelling as judgment, if not
more so. The love we receive from Christ must, if we have
really grasped it, be transformed into love for our fellow men.
Certainly this was so in Paul's experience, to the extent that in
Chadwick's understanding of Paul it is seen as the one foundation and one reason for his ministry.[12] Although this is to
overestimate its importance it is equally wrong to underestimate
it. As Chadwick points out, the teaching of 1 Corinthians 13
falls specifically in the context of the exercise of gifts within the
church which, although not confined in their exercise to pastors,
are not unrelated to them either. The pastor may apparently
have all the spiritual gifts he could wish for, but unless matched
by an equal spirit of love they would be misused and useless.[13]
The love of men is essential to persevere in pastoral ministry
but that, in turn, can come only from the love of Christ.

It is noticeable that all Paul's motives derive from God in
Christ. It is the call and grace of God, the desire to please God,
the awareness of the judgment of Christ and the overwhelming
sense of Christ's love which sustains his ministry.

---

[11] I. H. Marshall, *1 and 2 Thessalonians*, p. 87.
[12] Chadwick, *Pastoral Teaching of St Paul*, p. 270.   [13] *Ibid.*, p. 247.

IMAGES AND RELATIONSHIPS

With Paul's commitment to pastoral care it is curious that he uses the image of the shepherd only once in his writings (Eph. 4:11) and then in a way which firmly links the work of the pastor with that of the teacher.[14] None the less his writings are rich with other imagery which not only illustrates the work of the pastor but defines his relationships too. It is not our intention to provide a comprehensive review of the range of pastoral metaphors in Paul[15] but to select those which are particularly pertinent to and suggestive of the continuing pastoral task.

Slave, servant, steward and his master

The proper place to begin is with a group of images which, although having different individual emphases, call to mind essentially the same picture. It is proper to begin with the slave, servant and steward because these words are the ones used most frequently by Paul to speak of his own function within the church. It is also proper because they define Paul's relationship with his Lord. Although he was fond of telling the churches that he was their servant or slave Paul never made them his master. He was a servant (*diakonos*) of the gospel (Eph. 3:7; Col. 1:23), of the new covenant (2 Cor. 3:6), of God (2 Cor. 6:4) and of Christ (2 Cor. 11:23). Similarly, he is a slave (*doulos*) of Christ (Rom. 1:1; Gal. 1:10) and a steward (*oikonomos*) of Christ (1 Cor. 4:1). Whenever he gets anywhere near saying that he is a servant of the churches (1 Cor. 3:5; 2 Cor. 4:5 and Col. 1:25) he is careful to qualify it so that the determining authority for his work is clearly God in Christ.

What of the differences between the words? The picture of the slave serves to stress that the Christian worker owes total allegiance to his Lord and that he no longer belongs to himself but has been bought by the death of Christ and so is completely possessed by God.[16] The picture of the servant speaks of the need for humility in Christian work and that service needs, in accordance with the original meaning of the word and teaching of Christ, to be of a practical and humble kind on behalf of his

[14] Commentators are divided on whether 'pastor-teacher' refers to one or two offices, but see M. Barth, *Ephesians 4–6*, pp. 438f. See also the helpful comments of J. R. W. Stott, *The Message of Ephesians. God's New Society*, pp. 163f.

[15] Chadwick, *Pastoral Teaching of St Paul*, pp. 108–194.

[16] *Ibid.*, pp. 127f. and K. Hess, 'Serve', *NIDNTT*, vol. 3, pp. 544–549.

Christian brothers. But it says more than this. Jesus' identification of himself as a servant in Mark 10:45 not only defined the style of his leadership but identified him with the suffering servant of Isaiah. By using the same terminology Paul applies the saying of Jesus to his own ministry and indicates that suffering is a mark of leadership in the church (2 Cor. 4:10–12; 6:4–10 and Gal. 6:17).[17] The picture of the steward maintains the same close identification between a worker and his master but develops it in a more active sense. The steward is an 'assistant to another as the instrument of his will'.[18] He completely identifies with the aims of his master and knows how his master would wish his desired objectives to be brought about. Moreover, his master has put all the necessary resources for their achievement at his disposal. The relationship between master and steward is close and it gives the steward a certain independence from the criticisms and designs of others. He is, however, unlikely to abuse his master's trust, for the steward knows that accountability is another mark of their relationship.

It should be added that not only does the idea of servanthood define the relationship between the servant and his master but between the servant and his 'fellow-servants'. Paul used this as a description of his colleagues in Colossians 1:7 and 4:7 and was even more fond of the related expression 'fellow-worker' (Rom. 16:3, 9, 21; 2 Cor. 8:23; Phil. 2:25; 4:3 and Col. 4:11). The concept of servanthood focuses not on the status differences between servants but on their common lot as servants. And that is the way Paul develops it in Romans 14:4. It is 'to his own master he stands or falls' and he is not, therefore, to be judged by his fellow-servants.

Father and children
The idea of a pastor being the father of his people is particularly appropriate when the pastor has brought his people to birth in Christ, and it is essentially used in that connection by Paul (1 Cor. 4:15; Gal. 4:19; 1 Thes. 2:11; 1 Tim. 1:2; Tit. 1:4 and Phm. 10). Paul does not usually use it to signify his authority over them (although 2 Cor. 2:9 should be noted), but to mark his close relationship and his paternal love for them. It is his joy to provide for his children, not to be supported by them (2 Cor.

---

[17] C. Kruse, *New Testament Foundations of Ministry*, pp. 82f. and 110–114.
[18] K. H. Rengstorf, *'Huperetēs'*, *TDNT*, vol. 8, p. 539. See also pp. 530–544.

12:14). As their father it is appropriate that he should serve as a model for their development (1 Cor. 4:16). He desires what any father desires of his children and it is in that spirit that he 'encourages, comforts and charges' them (1 Thes. 2:12) or even 'warns' them (1 Cor. 4:14). Such a picture may seem unnecessarily condescending in our present day until one remembers Robert Banks' wise insight that 'Paul's model is the parent-*adult* child rather than the parent-*infant* child'.[19] There is no concern on Paul's part to keep them childishly dependent on him.

Nurse and infant

The closely related metaphor of a nurse and child which occurs in 1 Thessalonians 2:7 also uses parental imagery to describe the relationship between pastor and people. This time, however, the picture in Paul's mind highlights the feminine role within the family and accentuates the aspect of tender loving care in the relationship. That Paul is speaking of a mother nursing her own children rather than a professional nurse caring for the children of others is confirmed by his actual wording of this verse.

Paul frequently found himself exhorting other Christian leaders to lead with gentleness and patience (Phil. 4:5; Col. 3:12; 1 Thes. 5:14; 1 Tim. 6:11 and 2 Tim. 4:2), both of which were fruits of the Spirit's work (Gal. 5:22–23). In his world as in ours, gentleness was not always greeted as a wholly desirable quality. Some regarded it as mere flattery and believed that more radical surgery was needed if men were to be improved. Boldness and abusive scolding were considered essential by many of the wandering philosophers if their teaching was to have any impact.[20] The same tendency to be over-zealous in correcting the faults of others was, and still is, to be found in the church and those same abrasive qualities are often highly prized among preachers. But Paul shows that, bold (1 Thes. 2:1–2) and achievement-orientated though he was, gentleness was not only effective, but right. And he was not afraid to admit that he exhibited both gentleness and patience in his pastoral work (2 Cor. 10:1 and 2 Tim. 3:10). That such qualities were able to override his natural personality was amazing and perhaps it

[19] Banks, *Community*, p. 176.

[20] A. J. Malherbe, 'Gentle as a Nurse. The Gnostic Background to 1 Thessalonians ii', *Nov. T* 12 (1970), pp. 203–217.

happened only because he had realized just how gentle and patient Christ had been with him (1 Tim. 1:16).

Teacher and learners

Paul's writings are permeated by the language of the classroom. He portrays himself as a teacher of the truth (1 Cor. 4:6; Col. 1:28; 2 Thes. 3:6; 1 Tim. 2:7; 6:1; 2 Tim. 1:11 and 3:10), and shows himself, like an anxious teacher, to be constantly concerned lest his pupils remain ignorant (Rom. 11:25; 1 Cor. 10:1; 12:1 and 1 Thes. 4:13). He urges the privilege of teaching on others, particularly as the original apostles begin to fade from the scene (1 Tim. 4:13; 6:2; 2 Tim. 4:2 and Tit. 2:7) and insists that teaching, preaching and the provision of guidance are indispensable (Eph. 4:11–12).[21] Part of God's gift to the church is the provision of teachers (1 Cor. 12:28; Eph. 4:11; 1 Tim. 5:17 and 2 Tim. 2:2). The substance of their teaching is to be found in the Scriptures (1 Tim. 4:13; 2 Tim. 3:16; 4:2) and in the traditions which stretch back to Jesus himself (1 Tim. 6:3; 2 Tim. 2:2). So basic is the concept of teaching that he can describe conversion as 'learning Christ' (Eph. 4:20) and can condemn those outside of Christ as ignorant (1 Cor. 15:34; Eph. 4:18).

Such a survey makes it hard to disagree with Alexander Maclaren's view that, 'The Christian Ministry in the Apostle's view is distinctly educational in its design.'[22] Or with John Stott's similar assertion that, 'The Christian pastoral ministry is essentially a teaching ministry, which explains why candidates are required both to be orthodox in their own faith and to have an aptitude for teaching (*e.g.* Tit. 1:9; 1 Tim. 3:2).'[23] The concept of teaching, however, should not be isolated from other aspects of the pastoral role, nor should it be misunderstood as merely a highly developed verbal reasoning, or else it becomes a cerebral and barren activity which fails to communicate the life of God to those who listen. As such it is untrue to the real picture of the pastoral role within the New Testament. Only the wider picture will serve to ensure that the metaphor of the teacher remains healthy.

Accepting the importance of teaching, we may note the wisdom of Paul's approach. His basic method, most evident in

---

[21] M. Barth, *Ephesians 4–6*, p. 483.

[22] Maclaren is cited by Chadwick, *Pastoral Teaching of St Paul*, p. 321.

[23] J. R. W. Stott, *The Message of 2 Timothy. Guard the Gospel*, p. 108.

Romans and Ephesians, is a sustained exposition of the truth. Usually he builds on what the readers already know, mixing the familiar with the unfamiliar, and gently leads them on from where they already are to develop their understanding further (*e.g.* 1 Cor. 3:16; 5:6; 6:2, 3, 9, 15, 16, 19; 8:1, 4, etc.). He encourages them to learn from their own experience (1 Cor. 12:2; Gal. 3:1–5 and 1 Thes. 2:1) and frequently refers to his own experiences as an illustration of some truth. He also raises questions as a means of exploring new issues with his readers (*e.g.* 1 Cor. 7:16). In all this he displays acute knowledge of their local situation and uses their local context as an aid to learning.

Not all teaching is readily accepted, nor are all pupils eager to learn, and Paul was not free from such frustrations. Some of his teaching, therefore, involved rebuke and discipline, but as Chadwick points out such admonition is really a preliminary to effective teaching rather than teaching itself.[24] When all other strategies had been exhausted he occasionally resorted to the use of irony (1 Cor. 4:8–13 and 2 Cor. 10:13), outright denunciation (Gal. 1:6–9) or even active discipline (1 Cor. 5:1–13). Whenever such a course was forced upon him he kept in mind that the two purposes of discipline were the restoration of the offender and the maintenance of purity in the church.[25] Teaching was not primarily, however, correcting the wayward so much as instructing the ignorant.

Example and imitators

On a number of occasions Paul invites his readers to imitate him (1 Cor. 4:16; 11:1; Phil. 3:17 and 1 Thes. 1:6; 2:14). A recent excellent study, by W. P. de Boer,[26] has explored the concept of imitation in depth and provided not only a fuller understanding of what Paul had in mind but answered some of the unease arising from Paul's invitation.

To begin with, de Boer points out that Paul offers himself as a model only to those churches which he founded. Others are told to imitate Christ (Rom. 15:1–7; Col. 3:13). This provides the clue for our interpretation of Paul's request. It is essentially an

---

[24] Chadwick, *Pastoral Teaching of St Paul*, p. 319.

[25] J. Calvin, *The Second Epistle of Paul to the Corinthians and the Epistles to Timothy, Titus and Philemon*, p. 29 and J. T. McNeill, *Cure of Souls*, p. 81.

[26] W. P. de Boer, *The Imitation of Paul*.

aspect of the father-child relationship. Children naturally imitate their fathers and in the ancient world it was not despised as an artificial and restraining thing for the child to do. Rather it was the means of calling the children to be what they already were and of bringing to full expression what they already were by virtue of their birth.[27]

Then, de Boer points out that Paul is not asking his converts to imitate his eccentricities, 'he is not seeking a copy of himself which will reproduce him in the finest detail'.[28] Abstinence from marriage and manual labour may be advocated, but not as part of this call to imitate Paul. The call is to imitate Paul in his humility, self-denial, self-giving and self-sacrifice. It is particularly linked with the self-giving of Christ himself. What Paul is asking for is an imitation of the way of the cross. Just as this, the heart of the gospel, was the norm for the apostle's life-style, so in this respect the apostle was to be the norm for his churches' life-style. They too were to walk the way of the cross.

A third conclusion reached by de Boer is that Paul's use of himself as an example is crucial to his instructional method (1 Cor. 4:16–17). This is one reason why his teaching is more than cerebral. They can learn about the gospel through words but they can also see the gospel embodied in the apostle himself, for all he does is a reflection of what the gospel does and all he is is a reflection of what the gospel is.[29] Paul is a living example of the very thing he is teaching (1 Cor. 4:17). The aptness required to teach (1 Tim. 3:2) is more, then, than a verbal ability to explain truth clearly. It is a requirement to live the gospel.

If it was true in Paul's day that men learnt by visual means, it is even more true today in our much more visual age. The power of example remains one of the most potent influences in men's lives and is of crucial significance for the work of the pastor.

Priest and sacrifice
In a unique reference in Romans 15:16 Paul speaks of his calling as 'to be a minister of Christ Jesus to the Gentiles with the priestly duty of proclaiming the gospel of God, so that the Gentiles might become an offering acceptable to God, sanctified

---

[27] *Ibid.*, pp. 1–16, 206 and 213.
[28] *Ibid.*, p. 207 and Schütz, *Anatomy*, pp. 226–232.
[29] de Boer, *Imitation*, p. 213 and Schütz, *Anatomy*, pp. 227f.

by the Holy Spirit'. Although he may simply be commenting on his work as a holy service to the Lord, as C. E. B. Cranfield suggests,[30] the description of his work as the work of a priest does seem more probable. The thought here is certainly not that the priest offers God to men through ritual or sacrament, but rather that he offers men to God by bringing them into obedience to the gospel.[31] Paul's comment stands as a reminder that all the pastor's work, and not simply the conduct of church services, is an act of worship to a holy God. The sacrifice which is pleasing to God is not ceremonial, but the increasing faith and developing holiness of the members of the church.

Helmsman and ship

A much neglected gift of the Spirit is mentioned in both Romans 12:8 and 1 Corinthians 12:28. It is variously translated as 'leadership' or 'administration'. In Greek literature it is the word used for a ship's helmsman. Although it does not receive much prominence it is a suggestive picture and must refer to the gifts necessary to steer a congregation – gifts which, as has been pointed out, increase in importance in times of storm.[32] Leadership, management, government and administration all conjure up the techniques of the latest so-called 'human' sciences, but it is a pity to devalue what Paul claims to be a spiritual gift because of this image. All these words have to do with sensitive uniting of people towards a common goal and that not only requires great skill but the grace of the Holy Spirit as well. In the later church this was a picture which was to be developed. But even as it stands it is fitting description of the pastoral task.

Other images could be added. The pastor is a workman who must be concerned about the quality of his work (Col. 4:17; 2 Tim. 2:15), an ambassador who announces his master's message even in the church itself (2 Cor. 5:20; Eph. 6:20), a farmer who works hard to produce crops (1 Cor. 3:6–9 and 2 Tim. 2:6), a builder who is careful about his foundations (1 Cor. 3:9–15), a soldier who has learnt to deny himself for the sake of the war he fights (2 Tim. 2:3–4) and an athlete who has learnt self-discipline (2 Tim. 2:5).

---

[30] C. E. B. Cranfield, *The Epistle to the Romans*, vol. 2, pp. 755f. See his n. 1, where he admits the balance of commentators to be against him.

[31] J. Calvin, *The Epistles of Paul to the Romans and to the Thessalonians*, p. 310.

[32] H. W. Beyer, '*Kubernesis*', *TDNT*, vol. 3, pp. 1035–1037.

Each of the images conveys the impression of the closest of relationships between the apostle and his churches. They confirm H. T. Mayer's conclusion that, 'the primary characteristic of Paul's pastoral activity was his complete identification of himself with the dreams, the hopes, the fears, the needs of the people'.[33]

STRATEGY AND TACTICS

Some indication of Paul's tactics has already been given in reference to his teaching method and his offer to serve as a model, but this needs to be supplemented at a number of fundamental points.

Firstly, Paul's basic approach is to provide a positive climate for his instruction wherever possible (1 Cor. 1:4–9; 11:2; 2 Cor. 7:4, 13–16; Eph. 3:14–19; Phil. 1:3–6; Col. 1:3–8; 1 Thes. 1:2–3; 2 Thes. 1:3–4 and 2 Tim. 1:5). His encouragement is not manufactured or just inserted for effect, but is genuine, for he is quite capable of withholding any positive comment if the occasion deserves, as in Galatians or 1 Corinthians 11:17. Nor is his intention mere flattery in order that he may manipulate his converts more easily, as some have proposed.[34] It is rather, as Calvin puts it in his comment on Paul's thanksgiving in 1 Thessalonians 1:2, that, 'He does so . . . not so much to commend them as to encourage them to perseverance. It is a powerful stimulus to the pursuit of progress to consider that God has bestowed superlative gifts upon us for the purpose of perfecting what he has begun, and that we have moved in the right direction towards achieving our goal under his direction and guidance.'[35]

The commendations draw attention to a fundamental presupposition of Paul's pastoral care. They are principally thanksgivings for what God is doing in his readers' lives, rather than celebrations of their personal virtues. So Paul builds on the work God has already begun and seeks to bring it to full expression. Where that work is absent there is no point in building, since more fundamental issues have to be encountered first and God must first give spiritual life (1 Cor. 2:13–14).

---

[33] H. T. Mayer, *Pastoral Care. Its Roots and Renewal*, p. 35.
[34] G. Shaw, *The Cost of Authority. Manipulation and Freedom in the New Testament*, pp. 30f.
[35] Calvin, *Romans and Thessalonians*, pp. 333f.

Secondly, Paul is always careful to relate the practical to the doctrinal. Not even the most material of issues, like, for example, the collection for the saints in Jerusalem, is justified on pragmatic grounds. There is always a doctrinal underpinning. So in 2 Corinthians 8 and 9 Paul is neither content simply to set out the need for such a collection and the relief it will bring, nor to spur the Corinthians to generosity by quoting the example of others. Intermingled with those arguments are weightier doctrinal arguments drawing lessons from the incarnation (8:9), the honour of the Lord (8:19), the God-given laws of supply and demand (9:7–11), the progress of the gospel (9:12–13) and the grace of God (9:14–15).

Similarly, we could take the question of unity within the local church which Paul deals with in Ephesians 4:3–6. He does not argue that they should be one in spite of the diversity of their personalities and their gifts, simply because life is more comfortable that way or because of what the neighbours would think if they continued to fight. He goes to the heart of the matter. The very nature of their triune God, who is one, demands that they be one with each other. Division within the fellowship is an indication that they do not belong to him. Or, take Philippians 2:1–11, where the lack of unity seems to have arisen because of the clashing of some forceful personalities. The ground of Paul's argument is not that they should get on with each other because it is easier if they do than if they fall out with each other; it is that if they have appreciated the meaning of the incarnation at all they will be humble enough to serve one another. Putting oneself forward is an indication that the individual has failed to grasp an elementary truth concerning Christ. In Paul, the indicative always precedes the imperative.[36] Whatever the issue, Paul takes his readers back to the doctrinal truth which should determine their behaviour. Whereas in the Gospels and in Hebrews these truths are essentially Christological, in Paul they are drawn from a much wider range of doctrine, although they retain a Christological heart.

On this basis Paul issues a range of exhortations and expresses them in many different forms. Victor Furnish[37] has argued that the exhortations do not simply take the form of imperatives but include questions (*e.g.* Rom. 6:2), examples (*e.g.*

[36] Ridderbos, *Paul*, pp. 252–258.
[37] V. P. Furnish, *Theology and Ethics in Paul*, pp. 92–98.

1 Cor. 16:1), expresssions of confidence (*e.g.* Gal. 5:10 and Phm. 21), prayer (*e.g.* Rom. 15:5–6), the telling of a story (*e.g.* Gal. 4:22–30) and indicative statements (*e.g.* Rom. 5:1ff. and Gal. 4:31; 5:1).

The distribution of these exhortations warns us against the commonly accepted view that Paul's epistles begin with doctrine and then go on to draw out its practical implications. Although there is some ground for accepting this idea (*e.g.* Rom. 12:1; Eph. 4:1), such a division is in danger of leading us to a superficial view of Paul's strategy. Rather Paul intersperses his doctrinal teaching with practical exhortation and impregnates his applied teaching with doctrinal truth.[38] The two are not divorced and there is never ground for saying 'now the doctrine is over, let's be practical'. Doctrine is practical and practice is doctrinal.

A third feature of Paul's strategy, consistent with his aim of producing maturity, is his concern to enable believers to work things through for themselves. He is sometimes seen to impose his dogmatic ideas on the church but, in fact, he adopts this approach rarely and only when the central truths of the gospel are at stake, as in Galatians.[39] His main approach is much less forceful. He does not impose discipline on the church at Corinth but rather invites them to take the initiative in disciplining their errant member (1 Cor. 5:5). He is careful to distinguish between what had been revealed to him and what was his more personal – but worth-while nevertheless – opinion (1 Cor. 7:10, 12, 25, 40) where people are perfectly free to make up their own minds (1 Cor. 7:36–37). He is sympathetic to arguments which run counter to his own and even provides his opponents with arguments which could be used against his own position (1 Cor. 8:1–13; 10:23–33). Above all, his approach is to invite recognition that what he says is true (Phil. 3:15). He is confident that the recognition will be granted either because of the sheer logic of his argument (as in 2 Cor. 10 – 13) or because he is only reminding them of what they already know (Rom. 15:15; 1 Cor. 15:1; 1 Thes. 4:2). It was only by adopting this approach that they would be able to become responsible for their own spiritual condition.

[38] *Ibid.*, pp. 106–111 and Lloyd-Jones. *Darkness and Light*, pp. 11–24.
[39] H. von Campenhausen. *Ecclesiastical Authority and Spiritual Power in the Church of the First Three Centuries*, p. 51.

This strategy was no mere technique on Paul's part devised to ensure their greater or more willing compliance. It was the only strategy which was consistent with the gospel.[40] The gospel had called men to freedom (Gal. 5:1) and it would have been totally inconsistent to curtail their liberty by imposing new chains on them, even if Paul had manufactured the chains himself and believed them to be in the best interests of his converts. Freedom was of the essence of the gospel. Moreover, he expresses confidence about their ability to instruct each other (Rom. 15:14) because they too had the Holy Spirit (Rom. 8:9–11; 1 Cor. 2:6–16; Eph. 1:17; Phil. 1:9–10; 1 Thes. 4:8). Instruction, then, is not only conducted in a 'relationship of trusted motive',[41] but need not even be conducted by the apostle himself at all. Church members can ably and legitimately engage in mutual instruction.

Paul's pastoral strategy is summarized by the words encouragement, enabling, exposition, example and exhortation. He worked to enable Christians to be mature in their thinking, living and serving. His attitude was one of confident encouragement. His method was to expound truth and to be an example of that truth; from that basis he would exhort the churches to greater things. If rebuke was required he was not afraid to administer it, but did so in the context of a committed and loving relationship.

AUTHORITY AND STRUCTURE

The question of apostolic authority has recently been a storm centre for New Testament scholarship with some claiming that Paul was strongly authoritarian[42] and others resisting such a claim.[43] It has also been a storm centre at a local church level with the renewal movement questioning institutional church leadership and claiming it to be ineffective whilst discovering a greater authority in charismatic leadership.

Obviously Paul believed he had authority in the church

---

[40] *Ibid.*, pp. 46f.

[41] W. Oates, *The Christian Pastor*, p. 71.

[42] Shaw, *Cost of Authority*, and W. Munro, *Authority in Paul and Peter*, who attributes the claim to authority to Paul's successors rather than Paul himself.

[43] Banks, *Community*, pp. 175–187; von Campenhausen, *Ecclesiastical Authority and Spiritual Power*, pp. 30–55; Schütz, *Anatomy*, *passim*, and J. D. G. Dunn, *Jesus and the Spirit*, pp. 271–300.

because he spoke about 'the authority the Lord gave us' (2 Cor. 10:8; 13:10). The question is what did he mean by that and what, if any, are its implications for subsequent church leaders? We have already discussed a number of relevant issues, but now they need to be focused on the question of authority. As the founding father of a number of the early churches Paul exercised a natural authority over them and it is among them that his authority is chiefly, though not exclusively, displayed.[44] This is what determines the kind of authority he exercises.

Firstly, he has an authority in the gospel because it was by preaching the gospel to them that they were brought to birth and it was through the gospel that they now lived. The gospel was more than a verbal announcement; it was a power and a force which had effect in the lives of his hearers. The apostle embodied it and conveyed it to them. And having conveyed new life he continued to be responsible for its healthy growth and expression. This not only explains his continuing authority but limits it too. He only has authority as far as the gospel is concerned. Wherever that is threatened or wherever Christians fail to reflect it, there he speaks with authority. But the further away he gets from issues central to the gospel the weaker, in one sense, his authority becomes. In dealing with issues not central to the gospel, as for example in 1 Corinthians 7, he retains authority as a wise and godly pastor and people ignore his advice at their peril, but he cannot exercise final authority in them. So his authority is not a personal possession, neither is his power a personal quality. Authority and power exist only in so far as Paul is an agent of the gospel.[45]

Secondly, if his authority stems from his parental relationship, it must be an authority which has the interests of his children at its heart. This is plainly understood by Paul in that, on the only two occasions where Paul speaks of his authority, he states that it was given to him 'for building you up rather than pulling you down' (2 Cor. 10:8 and 13:10). The purpose of his being granted authority by the Lord is neither that his own status can be enhanced, nor that his personal whims can be satisfied, but that his converts might grow to maturity.

How was this to be conveyed subsequently when Paul was

---

44 B. Holmberg, *Paul and Power*.
45 Dunn, *Jesus and the Spirit*, pp. 278–280 and Schütz, *Anatomy*, pp. 224 and 281–282.

no longer available? In an influential article Ernst Käsemann[46] has proposed that the New Testament gives two answers, not one, to that question. The first answer, nearer to Paul, is that the church is a community where authority is located in charismata. The second answer, which arose after the failure of the unstructured community to protect itself adequately against assailants, provided for the creation of offices in the church, which was now viewed as an institution. This he sees as the very antithesis of Paul's view of the church.

Critics have not been slow to expose the problems raised by the antithesis Käsemann proposed. Schütz has developed an aspect of Käsemann's own argument to show that, although Paul does not elaborate a complex church order, there is an implicit order in what Paul states about the functioning of charisma. Käsemann asserted that no spiritual gift had any value or rights on its own account but was justified only in so far as it was an act of service. He pointed out that since gifts were not all equally distributed, but each received an individual manifestation of the Spirit for the common good (Rom. 12:3; 1 Cor. 3:5; 12:7, 11; Eph. 4:7), there was no place for ecclesiastical egalitarianism. Furthermore, the gifts were to be used for one another (1 Cor. 12:12–26) and in the fear of the Lord (Rom. 12:11; Eph. 5:21 and Phil. 2:3).[47] Schütz argues that this displays an implicit order which structures the common life by distinguishing between gifts and which orders the individual life by setting boundaries on the self.[48]

Dunn, whilst fundamentally agreeing with Käsemann's distinction, has shown how the exercise of gifts was not permitted to degenerate into anarchy in the church. Authority could be claimed by a member only in the exercise of his gift and not beyond it. Guide-lines were clearly laid down which provided for government and discrimination to be exercised in the matter and which gave an important place to the community acting as a corporate body (1 Cor. 14:1–40).[49] Authority, then, although residing in those who could demonstrate the Spirit, was also distributed in a network of relationships and was never located in a few individuals.

[46] E. Käsemann, 'Ministry and Community in the New Testament', in *Essays on New Testament Themes*, pp. 63–94.

[47] *Ibid.*, pp. 76–78.   [48] Schütz, *Anatomy*, pp. 257–263.

[49] Dunn, *Jesus and the Spirit*, pp. 280–297.

Ronald Fung[50] has further criticized Käsemann for basing his theory on selective evidence. He grants that Paul becomes more concerned about official ministries later in his life, but shows that from the beginning of his missionary activity Paul had displayed a concern that church life should be governed wisely (*e.g.* Acts 14:23, see also 1 Cor. 12:28; Gal. 6:6; Phil. 1:1; 1 Thes. 5:12). But perhaps the most severe weakness in the matter is that in the New Testament there is no serious opposition between spiritual charisma and ecclesiastical office. The only way in which such a divorce can be maintained is by reading more into the pastoral epistles about the nature of the ordination of leaders referred to there than is warranted. This Käsemann does whilst ignoring the close correspondence between the qualifications such leaders were required to have (1 Tim. 3:1–13; Tit. 1:5–9) and the spiritual gifts listed by Paul in Romans 12:3–8 and Ephesians 4:11. Paul was working on the fundamental assumption that those who exercised the office would possess the corresponding charisma.

The test of all authority in the New Testament, whether it be apostolic, charismatic or official, is one. It is a test of function. No-one is ever placed in an impregnable position, even if he is the apostle Peter himself (Gal. 2:14)! No gift of the Spirit is ever exempt from a process of evaluation. No office ever commands unquestioning loyalty. The present concern to find the right structure, as if one is inherently more biblical than another, would be foreign to Paul's understanding. The question is never settled by who the person claiming authority is, neither is it settled by what gift he exercises, or by what office he holds. The question is rather, 'What function does he perform?' Unless the apostle is true to his commission to advance and guard the gospel he may be a false apostle. Unless the spiritually gifted serve one another and build up the church they may be spiritual counterfeits. And unless the leader commands spiritual respect within the church he has in practice disqualified himself from office, whatever happens in theory.

Once the tests prove satisfactory there is an authority which the church must recognize and to which it must respond (1 Thes. 5:12; 1 Tim. 5:17) and even obey (Phil. 2:12). For such

---

[50] R. Y. K. Fung, 'Charismatic versus Organised Ministry', *EQ* 52 (1980), pp. 195–214.

leadership is a gift from God to his people to ensure their progress and preserve their purity (Eph. 4:11–16).

CHARACTER AND INTEGRITY

Something has already been said regarding the character of the pastor. In Paul's eyes he must be a patient and gentle teacher who is firmly committed to the truth. But his troubles with the church at Corinth caused him to reveal a much deeper side to pastoral life than this. Pastoral life can be a great joy and bring tremendous rewards, but it can also be painful and costly and no-one can be more vulnerable to the wounds inflicted by others than the true pastor.

He reveals in 2 Corinthians how some of his own children had criticized him for being fickle (1:15–17), speaking with a double tongue (1:13; 10:1, 10), of lacking credentials (3:1), of being untrustworthy with money (8:20–21), of acting in a worldly fashion (10:2), of being proud and deceitful (10:8; 12:16), of not being an original apostle (11:5) and of lacking dignity (11:7). The misunderstandings had led to a rupture in relationships, with the Corinthians not communicating with Paul in any meaningful way (7:2). It was all the harder because it was a family relationship which was disrupted and because Paul took such delight in them (12:14–15; 7:3–4). It was also hard because it came on top of all his other pressures (11:22–28). What is more, he was innocent. The strife had been stirred up by impostors (11:13), who in contrast to Paul had no legitimate place in the church at Corinth (10:13).

The amazing thing is just how much Paul seems to accept the situation as part and parcel of the pastoral life. Of course such experiences were not easy. But they were of the essence of pastoral service. Paul could be criticized for lacking personal charisma, but that is how it should be, because it ensured that what people saw in him was the power of God and not his own brilliant personality (4:7). More significantly still, such weakness and such suffering proved the genuineness of his ministry since it identified him with Christ (4:10; 13:4).

Throughout the letter there runs the tension between power and weakness. The Corinthians wanted Paul to be an apostle of power. They wanted their apostle to be the entertainingly persuasive preacher, the subject of sensational spiritual experiences, the worker of great spiritual feats, and a dynamic personality to boot. Who doesn't want their pastor to be the same today? Paul insists that such spiritual experiences were not unknown to him (11:6; 12:1–4) even if the Corinthians were unaware that he had had them. But he argues that they are not of the essence of ministry and therefore he will not boast of them. The essence of ministry is the closeness of one's identification with Jesus Christ; a Jesus who was crucified in weakness (11:3–4; 13:3–4). Since the cross was at the centre of his gospel he would boast not about his power but his weaknesses (11:30; 12:7–10). They were the true credentials of his calling and the means through which God conveyed his power.

This perspective on ministry was as ill-suited to the spirit of Paul's age as it is to our own. They, too, worshipped the idols of success, power, knowledge, strength and victory. Weakness was a quality to be avoided and those who displayed it were to be shunned. But that was the way God had chosen to work (1 Cor. 1:18 – 2:5) and it was pointless to pretend otherwise. Those who did so, automatically disqualified themselves from true Christian service. God's methods have not changed and he still chooses to work through the same weak vessels so that men might realize that it is he, not they, who is at work.

In juxtaposition, Paul shows a recurring concern to present himself as a man of integrity. It is evident in the following areas: in his attitude to money (Acts 20:33–35; 1 Cor. 9:15–18; 2 Cor. 12:14–18 and 1 Thes. 2:7–9), in his refusal to put a stumbling-block in anyone's way (2 Cor. 6:3), in the way he made his plans (2 Cor. 1:12 – 2:4), in his general character (1 Thes. 2:10; 2 Tim. 3:10), in his desire to make spiritual progress (Phil. 3:12–14), in the methods he adopts to preach the gospel (2 Cor. 4:2) and in his living out of the gospel he preached (1 Cor. 4:17 and 2 Cor. 1:18–19). The same standard of integrity is required of local church leaders too, as a perusal of 1 Timothy 3:1–13 shows.

His concern is not simply that the world is populated by actors and that the church provides many with a secure stage on which to perform. Nor is it just a negative fear that the gospel will be prevented from making progress if its propagators are discovered to be frauds. It is rather that the very nature of the gospel which he preached was a gospel of sincerity and truth (2 Cor. 1:18–19). To be anything less than scrupulously honest oneself, therefore, was a denial of the gospel one claimed to believe. It was tantamount to practical unbelief. This was no personal idiosyncrasy arising from an over-sensitive puritan conscience but a fundamental issue relating to the gospel itself.

In the light of this it can be seen that Paul's boasting of weakness and his concern to protest his integrity are not contradictions but find coherence in the gospel. The gospel determines everything about the pastor – his motives, authority, methods and character are all governed by the good news of Jesus Christ.

CONCLUSION: THE PASTORAL EPISTLES

Paul's final glimpse of the ministry also provides us with his most systematic treatment of the subject. In the pastoral epistles Paul is handing on the torch to the next generation and in so doing provides them with a pastoral directive[51] in which his essential thinking about the ministry is crystallized. Many have argued that the picture of the ministry presented in these letters contrasts with Paul's earlier views about the ministry, to the extent that many have not considered these letters genuinely Pauline. It is easy to overstress the contrasts and underrate the similarities, which have been shown to be numerous.[52] The picture of ministry presented in Timothy and Titus is consistent with Paul's earlier writings. It is also easy to overestimate the degree to which the church had developed and become institutionalized.[53] Believing, then, that these letters are from Paul and were written towards the end of his life, what can we learn from them about pastoral ministry?

The days in which Timothy and Titus were serving were different from the initial days of the Christian mission. The churches had grown and developed in numerous ways and had to face problems common to all second generation leaders. They faced opposition, much of which arose from internal arguments. They faced desertion as many once enthusiastic converts renounced their Christian faith (2 Tim. 1:15). They faced the threat of doctrinal error to an unprecedented degree. The element of spiritual conflict in ministry was therefore very much

---

[51] The phrase comes from G. W. Barker, W. L. Lane and R. Michaels, *The New Testament Speaks*, p. 235.

[52] Martin, *Foundations*, vol. 2, pp. 303f.

[53] Cf. Dunn, *Unity and Diversity*, pp. 341–366 and D. J. Tidball, *An Introduction to the Sociology of the New Testament*, pp. 123–136.

to the forefront of Paul's thinking. Timothy and Titus were to fight for the faith (1 Tim. 1:18 and 2 Tim. 2:1–10). But underlying the command to fight was the crucial assumption that they knew what they were fighting for. Before they took to the battlefield they had to be sure that they were holding on to the gospel. If their confidence in it had waned, as the confidence of many had, there was no point in fighting. And if they were not clear as to what it was they were to defend, there was no point in going to war (2 Tim. 1:14). So it was fundamental to their ministries that they should be exhorted to hold fast to the revealed truth. Many had not. Given this context of a discouraging church and a hostile world, together with Timothy's timid character, it is no wonder that Paul encourages him to endure and not to throw in the towel. In the circumstances, endurance was no mean spiritual achievement.

But what sort of ministry was it that would enable him to endure, remain true to the gospel and fight for it? Firstly, it was a spiritually gifted ministry. Three times Paul points to the spiritual endowment which Timothy was to exploit in his ministry (1 Tim. 1:18; 4:14; 2 Tim. 1:6). Once more he points to the help of the Holy Spirit as a vital resource in enabling Timothy to accomplish his task (2 Tim. 1:14). Timothy, it seems, had no more been elected to an ecclesiastical office, regardless of his spiritual gifts, than had those in the assembly at Corinth. The spiritual dynamic remained a vital qualification for ministry.

Secondly, it was to be a godly ministry. The central designation which Paul applies to Timothy is that he was a man of God (1 Tim. 6:11; 2 Tim. 3:17). Godliness summarized so much of what was expected of him. He was to portray it in the purity of his speech and life (1 Tim. 4:12; 2 Tim. 2:22), in his diligent hard work (1 Tim. 4:15), in his sensitivity in relating to others (1 Tim. 5:1–21), in avoiding the temptations of the ministry (1 Tim. 6:3–10) and in the fact that he continued to make spiritual progress (1 Tim. 4:15). Godliness was also to mark his handling of the false teachers. He was to handle them with a ruthless graciousness. On the one hand he was to stand resolutely for the truth. What he was to teach was clear and non-negotiable (1 Tim. 4:11; 2 Tim. 3:14–16; similarly, Tit. 3:4–8). He was to be single-minded in refusing to be distracted by mentally entertaining but nevertheless spiritually futile questions (1 Tim. 4:7; 6:3–5; 2 Tim. 2:16–18; similarly, Tit. 3:9). On the other hand, he was to be alert to the dangers of defending the truth. He was to handle his opponents with gentleness (1 Tim. 3:3; 6:11; 2 Tim. 2:24; 4:2). Being right was no excuse for arrogance. The pattern of sound teaching must be defended, but it must be defended with love (2 Tim. 1:13). It was all too easy, then as now, to have the right message but to cancel it out because it was not conveyed by the right manner.

Thirdly, all this points to the essential view of the ministry being that of an informed teaching ministry. In contrast to those who did not know what they were talking about (1 Tim. 1:7), he was to be sure of what he believed and why he believed it (2 Tim. 2:2; 3:14–16). The core of his ministry was to be teaching, both positively in expounding truth (1 Tim. 4:6, 11, 13, similarly Tit. 2:15) and negatively in correcting error (1 Tim. 5:20; 2 Tim. 4:2). Three other features of this teaching ministry stand out. It was a teaching which was to be conveyed as much by example as by word (1 Tim. 4:12; similarly, Tit. 2:7). It was a teaching which was to be relevantly applied to specific social groups and not restricted to general principles (1 Tim. 5:1–22, especially v. 7; similarly, Tit. 2:1–10). It was also a teaching in which others were to share. The burden was not to fall completely on his shoulders (2 Tim. 2:2; also 1 Tim. 3:1–13; Tit. 1:5–9).

Leadership in the church was evidently plural leadership. For all the authority that Timothy and Titus might have as delegates of the apostle Paul himself, it was not envisaged that they would engage in a one-man-ministry. In fact, the point of the commission Titus received was to appoint elders in Crete (Tit. 1:15). Those who were to share as leaders in the church, whether elders or deacons, were expected to have impeccable qualifications. They were to be able to stand tests of their family and social lives as well as of their spiritual lives. They were to be tested as to their understanding of and loyalty to Christian truth. No part of their lives was irrelevant if they wanted to be recognized as leaders in the church of God. The status of a leader was already liable to be a temptation for some (1 Tim. 5:17–19) and Timothy is discouraged from being over-hasty in his appointments so that those who are not personally and spiritually mature enough for the task would not be unwisely pushed to the front (1 Tim. 5:22).

Ministry is obviously a demanding spiritual task which, like marriage, is not to be entered into lightly or unadvisedly. It is conducted in the full view of God the judge (2 Tim. 4:1). The standards which Paul set out for Timothy and Titus remain the ideals for which every pastor should aim. But the relevance of the pastoral epistles for today is much wider. The difficult situation in which Timothy and Titus ministered bears more than a passing resemblance to our own age. The church in which they served was one in which the first enthusiasms with their excesses had passed but where dead orthodoxy now threatened as a real possibility. The emergence of more established forms of leadership, with all the potential for mixed motives which that entailed, similarly relates to our own situation. So, the strategy which Paul advocated, a ministry which taught truth and defended it against all error, with an integrity which was beyond reproach, remains the vital strategy for our own day. Here and throughout his writings Paul reveals himself to be anything but a reluctant pastor. Rather he is a pastor among the pastors.

6

The general epistles

HEBREWS

According to Ralph Martin, 'Hebrews is best understood as a polemical writing'.[1] But this judgment, if it stands unqualified, is likely to be seriously misleading. Hebrews shows none of the anger or animosity usually associated with polemic. It is true that it argues its case passionately and warns of the dire consequences of falling away from Christ without reserve. Yet its persuasiveness arises from its spirit of understanding, sensitivity and compassion. It would be more fitting, therefore, to say that Hebrews is best understood as a pastoral polemic.

Whatever the precise identity or location of its readers, it is clear that they were in danger of giving up the Christian faith.[2] They stood at some distance from the original events of the gospel (2:3) and had already lost some of their spiritual leaders (13:7), yet the return of Christ did not seem near (10:36–39). Their faith had already taken its toll in suffering (10:32–34) and the Christian life did not seem to be paying sufficient dividends to keep them loyal. Their lack of motivation was aggravated by the activity of teachers who offered a more attractive alternative to pure Christianity. This, whatever its details, involved the adoption, or readoption, of aspects of the Jewish religion. Their drawing back was already showing in their lack of desire to achieve their full potential (5:12), their sub-Christian behaviour (13:4–5) and in their lack of commitment to the fellowship life of the whole church (10:25). Possibly, they had already become a separate house group which had broken away from the mainline church.[3]

The writer clearly wishes to provide a cogent answer to the false teachers who were having such a damaging effect in the church. So his arguments against their teaching are thorough

---

[1] Martin, *Foundations*, vol. 2, p. 357.
[2] For a discussion of the background see R. Brown, *The Message of Hebrews, Christ Above All*, pp. 13–26; F. F. Bruce, *The Epistle to the Hebrews*, pp. xxiii–xliv; and D. Guthrie, *Hebrews*, pp. 15–38.
[3] Guthrie, *Hebrews*, p. 23.

and take up a great deal of space in his letter. But his principal concern seems not to be his readers' possible return to Judaism, but their rejection of Christianity.[4] The lure of Jewish ritual was only partially responsible for their wavering faith and perhaps it would not have appeared so attractive had it not been for the other dimensions of their disillusionment. Some of it was attributable to sheer apathy (6:12).[5] This wider concern means, as Raymond Brown has written, that 'the letter appeals to all those severely tested believers to keep their faith firmly anchored to the moorings of truth, to maintain their steady confidence in Christ and to press on to mature Christian stability'.[6]

Hebrews has much to contribute to our understanding of pastoral ministry. We shall examine the writer's pastoral foundations, his pastoral method, his pastoral instructions and his comments on pastoral leadership before commenting ourselves on the letter's contemporary pastoral relevance.

If the Hebrews were to persevere in their faith they needed to be given clear reasons for doing so. So before the writer comes to any of the more immediate pastoral problems he invites them to undertake a detailed review of the Christ in whom they had placed their faith. In the course of their careful examination of Christ three outstanding themes about him emerge. Firstly, he is superior to all. Whether the challenge to his supremacy comes from angels (1:5 – 2:18), from Moses (3:1–19), from Joshua (4:1–13), from the high priest (4:14 – 5:10) or even from Melchizedek (7:1–28), he is proved to be greater than them all and simply unrivalled in his relationship with God. Secondly, the way from man to God which he inaugurated is a better way than the one which was already familiar to men under the old covenant (8:1 – 10:18). Point by point the comparison between the two ways is made and point by point the way of Christ scores until, in the end, there can be no doubt as to which way is preferable.

But the examination of Christ is still not complete for, even if the supremacy of Christ and his better way might convince the Hebrews of the truth of Christianity intellectually, they have other needs as well. They are a tried and tested people. A Christ

---

[4] *Ibid.*, p. 33.
[5] P. E. Hughes, *A Commentary on the Epistle to the Hebrews*, p. 73.
[6] Brown, *Christ Above All*, p. 13.

who is only high in the heavens might lack identification with them and be indifferent to their present distressing circumstances. What they need, in addition to a supreme Christ, is a Christ who is near and can be shown to sympathize with them. That will enable them to be convinced not only intellectually but emotionally too. So, thirdly, the writer dwells on the humanity of Christ. He does this not only by his frequent use of the unqualified name 'Jesus' and his general stress on the incarnation, but more specifically by emphasizing the humanity of Jesus (2:14), his temptations (4:15), his suffering (5:7-9) and his perseverance even to death itself (2:14; 13:12). Jesus Christ could be an effective Saviour only if he had fully experienced the human condition 'yet without sin' from which men needed to be saved. But the Hebrews need have no fear, for he had been made like them in every way (2:14) and he had experienced their circumstances first-hand (4:15). He was able, therefore, to sympathize.

So the writer's starting-point, in encouraging the flagging faith of the Hebrews, is to get them to distance themselves a little from their own problems and look carefully at their Saviour. Several times he invites them to take another look at Jesus and to linger over the vision they see (2:9; 3:1; 12:2-3). It is as if he invites them to switch on a television, but before doing so he has made sure that the set they are going to watch is correctly tuned and switched to the right channel. His pastoral duty is to ensure that they do not miss out, either because they were watching the other side or because they have a weak signal and a cloudy picture.

Once the pastoral foundation is laid, the writer builds on it and much can be learnt from his pastoral method. Five features can be identified. Firstly, he engages in *periodic exhortation*. Exhortation quietly dominates the letter, as one would expect in view of its stated aim (13:22). The successive exhortations are not saved up and collected at the end of his writing but placed throughout, as appropriate (2:1; 3:12; 4:11, 14; 5:11-12; 6:1; 10:35-36; 12:1, 12, 25 and 13:9). Some of the exhortations are written in the strongest terms so that his readers can be in no doubt about the seriousness of the author's intent. They are 'to pay more careful attention' (2:1), to 'see it' (3:12), to 'make every effort' (4:11). They dare not throw away their opportunities (10:35) but they are to throw away everything which would prove a hindrance (12:1). It is made clear that the cure for many of their spiritual ills lay within their own hands (12:12–13). It would have been useless just to tell them to 'pull themselves together' but now, knowing what they do about Jesus Christ, the next step is up to them. Are they going to make the necessary commitment of will to make a go of it spiritually or not?

A second feature of the writer's pastoral method is to issue *plain warnings* about the spiritual path they seem to be on (2:2–3; 6:1–8;[7] 10:26–31 and 12:25). He does not dwell on these warnings and clearly derives no sadistic pleasure from issuing them. None the less, he would be less than honest if he did not sound such ominous notes, for judgment is a reality which must be faced. Part of his pastoral responsibility is to ensure that his readers are fully acquainted with the facts and fully conversant with the consequences of their behaviour.

A third feature is his *gentle encouragement*. Whatever his personal disappointment may have been over their lack of maturity, he does not allow it to be responsible for the adoption of a harsh or sarcastic manner. The negative notes of judgment are quickly followed by positive notes of encouragement (6:9–10 and 10:32–35). The stick is accompanied by a juicy carrot. There is no room for the Hebrews to feel punished, rejected and worthless. The rebuke is firmly set in the context of love. Their past record gives grounds for confidence (10:32), as does the character of God himself (6:10). So there is every reason to believe that they will emerge from their present spiritual apathy and make good progress towards maturity.

Fourthly, in a related manner, the author introduces a number of *encouraging examples* as a stimulus to their perseverance. Hebrews 11:1 – 12:1 is an obvious case, but the reference to Abraham in 6:13–15 and to the leaders they had known (13:7) should also be noted. It is all too easy when adopting this strategy to depress rather than motivate people, because they have been dazzled by a galaxy of stars who bear little relation to their own paltry lives. The introduction of examples, therefore, demands great skill. But it is evident that the writer to the Hebrews possessed such skill. In talking of the giants of the Old Testament he is careful to draw his readers' attention to

---

[7] For a pastoral exposition of the difficulties of Heb. 6:1–8 see Brown, *ibid.*, pp. 108–116. His exposition excels at providing a pastoral interpretation of Hebrews.

those aspects of their lives with which they would readily identify. And he talks not only of Noah, Abraham, Joseph and Moses but of Abel, Enoch, Rahab and a host of unnamed heroes as well. These are the human examples, but he also presents Jesus as an example to be imitated. They are to contemplate him in order that they might not lose heart and give up (12:2–3).

The final aspect of his pastoral method to be noted is his *careful application*. Referring to Hebrews 10:19–39, Raymond Brown has commented that, 'he knows only too well that his exposition of these impressive themes in the earlier chapters is not likely to achieve a great deal if it is to remain unrelated to their everyday lives'.[8] He therefore builds on the rich doctrinal teaching earlier in his letter and presses the application of the truths home. Part of the immeasurable privilege of an expository preaching ministry is the opportunity to take the timeless truths of God's word and to match them to the needs of the hour. To fail in the task of application is to fail in one's duty as a pastor.

More briefly, Hebrews contains a number of concise pastoral instructions (13:1–6) on love, hospitality, those who are imprisoned, marriage and money. The particular issues were chosen presumably because they were the ones most relevant to the Hebrews and yet they are strikingly relevant to our own day too. None of these ethical instructions is well developed and yet each of them manages to incorporate some reason why they should be obeyed. Love because you are brothers. Entertain because you may entertain angels. Care for prisoners as if you yourselves were one of them. Honour marriage because God will judge immorality. Shun materialism because God has already said he will provide for you. Not even in these terse commands does the writer feel that he should ask for mindless obedience.

Given the Hebrews' interest in priesthood, it would not have been surprising for the writer to compare the leadership of the church under the new covenant with the priesthood of the old covenant, but no such comparison is made. The writer's only interest is to contrast the old priesthood with the high priesthood of Jesus (8:1 – 9:28). Jesus stands alone as the priest and shepherd (13:20) of God's new people. Indeed, it would be in conflict with the benefits made available through the work of

---

[8] *Ibid.*, p. 191.

Christ if a new priesthood were erected: whereas the privilege of entering the holy place had previously been restricted to the priests, now it was available to all believers (10:19–22). The idea of sacerdotalism is therefore not only against the general spirit of the teaching of Hebrews but contrary to its specific understanding of the work of Christ.

Congruent with this understanding of the priesthood of all believers is the encouragement given in Hebrews for the members of the church to engage in mutual upbuilding (3:13; 10:25; *cf.* 6:10; 12:15). Ministry is a task in which every believer takes part and for which every believer will be equipped by 'the great Shepherd of the sheep' (13:20–21).

In spite of this Hebrews mentions the leaders of the church on three occasions (13:7, 17 and 24). They were considered by the author to play a crucial, not incidental, role in the spiritual development of the members of the church. Thus the responsibilities of both leader and led are outlined. Leaders were to earn respect by the example they set (v. 7). They were to be watchful. At a time when false teaching was making headway and many were dropping away, their vigilance was all the more necessary. But they should remember that they were accountable (v. 17), so there was no room for them to become authoritarian. On the other hand, members were to imitate their example (v. 7), obey their instructions, submit to their authority and co-operate with their leadership (v. 17). It is apparent that the writer's intention in stating this is not so that the church would run like a well-oiled machine. Nor is it that, as a leader himself, he had vested interests and wanted to ensure that his fellow leaders were to have an easy life. The intention is that the members themselves might benefit and this is most likely when they willingly comply with the leadership that is enjoined and intended to be of advantage to their spiritual growth. Both authoritarianism and anarchy are prohibited by these injunctions. For both sides must submit their attitudes and behaviour to the ultimate goal of preserving the safety of the flock and ensuring its development to maturity.

The contemporary pastoral relevance of Hebrews is many-sided even if its initial appearance, with its ostentatious Jewish dress, is not so encouraging. Many today find themselves in a similar situation to the Hebrews and need to be encouraged to persevere. Apathy, unbelief, the seduction of other faiths, discouragements because of ridicule or suffering, misunderstandings regarding the pilgrim nature of Christian discipleship and sub-standard Christian behaviour are all rife. Hebrews, then, has much to say to us. But let us be careful how we use it. To filter its exhortations and warnings out of their context is liable only to discourage us further. They become positive incentives to perseverance only when firmly kept in the context of the teaching about Christ. The antidote to Christians who are tempted to repudiate their faith is to let Christ, in all his fullness, fill their vision.

JAMES

James is unique among the letters of the New Testament. The enigma of its background and style together with its relatively undeveloped theology have often led to it being disparaged. Those who look to Scripture for something more sophisticated, however, are in danger of missing a letter of tremendous pastoral significance.

Arguing that James, the leader of the church in Jerusalem, was its author, James Adamson has adjudged that, 'the Epistle of James is a quasi-prophetic letter of pastoral encouragement, and, no less, of pastoral rebuke, proceeding from an unquestioned right of pastoral vocation and authority'.[9] He sees James as writing with all the authority of being close to the source of the faith, and since, unlike most other New Testament letters, it does not appear to have been caused by any particular crisis or persecution, he argues that it is catholic both in contents and readership. It is obvious that James' letter is thoroughly pastoral in orientation, and, in the absence of any more specific information about the situation or its addresses, others have seen it as a general letter which arose purely out of James' pastoral experience.[10]

A more specific understanding of its background would enable us to appreciate James' pastoral strategy more fully and a recent, if tentative, suggestion by Peter Davids is most fruitful in this regard.[11] Davids argues that the internal evidence indicates that it was written to Palestine before AD 70 because it reflects an economic situation where farming had been concen-

---

[9] J. Adamson, *The Epistle of James*, p. 20. [10] Guthrie, *NT Introduction*, p. 764.
[11] P. Davids, *The Epistle of James*, pp. 28–34.

trated in the hands of a rich few, whilst many 'free' labourers were scarcely able to find subsistence and were grossly oppressed. The wealthy families belonged to the high priestly circle and would have been unlikely to provide for or encourage any they knew to be Christians. Some had grasped the economic changes as an opportunity to be redeployed as merchants, which was known to be the quickest way to get rich. And these often became proud of their self-sufficiency and indifferent to the needs of others. A rich man entering a poor church would, therefore, have been welcomed most warmly as a potential economic lifeline.

The church was almost certainly facing difficulties which were imposed on it, not so much by direct opposition to its faith as by the economic context in which it lived. It was a situation which took its toll on its community life. As Davids has commented, 'The tests of faith were breaking the church apart as people yielded to the pressure. The call is for internal unity and charity with an attitude of prophetic denunciation toward the rich yet a refusal to engage in hatred or violence. The Lord's intervention, not man's, is sought. The outward collapse raises eschatological expectation.'[12]

It would be wrong to force every issue raised by James into this economic straitjacket. None the less it is a key which helps to unlock much of the letter. It provides both an explanation for James' concentration on riches and poverty, and it suggests why he includes several other topics which deal with the repercussions of the economic pressure they were experiencing.

It is clear that the people to whom James writes were acutely aware of their testing situation (1:2). The source of the testing was both internal and external. Inwardly, they were subject to evil desires (1:14; 4:3). Outwardly, they were subject to the pressures of their environment, the seduction of the world (4:4) and the activity of the devil (4:7). The testing could have been an obstacle to spiritual progress, but James encourages them to see all these as a potential means of growth (1:2–4). The very trials which they wished to escape would, if they persevered, be the means of bringing them to maturity. But they would never reach it unless they stood firm against all odds (1:3–4 and 5:7–11).

---

[12] *Ibid.*, p. 34.

James undertakes an examination of seven forms which the testing took. Though his theological answers seem superficial in comparison with others, he is concerned to relate each test to a theological truth. His distinctive strategy is to stick largely to the issue itself but to inject God the Father into his discussion so that attitudes and behaviour are formed in relation to him. There is little reference to Jesus Christ. But the two specific references he makes, in 1:1 and 2:1,[13] and other implicit ones stress his Lordship and ascension. Perseverance is therefore encouraged not, as say in Mark, Paul or Hebrews, by Jesus' example in suffering, but by his victory over the forces which opposed him and to which James' readers were currently subject. The theology which emerges, then, is not a repetition of accepted doctrine but a theology of the pastoral issues themselves.

The first stumbling-block to progress was hypocrisy (1:21–27; 2:14–26). Many had come to receive the gospel (1:21) and claimed to have faith (2:14), but they did not live by the gospel or show any evidence of faith. Rather, they heard the word and never thought about applying it (1:22–24) and boasted a faith which was spurious (2:15–19). James ties his discussion firmly to the will of God (1:20, 26–27) and insists that the religion God wants is a practical religion. In this connection he develops a theology of valid faith and shows how the genuine article can be distinguished from a convincing fake (2:20–26). So if the hypocrisy is their own they must abandon it for a living faith. If the hypocrisy is seen in others, they can rest assured that their claim to believe is fraudulent.

Secondly, there was the fundamental question of wealth and poverty and its corollary in terms of social prejudice in the church (1:9–11; 2:1–13; 4:13 – 5:6). James' words on this issue are particularly reminiscent of the teaching of Jesus and stress the transposition of earthly status which occurs in Christ and the reversal of fortunes which will take place in eternity. A great sympathy is displayed for the poor while the rich are accused of self-sufficiency and indifference, of self-indulgence and corruption, of usurping the prerogatives of God and murdering his creatures. The church dare not conform to the snobbish mould of the world. Its attitudes and behaviour

[13] *Ibid.*, pp. 39f. and Adamson, *James*, pp. 23–25.

should rather be formed by what it knows of God. God has chosen the poor (1:9). God disposes of men's lives (4:15). God hears the cry of the oppressed and will judge his oppressors (5:1, 4–5).

The third area of disappointment was to be found in the teachers who failed to be consistent (3:1–12). Their words were crucial to the spiritual growth of the community and had been greatly used to that end. But they failed to realize the need for absolute vigilance, and the good they had done had often been undone by unwise and inconsistent speech. In fact, such indiscipline was more damaging than if they had kept silent in the first place. James points such teachers to the exacting standards they would be required to reach by God's tribunal.

The fourth cause for concern was the poor quality of relationships within the fellowship generally (3:13–18 and 4:11–12). It may have arisen from economic and social tensions, as Davids has suggested. It was certainly made worse by the failure of the leaders to correct it by their own example, assuming 4:13–17 to be connected to 4:1–12. In any case, the relationship certainly had to be improved and divine wisdom was needed if that was to be done. James distinguishes between two forms of wisdom as a way of motivating them to turn to God to ask for divine help. One thing on which they could rely, if they did so, was the generosity of God (1:5), for they would not find his answer a miserly one.

Fifthly, there was the test of unanswered prayer (4:1–12). The whole context in which prayer was offered seems to have been wrong. We cannot be sure of the substance of the prayers they were offering, but it would seem that they either used prayer as a weapon for their quarrels in the fellowship – each side praying that God would show himself to be on their side (4:2–3) – or, possibly, because of their financial difficulties, they were using prayer as a way of asking God to improve their economic situation and make life more comfortable (4:2–6). Either way they were praying but not receiving. James develops the theology of prayer by stating that they will never receive answers while their prayers are so self-centred. Submission to God, with all the moral consequences it entailed, was essential if God was to hear them.

The sixth guise the testing wore was suffering (5:7–12). The suffering referred to here almost certainly has to do with their unenviable circumstances of life. It probably relates to the persecution mentioned earlier in the chapter, but there is nothing to stop his message from applying generally to the 'inevitable disappointments, griefs, sorrows and annoyances which no human life can avoid'.[14] They were reacting badly to their suffering with the result that it was having a destructive effect on their relationships. Clearly, they were not prepared to wait until the Lord's return. They wanted better conditions and they wanted them now. To encourage patience James balances the judgment of God with the compassion of God. On the one hand they should behave themselves or else! On the other hand, why worry? The God in whom they trusted was used to having his servants ill-treated, but look how he finally settled his accounts in favour of his people (5:11).

The final test to be mentioned was illness (5:13–20). James does not present a complete theology of sickness. Rather he adds a few more pieces to the mosaic of the teaching of Scripture on this subject. James connects illness on the one hand with confessing sin and on the other hand with believing prayer. He does not assume an automatic connection between sickness and sin, but they may well not be unconnected, and he sees ministry to the sick as an opportunity to explore any possible connection and to provide ministry for the whole person. To be concerned about bodily health but not spiritual wholeness is a misguided concern. He writes, without the slightest hesitation, that acting in the context of this wider framework the elders, praying in faith and anointing with oil, will see healing take place. The elders are brought into play here not in opposition to the charismatically gifted healers we meet in Paul's letters but simply, given James' Jewish background, as the natural representatives of the leadership of the church. Their action was to turn another potential obstacle to faith into a means of growth.

The letter to James gives little insight into the organization of the church.[15] Again, because of his Jewish background, he refers to the church as a 'synagogue' (2:2). He refers to teachers (3:1) but it is not clear if they are settled officers or not. He also refers to elders (5:14) but gives no further information as to their responsibilities apart from their pastoral duty to the sick. Clearly they were not expected to sort out the problems of the church

---

[14] C. L. Mitton, *The Epistle of James*, p. 19. [15] Ladd, *Theology of NT*, p. 590.

on their own and they are not told to use their authority to do so. Improvements in the communities to which James writes could come only if every member of the church worked for them.

In a way, James' letter is best seen as pastoral first aid. He takes the immediate symptoms and problems and hands out medicine which will both bring immediate relief and prevent the patient from getting worse. He is not unaware of the deep issues which lie behind the symptoms nor ignorant of the advanced theological remedies which will need to be brought into play; he suggests what some of these might be (*e.g.* the doctrine of God) without developing them. He is not unconcerned about the long-term goal of the patients' health. He longs for them to be mature and complete. But they are a long way from that. The immediate situation demands a strategy which is full of imperatives and not a little confrontational, and yet it is not without tenderness. Simple but frequent references to God should be sufficient for the patient's condition at the present time. And James leaves the impression of a God who is as much one of generous and creative love as he is of strong and sovereign judgment. James' pastoral strategy is robust, but that exactly matches the robust faith which he is seeking to encourage.

1 PETER

1 Peter excels as a pastoral letter in spite of vigorous competition from other New Testament letters. It breathes a pastoral spirit and is a model of a pastoral charge.[16] Its excellence lies not only in the content of its pastoral theology but in the manner in which it is conveyed. It is written with a gentle sympathy which shows the writer's understanding of his readers' situation. It exemplifies the very attitudes it seeks to encourage. Thus, although the author is an apostle (1:1), he 'keeps himself in the background and makes no parade of the apostolic status he assumes'.[17] On the contrary, he seeks to find a common basis with those whom he would exhort (as in 5:1) and a humble transparency is apparent throughout the letter.

The purpose of the letter is to encourage believers to stand

---

[16] E. G. Selwyn, *The First Epistle of Peter*, p. 1.
[17] A. F. Walls, 'Introduction', to A. M. Stibbs, *The First Epistle General of Peter*, p. 31.

fast in 'the true grace of God' (5:12). Several different proposals are currently canvassed as to his readers' exact circumstances. Three of the most persuasive are that his readers are about to undergo a fiery persecution, that they are young converts presenting themselves for baptism or that they are social and economic aliens, homeless in the world and in desperate need of a spiritual home.[18] Persecution might cause some to retract their Christian confession; young converts, after the initial stage of enthusiasm had passed, might be tempted to waver in their commitment to Christ; those enduring the constant pressure of non-acceptance might project their unsettled feelings on to their faith. Each of these proposals has in common the idea that the readers in the churches of Asia Minor, to whom the letter was addressed, were in a spiritually vulnerable state.

Peter's concern for them leads him to address the relevant issues directly. The nature of their salvation is expounded (1:2–12) and the assurance is given that they have found a spiritual home (2:4–11). The behaviour expected of Christians, both within the church (1:13 – 2:3; 4:7–11; 5:1–9) and outside in the world, is carefully unfolded (2:13 – 4:6). Then the theme of suffering is introduced (4:12–19) and reinterpreted as it is cast in a Christological light. The various pressure points of their pluralistic world are carefully examined and directions given so that hope, humility, self-control and endurance can be stimulated.

F. W. Beare may well be right in stressing that the appeal of the letter is to 'the living relationship which has been established between the Christian believer and God through the life, death, and resurrection of Christ and through entrance into the Christian community by baptism'. In this sense his comment that the epistle is not a theological treatise but one in which the central doctrines of Christianity are presupposed rather than expounded is fair.[19] But Beare's strong contrast between the appeal to doctrine and to Christian living is injudicious. In fact, the whole basis of Peter's appeal is doctrinal. It is more true to say, with Donald Guthrie, that 1 Peter shows 'the indissoluble link between doctrine and practice'.[20] One characteristic of

---

[18] For a review of the various theories see Guthrie, *NT Introduction*, pp. 771–803. For the theory about their sociological situation see J. H. Elliott, *A Home for the Homeless. A Sociological Exegesis of 1 Peter and its Situation and Strategy*, pp. 59–100.

[19] F. W. Beare, *The First Epistle of Peter*, pp. 31f.

[20] Guthrie, *NT Introduction*, p. 791.

Peter's writing alone is sufficient to justify the point. On ten occasions in his brief letter Peter explicitly links an ethical or spiritual injunction to an incontrovertible reason for obedience to it by the use of 'because' (1:16, 18; 2:15, 21; 3:9, 18; 4:1, 8; 5:5, 7).[21] Once the reason is practical (4:8) and four times it refers to the suffering and death of Christ (1:18; 2:22; 3:18; 4:1), but six times, counting one in common with the death of Christ, the motive for behaviour is firmly connected with God himself. His character (1:16), will (2:15), call (2:21; 3:9), ways (5:5) and care (5:7) are all used as determinants of Christian living.

Peter, then, firmly establishes a doctrinal foundation as the basis for his exhortation. And it is a foundation which is essentially theocentric not, as in most other New Testament writers, Christocentric. In Beare's words, the letter 'begins from and constantly returns to the thought of God as Creator, Father and Judge, as the One whose will determines all that comes to pass, who shapes the destiny and determines the actions of those whom He has chosen for his own, who sustains them through the sufferings which He sends to test them, and who at the last will vindicate them and reward them eternally'.[22]

Peter's conscious strategy in strengthening the vulnerable faith of his readers is to remind them of their God. He is so intoxicated with the approach that even his incidental references are bent to the same purpose.[23] He begins with the assurance that they have been chosen by God (1:1–2) and constantly returns to the same thought (1:15; 2:9, 21; 3:9; 5:10, 13). They were God's own people (2:9). But what sort of a God was he? Peter emphasizes his holiness (1:15–16) and his sovereignty as creator (4:19). He is the impartial judge of all the earth (1:17; 4:5). And yet he had become their father (1:17) and is a God of mercy (1:3), grace (5:10) and patience (3:20). Every aspect of Peter's portrait of God carries with it either the incentive for Christians to live holy lives (*e.g.* 1:17) or to substitute trust for anxiety, as, for example, in the situation of facing persecution (4:19).

Although Peter is essentially theocentric in his approach he does not omit reference to Jesus Christ. Three features of Peter's references to Jesus are particularly noteworthy. Firstly, Jesus is

---

[21] Selwyn, *First Peter*, p. 64.   [22] Beare, *1 Peter*, p. 33.
[23] Stibbs, *First Epistle of Peter*, p. 178.

held up as their pattern in suffering (2:21–25; 4:1). Peter's interest in the death of Jesus is not exhausted by this exemplary motif, but this is where his chief pastoral interest lies. In speaking of Christ as an example Peter uses a word which is unique in the New Testament, and rare elsewhere. The suffering of Christ, which he emphasizes was voluntary and undeserved, was like some writing which a child was expected to trace or copy over. The suffering of the Christian was to be that careful and exact in its copying of Christ.

Secondly, Peter puts no full stop after speaking about the death of Christ but stresses 'the glories' that followed it (1:11). The example of Christ's suffering did not stand alone. Hope was offered because of his resurrection and the inheritance which it made available to believers (1:3–4; 5:10). Christ's resurrection put him in a position of unquestioned authority in the universe (3:22) and therein lies the hope for the suffering Christian.

Peter, thirdly, speaks of Christ as the 'Chief Shepherd' (2:25; 5:4). The term is remarkable because it occurs only in Peter, although something approaching it occurs in Hebrews 13:20. It is a moving designation of Christ and all the more so given that it comes from the pen of a man who had met with the resurrected Christ in such an unforgettable encounter and been commissioned to 'feed my sheep'. All the biblical imagery of the shepherd reaches its climax here. Jesus is the true pastor of his flock. Others must model themselves on him and can work only under his direction. They can never become independent of him and always remain answerable to him. The flock is never theirs, but his (5:2). And even if earthly shepherds fail, the sheep can rest in the sure knowledge that there is one who looks after them who will never fail.

Peter exploits the shepherd motif more than any other New Testament writer to speak to his fellow elders about their responsibilities (5:1–4). He writes with all the love of a devoted shepherd who has gained years of wise experience. He is aware of the great privilege of the task but is more concerned about the pitfalls. The task is to care for the flock and to oversee their welfare (v. 2). Clearly the episcopal duty mentioned here, as in 2:25, is synonymous with the pastor's duty of caring and the overseers are synonymous with the pastors. No separate office or rung on the status ladder is envisaged. So much might have been obvious to Peter's readers. But the task may be done well or badly, and so Peter's concern is to speak to the manner in which it is undertaken. Three contrasts are presented to them. They are not to serve grudgingly, but willingly; not greedily, but eagerly; not arrogantly, but as examples. And when the going gets tough and the task seems unrewarding they are to remember that they do not work for earthly gain but for a 'Chief Shepherd' who will one day reward them with a more worth-while recognition than this life can ever offer.

This is the only mention, in 1 Peter, of the actual structure of the church, although much else is said about its nature. Selwyn has pointed out that there are no direct references to the church as such, and none to Paul's favourite picture of the church as a body. But Peter does refer to the people of God acting corporately as a people, a priesthood, a nation (2:9) and a flock (5:2).[24] Each of these suggests coherence and order. The church is not a collection of unrelated individuals but a group who relate to one another under a common allegiance.

Much, however, is said about internal relationships within the church. Its members are to love each other as brothers (1:22; 3:8; 4:8) and offer hospitality (4:9). The functioning of the church was not conceived of organizationally but, as in Paul, charismatically (4:10). God's gifts were the fuel which would make the church spark into life and move forward. But Peter seems aware of the need to make sure that these gifts were not abused as personal status symbols and their nature as an administration of God's grace is kept clearly in view (4:11). One particular area is mentioned where relationships in the church may have been fragile – the area of the generation gap. The arrogance of the young men and the caution of the elders was a recipe for division and Peter calls on the younger men to exercise humility (5:5–6). But his call for them to be humble is only a specific application of a general call he had issued earlier (3:8). 1 Peter gives no encouragement to view the church as an institution. Rather with the rest of the New Testament it portrays it as a family where brothers struggle to understand each other and work at relating to each other, whether it comes easily or not, because they share a common father.

Peter's pastoral approach is epitomized by his final assurances

---

[24] Selwyn, *First Peter*, p. 81.

to his readers in 5:10–11. The verses evince a pastoral realism. He is fully aware that his readers are going to suffer and it is a cruel deception to write in a triumphalist vein which pretends that, now they are God's people, they would be exempt from suffering. Whilst they remain in this fallen world that can never be the case. But the verses also evince pastoral encouragement. Peter's readers will not only survive the experience of suffering but emerge from it, without lingering scars, fully restored and strong. Their faith will be intact.

This confidence does not arise because of any qualities found in the believers themselves, but because of the nature of the God whom they have believed. He is, firstly, the God of all grace. His undeserved and all-sufficient love will be adequate for the needs of his suffering people. Even when they face the direst circumstances they will find that they have not come to the end of God's grace. He is, secondly, the God of election. He has called them for a purpose and that purpose will not be frustrated – they will share in the 'eternal glory of Christ'. And he will be true to his word (2:23–24). Then, thirdly, he is the God of power. He is stronger, therefore, than any forces which oppose him or threaten his people. His power will not diminish with the passing of time but remain impregnable for ever.

Peter's reassurances would be absurd if it were not for the fact that this God had revealed himself. But since he has made himself known in Christ, Peter is able to use the most tender vocabulary of pastoralia. He can assure his readers that God will personally 'restore, establish and strengthen' (5:10, RSV) them. Each word is full of meaning. The word 'to restore' is that used of mending a broken net, knitting a broken bone or refitting a damaged vessel. The word 'establish' refers to their need to be made stable and formed part of the commission of Christ himself to Peter (Lk. 22:32). Having been made whole and enabled to stand firm it could be that the third word, 'strengthen', carries with it the idea of being strengthened for active service.[25] The purpose of their restoration is not so that they can be the objects of wonder, like restored pictures in a museum, but so that they can be returned to the battlefield to continue their part in the defeat of the devil.

Peter seems to write with a special tenderness which, no

---

[25] Stibbs, *First Epistle of Peter*, p. 174.

doubt, arose from his own experience of defeat and his subsequent restoration, stabilizing and recommissioning by the Lord himself. He learnt from the chief pastor what it meant to be a pastor and he appears to have learnt his lesson well. Peter writes with the same graciousness that characterized Jesus and without the faintest indication of the volatility, superiority or condescension of his own earlier life. Instead, knowing the frailty of the human frame, he writes as a true pastor to strengthen the church so that they might stand firm.

2 PETER AND JUDE

2 Peter and Jude are rightly classed together as polemical documents. Jude is a letter which embodies what may possibly have been a sermon[26] and is almost wholly taken up with the unqualified denunciation of certain false teachers and their antinomian way of life. It is both vigorous and colourful in style.[27] 2 Peter, whilst not so exclusively consumed with exposing the danger of the same or similar false teachers, still has their infiltration as the principal item on its agenda. At the same time, it is much more than that and can be most helpfully seen as Peter's farewell speech.[28] The letters, then, are not primarily of pastoral interest except in so far as it is right to note that, from time to time, such an emergency situation is created in the church through the spread of heresy that it is right to adopt a strategy of fierce polemic, when all other strategies have failed. Though contrary to the tolerant nature of our own day, such an approach is canonized in Scripture.

The details of the letters are not, however, without pastoral interest. Richard Bauckham's recent commentary on Jude insists that the letter, even if it is an unqualified denunciation, is not mere denunciation. He insists that the denunciations of verses 5–19, which are usually considered the important verses, are included only as an explanation of the background to the appeal issued in verse 3.[29] Jude's purpose in writing is to urge his readers to 'contend for the faith'. They are being alerted to danger and called to resistance.

---

[26] R. J. Bauckham, *Jude, 2 Peter*, p. 3.
[27] J. N. D. Kelly, *The Epistles of Peter and Jude*, p. 228 and Guthrie, *NT Introduction*, p. 916.
[28] Bauckham, *Jude, 2 Peter*, pp. 131–135.   [29] *Ibid.*, p. 41.

The call to arms is taken up again in verses 20–23, where the church is told how it can resist. A five-fold course of action is presented to them. They are to build themselves up in the apostolic faith; they are to pray in the Spirit; they are to maintain their place in God's affection by their obedience; they are to wait with hope for the Lord's return and they are to exercise compassionate church discipline. Verses 22 and 23 are especially relevant, even though textually they are very difficult.[30] Jude asks that the church exercise the standard discipline as outlined in Matthew 18:15–19. Yet, one senses that at the same time he is concerned to apply gentle pressure to the brake. The hatred of sin is unmitigated, but wherever that is so it becomes especially important that the objective of discipline is kept firmly in view. The aim is not to destroy but to save. The hatred of sin and fear of judgment should be incentives to rescue people from judgment, but they can too easily turn into an excuse for a witch-hunt and the setting up of kangeroo courts.

It is fitting that the letter ends with such a powerful and comforting doxology. Those who were about to enter a fierce battle would need to be assured of their safety and, more crucially, of whose side was going to win.

Peter's strong denunciation of false teachers is set in the middle of a letter which gives evidence of a number of other concerns as well. Overall, Peter seems to fear that his readers are not making progress in the Christian life as they should and he writes about the various causes which might be hindering them. To paraphrase Michael Green, Peter not only harries the heretics but encourages the faithful.[31]

Four possible causes of their spiritual ineffectiveness are identified. Firstly, there is their own lack of effort. It is the sandwich with which the letter opens and closes (1:3–11; 3:11–14). Some may have been doubting if God had done his part or whether they had been provided with inadequate resources to make a go of it spiritually. Peter assures them that what is lacking is nothing which God can supply. He has made more than adequate provision for them. The missing factor is their own determination. Indeed, the very generosity of their God should act as a powerful stimulus to growth.

[30] *Ibid.*, pp. 108–111; M. Green, *2 Peter and Jude*, pp. 186–189 and Kelly, *Epistles of Peter and Jude*, pp. 288f.

[31] Green, *2 Peter and Jude*, p. 123.

A second possible cause of ineffectiveness lay in their doubts about the authenticity of apostolic testimony or Old Testament scripture (1:16–21).[32] If they were not convinced of the truth of what they believed it was unlikely that they would invest much effort in following it. Thirdly, they were disturbed by false teachers; these probably were the ones who had cast doubts on the genuineness of the message they had believed (2:1–22). It was obviously no good arguing with these men – they were past that. All that Peter does, therefore, is to assure his readers that they were destined for certain judgment. Fourthly, they were discouraged by their circumstances and the delay in the Lord's return (3:1–10). Peter's patient explanation of the Lord's non-arrival quickly turns into an urgent appeal for holy living.

In spite of the ferocity with which Peter writes about the false teachers, the letter is essentially gentle. He does not write to command but to encourage. He does not write from a position of authority but as a brother (1:10) and 'dear friend' (3:1, 8, 14, 17). His strategy, too, is eloquent in gentleness. He does not treat them as ignorant but simply writes to 'remind' them of what they already know (1:12; 3:1–2, 8 and 15). He displays sensitivity as if handling a recently bruised patient, but he reminds them that the soreness they presently feel is not the norm in life. The approach, therefore, is calculated to get them up off their beds and back in action, exploiting to the full the life that God has given them.

'Guard' and 'grow' are the two imperatives Peter presses right to the end (3:17–18). And yet the final impression he makes is not one of demand but of reassurance. For all their uncertainties, they are secure. For all their negligence, the atmosphere in which they are to grow is one of grace. For all their conflicts, the one they follow is Lord and he has glory both now and forever.

---

[32] The point is not their interpretation of Scripture but its authenticity. See Green, *ibid.*, pp. 89–92.

HISTORICAL SURVEY

7

The early centuries

The development of the pastoral role beyond the New Testament period is complex. Many factors determined the particular forms the ministry took, but among them four factors stand out. The church itself was subject to the natural processes of institutionalization. Divisions and the resulting need both to define and to defend orthodox belief had their effect. The men who moulded the ministry were children of their cultural and intellectual environment and often unconsciously shaped the ministry to conform to it. Then there was the wider social context. The church began the period as a persecuted minority and ended as the recognized religion of the empire and the baptizer of its culture. The ministry inevitably adapted to meet the changing fortunes of the church. In fact, it would have been of no use to anyone had it not done so.[1]

In the creative turmoil of these early centuries many rich works were brought to birth, which gave an insight into the work of the ministry, and some of these still speak with a voice which is amazingly relevant to our own day. To pass over them as merely the dusty and obsolete works of yesteryear is to leave ourselves the poorer. Besides their personal value, these writings will enable us to see the unfolding of the pastoral tradition and understand better how it can be authentically adapted to the needs of today.[2]

In the light of this it is not our purpose to trace the tortuous complexities of the development of ministerial structures, which has in any case been done elsewhere,[3] so much as to expose the heart of the pastoral role.

[1] See W. A. Clebsch and C. R. Jackee, *Pastoral Care in Historical Perspective*, pp. 14–31. Their neat scheme of adaptations is perhaps too tidy, but the attempt at a scheme is certainly stimulating.

[2] *Ibid.*, pp. 74–76.

[3] *E.g.* H. von Campenhausen, *Ecclesiastical Authority and Spiritual Power*; T. M. Lindsay, *The Church and the Ministry in the Early Centuries*; J. T. McNeill, *A History of the Cure of Souls* and G. H. Williams, 'The Ministry in the Ante-Nicene Church' and 'The Ministry in the Later Patristic Period', in H. R. Niebuhr and D. D. Williams (eds), *The Ministry in Historical Perspective*.

THE POST-APOSTOLIC PERIOD

Nearly all the earliest writings of the post-New Testament era have something to say about ministry. *The Didache*, an early document, continues to recognize the value of itinerant teachers and inspired prophets, but equally warns that not all who claimed this authority were genuine. So it lays down precautionary guide-lines for their reception. They are suspect if they stop longer than three days, their behaviour would be the proof of the validity of their prophecy and they were to be dismissed as charlatans if they asked for money for themselves whilst in a trance.[4] But it is already clear that local leaders were assuming greater significance and rivalling the itinerant prophets and preachers. Echoing the pastoral epistles, *The Didache* says,

> You must choose for yourselves overseers and assistants who are worthy of the Lord: men who are humble and not eager for money, but sincere and approved; for they are carrying out the ministry of the charismatics and teachers for you. Do not esteem them lightly, for they take an honourable rank among you along with the charismatics and catechists.[5]

Several of the early writings suggest an increasing divorce between the clergy and the laity[6] and an increasing stress on the need to obey the clergy, but none more so than the *Letters of Ignatius* (*c*. AD 110). They reveal that a three-fold ministry of bishops, priests and deacons is not only in existence, but of the essence of the church.[7] Time and again he enjoins obedience to the bishops as pre-eminent. Bishops had power conferred on them by God[8] and were to be followed like sheep.[9] To obey them was to obey the voice of God,[10] for 'every man who belongs to God stands by his bishop'[11] whereas to act independently was to act in a worldly fashion.[12] He writes,

[4] *The Didache*, 11 and 12, in M. Staniforth (trans), *Early Christian Writings*, pp. 232–234.
[5] *Ibid.*, 15, pp. 234f.
[6] E.g. *The First Epistle of Clement to the Corinthians*, 42–47, 53 in Staniforth, *ECW*, pp. 45–48 and 53.
[7] *The Epistles of Ignatius*, 'To the Trallians', 3, in Staniforth, *ECW*, p. 96.
[8] 'To the Magnesians', 3, *ibid.*, p. 87.   [9] 'To the Philadelphians', 2, *ibid.*, p. 111.
[10] 'To the Philadelphians', 7, *ibid.*, p. 113.
[11] 'To the Philadelphians', 3, *ibid.*, p. 112.   [12] 'To the Trallians', 2, *ibid.*, p. 95.

This is why it is proper for your conduct and your practices to correspond closely with the mind of the bishop. And this, indeed, they are doing; your justly respected clergy, who are a credit to God, are attuned to their bishop like the strings of a harp, and the result is a hymn of praise to Jesus Christ from minds that are in unison, and affections that are in harmony.[13]

Follow your bishop, everyone of you, as obediently as Jesus Christ followed the Father. Obey your clergy too, as you would the Apostles; giving your deacons the same reverence that you would a command from God.[14]

This hierarchical mentality, motivated, no doubt, as it was by the desire to protect the flock, was not apparently universal and Ignatius' contemporary Polycarp (*c.* 110) writes in an altogether different spirit. Although he encourages obedience to the clergy and deacons he does not mention the office of bishop, but emphasizes the qualities desired of the clergy instead.

As for the clergy, they should be men of generous sympathies with a wide compassion for humanity. It is their business to reclaim the wanderers, keep an eye on all who are infirm, and never neglect the widow, the orphan and the needy. Their care at all times should be for what is honourable in the sight of God and men. Any show of ill-temper, partiality and prejudice is to be scrupulously avoided; and eagerness for money should be a thing utterly alien to them. They must not be over ready to believe ill of anyone, nor too hasty with their censure; being well aware that we all of us owe the debt to sin.[15]

The lack of uniform development is apparent elsewhere in the literature of the period. Justin Martyr (*c.* 100–165) speaks of the bishop as the president of the eucharist, not as a priest, and he does not mention presbyters at all.[16] In contrast the *Apos-*

---

[13] 'To the Ephesians', 4, *ibid.*, p. 76.
[14] 'To the Smyrnians', 8, *ibid.*, p. 121.
[15] *The Epistle of Polycarp to the Philippians*, 6, in Staniforth, *ECW*, p. 146.
[16] *Justin Martyr, First Apology*, 66, 67, *A-NCL*, vol. 2, pp. 64–65. See also H. T. Mayer, *Pastoral Care, Its Roots and Renewal*, pp. 37–50.

tolical Constitutions (*c.* 250) portray the bishop very much as a high priest, teacher and judge.[17] This is a picture which had come to full fruition in Tertullian (*c.* 160–220), before his conversion to Montanism, with his strict outlook and emphasis on penitential discipline.[18]

Meanwhile in Egypt, Clement of Alexandria (*c.* 155–220), whilst usually recognizing a three-fold structure for the ministry and seeing its structure as an imitation of angelic glory, does not elevate the bishop above the clergy as much as other writers. His own life, together with that of his pupil Origen (*c.* 185–254), rejuvenated the role of the Christian teacher or scholar. Pastorally, Clement reveals a great concern for the spiritual progress of the Christians and advocates the value of submitting oneself to a pastor as a means of achieving it. Thus, in his sermon *The Rich Man's Salvation*, he urges his hearers,

> For this purpose, my wealthy friend, you should set over yourself some man of God as trainer and pilot. Give him your respect and fear. Be at pains to listen to his rebuke. Your eyes will be the better for tears, your soul from some break in its continuous pleasures. You will fear the anger of such an adviser. His grief will cause you pain. You will anticipate him when he pleads for your pardon. Let him spend wakeful nights for you in prayer; let him be your ambassador in God's presence and prevail with the Father by the magic of supplication. Honour him, as an angel of God, and he shall pray for you, grieved not by you but for your good.[19]

Real developments in the pastoral role did not lie, however, in Alexandria, but in Carthage and Rome. In Carthage Cyprian (*c.* 200–258) presided over the church during the tumultuous years of the Decian persecution and of its resulting schisms. He is remembered most for his teaching on the unity of the church, the sacerdotal authority of the bishop and his insistence on the rebaptism of heretics.[20] He comes down to history as a theological combatant, but he was in reality more of a pastor and administrator and his actions and policies, rightly or wrongly,

---

[17] *Apostolical Constitutions*, II, 1–63, *A-NCL*, vol. 17, pp. 26–92.
[18] Tertullian, *On Baptism*, 17, *A-NCL*, vol. 11, pp. 250–252.
[19] Cited in R. B. Tollinton, *Clement of Alexandria*, vol. 1, p. 320.
[20] See G. S. M. Walker, *The Churchmanship of St Cyprian*.

were motivated by a genuine concern for the welfare of the church and its members.

Cyprian sought to institutionalize in the office of the bishop the charisma which Tertullian and others sought through Montanism. Yet the priestly, rather than the prophetic, nature of the ministry was uppermost in his thinking. Presbyters were priestly only in so far as they were participating in the sacrificial office of the bishop. The bishop was the essential focus of the worship and unity of the church and derived his status from apostolic succession. He wrote, 'they are the church who are a people united to the priest and the flock which adhere to its pastor. Hence you ought to know that the bishop is in the church and the church is in the bishop.'[21] Yet the bishop, for all that, was to be elected by the people and could equally be deposed by them.

Cyprian's emphasis on the authority of the bishop was motivated, in part at least, by a desire to steer a straight course for the church through the stormy waters of his day, which threatened to break it up. Thus, his decision to flee Carthage in 250 rather than face martyrdom, from which he did not ultimately shrink, was a 'calm decision' based on the belief that the best interests of the church were served by his being able to continue to administer the church from exile rather than adorn her as a martyr.[22] The same concern for a steady hand on the tiller can be seen in his dealing with the question of the re-admission of the lapsed to the church following the Decian persecution and in his disputes regarding the problematic bishops of Spain and of Arles.

The true pastoral character of Cyprian is more evident in his letters and minor works than in these ecclesiastical disputes. In 252 the Great Plague reached Carthage and the Christians were blamed for this and all the other ills which had befallen the city. Cyprian's response was to call his church together, urge on them the duty of prayer and then organize them into a practical care scheme which covered the whole city. They raised funds, nursed victims, and buried the dead whether they were members of the church or not. Such self-giving was no more than was called for by Christ and ensured the continuing of the gladiatorial contest between Christ and Satan. Refusing to give

---

[21] Cyprian, *Epistles*, 68, 8, *A-NCL*, vol. 8, p. 248.
[22] E. W. Benson, *Cyprian: His Life, His Times, His Work*, p. 85.

alms was sinful, whereas giving them maintained the freshness of one's baptismal experience.[23]

The suffering imposed by persecution raised the greatest questions of the day and led Cyprian in response to develop the idea of probation. This life was a contest:

> Behold a lofty and great contest, glorious also with the reward of a heavenly crown, inasmuch as God looks upon us as we struggle, and extending his view over those whom he has condescended to makes his sons, he enjoys the spectacle of our contest. God looks upon us in the warfare, and fighting in the encounter of faith; his angels look on us, and Christ looks on us. How great is the dignity, and how great the happiness of the glory, to engage in the presence of God, and to be crowned, with Christ for a judge! Let us be armed, beloved brethren, with our whole strength, and let us be prepared for the struggle with an uncorrupted mind, with a sound faith, with a devoted courage.[24]

Through suffering, God was at one and the same time imposing the discipline of love and censuring sin. If Christians could but bring themselves to accept it, trusting in his paternal care, they would be elevated and purified by it. Certainly they should do all within their power to relieve suffering. Yet men should look beyond death to eternal life and welcome martyrdom.[25] It was a path Cyprian willingly trod in conformity with his Lord's example in the year 257.

H. T. Mayer has accurately summarized Cyprian's contribution to our understanding of pastoral care:

> In one of his letters, Cyprian presents a classically beautiful picture of the bishop working as the shepherd of his flock. The bishop expends his energy without reservation to care for every need of his sheep. He finds their scratches and wounds and pours in oil and wine, he combs their fleece, he beds them down at night, he knows each one by name, he loves each one. It's a moving pastoral picture. The problem is that the bishop has taken over sole responsibility for

---

[23] *Ibid.*, pp. 246–249.

[24] *Ibid.*, p. 259; Cyprian, *Epistles*, 55, 8, *A-NCL*, vol. 8, p. 186.

[25] Cyprian, *On the Immortality*, *A-NCL*, vol. 8, p. 467.

nurturing Christians. As a consequence, the people become quite content to turn all their baptized responsibility over to this great father-figure.[26]

At the end of this initial period of the history of the church the ministry had become hierarchically structured with the bishop reigning supreme in discipline as judge, in doctrine as teacher and in pastoring as preacher. Under his authority, a defined system of penitence had emerged for those who fell into post-baptismal sin. Simultaneously, numerous minor offices had proliferated at the lower end of the scale including grave-diggers, door-keepers, acolytes and exorcists. The aims of the pastor remained spiritually clear and rich, but the responsibility for their fulfilment no longer lay within the fellowship as a whole, having become a specialized function.

THE POST-CONSTANTINIAN PERIOD

Following the conversion of the emperor Constantine in 312, the Christian faith was not only granted toleration but became the official faith of the empire. Although some factors, such as the threat of heresy, remained constant, the new situation called for a reorientation of pastoral care. A church composed of members who stood the chance of facing persecution is different in character from a church composed of members for whom it costs little and to which it is even socially advantageous to belong.

The period from Constantine to the beginning of the medieval era produced an abundance of writing about pastoral care which reflects in a detailed and self-conscious manner on the skills a pastor requires and the standards he is expected to reach. It reveals the magnitude of the task and the variety of human need confronting the pastor and, although devoid of anything like technique in the modern sense, its authors are conscious of the need for elementary pastoral psychology.

Two broad streams will occupy our attention. The one flows from the Cappadocian Fathers, Basil of Caesarea and Gregory of Nazianzus through John Chrysostom to Gregory the Great. The other flows from Ambrose of Milan to Augustine of Hippo.

[26] Mayer, *Pastoral Care*, p. 64.

Basil of Caesarea (329–379), his brother Gregory of Nyssa (330–395) and their friend Gregory of Nazianzus (330–389), collectively called the Cappadocian Fathers, were trained in rhetoric and ascetic living before being called to the priesthood. They were a formidable theological team and were responsible for the defeat of Arianism. Yet, for all that, they were gifted pastors, as their writings show. Basil shows it in his correspondence whilst Gregory of Nazianzus displays it in his *Oration II, In Defence of his Flight to Pontus*. As often happened then, Gregory had resisted the summons to the bishopric of Nazianzus, and fled. He wrote explaining the reasons for his discourteous behaviour and why he had changed his mind. In so doing he gives a graphic insight into the ministry. Gregory's *Oration II* is the bud which develops into an emerging flower in Chrysostom and into full bloom in Gregory the Great.

John Chrysostom (344–407) had a similar background before being called to the priesthood in his native Antioch. He distinguished himself as an eloquent preacher and from the pulpit exercised tremendous influence and power over both mobs and emperors alike. In 398 he became patriarch of Constantinople where his influence continued. Here his uncompromising spirituality and diplomatic naivety led to numerous troubles, with, among others, the Empress Eudoxia, which finally resulted in his being deposed. Only after his death was he finally vindicated. His work *On the Priesthood*, written while he was probably still a deacon in 386, is in the form of a supposed conversation with his friend Basil. Chrysostom wrote to justify his action in securing the election of Basil to a bishopric while he had evaded it himself, despite a prior agreement with his friend that they would stand or fall together.

Gregory the Great (540–604) continues the same tradition of writing in his *Pastoral Rule*, in which he reaches a new level in his discussion of the complex sensitivity demanded in pastoral care. A former lawyer and prefect of the city of Rome, Gregory renounced the world and entered a monastery in 575. But he was forced back into public affairs and become pope in 590. He was an outstanding moral theologian and skilled pastor. Much concerned with the Lombard invasion of Rome, he forged the character of the papacy for the centuries to come and acted as the bridge between the ancient church and the medieval world.

For each of these writers the pastoral ministry was a high

and holy calling. Gregory of Nazianzus fled because shepherding people was harder than ruling a flock of sheep. The pastor 'like silver or gold, though in circulation in all kinds of seasons and affairs, (must) never ring false or alloyed, or give token of any inferior matter'.[27] The need to outstrip other men in virtue was only part of the difficulty of the office, 'For the guiding of man, the most variable and manifold of creatures, seems to me to be the art of arts and science of sciences.'[28] The doctor, by comparison, had an easy time, for the pastor was involved in 'the diagnosis and cure of habits, passions, lives, wills and whatever else is within us by the banishing from our compound nature everything brutal and fierce and introducing and establishing in their stead what is gentle and dear to God'.[29]

Chrysostom, too, was overwhelmed by the requirements of the task. The pastor needed to be unsullied in holiness and possess the virtues of an angel, for there was no way in which his faults could be concealed from the public.[30] The task could never be given to a commonplace or unprepared man.[31] He must be 'dignified yet free from arrogance, formidable yet kind, apt to command yet sociable, impartial yet courteous, humble yet not servile, strong yet gentle' to contend against all the difficulties he would face.[32] As if that was not sufficient, 'the priest ought to be sober-minded, and penetrating in discernment, and possessed of innumerable eyes in every direction, as one who lives not to himself alone but for so great a multitude'.[33]

Apparently the members of the church did nothing to lessen the pastor's burdens. They would listen to sermons, 'not for profit, but for pleasure'; sitting like critics in the theatre or spectators at the games rather than humbly submitting themselves to the word.[34] The administrative and pastoral duties of the priest equally contain many hidden pitfalls. Among the pretexts for fault-finding is the familiar cry, 'he didn't visit me'.

---

[27] Gregory of Nazianzus, *Oration II. In Defence of his flight to Pontus*, 9, 10, *NP-NF* Second Series, vol. 7, p. 207.

[28] *Ibid.*, 16, p. 208. See also 95, p. 223.   [29] *Ibid.*, 18, p. 208.

[30] John Chrysostom, *On The Priesthood*, IV, 2, and III, 14, *NP-NF* First Series, vol. 9, p. 75 and p. 52.

[31] *Ibid.*, III, 10, p. 50 and IV, 1, 2, pp. 62f. See also Gregory the Great, *The Book of Pastoral Rule*, I, 1, 2, *NP-NF* Second Series, vol. 12, pp. 1–3.

[32] Chrysostom, *On the Priesthood*, III, 16, p. 55.   [33] *Ibid.*, III, 12, p. 51.

[34] *Ibid.*, V, 1, p. 70 and V, 5, p. 72.

Chrysostom knew that the healthy as well as the sick demanded a visit from the priest, but not so that they could grow in piety, but only so they could boast they had had the honour. He warned,

> For merely from their mode of accosting persons, bishops have to endure such a load of reproaches as to be often oppressed and overwhelmed by despondency; in fact, they have also to undergo a scrutiny of the way in which they use their eyes. For the public rigorously criticise their simplest actions, taking note of the tone of their voice, the cast of their countenance, and the degree of their laughter. He laughed heartily to such a man, one will say, and accosted him with a beaming face, and a clear voice, whereas to me he addressed only a slight and passing remark.[35]

Yet the picture was not all gloom and despondency. Indeed these writers were only too aware of the help and blessing they received from God in undertaking their task. Gregory the Great agreed with his predecessors in stressing the demands of the office:

> It is necessary, then, that in thought he should be pure, in action chief; discreet in keeping silence, profitable in speech; a near neighbour to everyone in sympathy, exalted above all in contemplation; a familiar friend of good livers through humility, unbending against the vices of evil-doers through zeal for righteousness; not relaxing in his care for what is inward from being occupied in outward things, nor neglecting to provide for outward things in his solicitude for what is inward.[36]

Yet he asserted that even the pitfalls of office could be a means of grace. In a moving passage he likens the pastor to the laver in the temple. People washed their sin away through confession, and just as the laver collected the dirt of the worshippers, so the pastor's mind was in danger of collecting the dirt of the confessors and being tempted by it himself. 'But of this the pastor ought by no means to be afraid, since, under

---

[35] *Ibid.*, III, 16, p. 58.   [36] Gregory the Great, *Book of Pastoral Rule*, II, 1, p. 9.

God, who nicely balances all things, he is more easily rescued from his own temptations as he is more compassionately distressed by those of others.'[37]

All manner of imagery is pressed into use to explain the glories of the pastoral life.[38] Often the purpose is to contrast the complexity of pastoral work with the simplicity of the work of others, as in the case of the ordinary shepherd and the medical doctor already mentioned. Chrysostom also contrasts the pastor to the king[39] and argues that the pastoral office exceeds that of the monarch. Later he compares the care needed in choosing the bishop with the care shown in selecting a military dignitary or a captain of a merchant ship.[40] He claimed that he would never want to be a ship's captain, full as the ship would be with rowers and laden with expensive cargo, lest he would sink the ship. But this fear was purely on behalf of material wealth. How much more care should be exercised over spiritual wealth?

The picture of the pastor as a navigator skilfully piloting the ship of the church was frequently employed by the early fathers of the church. Clement of Alexandria had written of Christians who 'look to the Lord with steadfast gaze, like sailors on the watch for the nod of a good pilot to see what are his wishes, his commands, his signals, what watchwords he gives them, where and whence he proclaims the harbour'.[41] With so many looking to the pastor to bring them safely through the storms, currents and obstacles into harbour, it was no wonder that someone like Gregory of Nazianzus confessed to a preference for staying on dry land and subsisting as a humble farmer rather than taking to the more adventurous life of the sea.[42]

The medical metaphors stress the way in which different illnesses, and even different patients, cannot all be treated by the same remedy. 'As then the same medicine and the same food are not in every case administered to man's bodies, but a difference is made according to their degree of health or infirmity; so also are souls treated with varying instruction and guidance.'[43] 'For the things that profit some

[37] *Ibid.*, II, 5, p. 14.
[38] See further R. Brown, 'An Early Christian Conception of the Ministry', *The Fraternal* (July 1978), pp. 3–11.
[39] Chrysostom, *On the Priesthood*, III, 1, p. 45.   [40] *Ibid.*, III, 7, p. 49.
[41] Cited by R. Brown, *Pastoral Care: An Early Christian Perspective*, p. 17.
[42] Gregory of Nazianzus, *Oration II*, 100, p. 224.   [43] *Ibid.*, 30, p. 211.

often hurt others; seeing that also for the most part herbs which nourish some animals are fatal to others; and the gentle hissing that quiets horses incites whelps; and the medicine which abates one disease aggravates another; and the bread which invigorates the life of the strong kills little children.'[44]

Unlike the doctor, the pastor often has to treat a patient who refuses to admit the truth of his condition and hides his sin.[45] But the only remedy open to the pastor is one of persuasion. Force is not permitted.[46] Even where wrong is admitted the punishment applied must not so much fit the crime as the criminal, 'lest, while wishing to mend what is torn, you make the rent worse, and in your zealous endeavours to restore what is fallen, you make the ruin the greater'.[47] What skill was required! In Gregory of Nazianzus' words,

> Some are led by doctrine, others trained by example, some need the spur, others the curb; some are sluggish and hard to rouse to the good, and must be stirred by being smitten with the word; others are immodestly fervent in spirit, with impulses difficult to restrain like thoroughbred colts, who run wide of the turning post and to improve them the word must have a restraining and checking influence.[48]

The body of Gregory the Great's *Pastoral Rule* is a detailed commentary on just this point. Proposing thirty-six contrasting types of member, Gregory shows how each is to be handled and what are the special strengths and weaknesses and unanticipated traps in each case. He speaks of rich and poor, of the impatient and the patient, of the whole and the sick, of the slothful and the passionate, of the obstinate and the fickle, of the married and the single, of trouble-makers and peacemakers, of impulsive sinners and calculating sinners, to name but a few. Let us take the patient and the impatient as an illustration of his approach.[49]

The trouble with the impatient is that they unintentionally

---

[44] Gregory the Great, *Book of Pastoral Rule*, III, Prologue, p. 24 and Chrysostom, *On the Priesthood*, IV, 4, p. 65.

[45] Gregory of Nazianzus, *Oration II*, 19, p. 209.

[46] Chrysostom, *On the Priesthood*, II, 3, p. 41.   [47] *Ibid.*, II, 4, p. 41.

[48] Gregory of Nazianzus, *Oration II*, 30, p. 211.

[49] Gregory the Great, *Book of Pastoral Rule*, III, pp. 29–31.

commit sin, undoing the good they are capable of, and afterwards are hardly aware that they have done so. 1 Corinthians 13:4 and Proverbs 19:11 are used to show that impatience is a sin. Underlying it is the deeper sin of arrogance. With many other scriptures, such as Galatians 6:2, Proverbs 16:32, Luke 21:19 and Proverbs 29:11, the impatient man is encouraged not to ruin the good he might achieve. Further, he must understand that God has made us so that reason, not passions, controls the soul, and the soul the body. The impatient man is given to avenging himself and Gregory, therefore, concludes by reminding him of the judgment to come.

Whatever the Bible may say about patience as a virtue the patient are not exempt from their own temptations, and Gregory exhorts them 'that they grieve not inwardly for what they bear outwardly, lest they spoil with the infection of malice within a sacrifice of so great value which without they offer whole'. God sees the inward malice even if others do not. The patient must be encouraged to love those they bear with. Paul adds to the words 'love is patient' the words 'love is kind'. When affronted, the patient man often copes well with it at the time but often later recalls the hurt and then exaggerates it. So the patient one, 'led captive after victory, blushes from having borne things calmly, and is sorry that he did not return insults, and seeks to pay back something worse, should opportunity be afforded'. They must therefore guard their heart after a victory has been won.

Gregory the Great commenting on the man cared for by the good Samaritan pointed out,

> both wine and oil are applied to his wounds; the wine to make them smart, the oil to soothe them. For whosoever superintends the healing of wounds must needs administer in wine the smart of pain and in oil the softness of loving-kindness, to the end that through wine what is festering may be purged, and through oil what is curable may be soothed.[50]

There can be no better exemplar of that art than Basil of Caesarea. A forceful organizer and protagonist for the truth, he is, none the less, seen in his letters to be a gentle pastor,

---

[50] *Ibid.*, II, 6, p. 16.

concerned about the apparently trivial concerns of the nobodies in his flock.[51] He could pen a moving letter of comfort believing that 'every grief finds consolation in communication with sympathising friends'[52] but it is in the letter where rebuke is mixed with entreaty that he excels.

To a lapsed monk,[53] Basil can begin, 'I do not wish you well, for there is no joy for the wicked.' Wine indeed, which was made to smart even more by his bishop's exposition of his grief and condemnation. But he has not forgotten the oil and invites the monk to remember the mercies of God. He is encouraged not to despair but to arise and return and be assured that his bishop, having recovered his as-good-as-dead charge, will tend him carefully. 'Do not sink back. Remember the days of old. There is salvation; there is amendment. Be of good cheer; do not despair . . . The doors are not yet shut; the bridegroom hears; sin is not the master.'

Another excellent example of the mixture of wine and oil comes in a letter to a fallen virgin. Basil does not spare her blushes, if she was still capable of any, but grievously laments her fall and writes in the strongest terms about both her sin and the sin of the one who had the 'mad audacity' to cause her to fall. But again the supply of wine is limited, so that she does not become insensitive to the persuasiveness of the gospel:

> The great physician of souls, who is the ready liberator, not of you alone, but of all who are enslaved by sin, is ready to heal your sickness. From him come the words, it was his sweet and saving lips that said, 'They that be whole need not a physician but they that are sick . . . I am not come to call the righteous but sinners to repentance.' What excuse have you? What excuse has anyone, when he speaks thus? The Lord wishes to cleanse you from the trouble of your sickness and to show you light after darkness. The good Shepherd, who left them that had not wandered away, is seeking after you. If you give yourself to him he will not hold back. He,

---

[51] Basil of Caesarea, *Letters*, NP-NF Second Series, vol. 8, *e.g.* LXXXIV concerning an old man, LXXXVI and LXXVII regarding a presbyter deprived of his living, and CVII-CIX on a widow's interest.

[52] *Ibid.*, CLXXXIV to Eustathius, p. 222. See also CXXXIX on persecution and CLXXXII on Eusebius' exile.

[53] *Ibid.*, XLIV, pp. 146f. and the parallel letter XLV, pp. 147–149.

in his love, will not disdain to carry you on his own shoulders, rejoicing that he has found his sheep which was lost. The Father stands and awaits your return from wandering. Only come back . . .[54]

The exhortations of these pastors were soaked in biblical allusion and quotation, not because the literary power of Scripture was more persuasive than their own but because they saw Scripture as their primary pastoral medicine. Chrysostom wrote, 'there is but one method and way of healing appointed . . . the powerful application of the Word'.[55] It should be the ambition of every pastor, therefore, to let the word of Christ dwell in him richly. Only so would the pastor be able to speak with effectiveness and, but for that, souls under his care would be no better off than ships subject to the continuous tossing of a stormy sea.[56] For Chrysostom, preaching belongs in a pastoral context. To be a preacher is to enter upon a life of toil. Careful study is demanded and none is exempt from it, least of all those who seem to have great natural abilities in the pulpit.[57] The preacher is not to be governed either by the acclamation or criticism of the crowds. Rather he should strive to present workmanship which is pleasing to God. That alone should be his test.[58]

Every duty of the pastor is a potential snare and every pleasure a potential temptation. In writing of preaching, a skill at which he was so gifted, Chrysostom is at pains to point out the way in which applause and criticism are both waiting to trap him. Slander and envy would be voiced. It seems that his hearers were as fond then of roast (or is it minced?) preacher for Sunday lunch as congregations are now. But he must treat their comments like a father with his young children and take little account of them. He needed to show equal indifference to their praise. Public fame was a many-headed monster which seemed almost unconquerable and would destroy the preacher, either through pride or through convincing him to trim his message to please his congregation, and the preacher must be determined to defeat it.[59]

[54] *Ibid.*, XLVI, p. 152.   [55] Chrysostom, *On the Priesthood*, IV, 3, p. 64.
[56] *Ibid.*, IV, 4, 5, pp. 65–66.   [57] *Ibid.*, V, 5, pp. 71f.   [58] *Ibid.*, V, 7, p. 73.
[59] *Ibid.*, V, 8, p. 73 and V, 2, p. 71.

There were temptations outside the pulpit as well. The need to be able to mix with people up and down the social spectrum and converse easily with the high-born as well as the low meant he needed to be a many-sided man, yet without compromise or pride.[60] Similarly the privilege of providing spiritual direction for others could too easily provide the pastor with the opportunity to 'turn the ministry of government to the purpose of domination'.[61] But pleasing men or pleasing self instead of pleasing God would lead to alienation from God. As Gregory the Great starkly puts it, 'a servant whom the bridegroom has sent with gifts to the bride is guilty of treacherous thought if he desires to please the eyes of the bride'.[62]

Other besetting temptations facing the early pastors seem to have included money. Basil rebukes some minor rural bishops for taking money for admitting people to the priesthood.[63] But the temptation seems to have been widespread.[64] Chrysostom speaks in fuller terms about the seductiveness of certain women, the temptations of patronage and honours and the frustrations of having people under their care who are taken up with the cares of the world and of wealth. In the face of this he urges that 'the soul of the priest ought to be purer than the very sunbeams'.[65]

Like earlier writers these men believed in the authority of the pastoral office: 'What priests do here below, God ratifies above and the Master confirms the sentence of his servants.'[66] But in contrast to earlier writers, authority was not their concern. They were more concerned about the skilful performance of pastoral duties and the training of sensitive pastoral characters. They were aware of the vital influence of example. 'Every preacher should give forth more by his deeds than by his words, and rather by good living imprint footsteps for men to follow than by speaking show them the way to walk in.'[67] The church took its character from the character of the priesthood and the priests dare not fail, for the people's sake, let alone for the judgment

---

[60] *Ibid.*, VI, 4, p. 77.
[61] Gregory the Great, *Book of Pastoral Rule*, II, 6, p. 16.
[62] *Ibid.*, II, 8, p. 19. [63] Basil, *Letters*, LIII–LIV, pp. 156–158.
[64] R. Brown, 'An Early Christian Conception of the Ministry', pp. 7f.
[65] Chrysostom, *On the Priesthood*, VI, 2, p. 75. See also VI, 2, 3, and 4, pp. 75–77.
[66] *Ibid.*, III, 5, p. 47.
[67] Gregory the Great, *Book of Pastoral Rule*, III, XL, p. 71.

they themselves would face.[68]

It is no wonder that Gregory of Nazianzus referred to the work of the ministry as 'no slight task',[69] nor that many resisted the office. But what convinced them to accept it in the end was the greater fear of disobedience to God. For, as Gregory said in explaining his change of heart, 'we have, against our fear of office, a possible help in the law of obedience, inasmuch as God in his goodness rewards our faith and makes a perfect ruler of the man who has confidence in him, and places all his hopes in him'.[70]

In the same year that John Chrysostom wrote *On the Priesthood*, Ambrose of Milan (339–397) wrote a work entitled *On the Duties of the Clergy*. Ambrose, the son of the prefect of Gaul, had himself entered upon a career in imperial administration and was made the governor of Upper Italy, centred on Milan, in 370. Four years later, on the death of Auxentius, the bishop of Milan, Ambrose was chosen to succeed him. Though a convinced Christian, he had not yet been baptized and therefore was hurriedly initiated into the church and rose through its ranks to the episcopacy within eight days. Ambrose was an outstanding preacher and administrator who left the stamp of an aristocratic Roman (trained in the upper echelons of the civil service of his day) on the church.

His work *On the Duties of the Clergy* is not really a textbook in pastoral theology so much as an exhortation to ministers to live virtuous lives and to hold fast to perfect duties. Building on the work of Cicero he extols the four pagan classical virtues of wisdom, justice, fortitude and temperance, to which he adds the Christian virtues of faith, hope and love.[71] His view of the ministry has to be constructed by teasing out the assumptions behind this work and by using passing references elsewhere. Ambrose widens the already-existing gap between clergy and laity. Priests are clearly seen to enjoy a different status than ordinary Christians and by virtue of their ordination were reckoned to be better Christians. He takes duties and exhortations which the New Testament lays upon all Christians and although, in passing, he recognizes their general validity, he ignores that fact in his desire to urge them on the priests. To

---

[68] Gregory of Nazianzus, *Oration II*, 82, p. 221.   [69] *Ibid.*, 35, p. 212.
[70] *Ibid.*, 113, p. 226.
[71] Ambrose, *On the Duty of Clergy*, NP-NF Second Series, vol. 10, pp. 1–89.

him, a good but ordinary member of the church was hard to distinguish from a good-living pagan.[72]

Superior to the priests was the bishop, the father of the priests, who derived his authority from apostolic succession. The bishop's power lay in his office rather than in his person, so although personal holiness could be helpful to his work it was the position not the person that really mattered. The bishop was the successor to both the Old Testament prophet and priest, and therefore had the obligation, on the one hand, to engage in stern rebuke, and on the other, to work for healing. Ambrose uses Elijah, Nathan and Jeremiah as his models for asserting that bishops must confront wrong and proclaim against evil. To be silent was a dereliction of duty of the utmost magnitude.[73]

Ambrose practised what he preached. His clashes with pagans and with Arians involved him in confronting emperors, empresses, soldiers and heretics alike. His involvement in public affairs was unprecedented. His belief that priests should judge laymen, but that they were not subject to the judgment of laymen, gave him a high-minded confidence which enabled him to resist the interference of the state in the church whilst, in contrast, it enabled him to withstand even an emperor until public penance had been done for sin. Not for nothing has Ambrose been seen as the first medieval prelate.

The significance of Ambrose lies as much in the effect he had on Augustine of Hippo (354–430) as it does in his own episcopal career. It was through Ambrose's learned preaching that Augustine had been converted, and as a bishop Augustine looked to Ambrose as his model. From a middle-class background, Augustine was a teacher of rhetoric and deeply involved in philosophical and Manichaean teaching before his conversion. He was press-ganged into the priesthood in 391 while on a visit to Hippo and became the bishop there in 396. Many consider him to be an ideal pastor and an exemplary preacher.

As a pastor, Augustine knew the immense responsibilities he had accepted when he became a bishop. Preaching on the anniversary of his consecration he listed them as:

> To rebuke those who stir up strife, to comfort those of little courage, to take the part of the weak; to refute opponents,

---

[72] Mayer, *Pastoral Care*, pp. 51–72.   [73] Williams, 'Later Patristic Period', pp. 72f.

to be on guard against traps, to teach the ignorant, to shake the indolent awake, to discourage those who want to buy and sell, to put the presumptuous in their place, to mollify the quarrelsome, to help the poor, to liberate the oppressed, to encourage the good, to suffer the evil and to love all men.

To be preaching, disputing, reproving, edifying, to be on hand for everyman – that is the great burden and one which lies heavily on me.[74]

These duties he carried out meticulously. Unlike Ambrose, Augustine's door was open to all. As F. van der Meer has written in his monumental study of Augustine as a bishop,

Augustine knew well that these petty worries were a primary duty. Mundane preoccupations often brought with them the opportunity to give good advice or rebuke to a sinner, they brought with them the possibility of quiet influence and of setting a good example, a chance to bring enlivening of consciences and give spiritual direction. Administration was the least among the thieves of his time. That vile blood-sucking creature . . . was left by Augustine to his accountant, but for the rest, there was hardly anything on which he would turn his back for Augustine knew that many an opportunity of serving a soul begins with a chance encounter.[75]

Augustine's pastoral care was exemplary. He was the first to introduce monastic living into a cathedral and his life in the community, which was situated at the heart of the town, was open for all to see. Having renounced luxury as hostile to spiritual growth he maintained a simple life-style and lived on a frugal diet of vegetables and pot-herbs and wore clothes that others had given to him.[76] The same high standards were expected of his monastic brothers. He believed that they should work for their living rather than rely on gifts – a system which was subject to abuse. Equally high standards were expected of his clergy, and usually obtained. The records contain a number of cases where the required standards were not reached and tell of Augustine's firm, yet sympathetic, handling of the

[74] Cited in F. van der Meer, *Augustine the Bishop*, p. 268.   [75] *Ibid.*, p. 269.
[76] On Augustine's personal life-style see, *ibid.*, pp. 234–241.

offenders.[77]

Augustine's pastoral care was also comprehensive. For much of his life Augustine was engaged in controversy against the Manichaeans and the Pelagians, and for thirty years he was in dispute with the schismatic Donatist church of Africa and did much to bring about its eventual reconciliation. Even though his disputes were often polemical, his motivation was always pastoral. 'What he has chiefly taught posterity as a pastor of souls is to see those who hold heretical beliefs as strayed sheep rather than as carriers of loathsome infection, the strayed sheep for which as a bishop of the true church, he bore as much responsibility as he did for the herd that was guarded secure in its fold, the herd that knew its home full well and was comfortable in that knowledge.'[78]

Then, too, his pastoral care was marked by faithfulness. He lived at the time when Rome was sacked by Alaric (410) and when North Africa was crumbling under the invasion of Vandals. Such terrifying events were often spiritually productive and it was certainly no time for the clergy to seek their own safety. It was then that they had a job to do and their solidarity with the flock became most apparent:

> God forbid that this ship of ours should be prized so lightly that the sailors, and especially the pilot, ought to abandon it when it is in danger, even if they can escape by taking to a small boat or even by swimming.

> . . . when these dangers have reached their height and there is no possibility of flight, do we not realize how great a gathering there usually is in the church of both sexes and of every age, some clamouring for baptism, others for reconciliation, still others for acts of penance: all of them seeking consolation and the administration and distribution of the sacraments? If, then, the ministers are not at hand, how terrible is the destruction which overtakes those who depart from this world unregenerate or bound by sin![79]

All this needs to be borne in mind when discussing the other

[77] *Ibid.*, pp. 225–234.   [78] *Ibid.*, p. 128.
[79] Cited by Williams, 'Later Patristic Period', pp. 73f. from Possidus, *Life*, 135, 131.

side of Augustine's contribution to our understanding of the ministry, namely, its sacramental character. Sacraments were vital to the life of the church both in providing it with external visibility and also with internal unity. But Augustine's views were forged against the background of the Donatist schism and these led him to affirm two ideas which were to leave their mark on the future of the ministry. He believed that sacraments could be valid outside the true church but ineffective, and this led to the view that the personal character of the celebrant was incidental to the validity of the sacrament. Its validity was determined by the one true church, not the celebrant. Sacraments therefore were valid *ex opere operato*, a view which however worthy in theory has often led to their being spiritually debased in practice.

A second affirmation concerned the nature of valid ordination. Did it depend on the moral worth of the ordinand? Augustine's answer was that it did not, but that ordination conferred an indelible character on the individual ordained and that ordination was the permanent possession of the individual priest.[80] With Augustine the final nail in the coffin of corporate ministry in the local church was hammered in. Ministry was now a new order, for a select few, who had undergone a solemn ordination. It was a prize which could not be taken away from them and, sadly, a status which denied the rest of the church the privilege of exercising the gifts of God in ministry to each other.

In addition Augustine made a vital contribution to our understanding of preaching. We know that he was a popular preacher and fortunately we can detect something of his method from two works: his *Fourth Book of Christian Knowledge*[81] and his *Instruction for Beginners*.[82] Among the wealth of his teaching a few elementary points are worth recalling.[83] The purpose of his preaching was the exposition of the Bible, although his method of exegesis would not be in fashion today. The text of the Bible always determined the subjects and direction of his sermons. It was a sufficient textbook for it touched on the whole of human

---

[80] Williams, 'Later Patristic Period', pp. 74–76 and T. Rowe, *St Augustine, Pastoral Theologian*, pp. 57–75.

[81] Augustine, *On the Catechising of the Uninstructed. NP-NF* First Series, vol. 3, pp. 283–314.

[82] Augustine, *On Christian Doctrine*, IV, *NP-NF* First Series, vol. 2, pp. 574–597.

[83] See the excellent studies of Rowe, *St Augustine, Pastoral Theologian*, pp. 24–56 and van der Meer, *Augustine the Bishop*, pp. 405–467.

life and was easily applied to current affairs. The preacher was accountable to God for discharging the duty of proclaiming it without fear or favour to the people listening, and for remembering that his life was a more effective preacher than his words would ever be.

The purpose of preaching was three-fold. It was to explain, edify and persuade. These aims were derived from the rhetorical teaching of Cicero and were used to show that a variety of approaches and styles were needed in the sermon. He did not overplay the need for oratory and saw that it could be harmful to the interests of the gospel. Nonetheless, the preacher should give consideration to his aims and how he seeks to fulfil them. Each purpose corresponds to a separate style of delivery. Explaining demands a quiet style which convinces the hearers of the truth. Edifying means that the congregation must be pleased and their attention held by the sermon. Persuasion involves a grander style which inspires people to action. This last aim was always present in the preaching of the gospel. 'The end of eloquence is to persuade . . . In any of these three styles an eloquent man speaks in a manner suitable to persuasion, but if he does not persuade, he has not attained the end of eloquence.'[84]

Augustine's style seems to have been essentially spontaneous, although not by any means unprepared, and the reports of his preaching pay tribute, on every hand, to the marvellous rapport he had with his congregation. Audience participation in the sermon was common and for the most part welcome. On reading his *Instruction for Beginners* it soon becomes apparent that this was no accident, but an art which Augustine consciously studied.

In that work Augustine sets out to help a Carthaginian deacon called Deogratius in his task of preparing people for baptism. He stresses that Deogratius' approach must be determined by the nature of his audience. If it is just a single individual he must sit with him and have a conversation. If a group, then a sermon is a right and proper approach. But what of the background of the catechumen? Those who are educated and have already read much should be led on by being told, 'Of course, you already know this.' But they must be warned against im-

[84] Cited by Rowe, *St Augustine, Pastoral Theologian*, p. 50. See *On Christian Doctrine*, IV, xvii, xix, xxii–xxvi, pp. 586 and 593–595.

bibing heresy. Professional speakers require harsher treatment. They must be warned to be more concerned about immoral behaviour than inaccurate grammar. But their interests can be exploited to encourage them not to rest content with anything less than the allegorical – the real – meaning of Scripture. The teacher must not only study his pupils, but also their motivation in coming, if he is to be successful in his task. Very practically, Augustine even examines why pupils get weary and suggests ways in which their attention can be held. The method which Augustine recommends is that of telling the story of salvation. This is much to be preferred to discussing the theory of salvation. It needs to be done comprehensively but briefly and must be done with a right use of emotion, for it is a story that must persuade the learner of the love of God.

Through these writings Augustine may justly be claimed to be the father of homiletics. Before, some had used their rhetorical education both to enhance their own gifts as preachers and to urge others to study the craft carefully. But Augustine is the first to reflect and teach some of those lessons systematically for the benefit of the church.

Finally, Augustine was no simple practitioner but must be acknowledged as a pastoral theologian. More than anyone else in the early church he was creative in his thinking and produced theology of some weight, including *The City of God*, which sought to integrate the teaching of the Bible and the church with his own experience, his own conflicts and his people's needs. His prolific writing arose out of pastoral needs whether it was the need to reclaim heretics, to convince sceptics or to encourage wavering believers. Given that his writing was forged in the heat of the battle it is not surprising that he was no systematic theologian and that it is impossible to summarize his contribution briefly.[85] Much of the writing, and some of his practice, belongs to another age and another world of thought. But Augustine stands as a model for those who wish to try to present the gospel relevantly to their own day.

---

[85] The best guide is Rowe, *St Augustine, Pastoral Theologian*.

CONCLUSION

At the gate of the Middle Ages the ministry had assumed once more the character of the Old Testament priesthood and had, to a great extent, forsaken the New Testament vision of a spiritually gifted body where, under responsive leaders, members were engaged in corporate ministry. The more prominent exercised gifts to the exclusion of others with the result that members of the body were no longer seen as having equal worth. It was the outworking of the growth and changing circumstances of the church which had become culture-bound. In spite of its mistakes, however, there shine from these days rich jewels which sparkle in the gathering gloom and reflect a penetrating understanding of the life of the true pastor. Both the negative warnings and the positive examples still have much to say to our own day.

8

The Middle Ages

The strange world of the Middle Ages relates little to our own age. The clergy entered the Middle Ages well equipped with Gregory the Great's *Pastoral Rule*. It was an ideal which was never questioned and all paid lip-service to it. But it was equally an ideal which was never reached, apart from some notable exceptions to be found in the monastic orders. But Gregory had not only sowed the seeds for a fruitful pastoral ministry, he had also sowed the seeds of ministerial decay. His pontificate had seen the accumulation of vast lands in the hands of the papacy which, consequently, forsook the care of souls for the care of estates.[1]

The Roman empire, now as defunct as a spent battery, needed replacing with a new civilization and the papacy was to be the main channel of reconstruction. The civilization which arose was one where society was to equal the church and the church was to equal the papacy. Reconstruction demanded that the church took an increasing part in secular affairs. In 754, Pepin, king of the Franks, conferred the keys of ten cities on the pope and thus recognized in law what was already the situation in practice (and was to remain so until 1870). Pepin's son, Charlemagne (742–814), did much to bring about the concept of the Holy Roman Empire through his military conquests and on Christmas Day, in the year 800, at mass in St Peter's, Pope Leo III crowned him emperor. Whatever other implications that act contained, it symbolized the claim of the pope to be superior to the king.

Charlemagne was not slow to see this implication, and when it came to the crowning of his own son, thirteen years later, he insisted that he crown himself rather than be crowned by ecclesiastics. But the grip of the papacy over rulers tightened. One of the battlefields between them was the right of secular rulers to make ecclesiastical appointments and this conflict reached its climax in a dispute between Pope Gregory VII

[1] R. H. Bainton, 'The Ministry in the Middle Ages', in H. R. Niebuhr and D. D. Williams (eds), *The Ministry in Historical Perspective*, p. 86.

(1023–1085) and the German king Henry IV. When King Henry refused to stop lay investitures Gregory threatened him with excommunication. Henry replied by getting the diet at Worms to depose Gregory. But Gregory was not to be beaten. He excommunicated the king in 1076 and absolved his subjects from the duty of obeying him. Finally the king was forced to go as a humble penitent to Gregory, standing barefooted in the snow for three days before he was forgiven. Such was the power of popes!

It was a power which reached its height under Innocent III (1160–1216) who, following Gregory VII, claimed that 'the priesthood is the sun, and the monarchy the moon; kings rule in their individual kingdoms, but Peter reigns over the whole earth . . .'[2] He believed himself to be a universal arbiter and statesman. He frequently tested his strength against kings and meddled in political affairs all over Europe as well as initiating the abortive Fourth Crusade.

Nonetheless in reality papal power was on the wane. It had served its purpose as far as the secular rulers were concerned and, having given what it had to give, was increasingly ignored. It more and more suffered from the problem, as R. W. Southern has aptly described it, of inflation.[3] The papal court was the centre of a vast administrative machinery and, like so much bureaucracy, its ravenous appetite for growth was not matched by an increase in efficiency. The tendency to centralize in the church was aided by bishops who increasingly looked to Rome to champion their cause against their kings. But the growing mass of business disguised a real decline in influence. Inflation, too, meant that its money was running out and that the preferments and benefices it had to give were decreasing in value. The same was true of its power of excommunication, which had to be restricted to prevent it from complete devaluation. To a lesser extent, the same was also true of its granting of indulgences.

All this had serious consequences for the ministry lower down the ecclesiastical hierarchy. It was hard to maintain a pure view of the ministry when the church had become so inextricably bound up with the affairs of this world. During the Middle Ages, Europe had nearly five hundred bishops who

---

[2] See H. Bettenson (ed), *Documents of the Christian Church*, pp. 155f.
[3] R. W. Southern, *Western Society and the Church in the Middle Ages*, pp. 133–169.

now had to concern themselves, as landowners, with the affairs of business, as judges and legislators, with the administration of law, and as political magnates, with military activity; activities which had been forbidden to priests of John Chrysostom's time. Samuel had become their model rather than Christ. It was hardly surprising, therefore, that those who occupied the episcopal thrones were most often connected with the great families or were the appointees of kings. This being so, a legion of other evils followed. Simony, nepotism, pluralism, absenteeism and moral incontinence were common. The lower clergy were, for the most part, no better. In addition to the problems found among the bishops, illiteracy, drunkenness, abuse of power and an overbearing desire for material gain at the expense of the poor were rife.[4]

Force of circumstances may well have been responsible for the ministry straying down this path. Society was in need of reconstruction; kings needed advisers and the people needed leaders and defenders, and the clergy were the only literate people in a position to oblige. But if necessity had initiated the problem, success had aggravated it. The ministry, as a spiritual force, was at its lowest ebb.

The period saw a number of genuine attempts at reform. Gregory VII brought to a head, albeit without achieving complete success, a reform of the clergy which had begun long before. The revival of monasticism at Cluny, the renewed study of canon law as seen in the writings of a man like Bishop Buchard of Worms[5] and the concern of the German emperors conspired to put reform on the agenda. In his first synod, held in Rome in 1074, Gregory decreed against simony and concubinage, which he described as the heresy of Nicolaitanism, and made it clear that he expected his decrees to be published, obeyed and enforced throughout the empire. Under Gregory, celibacy became part of canon law and priests were instructed to adopt the tonsure and wear distinctive clothing as an encouragement to their morality. But Gregory VII's reforms were bound up with his opposition to lay patronage and his augmenting of the power of the pope. It is probably because of these attacks on the vested interests of others that he met with

---

[4] G. G. Coulton, *Ten Medieval Studies*, pp. 122–152.

[5] For the contribution of Buchard of Worms see Clebsch and Jackee, *Pastoral Care in Historical Perspective*, p. 24.

such opposition and was only partially successful.[6]

Innocent III, for all his worldly faults, made reform the great objective of his pontificate and was able to bring many of Gregory VII's desired goals to completion. He was not unaware of the spiritual responsibilities of his office, as a sermon on Matthew 24:45 shows. The pope, he says, must 'show fidelity, prudence and pastoral zeal, feeding the flock by personal example, by teaching and by dispensation of the sacraments, with godly wisdom and unshaken loyalty to the apostolic faith'.[7] And he seems particularly alert to the pastoral significance of the clergy: 'The shepherd must be diligent in his pastoral care so that there will be no sick sheep in his fold from whom contagion will threaten the whole flock.'[8] Something of the same pastoral understanding is seen in the canons of the Fourth Lateran Council which met, under his direction, in 1215. It tried to regulate pastoral care and saw the need for the pastor to be as skilled as the physician in his application of cures. It also recognized a connection between sin and bodily sickness.

But these positive statements are overshadowed by the faults in the clergy which were still a major preoccupation for Innocent III. The sins which he attacked were largely the same as those attacked by Gregory. But one improvement was that his enforcement of celibacy now met with little opposition, although there were still violations to be checked.

In addition to popes, various other bishops and spiritual leaders attempted to raise the standard of clerical life during the Middle Ages. The widespread adoption of the Rule of St Benedict, with its encouragement to subjugate one's own desires in submission to God and one's superiors, did much to elevate spiritual life both within and outside of the monastery. Lay folk were encouraged to adopt at least the initial emphases of the rule and then interpret their lives within the norms it laid down. Later on, the founding of the Orders of St Francis (1182–1226) and Dominic (1170–1221) did much to revive spirituality and bring it within the grasp of ordinary folk.[9] Not all such attempts were incorporated within the Catholic Church

[6] G. S. M. Walker, *The Growing Storm. Sketches of Church History from AD 600 to AD 1350*, pp. 74–95.   [7] *Ibid.*, p. 163.

[8] C. E. Smith, *Innocent III: Church Defender*. Smith gives detailed documentation of Innocent III's attempts at pastoral reform.

[9] For the contribution of these orders to pastoral care see McNeill, *Cure of Souls*, pp. 122–162.

and sadly some, such as that of the Waldensians, which might have benefited the church through its reforms, were ejected and severely persecuted in their search for a purer faith.

Some bishops fought nobly to improve the standard of the secular clergy. A man like Bishop Hugh of Lincoln (1135–1200), who impressed everyone with his own personal holiness, instituted measures aimed at clerical reform. He was much more conscientious about the performance of his spiritual duties than most, and aware of the spiritual realities involved. On one occasion he refused to demand payment from a widow of the tax due to him because of her husband's death. It would have meant her losing her ox, the only means of livelihood she had. His bailiff protested, saying that he would soon ruin his finances if that was the way he was to conduct his affairs. But Hugh replied, 'Look, my friend, here is plenty of earth, I can keep all this without depriving the widow of her ox. What is the use of possessing so much earth if one loses heaven? If we are over-strict in demanding payment for debts that are not just we may become bankrupt before God.'[10]

One of the greatest English reformers was John Pecham, who was archibishop of Canterbury from 1279 to 1292. On his appointment he called for a council to meet him at Reading and then, later that year, at Lambeth where he re-enacted previous legislation and added his own canons to purify the priesthood. The Fourth Lateran Council had insisted that annual communion and confession be made and Pecham, in turn, insisted that his clergy instructed the laity before they made their Easter communion.[11]

His comprehensive visitations meant that the execution of his injunctions was not left to chance. Following his second visitation of the diocese of Canterbury, he addressed the clergy about their responsibilities and put an equal stress on those of a spiritual and those of a temporal nature. As to the spiritual duties, he enjoined that the sacraments and offices should always be recited reverently, that if they were too ignorant themselves to act as preachers and confessors they should make use of friars to carry out these duties, that excess revenue should be devoted to charity and that they should exercise hospitality. It is clear that he did not meet with automatic obedience.

[10] J. Clayton, *St Hugh of Lincoln*, pp. 90f.
[11] D. L. Douie, *Archbishop Pecham*, pp. 133–136.

Twenty-nine churches in south-east Kent alone did not reach the required standard. Incontinence was rife, nine rectors were non-residents, one was extremely violent and quarrelsome and church vestments and property were ill-kept.[12] It seems that he had little effect, despite all his hard work, by the end of his life.

Pecham's reforming zeal inevitably led him into conflict with those who stood to lose by it. One of these conflicts gives an insight into Pecham's feelings about the opposition he faced and the state of the church. Tedisius de Camilla was the dean of Wolverhampton. He was non-resident and had failed to proceed to the priesthood in the required amount of time, added to which he failed to appear before the archbishop to answer charges against him when summoned to do so. In the ensuing correspondence Pecham wrote to the pope as follows,

> Formerly Mother Church nourished her children by means of the pastoral office, but now her maternal bowels are wrung, when she sees Solomon dissect her child at the demand of the wolf. The cautery which should have been applied to the gangrene drops from the hand of the careless physician, when the werewulf, lest his misdeeds should be made manifest by the daylight, and the bonds of iniquity loosed, has recourse to the subterfuge of a fraudulent appeal.[13]

When John Pecham served as archbishop the effects of the Fourth Lateran Council, which had stimulated the demand for works of pastoral theology and numerous popular books of spirituality, were still being felt. One of his predecessors, Stephen Langton, had required his priests to draw up a syllabus of instruction for their people. Pecham built on the work of William of Bruges to produce a work of his own called *Ignorantia Sacerdotum*. In it he dealt with the creed, the ten commandments, the sacraments, the seven deadly sins and the seven acts of mercy. Others often added the Lord's Prayer and the Ave Maria to their instruction. Under Pecham, then, a sincere attempt was made in England to reform the priesthood.

The tradition of writing to which Pecham contributed in his *Ignorantia Sacerdotum* is still to be seen in one of the few instruc-

---

[12] *Ibid.*, pp. 153–155.   [13] *Ibid.*, p. 148.

tion manuals for the clergy to survive from the fifteenth century. John Myrc's poem, *Instructions for Parish Priests*,[14] is thought to have been written in 1450. John Myrc was Canon of Lilleshall but, other than that, we know nothing of him. It bears the clear marks of the same sort of exposition of Christian teaching as we saw in Pecham. But its value for us lies in two other areas. Firstly, it gives a rare insight into the instructions given to priests during the Middle Ages.[15] Secondly, in doing so it reveals the nature and state of the priesthood at the time.

It begins by stressing the importance of preaching, but then says nothing more about how it is to be done.[16] It is clear that ignorant clergy abounded everywhere and were considered to be doing a great evil to the church. At one stage in the poem (lines 623–626) priests are instructed not to baptize if they are drunk, because they would not be in control of their speech! Generally they are told to eschew women, coarse jokes and immodest behaviour and to keep up their tonsures. Positively, they must be gentle, modest, given to hospitality and the reading of the psalter. Care must be taken in the teaching of the Christian faith and in ensuring that those who participate in baptisms and weddings do so with a due sense of responsibility. Reverent behaviour in church is enjoined and the priest is to rebuke people for lolling about on the floor and engaging in idle chatter during the service. Among the other duties referred to is the care of the graveyard.

Two impressions remain from these *Instructions*. Firstly, the general standard of the priesthood must still have been very low in John Myrc's time to merit the sort of instructions he sees fit to write. Secondly, the dominant impression of the clergy is that they had become the dispensers of the sacraments. There is little by way of the pastoral care which was characteristic of the early fathers of the church. The pastoral dimensions of the *Instructions*, such as they are, revolve around the saying of the mass, the administration of extreme unction and communion for the sick, the hearing of confession and the pronouncement of penance and excommunication. The priests of the new covenant had sold their birthright for a mess of pottage. Instead

---

[14] J. Myrc, *Instructions for Parish Priests*.
[15] Other texts from the earlier period can be found in E. McCracken (trans and ed), *Early Medieval Theology*. LCC, vol. 9, pp. 371–399.
[16] See the quotation in Bainton, 'The Ministry in the Middle Ages', p. 99.

of being the pastors of a more splendid covenant of the Spirit, they had regressed to being the priests of the old covenant of the law. The inner life had once more been supplanted by the external rite.

Although there may be much to gain from some medieval works of devotion, and though there are some notable exceptions, there is little in this period which relates, except by way of tragic warning, to the pastoral ministry today. Rather, an examination of the futile attempts to reform the ministry during the centuries of the Middle Ages underlines the need there was for a reformation. Nothing less than a radical renewal of the church seemed capable of making any impression on the generations of false shepherds who, rather than feeding their sheep, looked after their own interests while their flock suffered the ravages of the wolves.

9

The Reformation and its legacy

The two great questions of the Reformation, according to Paul Avis,[1] were, 'How can I obtain a gracious God?' and 'Where can I find the true church?' It was a necessary corollary of both those questions that the pastoral ministry should undergo a fundamental reformation.[2] It was a reformation which, however ill thought through to begin with, was to put the ministry in touch once more with its biblical and early church roots.

MARTIN LUTHER

Martin Luther (1483–1546) set about demolishing the medieval view of the papacy and priesthood in 1520 in a tract addressed *To the Christian Nobility of the German Nation Concerning the Reform of the Christian Estate*.[3] The pope, he argued, had erected three illegitimate claims which now protected him like three strong walls; the claim that the spiritual estate was superior to the secular estate, the claim that the pope alone could interpret Scripture and the claim that the pope alone could call a council. The tract ended with practical proposals for the reform of the ministry, which contain the seeds of much of his later thought. Having stormed the outer walls Luther next advanced on the papal citadel in a tract, also published in 1520, entitled *The Babylonian Captivity of the Church*.[4] Here the Roman view of the sacraments was questioned. While that remained unaltered there could be no reform.

In reconstructing the doctrine of the church a number of basic tenets were soon stated and repeatedly affirmed. The true church was to be found wherever the word of God was preached, 'if the word of God is present in its purity and is active, the Church is there'.[5] 'The sure mark by which the

---

[1] P. D. L. Avis, *The Church in the Theology of the Reformers*, p. 1.
[2] *Pace* Clebsch and Jackee, *Pastoral Care in Historical Perspective*, p. 14.
[3] M. Luther, *Luther's Works*, vol. 44, pp. 123–217. See also G. Haendler, *Luther on Ministerial Office and Congregational Function*.
[4] *LW*, vol. 36, pp. 5–126. [5] *LW*, vol. 28, 'Lectures on 1 Timothy', p. 302.

Christian congregation can be recognised is that the pure gospel is preached there. For just as the banner of an army is the sure sign by which one can know what kind of Lord and army have taken to the field, so too the gospel is the sure sign by which one knows where Christ and his army are encamped . . .'[6]

The ministry, then, became a ministry of the word and the pastor a teacher of the flock, not a dispenser of the sacraments. The administration of external rites without the requirement of inner faith was a wicked abuse and criminally misleading. Those set apart by the church to be its leaders were essentially seen as preachers. They were also referred to as pastors but that designation was not common until the eighteenth century.[7] Preaching was their specific responsibility and their ordination was a setting apart to the responsibilities of that office, not to some priestly status. Pastoral care took the form of the application of the word of God to the needs of the people and the encouragement of the people to have faith in that word.

Further, the ministry was transformed, once more, into the ministry of the whole church. It was no longer the exclusive province of an élite sacred order. The church had a right to appoint ministers and even more of a right and duty to dismiss them if they were not preaching the gospel. And since that stricture applied to many of the established clergy of his time, Luther urged the Christians 'to avoid, to flee, to depose and to withdraw from the authority' that they were exercising.[8] More radically still, Luther asserted that

> the ministry of the Word belongs to all. To bind and to loose clearly is nothing else than to proclaim and to apply the gospel. For what is it to loose, if not to announce the forgiveness of sins before God? What is it to bind, except to withdraw the gospel and to declare the retention of sins? Whether they want to or not they must concede that the keys are the exercise of the ministry of the Word and belong to all Christians.[9]

[6] *LW*, vol. 39, 'That a Christian assembly or congregation has the right and power to judge all teaching and to call, appoint and dismiss teachers, established and proven by Scripture', p. 305.

[7] See Lewis Spitz, 'Luther. Ecclesiast, A Historian's Angle', in P. N. Brooks (ed), *Seven-Headed Luther*, p. 115.

[8] *LW*, vol. 39, pp. 301–314, especially p. 308.

[9] *LW*, vol. 40, 'Concerning the Ministry', p. 27.

Luther himself was much involved in pastoral work, as his numerous writings and letters show. To be a pastor seems to have been part of Luther's nature rather than a responsibility he adopted once the Reformation had begun. His correspondence whilst he was still an Augustinian monastic visitor shows him to have been greatly concerned for the well-being of his flock and the recovery of the occasional lost sheep.[10] But once the Reformation dawned it was a gift which was able to be developed more fully. From then on he was tirelessly involved in providing spiritual counsel to individuals and in reconciling those who had fallen out with each other.[11] It was this work of peace-making on which he was engaged at the very end of his life when common sense and poor health should have really dictated a rest. Two brothers, the counts of Mansfeld, were quarrelling with each other and Luther set out in the depth of winter to journey to Eisleben to establish peace. He succeeded in effecting the reconciliation, but had left himself greatly weakened and died the day after his triumph.

One event demonstrates his pastoral qualities superbly. In August 1527 the plague came to Wittenberg and Luther stayed, despite being ordered by the elector John to leave with the rest of the university for Jena, and in spite of difficult family circumstances which would have provided more than enough justification for his flight. In reply to a question posed by John Hess of Breslau, where the plague had also struck, Luther set forth his attitude. He does not commend foolhardiness in the face of the plague and mentions practical steps which should be taken to avoid its spread. Unless there were spiritual and civic duties which kept people in Wittenberg, he argued that they should leave. But, he was a pastor and,

> Those who are engaged in a spiritual ministry such as preachers and pastors must likewise remain steadfast before the peril of death. We have a plain command from Christ, 'A good shepherd lays down his life for the sheep but the hireling sees the wolf coming and flees' (John 10:11). For when people are dying they most need a spiritual ministry which

[10] J. Atkinson, *Martin Luther and the Birth of Protestantism*, pp. 132–135.
[11] R. Brown, 'Luther as a Pastoral Counsellor', unpublished lecture. See also, *Luther: Letters of Spiritual Counsel*, translated and edited by T. Tappert.

strengthens and comforts their consciences by word and sacrament and in faith overcomes death.[12]

To Luther, his duty was clear.

One of the recurring themes of Luther's pastoral guidance was that of consolation. The most outstanding work, but by no means the only work, of consolation was that of 1519 addressed to the elector Frederick the Wise who was unwell. After reviewing seven sources of evil Luther contrasts them with seven sources of blessing which were so much greater and the experience of which would all but eclipse the evil. The final blessing was the contemplation of the risen Christ. 'Here', Luther wrote, 'the heart can find its supreme joy and lasting possessions. Here there is not the slightest trace of evil, for, "Christ being risen from the dead, will not die again. Death no longer has dominion over him" (Rom. 6:9).'[13]

The theme of consolation was one often addressed by Luther in his sermons. His own experiences in life doubtless contributed much to the frequency with which this note was sounded. Man needed consolation not just when facing ill-health or death but when doubts, despair, turmoils and temptations invaded his spirit.[14] To Luther such experiences came from God's direct dealing with man. God presented himself to man as a judge, making him unhappy when he had moved outside his will; as an enemy, enticing him to put out hope completely in him alone; as a tempter, testing the deep quality of his faith; as a hidden one, calling him to believe in spite of unanswered faith and an arbitrary one, who though apparently undependable or capricious inspires the deepest faith of all, a faith that believes God's answer will be 'Yes' even when to all appearances it seems to be 'No'.

Warren Horland has pointed out, in reference to God presenting himself to man as the arbitrary one, that Luther preached thirteen times on Jesus' rejection of the Canaanite woman and his calling her a dog. Luther commented, 'If this had been said to me I would have run off. This is the hardest text of all, to be called a dog.' But what faith arose from the

---

[12] *LW*, vol. 43, 'Whether one may flee from the Deadly Plague', p. 121.

[13] *LW*, vol. 42, 'Fourteen Consolations', p. 163.

[14] C. W. Horland, 'Anfectung in Luther's Biblical Exegesis', in F. H. Littell (ed), *Reformation Studies. Essays in Honour of Roland H. Bainton*, pp. 46–60.

woman as a result! In spite of apparent rejection she refuses to abandon her quest and discovers underneath a God who does accept her.[15] His fascination with his text could be biographically motivated, for he certainly knew enough of rejection and despair. But it was just such experiences, according to him, which were the anvil on which all true theology was forged.

In his delightful study of 'Luther as a Pastoral Counsellor',[16] Raymond Brown has concluded that Luther's pastoral motivation is to be found in Christology rather than human altruism. The incarnation and the judgment, in particular, are seen by Luther as incentives for loving and caring. The Christian must love because in the first coming of Christ God was generous to us, and in the second coming of Christ man is accountable to him. It is true that Luther worked against the backdrop of an active devil. But the greater vision he kept before him was of a loving God who had chosen to use men to be his messengers. No more apt summary of his understanding of pastoral care can be found than that Luther himself gave in *The Freedom of a Christian*, 'Surely we are named after Christ, not because he is absent from us, but because he dwells in us, that is because we believe in him and are Christs one to another and do to our neighbours as Christ does to us.'[17] What higher motivation could there be to engage in such a difficult task as the pastoral ministry with all its trials and temptations?[18]

MARTIN BUCER

Many of the Reformers made some contribution to a renewed understanding of pastoral care in the church. Ulrich Zwingli (1484–1531), the Swiss reformer, published a tract called *The Shepherd*[19] in 1524. It was the first systematic treatment of the subject provided by a Reformer, but was unfortunately a hurried work and shows more concern to expose the evils of the Roman priesthood than to construct a positive approach to the work of the pastor. It was written partly to persuade those on the brink of forsaking the church of Rome to join the side

---

[15] *Ibid.*, p. 59.   [16] R. Brown, 'Luther as a Pastoral Counsellor'.
[17] *LW*, vol. 31, 'Freedom of a Christian', p. 368.
[18] *LW*, vol. 54, 'Table Talk', No 453, pp. 73f.
[19] The work has never been translated into English, but details of it can be seen in McNeill, *Cure of Souls*, pp. 192–196.

of the Reformers, and was effective in that regard. Before devoting the second part to a denunciation of Rome, Zwingli does stress the need for pastors to be on guard over their sheep to prevent them from falling into sickness or danger. He saw pastors as a gift from God for the protection of the flock and argued that the sheep were never so healthy as when they were fed on the pure word of God without any human addition to it.[20]

The supreme accolade of 'Pastoral Theologian of the Reformation' must, however, without doubt be awarded to Martin Bucer (1491–1551). Trained as a Dominican, he was converted to Lutheranism in 1518. He was released from his order in 1521 and was one of the earliest Reformers to marry. Most of his life was devoted to the interests of the Reformation in Strasbourg where he was a great influence on John Calvin during his time there. He was expelled from Strasbourg in 1548 for resisting the emperor's will and he spent his final few years in England, where he became a Regius professor at the University of Cambridge. His major contribution to the Reformation lay in copious ecumenical negotiations in which he engaged and for which he seemed to have an endless capacity, and in his production of ecclesiastical constitutions and liturgies. Both of these activities demonstrate his central concern for the church, so it is fitting that he should have been the one to write the most constructive and systematic pastoral theology of his day.

Bucer's major work *On the Care of Souls*, written in 1538, has sadly never been translated into English.[21] Its twelve chapters, plus a concluding summary, are a comprehensive statement of the church and its ministry and how to care for particular cases within the church, all liberally supported, at each point, by reference to Scripture.

The work begins by stressing that the church should be characterized by close and deep fellowship between Christians, not only of a spiritual nature but of a material kind as well. The true church would be marked by unity, for all Christians are united in Christ. Ephesians 4:1–6, 15–16; 1 Corinthians 1:18–27; 8:1–13; 12:12–13; Romans 12:4–6; Acts 4:32, 34a and 35b; 2 Thes-

[20] See W. Pauck, 'The Ministry in the Time of the Continental Reformation', in Niebuhr and Williams, *Ministry in Historical Perspective*, p. 116.

[21] M. Bucer, 'Von der Waren Seelsorge . . .', in *Martini Bucer Opera Omnia Series I: Deutsche Schriften*, vol. 7, pp. 67–245. I am grateful to my former colleague Mr Tony Lane for his willingness to read this work and provide me with a guide to it.

salonians 3:11–13 and Jeremiah 23:5–6 form the basis of his argument.

Within the church there is the need for Christ to reign supreme through his Holy Spirit. Therefore whoever did not serve Christ through the preaching of his word or through applying his discipline proved themselves to be Antichrist. Although Christ rules supreme in the church he usually exercises his ministry through his ordinary ministers, as the commissions of Christ in the Gospels, together with 1 Corinthians 3:5–17; 4:1; 2 Corinthians 3:2–6; 1 Thessalonians 1:4–5 and 2:13 make clear. Bucer drew out two implications of this assertion. On the one hand, the power always belongs to Christ and no minister could claim it as his own. On the other hand, the minister was acting with the power of Jesus Christ and therefore to belittle his office or ignore his teaching was to belittle or ignore Christ himself.

Although Bucer subsequently argued that the church should be composed of four offices, those of preachers, elders, teachers and deacons,[22] in *On the Care of Souls* his thinking does not appear to have crystallized as much, for there he speaks in a looser way and only of shepherd-teachers (elders) and ministers of alms (deacons). The aim of the elders, who had taken over the pastoral ministry from the apostles, was to ensure the continuing discipleship of those within the church and to enable them to grow in holiness and to reach adulthood in Christ. This was to be done through supplying any lack they had in their understanding of life through teaching, warning, punishment, comfort and pardon. One thing was clear to Bucer, such a large task could not be accomplished by one man and God had not intended that it should be, for he had not given all his gifts to one or two people. He insisted, therefore, that the churches appoint a number of elders.

Next Bucer turns to the sort of persons elders should be and here for his discussion he relies chiefly on the qualifications set out in the pastoral epistles. They should be trusted and loved by the congregation, gifted and zealous, holy and disciplined themselves and able to discipline their family. Perhaps with the initial enthusiasm characteristic of all who experience novelties, he argues that marriage helps the pastor, whereas celibacy could

---

[22] Pauck, 'Ministry in the Continental Reformation', p. 127.

lead only to trouble. He believed that Paul's teaching in 1 Corinthians 7 had been taken too far by the church fathers. The pastor was required to meet high standards continuously and faults which might be tolerated in others were not to be entertained in those who occupied such a high office. Bucer believed that while failure to maintain the standards required might not be a ground of excommunication, it may well lead to the elder withdrawing from office. He stated that false teachers should certainly be removed from office.

In a number of ways Bucer's work has a remarkably contemporary ring in its view of the ministry. His insistence on a plurality of elders is one to which he returns again and again. The church lived by the gifts God had given and since there were many gifts there were also to be many elders. These elders should be drawn from across the social spectrum. It was wrong to choose them just from one type of status group, that is, the solidly middle strata of society. The source of the error he believed to lie in an overemphasis on learning. He believed that the upper middle and lower strata had a legitimate place in the ministry as well. By no stretch of the imagination could he be said to despise learning and yet he felt that it often assumed too much importance in the choice of an elder at the expense of godliness and spiritual zeal, which were also vital qualifications for office. Ministers were to be chosen firstly by discerning God's choice through prayer, then by discerning their gifts and zeal. It was a process in which the whole congregation should be involved and which should be ratified in a public service with due seriousness and prayer.

The thorough discussion given to the office of eldership should not mislead us into thinking that the ministry was confined to elders. In contemporary language Bucer believed in 'body ministry'. Not only was it crucial that 'one-man-ministry' be abandoned in favour of a plurality of elders, but that all Christians understand that they had a part to play in helping one another to grow in faith. The New Testament picture of the church as a body where each had a gift, the employment of which was vital to the health of the whole, had been restored.

The bulk of Bucer's work is taken up with the skill required in ministering to five particular sorts of people. Based on Ezekiel 34 Bucer argued, as we have seen, that the pastor should (1) bring to Christ and into the church those who had strayed through sin or error, (2) restore those who had lapsed, (3) restore those who whilst staying within the church had fallen into sin, (4) restore those within the church who were weak and ill and needed to be brought back to health, strength and active Christian living once more and (5) to keep and establish those who were already going on with Christ.

The first group must be actively sought by the elders with a view to reclaiming them. The second must be confronted with their sin, for only then would pardon and amendment come and the wounds be healed. The third group too should have sin made clear to them and penance prescribed. Sometimes stern measures were needed to have an effect here. The fourth group required a variety of remedies according to their particular state, but generally Bucer prescribed public worship and sought to fan their dying Christian commitment into flame once more.[23]

The final group, those who are already strong and healthy, are often pastorally neglected by the church, but Bucer had the discernment to see that they too needed to be fed. John 21:15–17; 1 Peter 5:1–4; Acts 20:18–28; 1 Thessalonians 2:5–12 and 1 Corinthians 5:2–13 serve as Bucer's starting-points here. As to the manner in which it is to be done, Bucer points out that all Christians should be engaged in helping one another and stresses that this sort of ministry was to be conducted personally and privately from home to home, not just publicly in church. As to the object of such pastoral care, Bucer says it is to encourage sound faith, by which he meant a faith which did not rely for justification on works but one which, having crucified evil behaviour, devoted itself to the love of one's neighbours. The aim was a life worthy of Christ which was continuously growing out of its relationship with Christ. Sound faith was essential if such a life was to be developed.

In addition to this general work we have a specific application of Bucer's pastoral approach in the advice he gives on visiting the sick.[24] Rejecting the Roman trust in external ceremonies and decrying the idea that the administration of the sacraments is to be left until someone was about to die, Bucer puts forward

[23] For a brief exposition of the particular approaches required see McNeill, *Cure of Souls*, pp. 178–180.
[24] M. Bucer, 'Visitation of the Sick', in D. F. Wright (trans and ed), *Common Places of Martin Bucer*, pp. 429–451.

a more constructive pastoralia for the sick. He begins with a pastoral theology of suffering.

> Since the Lord inflicts illnesses on men for the very purpose of drawing them to himself out of a lost world and moving them to seek him afresh with their whole heart, and by means of an illness often urges a whole family to repentance, we too should spare no effort in our dealings with the sick, to lead them together with their families fully back to the Lord, and to guide them to the point of acknowledging and adopting him with genuine faith as their only Saviour.[25]

The pastor is to gather the whole family together for instruction. They are to be given to understand that God created us healthy, but sin has ruined his creation. But God took mercy on us and through the suffering of Christ sought to restore his divine image in man. This the Lord brings about through his word and sacraments, which are dispensed through elders who have the power of the keys. Elders therefore are to be welcomed as one would welcome Christ. Sickness may be a punishment for sin, as in 1 Corinthians 11:30, but that is not to say that the worst afflicted are the worst sinners. 'On the contrary, the Lord often makes a spectacle of his dearest children to other men in order to summon us to repentance through the hardness of his judgment on the elect.'[26]

The manner of this teaching is to be compressed or expanded, softened or sharpened according to the need. What is important is that the visitor assures himself that the sick person has grasped and understood the teaching given. The pastor must then discern the most appropriate course of action according to the patient's past religious experience. In all cases it is right to urge them to put matters right with God and even to use strong terms to persuade them to do so if necessary. Bucer recommends the offer of private confession at this stage, but only as a first step, should the person recover, to public confession and absolution.

Bucer concludes,

> Since, then, we are bound to give account to the Lord for all

---

[25] *Ibid.*, p. 431.   [26] *Ibid.*, p. 433.

his sheep that we neglect and abandon to destruction, it is our duty when we learn of sickness, not to wait until we are summoned. We should offer our ministry even though not called for, and discharge it as faithfully as we can.[27]

With Martin Bucer the discipline of pastoral theology, which had been so evident in the early church, can be said to have been rediscovered. His writing not only contributed much to the reformation of the church in his own day but set the pattern and standard for many works on pastoral theology which were to be written subsequently.

JOHN CALVIN

Too often the Reformer of Geneva is presented in a one-sided manner. He is well known to history as an academic theologian and an ecclesiastic disciplinarian, but not as a pastor and a preacher.[28] His own shy, perhaps even introverted, personality has done little to alleviate the harshness of this portrait. Nonetheless, the truth is that John Calvin (1509–64) made a substantial contribution to the revival of the work of the pastor. His commentaries are full of pastorally sensitive comments; his letters are always pastorally discerning; his writings on the church give much attention to the question of pastoral care and the growth of the individual in Christ and, in his own life, he set a high standard of pastoring for others to follow.

John Calvin was no stranger to the hardships of life and, although that may well have led him to overactivate his psychological defence mechanisms in an attempt to protect himself from more suffering, it also gave him an understanding of the weaknesses and failings of men. He received his full share of bereavement, not only losing many of his dear friends but his only child to be born alive, who lived but for a short time after a premature birth in 1542.[29] He was deserted and let down by other friends, robbed by his servant, banished from Geneva from 1538 to 1541, and constantly opposed by those who took a laxer view of morality as well as suffering from ill-health.

---

[27] *Ibid.*, p. 436.
[28] T. H. L. Parker's recent biography of *John Calvin* does much to correct the picture. There are two other essays on Calvin as a pastor: Mayer, *Pastoral Care*, pp. 113–133 and J. van Zyl, 'John Calvin the Pastor' in *The Way Ahead*, pp. 69–78.
[29] Parker, *Calvin*, pp. 69f. and p. 102.

Added to this were the other disappointments of his family life. His younger brother Antoine had an unsuccessful marriage and his wife was accused, but acquitted, of adultery in 1548, only to be found guilty of the offence in 1557. Even more devastating to Calvin was the conviction of his step-daughter Judith for adultery, after which 'for a few days he was too ashamed even to leave his house'.[30]

A true picture of Calvin must give plenty of attention to his pastoral activity. Van Zyl says of him, that 'He robbed himself of sleep. His home was always open to anyone seeking advice. He was constantly in touch with all the affairs of church and state. He visited the sick and lackadaisical, and knew almost every citizen'. In January 1542, Calvin wrote: 'Since my arrival here (in September 1542) I can only remember having been granted two hours in which no one had come and disturbed me.'[31] We know that he took his fair share of routine pastoral work, for between 1550 and 1559 Calvin performed 170 weddings and about fifty baptisms. In addition to which he regularly presided over the Venerable Company of preachers who managed the ministry and the church alike.

The pastoral principles which Calvin sought to lay down for the Reformed church are to be found in the *Ecclesiastical Ordinances* of 1541 and his *Institutes of the Christian Religion*. The church is not in any way incidental to a Christian's spiritual development. 'We see that God, who might perfect his people in a moment, chooses not to bring them to manhood in any other way than by education of the church.'[32] The church is a school from which the Christian never graduates. As in any school, the emphasis falls on the teaching and instruction to be given, but Calvin, like all good educationalists, recognizes that the teaching is not given in a vacuum. There needs to be a genuine care for the pupils if the atmosphere is to be conducive to learning. So, for example, much attention is given to the care of the sick. The *Ordinances* laid it down that no-one was to be confined to bed for three days without the pastors being informed, so that they could bring comfort from God's word. People were not to be reluctant to send for them and it was certainly not to be left until death was at the door before the

[30] *Ibid.*, p. 102 and van Zyl, 'Calvin the Pastor', p. 76.
[31] van Zyl, 'Calvin the Pastor', p. 73.
[32] J. Calvin, *Institutes of the Christian Religion*, 4.1.5, p. 284.

minister was called.[33]

The teachers and administrators of the school fell into four categories. They were pastors, teachers (called doctors), elders or deacons. Other New Testament offices Calvin thought to have been only temporary and their duties to have been subsumed under these four. The work of the pastor was 'to proclaim the Word of God, to instruct, admonish, exhort and censure, both in public and private, to administer the sacraments and to enjoin brotherly corrections along with the elders and colleagues'.[34] High standards of life and doctrine were expected of them and two lists of offences were proposed. The first list contained such things as heresy, schism, criminal offences, 'dances and similar dissoluteness', which were to lead to dismissal. The second list, which chiefly involved laxity in performing one's duties or the pursuit of idle questions, was to lead only to fraternal admonition.[35]

Doctors had the responsibility of preserving the purity of the gospel and instructing the faithful in the truth.[36] Elders were senior laymen selected from the congregation to join with the pastors in the administration of discipline.[37] Deacons were to be employed in the distribution of alms or the care of the poor.[38]

The substance of the teaching was the word of God which, coupled with the sacraments, would 'uniformly display its efficacy' wherever it was received and welcomed, even if it did not always bear immediate fruit.[39] So strong was the theological conviction that this was God's chosen method of imparting life and growth that preaching became the primary task of the pastor. This conviction equally had implications for the character of preaching. It was to be the exposition of Scripture and to follow an essentially systematic method, because this would enable the word of God to speak most clearly for itself.

The most impressive feature of Calvin's Geneva is the seriousness with which the teaching of the word of God was taken. It was not sufficient to expound it publicly and then leave it to the people to adhere to it or not as they chose. The word was

[33] J. Calvin, 'Draft Ecclesiastical Ordinances', in *Theological Treatises*, p. 68.
[34] 'Ordinances', p. 58 and *Institutes*, 4.3.4, pp. 318f.   [35] 'Ordinances', pp. 60f.
[36] *Ibid.*, pp. 62f.   [37] *Ibid.*, p. 63 and *Institutes*, 4.3.8, pp. 321f.
[38] 'Ordinances', p. 64 and *Institutes*, 4.3.9, p. 322.
[39] *Institutes*, 4.1.10, p. 289. See also Parker, *Calvin*, pp. 89–96.

to be taught both publicly and privately, so that its message could be driven home with greater effect. Without such discipline Calvin envisaged the church would fall apart. Only the addition of private admonition and correction would save it from becoming lethargic. Following Bucer, and citing Paul in Acts 20:20 as his example, he wrote: 'Here especially is there occasion for the vigilance of pastors and presbyters whose duty is not only to preach to the people, but to exhort and admonish from house to house, whenever their hearers have not profitted sufficiently by general teaching . . .'[40]

The eldership system of discipline might appear to have all the overtones of 'big brother', but its spirit, when Calvin introduced it to Geneva, was very different. Far from being legalistic and crippling it was intended to be life-giving and spiritually wholesome. When seen in the context of the unreformed pastoral and penitential practices of the church of Rome it was a magnificent instrument for the protection and healthy development of the flock. It permitted the word of God to invade every area of the Christian's life and broke with the idea that spirituality should be confined within the church. It stressed the importance of not being indifferent to the word of God. It enabled lay folk to be involved in the pastoral care of the church. Pastoral care was no longer a matter for full-time professionals alone. It introduced a system which enabled the church to grow strong organically. Calvin referred to it as 'the sinews' of the church which allowed the body to adhere together.[41] If it did not go quite as far as that of the New Testament in permitting an even fuller mutual ministry, it was none the less a decisive step away from the pastorally suicidal path of Rome.

RICHARD BAXTER

The ripest fruit of the Reformation's pastoral theology is to be seen in the ministry of Richard Baxter (1615–91). Having served as a curate in Kidderminster, Baxter left to become an army chaplain, first at Coventry and then with the New Model Army, for five years, before being petitioned to return by the parishioners as vicar of Kidderminster in 1647. He stayed there

[40] *Institutes*, 4.12.1, 2, pp. 453–454.
[41] *Institutes*, 4.12.1, p. 453. Robert M. Kingdon, *Geneva and the Coming of the Wars of Religion*, gives a fascinating picture of the pastoral training given in the Academy of Geneva.

until 1661, when the Restoration changed his fortunes and led to his spending the rest of his life living in various places as a writer and private preacher who was periodically subject to imprisonments and fines for his activities.[42]

Baxter does not easily conform to neat categories. He was, in James Packer's words, 'a brilliant cross-bencher'.[43] He was ill-at-ease with much that he saw during the Civil War and even more out of place once the monarchy had been restored. The result was that much of his brilliance was channelled into his writing. Yet he was no mere theoretician, as his success at Kidderminster shows. On his arrival there in many of the streets only one family worshipped God, but when he left only one family in each side of the street did not. His congregation was a thousand strong, which, considering Kidderminster had only 800 homes and a population of 2,000, was remarkable. Six years after his leaving and despite much opposition he could claim that none had fallen away from God.[44] We can only guess what he might have accomplished had the circumstances of his life allowed him a more active ministry.

In *The Reformed Pastor* Baxter gives us a comprehensive insight into his philosophy of ministry. It was written in 1656 for the Worcester Association of Ministers. Baxter had been due to preach at a day they had set aside for humiliation and prayer, but ill-health, from which he suffered much, prevented him from keeping the appointment and so he set down, in expanded form, what he had intended to share. As a result we have a work which, although it betrays a paternalistic approach to ministry, is rightly considered 'the outstanding early protestant text on the subject'.[45] The work is an extended commentary on Acts 20:28 and shows Baxter's main concerns were the motivation and methodology of the ministry.

The ministry demanded 'skill, resolution and unwearied diligence' and was not a burden to place on the shoulders of a child.[46] But there were more basic requirements too. The pastor needed to be a converted man. If he was not, his preaching, rather than saving him, was likely to be a snare to him, for it

[42] G. F. Nuttall, *Richard Baxter*.

[43] J. I. Packer, 'Introduction' to R. Baxter, *The Reformed Pastor*, p. 9.

[44] *Ibid.*, pp. 11f.

[45] McNeill, *Cure of Souls*, p. 180. On the charge of paternalism see Mayer, *Pastoral Care*, p. 147.

[46] Baxter, *Reformed Pastor*, pp. 69f.

would lull him into a state of false spiritual consciousness and give him the impression that he was saved.

The pastor needed to be spiritually mature, seeking after godliness, and spiritually lively. If the pastor's spirituality grew cold so would that of the flock. But if he found himself at low ebb, he need not stay there. By resorting to the spiritual disciplines, by reading some stirring book or through meditating on some great subject he could rouse himself. To neglect these disciplines was not only harmful to himself but to his people. 'We are nurses of Christ's little ones. If we forbear taking food ourselves, we shall famish them; it will soon be visible in their leanness, and dull discharge of their several duties.'[47] The pastor should also be spiritually consistent. Baxter lamented the sort of man who would spend the whole week preparing to preach two sermons and yet not spend a single hour studying how to live all the week long. Nothing was more injurious to the success of the ministry.

Such care was to be shown, 'for you have a heaven to win or lose and souls that must be happy or miserable for ever'.[48] The work of the ministry was one of eternal significance and should therefore be approached with due seriousness. It was evident that Satan took it seriously and Baxter shows an acute consciousness of being engaged in spiritual warfare. The ministry was about demolishing the kingdom of darkness, but 'If you will be the leaders against the princes of darkness, (the tempter) will spare you no further than God restraineth him. He beareth the greatest malice to those that are engaged to do him the greatest mischief'.[49] Even so, Baxter's expectation was one of success. That this expectation was missing in so many ministers accounted for their lack of seeing people converted and growing. He confessed that he would find it hard to continue labouring where there was no fruit and believed it right, in such circumstances, to leave that parish and labour elsewhere, so that God might bring someone else into that place who could bear fruit.[50]

Baxter sets out a seven-fold remit for the pastor. Of prime importance was his labour for the conversion of the unconverted. Their needs should take precedence over the needs of the godly, just as a doctor would attend first to a dying man

[47] *Ibid.*, p. 61.   [48] *Ibid.*, p. 72.   [49] *Ibid.*, p. 43 and p. 74.
[50] *Ibid.*, pp. 121f.

rather than one suffering from mere toothache.[51] Secondly, enquirers under conviction of sin needed to be advised. Thirdly, those who were already Christians needed building up. Then, families needed to be watched, the sick needed visiting and offenders needed to be admonished. Lastly, the pastor needed to be conscientious in his exercise of church discipline. Baxter sets down the procedure for this, beginning with private reproof and leading, if necessary, through to public excommunication. To him, negligence here was as serious as negligence in preaching and in both cases the negligent pastor deserved to be dismissed from office.[52]

Superficially, Baxter's pastor appears to be stern, in deadly earnest, possessed of great authority, and perhaps even punitive. But that would be a one-sided reading of Baxter, who firmly places those aspects of pastoral ministry in the context of the need for a close and loving relationship between the pastor and his people. In one way or another he constantly reiterates this theme. The preacher is to know how to get inside people rather than assume that they will hear and obey because he has told them to, and that demands a close knowledge of the flock.[53] Each one is important and should be personally known.[54] Personal catechizing would beneficially bring pastor and people closer together. It would, for example, enable doubters to feel free to open up their minds to their pastors. 'By distance and unacquaintedness, abundance of mistakes between ministers and people are fomented.'[55] His general principle was that 'The whole of our ministry must be carried on in tender love to our people. We must let them see that nothing pleaseth us but what profiteth them; and that what doeth them good doeth us good; and that nothing troubleth us more than their hurt.'[56]

Since the pulpit was to be one of the chief methods of achieving a pastor's aims, Baxter has much to say about preaching. To him it was a sad thing to preach a congregation to sleep. But there was a worse crime, and that was for the preacher to preach himself asleep. The word of God was a living force and should produce life in its hearers.[57] But even more significant than preaching was his discovery of the value of personally catechizing people. He claimed it was no new inven-

[51] *Ibid.*, p. 95.   [52] *Ibid.*, pp. 104–111 and p. 171.   [53] *Ibid.*, p. 65.
[54] *Ibid.*, p. 90.   [55] *Ibid.*, p. 177.   [56] *Ibid.*, p. 117.   [57] *Ibid.*, p. 134.

tion, merely a restoration of the ancient ministerial work, and he was convinced of the expediency of the method. Speaking of his own parishoners, he wrote,

> But most of them have an ungrounded trust in Christ, hoping that he will pardon, justify and save them, while the world hath their hearts, and they live in the flesh. And this trust they take for justifying faith. I have found by experience, that some ignorant persons, who have been so long unprofitable hearers, have got more knowledge and remorse of conscience in half an hour's close discourse, than they did in ten years' of public preaching.[58]

His own practice was to devote Monday and Tuesdays to catechizing. Once the catechisms had been delivered he would see each family on a systematic basis. They would be visited a week beforehand and an appointment fixed for them to call on Baxter. When the time came he would spend about an hour with them, teaching and questioning their understanding of the catechism and giving them whatever spiritual direction was appropriate. In this way he saw about fifteen or sixteen families a week and covered the whole parish in a year. Baxter was an enthusiast for personal catechizing and devoted a major section of *The Reformed Pastor* to extolling its virtues and setting out its principles.[59] He believed it to be the chief means by which the church had been reformed in the past and the chief means of hope for the nation in the future.[60]

Baxter saw the pastor as essentially a teacher and bent all his efforts to that end. In addition to preaching and personal tuition, he frequently gave away Bibles and Christian books and held a regular Thursday evening house group where the group briefly went over his sermon once more and then discussed it before one of them would lead the rest in prayer.[61]

The Reformed Pastor at one and the same time reaches the heavens whilst having its feet firmly planted on the ground. It is an immensely spiritual book. It reveals the awesome spiritual dimensions of the pastoral office, the spiritual temptations to which pastors are vulnerable, the spiritual conflicts they have to endure as well as the spiritual resources which are theirs.

[58] *Ibid.*, p. 196. See also p. 43.   [59] *Ibid.*, pp. 172–256.   [60] *Ibid.*, p. 189.
[61] Packer, 'Introduction', *ibid.*, p. 13.

But without any indication of tension, the book also reveals an acutely practical mind. It is concerned about the number of people a pastor can have in his flock before he needs assistance, about the pastor's physical fitness and about the details of executing a plan for personally catechizing the parish. This mature balance displays the legacy of the Reformation at its best. In the light of the continuing value of Baxter's *Reformed Pastor*, who can doubt that it was providence that kept him from attending the meeting of the Worcester Association on 4 December 1655? Had he gone, his contemporaries might have benefited, but we might well have been left without one of the greatest works on pastoral ministry of all time.

THE WIDER LEGACY

The Reformation had planted an orchard in which a variety of fruit was grown. Richard Baxter's work may well have been the ripest and most delicious of the crop, but it certainly did not grow alone. Within the Reformed churches of the Continent there was much reflection on the nature of the ministry following the Reformation.[62] But its effect was far wider than the churches of Lutheranism and Calvinism.

In Anglicanism there was a new concern to raise the quality of spiritual care and the standards of the ministry.[63] One indication of the change can be seen in George Herbert's *The Country Parson* published, after his death, in 1652. George Herbert (1593–1633) came from an aristocratic English family and served as Public Orator for Cambridge University and, briefly, as a Member of Parliament before entering the ministry. He is better known for his poetry than for his prose, but *The Country Parson* affords a rare insight into mainstream Anglican, if not early Anglo-Catholic, views of the ministry. He probably wrote it when preparing himself to serve a larger parish, Bemerton, in about 1628.[64] He does not claim that he lived up to its ideals, only that it was 'a mark to aim at'.

'A Pastor', he wrote, 'is the deputy of Christ for the reducing of Man to the Obedience of God.'[65] From that definition all else

---

[62] For details see McNeill, *Cure of Souls*, pp. 181–191 and 209–216.

[63] *Ibid.*, pp. 218–239.

[64] For George Herbert's life see J. N. Wall's 'Introduction' to Herbert's *The Country Parson* and *The Temple*, pp. 1–53.

[65] *Ibid.*,I, p. 55.

followed. His personal manner was to be holy, just, prudent, temperate, bold, grave, patient and self-denying. He was to be generally sad, knowing little but the cross of Christ. If he were married – and celibacy was to be preferred – then his home was to be a model for the parish.[66] He was to be the centre of the life of the parish, loving its old customs where these were harmless. He was to show knowledge about rural matters such as tillage and pastorage, but also to act as the teacher, lawyer and doctor for his people.[67] He was to be a man of some status and George Herbert displays a consciousness of this in his attitude to different classes. The poor were to be shown charity and provided with money, whereas the better off were to be shown courtesy and provided with hospitality. Occasionally the poor might be invited to a meal but chiefly, it would seem, with the purpose of aiding the parson's humility.[68]

The spiritual duties of the parson were principally three-fold. Firstly he was to conduct the worship of the church and administer the sacraments both within the church and to the sick at home, for 'how comfortable and sovereign medicine it is to all sin-sick souls'.[69]

Secondly, he was to instruct people in the faith through preaching and catechizing. The pulpit was 'his joy and his throne' and it exercised tremendous spiritual power, for none ever left the church the same as he came in since the word preached would be his judge. The sermon consisted in taking a text and showing the congregation its plain meaning, after which a few pertinent observations were to be added. For all the high view Herbert had of preaching he was not blind to its limitations. Realistically (?) he wrote, 'The Parson exceeds not an hour in preaching, because all ages have thought that a competency, and he that profits not in that time, will less afterwards, the same affection which made him not profit before, making him then weary, and so he grows from not relishing, to loathing.'[70] Later, he admitted that in the sermon people could sleep or wander and therein lay the value of catechizing, for it was impossible to do this when being questioned. Catechizing infused knowledge into individuals, multiplied and built up the flock and inspired them to practise what they had

[66] *Ibid.*, III, p. 56; XXVII, p. 94; IX, p. 66; X, p. 68.
[67] *Ibid.*, XXXV, p. 109; IV, p. 58; XXIII, p. 87.   [68] *Ibid.*, XI, pp. 71f.
[69] *Ibid.*, XV, p. 77.   [70] *Ibid.*, VII, pp. 62–64.

heard. Although not taken to the same lengths as Baxter, the same confidence in the catechism is evident in Herbert.[71]

The third aspect of his work was visiting. On a Sunday after his public duties were completed, 'The rest of the day he spends either in reconciling neighbours that are at variance, or in visiting the sick, or in exhortations to some of his flock by themselves, whom his sermons cannot, or do not reach. And everyone is awakened, when we come and say "Thou art the man".'[72] Similarly, during the week the parson is tirelessly engaged in such personal care, adapting his approach to the needs of those he visits. Those religiously employed he commends. Those about their secular work he also commends, but advises them not to invest all their energies in such work but to work for heaven too. The idle

> he chides not at first, for that were neither civil, nor profitable; but always in the close, before he departs from them: yet in this he distinguisheth; for if he be a plain countryman, he reproves him plainly; for they are not sensible of fineness: if they be of higher quality, they commonly are quick, and sensible, and very tender of reproof: and therefore he lays his discourse so, that he comes to the point very leisurely, and oftentimes, as *Nathan* did, in the person of another, making them to reprove themselves.[73]

Herbert's rhetorical style and seventeenth-century outlook gives the appearance of a quaintness in his advice. His parson is as paternalistic as Baxter's pastor, but there are differences between them. There is a much gentler atmosphere in Herbert and, although alive to the serious spiritual nature of his duty, he lacks the spiritual intensity of the Puritans. Nowhere does Herbert refer to the need for conversion; rather he starts from the assumption that all have spiritual life even if it is less evident in some than others. Consequently, though many of the words and concerns may seem to be the same between Herbert and Baxter, the end product is very different.

The Reformation's legacy with regard to pastoral theology was not only wide in extent but profound in its effect. Among the Puritans there developed a widespread and detailed concern

---

[71] *Ibid.*, XXI, pp. 82–85.   [72] *Ibid.*, VIII, p. 65.   [73] *Ibid.*, XIV, p. 76.

with spiritual counselling, dealing with such issues as depression (which seems to have been a common problem), lack of assurance, afflictions, temptation and falling into sin. The great names of the Puritan era, John Owen, Thomas Brooks, Richard Sibbes, Robert Bolton, Thomas Manton, Thomas Goodwin and William Gurnall all adopted this pastoral perspective in their writing of theology.[74]

Three comments may be noted about their approach. Firstly, before any advice was offered they believed it necessary to discern the spiritual state of the one seeking counsel. There was a world of difference between how one handled a child of light walking in darkness and a child of darkness walking in light.[75] The remedy for the former was a careful examination of the causes of his problem followed by the application of Scripture and the prescription of practical steps to be taken. The latter could know no remedy until first he had come to life in Christ. Until the problem led to a conviction of sin and the law had done its work in moving them to repentance and to seek grace, any superficial spiritual counsel could be eternally misleading.

Secondly, the Puritans worked on the basis of what today would be called a case-study approach. Their writings are not only illustrated by their experiences in handling individuals and their problems, but constructed on the basis of those individuals and problems. The problem was approached with thoroughness. It was stated and all its possible causes would then be listed and examined. The answer was always anchored in Scripture and care was always taken to expose false leads. Depression, for example, may come because of sin, weak grace, failure in duty, lack of assurance, temptation, backsliding, adverse circumstances or uselessness.[76] The cure came not in dealing with the general but the specific cause, and the way in which it would affect different types of people.

Thirdly, the remedy was a mixture of the application of Scripture and practical advice. The one who showed evidence of justifying faith was encouraged to see the wider purposes of God in permitting his experience before being exhorted to believe the appropriate promises or teachings of Scripture. But

[74] E. Hulse, 'The Puritans and Counselling Troubled Souls', *Foundations* 8 (1982), pp. 6–28. For a deeper survey see P. Lewis, *The Genius of Puritanism*, pp. 63–136.
[75] Hulse, 'Counselling Troubled Souls', p. 23. The wording is that of Thomas Goodwin.
[76] *Ibid.*, p. 13 taken from William Bridge's *Lifting Up of the Downcast*.

he was not left with that alone. A study of the Scripture was intermingled with the giving of practical advice. Erroll Hulse has drawn attention to the example of Thomas Brooks in his advice to those who lack assurance. They were to be active in exercising grace, to be obedient, to follow the Holy Spirit diligently, to attend the ordinances regularly, to meditate on the scope of God's mercy, to examine the differences between believers and unbelievers, to seek to grow in grace, to seek assurance when the soul was in its best frame and to discover whether they were lacking in any of the things, like love or knowledge, which should accompany salvation.[77]

The intensity of their approach and possible morbid introspection it might encourage does not fit well with the spirit of our own times. Even so Peter Lewis' summary of their approach is an apt tribute to their skill:

The Puritans were physicians of the soul, skilled enough to avoid the vagueness and subjectiveness which leaves the anguished mind clutching at uncertain straws with uncertain hope. They believed the Word of God in Scripture to be comprehensive enough to cover every basic human situation and need, and knew their Scriptures well enough to apply, with responsible authority, the available salve to the exposed sore. They were also clear, logical and fearless enough to set before the confused believer his state in an orderly fashion, quietly and clearly making the 'patient' understand his particular stress, what it issued from and where relief from it lay. People were thus turned back from side-issues and from obsession with mere symptoms to the real needs and proper resorts of the soul in that condition.[78]

SUMMARY

The Reformation had thus profoundly affected the nature of the ministry. It had revived something of the spirit it originally had in the early church and set it on a much surer course for the future. It restored its spiritual character and rejected its compromise with the world. It renewed its spiritual heart and

[77] *Ibid.*, pp. 14f. and Thomas Brooks, *Heaven on Earth*.
[78] Lewis, *Genius of Puritanism*, p. 65.

rejected its reliance on external rites. It revived its spiritual power and rejected the silly threats of purgatory, releasing the word of God to be, once more, an effective spiritual instrument in the hands of skilful pastors.

10

The Evangelical Revival and its sequel

THE EVANGELICAL REVIVAL

The Evangelical Revival was to quicken concern for the nature and work of the ministry after almost a century of neglect and decay by the mainstream churches. For all John Wesley's (1703–91) loyalty to the Church of England and his reluctance to break from it, it was inevitable that the new wine of the Spirit-led revival should rupture the old wineskins of a worldly and complacent established church.

John Wesley's views on the ministry were originally, in theory, those of a perfectly orthodox Church of England clergyman. But whatever his theory, from his conversion onwards he engaged in practices which were to bring him into conflict with what was considered acceptable. Many considered his preaching irregular since he did not confine himself to accepted parish ministry. He rounded on his critics that his preaching was perfectly consistent with his ordination at which the Archbishop of Canterbury had charged, 'Take thou authority to preach the Gospel'. Was he to neglect his charge and stand idly by while others were neglecting it too? His use of lay-preachers was also considered irregular and a cause of concern. Wesley considered these a practical necessity and believed they could be justified theologically. So from early days the seeds of division had been sown. His own genius prevented this inherent tension from becoming an outright schism in his own day, but not from developing and imposing immense strains on the movement.

Writing to his brother Charles, John stated, 'Your business, as well as mine, is to save souls. When we took priests' orders, we undertook to make it our one business. I think every day lost which is not (mainly at least) employed in this thing; *sum totus in illo.*' ('I am complete in this work.')[1] But that was not

[1] J. Wesley, *The Letters of John Wesley*, vol. 5, 26 April 1772, p. 316.

the sum total of the work as he was shortly to admit. In a subsequent letter he wrote,

> This is the great work: not only to bring souls to believe in Christ but to build them up in our most holy faith. How grievously are they mistaken who imagine that as soon as the children are born they need take no more care of them! We do not find it so. The chief care then begins.[2]

How was this work to be carried out, in view of the vast masses who were being converted? The answer was to unite the converts into societies where they could encourage one another to flee the world and through the practice of the regular spiritual disciplines, including attendance at public worship, make progress in holiness. Under the umbrella of the society two smaller groups or cells operated.[3] The most common of these, the class meeting, provided for the pastoral care of the members of the society and acted as a disciplinary agent at the same time. In Wesley's view it was the core of the whole structure. Membership of a Wesleyan society meant essentially membership of a class and the possession of a class ticket. Here advice, reproof, comfort and exhortation were given and an offering made for the relief of the poor. It was as a means of collecting money that classes arose, but they quickly became meetings for fellowship and fraternal correction. In these groups those whose discipleship did not live up to standard could easily be detected and, if intransigent, could be expelled, or more often expel themselves. The class leader could also keep the preacher in close touch with the progress or needs of the flock.

The second cellular structure was the band, a form which Wesley had adopted from the Moravians and which existed before the advent of the class meeting. The bands were small group confessionals where people could pour out their hearts to one another as they had need and were particularly remedial and therapeutic in character. They were more intimate and intense than the class meeting and as a safeguard were usually

---

[2] *Ibid.*, 4 November 1772, p. 344.

[3] F. Baker, 'The People Called Methodist – 3. Polity', in R. Davies and G. Rupp (eds), *A History of the Methodist Church in Great Britain*, vol. 1, pp. 219–225.

composed on the basis of sex and marriage status.[4]

The cellular structure has proved its value time and again in the history of the church. It is an ideally flexible structure which lends itself to growth, since it can easily expand. It facilitates newcomers' entry to a larger group whilst providing them with supportive personal relationships and instruction at the level they need. At the same time the relationship between the leaders and the commitment of the groups to the overall society ensure that the society itself is strong, tight-knit and coherent. Wesley did not invent such a structure but he saw and exploited its pastoral potential during the years of the Evangelical Revival.[5]

The development of the Methodist societies was not originally intended to detract from faithful attendance at the parish church, but merely to provide a holiness society within the church. But it was unavoidable that their existence should eventually lead to a divorce between the society and the church, since the former provided a spiritual satisfaction absent from the latter. That being so, a host of supplementary questions demanded an answer. Who was to lead? What were their responsibilities? Did their duties include the administration of the sacraments? What was their status in relation to the ordained ministry? What was their relationship to their people to be?

In his famous sermon 'On the Ministerial Office' Wesley drew a sharp distinction between the work of the preacher and that of the priest. He made it clear that it had never been his intention that those whom he appointed as preachers should envisage themselves as priests with a right to administer the sacraments. His text, Hebrews 5:4, was chosen to expose the error of men who desired such a status and as a basis for warning them that if they assumed the office of priest they would be expelled from the connexion. 'Now, as long as the Methodist keep to this plan', he claimed, 'they cannot separate from the Church. And this is our peculiar glory.'[6] He urged his preachers to keep within their bounds and to be content to view themselves as the extraordinary messengers of God who would

[4] A. Skevington Wood, *The Inextinguishable Blaze*, pp. 186–195.

[5] See further, W. Dean, 'Successful House Groups – Lessons from History', *Church Growth Digest* (Autumn–Spring 1983–1984).

[6] J. Wesley, *Sermons on Several Occasions*, vol. 3, Sermon 115, 'The Ministerial Office', pp. 307–316.

provoke the regular messengers of God to better things, not take over from them.

It was not a distinction which was easy to maintain and increasingly the Methodist preachers became more and more indistinguishable from a regular ministry and sought, and in some cases were granted, ordination.[7] But a number of rules were designed to prevent them from becoming regular ministers. Originally they had been introduced as Wesley's personal assistants to help him in the government and growth of the societies. Their basic rules reveal the spiritual qualifications expected of them.[8] In summary they were:

1. Be diligent, never be unemployed a moment, never be triflingly employed.
2. Be serious. Let your motto be 'Holiness unto the Lord'.
3. Touch no woman.
4. Believe evil of no-one.
5. Speak evil of no-one.
6. Tell everyone what you think wrong in him, and that plainly, and as soon as may be, else it will fester in your heart.
7. Do nothing as a Gentleman . . . you are the servant of all.
8. Be ashamed of nothing but sin.
9. Take no money of any one.
10. Contract no debt without my knowledge.
11. Be punctual.
12. Act in all things not according to your own will but as a son of the Gospel.

Wesley never forsook this spiritual perspective on the pastoral leadership. He was far more concerned about the nature of its function than he was about the shape of the office. The test of ministry was practical. Was the man doing the work of an evangelist or not? If so he was fulfilling his ministry. If not, no office or title could ever turn him into a minister.[9] If his assistant was fulfilling his role as an evangelist then he was bound to

---

[7] See A. B. Lawson, *John Wesley and the Christian Ministry* and J. Kent, *Jabez Bunting: The Last Wesleyan*.

[8] Lawson, *Wesley and the Christian Ministry*, pp. 32f.   [9] *Ibid.*, p. 83.

incur pastoral responsibilities, for those whom he had fathered in Christ would 'desire him to watch over them, to build them up in the faith, and to guide their souls in the paths of righteousness'. It was a natural fatherly relationship which they enjoyed.[10]

It was entirely consistent with this understanding of the pastoral relationship that the pastor should exercise authority over his people. In Wesley's view the failure to grasp the importance of the principle of obedience to pastoral leaders was a major hindrance to the grace of God having full effect in people's lives. Yet he was not advocating authoritarianism. The authority was to be exercised persuasively and gently, not in a domineering fashion.

The convert needed guidance about matters which were 'indifferent'. If God had commanded something, there was no question but that he should do it. If God had forbidden something, there was no question but that he should avoid it. But what about the rest of matters which fell in between? That is where the pastor stepped in. 'The sum is, it is the duty of every private Christian to obey his spiritual pastor by either doing or leaving undone anything of an indifferent nature; anything that is in no way determined in the word of God.'[11] Wesley drove his message home by asking his hearers how seriously they had taken his oft-repeated teaching about the style of dress they were to adopt! Here was no unimportant issue. Failure to obey pastoral direction would grieve the Holy Spirit and cause deadness of soul.

The example Wesley chose on this occasion is instructive. Much of Wesley's teaching was practical and moral in character. Though competent as a theologian, he was essentially practical in orientation when instructing his followers. His great concern was that they should steadily conquer inward sin and aim for entire sanctification or perfection which he believed to be attainable in this life. His statements on the theory of perfection may leave something to be desired as far as clarity is concerned, but there can be no doubt about the importance he placed on every Christian aiming for perfection. His advocacy of perfectionism demonstrated both his rejection of antinomianism and the concrete nature of what he meant by holiness. Perfection meant

10 Kent, *Jabez Bunting*, pp. 11f.
11 Wesley, 'On obedience to Pastors', *Sermons*, p. 127.

perfect love.[12]

In setting out who these spiritual guides were to be, Wesley side-steps the question of church government in favour of devoting time to an outline of what the pastor should do.

> They are supposed to go before the flock . . . and to guide them in all the ways of truth and holiness; they are to 'nourish them with words of eternal life'; to feed them with the 'pure milk of the word': applying it continually 'for doctrine', teaching them all the essential doctrines contained therein; 'for reproof'; warning them if they turn aside from the way, to the right hand or to the left; 'for correction'; showing them how to amend what is amiss, and guiding them back into the way of peace; – and 'for instruction in righteousness'; training them up to outward holiness, 'until they come to the perfect man, to the measure of the stature of the fulness of Christ'.[13]

These objectives could be fulfilled only if there was a secure and trustful relationship between the pastor and his people. Wesley knew that no-one could guide a soul unless that person consented to it. If the consent was withdrawn it was impossible to continue to guide and a separation had in effect taken place. There was no spiritual value in trying to impose authority; authority rested on the consent being granted.[14]

The second generation of Wesleyans did not live up to the high ideals of their founder. The class meeting became increasingly repetitive and ceased to be an effective means of spiritual growth.[15] Pastoral leadership became increasing formalized like any other ecclesiastical ministry.[16] But what Wesley had achieved had far wider implications than for the Methodists alone. The repercussions of his view of the ministry and of pastoral care spread into the other mainline churches, which during the late eighteenth and early nineteenth centuries also revived under the warm winds of the Spirit.

---

[12] J. Lawson, 'The People Called Methodists – 2. Our Discipline', pp. 183–209 and R. Davies, 'The People Called Methodists – 1. Our Doctrine', pp. 168–173, in Davies and Rupp, *History*.

[13] J. Wesley, 'On Obedience to Pastors', p. 123.

[14] A. B. Lawson, *Wesley and the Christian Ministry*, p. 35.

[15] H. D. Rack, 'The Decline of the Class Meeting and the Problem of Church Membership in Nineteenth–century Wesleyanism', *Proceedings of the Wesleyan Historical Society* 39 (1973), pp. 12–21.

[16] Kent, *Jabez Bunting*, pp. 38–50.

REVIVED EVANGELICALISM

Wesley's effect on the Church of England can be traced in the ministry of a man such as Charles Simeon (1759–1836) of Cambridge, where he became vicar of Holy Trinity in 1782, remaining there until his death. Simeon conducted his ministry with a spiritual conscientiousness which was notably lacking in most of his fellow clergyman. It commenced in the face of great opposition, which made it impossible for him to visit his parishioners. So he organized a Bible study group and prayer meeting for the faithful few one evening per week. Out of this single meeting grew a system of group meetings, modelled on the pattern of Wesley, which he visited in turn. Others he cared for through a visiting society, members of which were responsible for visiting the sick, providing relief for the poor and at the same time bringing instruction for the souls of those they visited. The society operated quite simply by dividing the whole parish into areas and making a visitor responsible for the needs of that area. The visitors would then meet together once a month to share their needs and experiences.[17]

Simeon's contribution to pastoral theology extended beyond devising a system for the adequate pastoral care of his parish. Perhaps his greater contribution lies in the interest he showed in inspiring and training students who felt themselves called to the ministry. In 1792 he began sermon classes with fifteen to twenty students attending at a time. He advocated the use of notes rather than read sermons and gave very practical advice about sermon construction and delivery and how not to weary one's listeners. Then in 1813 on Friday evenings he began what has been called a 'one man's Brains Trust',[18] where he answered any questions students cared to throw at him. Numerous other meetings and small groups, during which Simeon would exercise scrupulous care in noting the details of any newcomers so as to follow them up later, meant that he made a tremendous impact on the next generation of Anglican clergymen and convinced many sceptics to become evangelicals. Unofficial though his work may have been, it succeeded in having a profound effect.

Simeon was not an original theologian but he was certainly

17 H. E. Hopkins, *Charles Simeon of Cambridge*, p. 47.
18 *Ibid.*, p. 89.

a pastoral theologian in the fullest sense of the term. As a pastor he was theologically literate and aware, and as a theologian he was pastorally sensitive and selective. 'His great achievement', wrote Douglas Webster, 'was the way in which he interpreted and stated the doctrines of Scripture so as to help men live their Christian life.'[19] His sermons and letters show him to have been a realist as far as the Christian life was concerned. He never underestimated its difficulties nor the Christians' need for support and encouragement.

His realism led him to reject a systematic approach to doctrine and helped him to discern the validity of certain doctrinal positions. So he refused to side totally with either the Calvinist or Arminian sides of the debate that then raged. He believed them right in what they both affirmed and wrong in what they denied.[20] The doctrine of election was the best possible antidote to despair and many weak and sickly Christians found it a great medicine. But to overstress the doctrine of the final perseverance of the saints was disastrous for many Christians who needed a voice of warning and for young Christians in particular who could be saved from being overconfident if confronted with the possibility of falling away.

Christianity was, to Simeon, not a doctrinal system to be accepted but a remedy to be applied. The primary evidence of regeneration was not the mental acceptance of facts but a brokenness of life and a self-loathing humility. He saw that Christians needed a strong doctrine of the church and sacraments if they were to progress, and this was to be found in his preaching. Certain teachings he considered pastorally hazardous. Among these were Wesley's idea of perfection, which he rejected as a delusion.

As a pastoral theologian Simeon was among both the most gifted and the most rare of his generation. He succeeded not only in shaping a true biblical theology which met the needs of the congregation, but in providing a model for ministry which many followed subsequently.

The Evangelical Revival not only brought new life and confidence to the evangelicals of the Church of England, but also an entirely new lease of life to the moribund, doctrinally

---

[19] D. Webster, 'Simeon's Pastoral Theology', in A. Pollard and M. Hennell (eds), *Charles Simeon 1759–1836*, p. 118. This whole section owes much to this article.
[20] *Ibid.*, p. 75.

sterile and socially paralysed churches of nonconformity. John Angell James (1785–1859) might serve as an early representative of the changes which occurred among them in their attitude to ministry. James became the minister of Carrs Lane Congregational Church, Birmingham, in 1806 and experienced seven years of ineffectiveness and discouragement before seeing any fruit for his labour. Resisting attempts to desert his calling he remained in Birmingham and eventually became a successful pastor, a popular preacher and a denominational statesman. In the course of his ministry his congregation more than quadrupled, until his church was regularly attended by two thousand people.[21]

In addition to the numerous ordination addresses which set out James' view of the ministry, he wrote one extensive work setting out the central question, as he saw it, facing the ministry in his time. It was called *An Earnest Ministry the Want of the Times*. He saw the ministry as a dignified and honourable office since, following 2 Corinthians 5:20, it was an embassy on behalf of God. Its grand object was the salvation of souls, in a broad sense, thus involving both the primacy of evangelism and a commitment to 'the sanctification, comfort, and progress of those who through grace have believed'.[22]

The ministry of his day was failing to achieve this objective, principally because it lacked earnestness. It was James' firm belief that earnestness usually accomplished its aims and that any obstacles could be overcome if people seriously applied their minds to it.[23] Spiritual insincerity and the absence of vocational commitment were the chief enemies of the ministry. The stamp of Baxter, and of Wesley, is firmly impressed on his writing.

Yet James does not rest content with a challenge to contemporary attitudes. He presses forward to practical remedies too. Nonconformists needed, in his view, to broaden their view of the minister so that less attention was paid to his teaching office and more to his pastoral work. The Church of England, he believed, had an advantage in that regard. The over-reliance on the pulpit had not only led to pastoral neglect but to the abdication of spiritual responsibilities by parents since, rather than

[21] R. W. Dale (ed), *The Life and Letters of John Angell James*.
[22] J. A. James, *An Earnest Ministry the Want of the Times*, p. 20.
[23] *Ibid.*, pp. 8 and 266.

instructing their children in the faith at home, they left it to the preacher's sermons to convert them at church.[24] His advocacy of new methods and a new spirit in the ministry provides not only an insight into the ministry of his day, but, considering that nonconformity had experienced something of the winds of revival not long before he wrote, it stands too as a reminder of the need for the perpetual reinvigoration of the ministry. He wrote,

> In calling for new methods, we want no new doctrines; no new principles; no startling eccentricities; no wild irregularities; no vagaries of enthusiasm; nor phrensies of passion; no nothing but what the most sober judgment and soundest reason would approve; but we do want a more inventive as well as a more fervid zeal in seeking the great end of the ministry. Respectable but dull uniformity, and not enthusiasm, is the side on which our danger lies. I know well the contortions of an epileptic zeal are to be avoided, but so also is the numbness of a paralytic one; and after all the former is less dangerous to life, it is more easily and frequently cured than the latter.[25]

Later nonconformity must be represented by Charles Haddon Spurgeon (1834–92), who could never have been accused of lacking in inventiveness or fervid zeal in seeking the great end of the ministry. As an enormously popular preacher Spurgeon was not involved in a routine pastoral ministry and was not in a position to undertake a normal range of counselling. Even so his writings and preaching reveal him to have been a large-hearted man and full of wisdom, if somewhat idiosyncratic in style. It is through his Pastor's College, however, that we learn most of Spurgeon's approach to pastoral theology and especially through his popular and anecdotal Friday afternoon lectures and his Annual President's Address to the College Conference. The college grew from a single student in 1856 to become probably the most important single influence on the shape of the Baptist ministry for generations. Spurgeon felt that a new college was needed because,

[24] *Ibid.*, pp. 174–187.   [25] *Ibid.*, p. 34.

No college at that time appeared to me to be suitable for the class of men that the providence and grace of God drew around me . . . It seemed to me that preachers of the grand old truths of the gospel, ministers suitable for the masses, were more likely to be found in an institution where preaching and divinity would be the main objects, and not degrees and other insignia of human learning.[26]

Spurgeon's statement captures the flavour of the ministry as he saw it. It was essentially a preaching ministry, a conservative evangelical ministry and a popular ministry. Spurgeon totally rejected modernism and could pour withering scorn, such as would have been worthy of the fiercest of the Old Testament prophets, on those who propagated it. Modern theology may contribute to the growth of grass in the graveyard, but it did so at the expense of closing down the chapels.[27] It was playing at speculation while men's souls were lost.[28] And commenting on one well-known preacher he said that he 'was orthodox compared with many in this advanced age; but one said of him that he taught that our Lord did something or other, which in some way or other was more or less connected with our salvation. Flimsy as that was, it is better than the doctrine of this hour'.[29]

The essence of the ministry for Spurgeon was preaching, and most of his efforts were concentrated in training the gift of preaching in his students. Preaching led to conversion and to growth in Christ, if it was of the right sort. To cater for the variety of people in the congregation one would certainly have to use a variety of styles in preaching,[30] but the message was always one and the style must always communicate. So whatever the style the preaching must be directed straight at the hearers. 'It is of no use to fire your rifle into the sky when your object is to pierce men's hearts. To flourish your sabre finely is a thing which has been done so often that you need not repeat it. Your work is to charge home at the heart and conscience. Fire into the very centre of the foe.'[31]

Effective preaching could come only from those who had faced affliction and had sensitively shared in the agony of

---

[26] C. H. Spurgeon, *The Early Years*, p. 384.
[27] C. H. Spurgeon, *An All-Round Ministry*, p. 102.   [28] *Ibid.*, p. 19.
[29] *Ibid.*, p. 373.   [30] *Ibid.*, p. 73.   [31] *Ibid.*, p. 125.

213

others. True, the whole range of life's experience should be recognized in the pulpit, but there were some men who preached as if 'they knew nothing of the broken bones which others have to carry throughout the whole of their pilgrimage'[32] and such preachers were of little use. The best sermons were those which were wrung out of broken hearts[33] and which were alert to the changing moods and phases of the soul.[34]

The same point applied generally to the ministry. Spurgeon saw the ministry as people-centred, the grand object being to serve the spiritual needs of the congregation as a mere steward of the Lord. 'Ministers are for churches, and not churches for ministers', he declared, adding that 'we must not dare to view them as estates to be farmed or gardens to be trimmed to our own tastes'.[35] To do so would be spiritually arrogant and pastorally futile.

Given this perspective, no complex techniques or grand academic apparatus was needed. Spiritual qualities were all-important. Firstly there was faith. Faith was not only the substance of the message to be preached, but it also needed to be exercised by the preacher.[36] Faith had to be rightly based on the truths of the gospel and the grace of God, but more than that, it had to be 'experimental', that is, not an experiment, but a doctrine which was experienced. The congregation would soon detect the difference between the man who had experienced and proved his doctrines and those who had not.[37] In addition to faith the next requirement was love. 'Love', said Spurgeon, 'is a practical theologian and takes care to deal practically with all the blessings of the covenant and all the mysteries of revealed truth.'[38]

Besides faith and love there was the Holy Spirit who in all aspects of the ministry was 'absolutely necessary'.[39] Without him nothing could be discerned and nothing effective wrought in the lives of the congregation; ministry was simply useless.

None of these nineteenth-century pastoral leaders had any great system or technique in pastoral theology. By the standards of academic theology they may even have been somewhat naïve. They were essentially practitioners who shared their burdens with their fellow ministers. Their common burden was

[32] *Ibid.*, p. 59.   [33] *Ibid.*, p. 71.   [34] *Ibid.*, p. 137.   [35] *Ibid.*, p. 264.
[36] *Ibid.*, p. 11.   [37] *Ibid.*, pp. 119f.   [38] *Ibid.*, p. 256.
[39] C. H. Spurgeon, *Lectures to My Students*, p. 384.

the need for a genuine spiritual sincerity, which sought to convey and apply the message of the Bible to the lives of men, if their ministry was to be used of God rather than being a mere social convenience and a status symbol.

One evangelical, at least, did attempt a more systematic approach to pastoral theology. Charles Bridges' *The Christian Ministry*[40] shared the same burden for the spiritual quality of the ministry as Simeon, James or Spurgeon, but tried to present it in a more orderly and comprehensive way. Having set out a general view of the ministry, Bridges then enquired into the causes for ineffectiveness and recognized that these may vary from the withholding of divine influence, the attacks of Satan, personal sin, sociological factors or – and this he believed to be the main cause of failure – the lack of a divine call. Next, Bridges explored the area of personal sin and in more depth he reviewed such shortcomings as the lack of faith and the failure to be totally committed to the task as well as covetousness, pride and refusal to rest and meditate.

The remaining half of the book is devoted to preaching and pastoral work. Very practical advice is given concerning sermon preparation, the place of the law in preaching, types of sermon and the qualities which should be found in all preaching. Pastoral work was related to preaching inasmuch as it was 'the personal application of the pulpit ministry to the proper individualities of our people'.[41] Bridges urged the necessity of doing this pastoral work systematically or else it would not be done at all and ministers would be guilty of negligence. Like a true parent, the pastor should walk among all his children giving them the direction and guidance they personally needed. Bridges then concludes by applying his principles to particular individuals such as the infidel, the young Christian and the backslider in a way reminiscent of the earlier works of Gregory the Great and Richard Baxter.

The Christian Ministry is a warm and spiritual review of the ministry which commendably sets out a classical evangelical understanding of the role of the pastor. It could not claim any originality nor real theological weight, but even today it serves admirably as an encouragement to the working pastor to attain high spiritual standards in his ministry.

---

[40] C. Bridges, *The Christian Ministry*. Original edition 1849.   [41] *Ibid.*, p. 344.

WIDER DEVELOPMENTS: SYSTEMS AND SCHLEIERMACHER

Concern for the quality of the ministry was not the exclusive province of evangelicals. Parallel to their concern was a widespread desire to improve pastoral care and to provide it with a better spiritual and theological foundation. The role of the clergyman in eighteenth-century England has been fairly described as 'an occupational appendage of gentry status'.[42] But in the nineteenth century, in spite of the powerful hold of tradition, much of that was to change. Sociologists describe what happened as the emergence of the clerical profession. Among the indicators of change were the growth of societies which provided a forum for clergy to discuss their work, the enormous increase in magazines and books produced for their benefit, and the founding of theological colleges as occupational training centres; the first significant one in the Church of England being that founded by Bishop Samuel Wilberforce at Cuddesdon in Oxford in 1854.[43]

Judged by the literature of the period there was a new desire to provide a comprehensive and systematic guide to the work of the minister. In some form or other these works dealt generally with the nature of the pastoral office and life and the spiritual requirements of the task, and then more specifically with the agreed basic elements of practical theology, namely, worship, homiletics, education and pastoral care. Four works might be mentioned as more significant and lasting representatives of this trend and of developments within it.

The earliest work was published in 1852, having been translated from the French. Vinet's *Pastoral Theology* was sub-titled 'The Theory of a Gospel Ministry'. It is a thoroughly evangelical and judicious work, written in the tradition of Richard Baxter, and deals with the agreed topics. Its outstanding characteristic is its wisdom as it honestly confronts the tightropes which a pastor walks. Vinet is concerned, for example, to maintain a balance between the dignity and authority of the office of the pastor and to debunk any pretensions to personal authority or views of the pastorate as a priestly caste. In dealing with the counselling of individuals he stresses the need to avoid being

---

[42] A. Russell, *The Clerical Profession*, p. 6.
[43] For a more detailed account see, *ibid.*, pp. 28–49.

over-directive whilst not neglecting the responsibility of discipline.[44] In similar vein the Scottish divine Patrick Fairbairn published a book, in 1875, called *Pastoral Theology*. It was a worthy and thoroughly biblical, if unimaginative, introduction to the task which befitted the reformed ministry of Fairbairn's day and proved a practical guide to many.

The third work came from the Dutch scholar, J. J. van Oosterzee, in 1878, and was called *Practical Theology*. As it was intended as a manual for theological students it is an elaborate work and enters each topic in some depth, providing a historical and literary guide to each subject before discussing contemporary principles. Its overriding concern is to demonstrate that practical theology is a science and 'as such it occupies its own distinguished place of honour in the organic whole of the Theological Sciences'.[45] Pastoral care is presented as one aspect of practical theology and although in many ways van Oosterzee presents a traditional picture of the pastor as a visitor caring for his flock, in another sense he updates the picture. For example, he acknowledges the growing problem of mental illness and recognizes the value of the elementary psychology of his day in dealing with it.[46] This work is the first substantive work to demonstrate the more scientific approach to pastoral theology which was to become commonplace in the twentieth century.

Lastly, one might point to Washington Gladden's book, *The Christian Pastor and the Working Church*, published in 1901, as typical of the state of development which pastoral theology had reached at the end of the century and from which it did not progress for much of the early twentieth century. Gladden took the view that pastoral theology was a branch of practical theology and its subject-matter was the pastor and the church at work. Then he somewhat arbitrarily decided that certain aspects which were generally thought to be within the scope of pastoral theology, such as preaching and worship, were only incidentally related to it whilst the work of shepherding and training (poimenics and catechetics) were central.

The result of Gladden's approach is to give a different shape to his work than that found in earlier textbooks. The church is clearly seen as a busy, complex organization and the aim of his book appears to provide the pastor with a science of leadership.

---

44 A. Vinet, *Pastoral Theology*, pp. 231, 275f., 287–295.
45 J. J. van Oosterzee, *Practical Theology*, p. 1.   46 *Ibid.*, pp. 580–583.

There is less concentration therefore on the pastor himself and on the spiritual dynamics involved. There is correspondingly a more comprehensive review of segments of the church's life so that the pastor's relation to women's work, the Sunday school, the mid-week service, revivals (*i.e.* evangelistic missions), missionary societies, his denomination and ecumenical responsibilities, all come in for comment. The church is recognizably much more like the church of the twentieth century, that is, a voluntary (even democratic) religious organization, rather than the expression of the spiritual dimension of a whole community. The church was viewed as a working body and the object of pastoral theology had become to improve the efficiency with which it worked. In effect this was to tip the balance of the scales away from theology in favour of science, administration and technique. This was to prove an uncertain foundation, as subsequent pastoral theology was often to deal purely with techniques, which so easily became anachronistic, and failed to ask the more vital and fundamental theological questions which would have kept the discipline in a more lively state.

In the shift towards a more modern approach to pastoral theology the work of F. D. Schleiermacher (1768–1834) is crucial. Van Oosterzee and Gladden, with many others, are the heirs of the perspective on practical theology initiated by him. Schleiermacher saw theology as a positive science concerning faith which he defined as 'a particular way of being conscious of God' (1).[47] He found the orthodox approach to theology, based as it was on revelation, inadequate for a post-Enlightenment world and argued that Christian truth needed reinterpreting for modern man. His theology was founded on the basis of his view of religion as a feeling or awareness of the infinite.[48] His understanding of practical theology is consistent with and constrained by his general approach.

Schleiermacher sets out his views on practical theology in a *Brief Outline of the Study of Theology*. He divides theology into three areas and argues strongly that each branch is vitally dependent on the others. Philosophical theology deals with apologetics and polemics. Historical theology concerns exegesis,

---

[47] F. D. Schleiermacher, *Brief Outline of the Study of Theology*, p. 19 paragraph 1. Subsequent references to the paragraphs in the work are included in brackets in the text.
[48] On Schleiermacher's theology see H. R. Mackintosh, *Types of Modern Theology*, pp. 36–101 and S. Sykes, *Friedrich Schleiermacher*.

the development of dogma, church history and the historical knowledge of the contemporary situation of the church. Practical theology builds on those and is the crown of the theological sciences. It is here that theology becomes useful. Schleiermacher regretted the division between the theologian and the clergyman and repeatedly warned of the disastrous consequences which would take place should the division be allowed to harden (6–12, 30). The clergyman, as a practical theologian, would become a mere technician and would be superficial in practice and indifferent to scientific progress. (30) He recognizes that no-one could become proficient in all the disciplines but argues that the clergy should be able to have an overview, an understanding of the organization of each of its branches, a way of quickly finding out information about it and some practice and confidence in using it (14–18).

Philosophical and historical theology determine how one is to conceive of the pastoral task. Practical theology is designed to tell how to carry that conception out and to specify procedures which will help to apply it to particular circumstances (260–265). Schleiermacher conceives of practical theology's task as 'stabilizing and advancing the community' and of 'effectively communicating religious ideas for the purpose of influencing the life of the community, or of conducting common worship and of serving to order and direct morality' (268–269). In J. E. Burkhart's words, 'practical theology therefore simply studies and indicates the appropriate rules, procedures and methods to be used in overcoming the gap between the ideal and the actual. Its task is not hermeneutical but technological.'[49]

Schleiermacher makes a distinction between 'church service', by which he means a local ministry, and 'church government', by which he means a trans-local leadership which deals with relationships between the churches (274). Church service has primarily to do with the edification of those whose religious consciousness has been quickened. The key to effective edification lies in effective communication, so much of Schleiermacher's attention is devoted to how the minister should communicate both in free forms such as the sermon and in set forms such as the liturgy (279–289). Once that is completed he

---

[49] J. E. Burkhart, 'Schleiermacher's Vision for Theology', in D. S. Browning (ed), *Practical Theology*, p. 48.

looks at those who were to be the recipients of the communication and deals with the slow developers in the congregation, children and those young in the faith, religious strangers (which leads to a digression into mission) and the wayward (290–301).

Church government determines such things as morality and worship, which are common to any order of churches; it is to be concerned with relationships between churches within that order and with other denominations too; it is to determine things which the local church fails to resolve itself and relations between the church and the state (309–324, 327). Government also has the responsibility of stimulating the scientific interest in theology and deciding what is to be published (330–334). At the heart of church government, as Schleiermacher understood it, there lies a certain tension in constant need of resolution. How could ecclesiastical authority be exercised without threat to the freedom of the individual believer or congregation (325)? And how could the scientific enterprise be stimulated without weakening the power of religious experience (330)?

Schleiermacher's contribution was profound and should not be underestimated. He raised the status of practical theology and showed how it could be integrated with other theological disciplines, not as their equal, but as their summit. He clearly advocated that the purpose of all theology, even at its most intellectual, must be to forward the welfare of the church. He showed that it was possible for practical theology to be a serious discipline in its own right and not an amateur among the professionals.

None the less there were some fatal flaws built into Schleiermacher's *Outline* which render it less useful as it stands. Firstly, Schleiermacher does not seem to have been able to match his own requirements. His outline of pastoral theology is very much in danger of being reduced to a 'mere technique', a superficial method which is not sufficiently integrated into the rest of theology. Many who have followed him have fallen into this trap. Secondly, as Karl Barth has said, 'many things are too brilliantly and hastily tossed off to be pedantically tested in detail or criticised specifically'.[50] The syllabus he proposes for pastoral theology does read curiously at times! It has about it the stamp of a hurried, rather than a mature work.

[50] K. Barth, *The Theology of Schleiermacher*, p. 169.

More fundamentally, however, the fatal flaw lies in the humanistic presupposition on which his whole theology is built. Barth's major criticism is correct here too. The minister is not seen as a messenger from God but merely the mouthpiece of the community. Barth wrote,

> Spiritual direction is the self-orientated end which, sanctioned basically by philosophical ethic and illustrated in a Christian form by the picture book of history, occupies a holy place in the church. What happens in the holy place is a meaningless question. 'It' *happens*. 'Religious power' is in full operation. Only the How can be the object of renewed research and discussion.[51]

In Schleiermacher, the minister serves the community and tries to generate and stimulate religious experience, seeking all the time to integrate the individual with the collective. But he does so unaided by divine assistance. God never enters and the Holy Spirit is absent in any living way. It is man-centred in the wrong sense and therefore never really permits the pilgrim to get off the ground in his journey to heaven. The cause of this fault lay not in Schleiermacher's practical theology but in the faulty theology which underlay it.

CONCLUSION

During the period under review in this chapter the survival and prosperity of pastoral theology owed much to the evangelical practitioners who, motivated by a concern to glorify God, sought a better structure for pastoral care in the church and devised better ways of training its pastoral leadership. But that impetus was taken up and developed well beyond the evangelical fold, so that pastoral theology also became a serious topic on the curriculum of theological faculties. It was there that a change of direction took place, paving the way for much of the twentieth-century approach to pastoral theology.

Schleiermacher's influence has been both good and bad. It has been good in raising the status of pastoral theology and establishing its respectability as an academic discipline. It has

---

[51] *Ibid.*, p. 170.

been bad in that many have swallowed his naturalistic approach to God and theology, which has all too easily led to having little of God and little theology left in pastoral theology.

11

Twentieth-century trends

THE GREAT LEAP FORWARD

The early twentieth century saw little development in the field
of pastoral theology. With few exceptions the dominant
approach was simply one of providing practical guides as
the work of the ministry and the new ideas of psychology,
which had been alluded to in the nineteenth century, were
largely ignored.[1] All this was to change after the Second
World War and fresh approaches and ideas were to be introduced which would have made the discipline unrecognizable
to its earlier proponents. Chief among these developments
was the new alliance between pastoral theology and psychology.

Seward Hiltner, the doyen of the new pastoral theology, has
attributed the change in the United States to the rise of the
religious education movement, the development of clinical
study in psychology, the recognition of the importance of wider
social issues and the work of A. T. Boisen.[2] Boisen not only
introduced the clergy to clinical training but put forward a
number of creative ideas on the relationship between
psychology and theology. He saw parallels between the
religious experience of the great prophets and mystics and some
forms of mental disorder and argued for a method of approach
to these human experiences which was both theologically and
psychologically adequate.[3] It was his embryonic views that
Hiltner was later to develop systematically.

These changes were quickly followed by the Second World
War, which not only gave rise to the need for chaplains for the
armed forces but also altered the questions and methods which
chaplains had traditionally asked and used. At the same

[1] England was more positive in its approach than the United States as the following
works show: L. Dewar and C. E. Hudson, *A Manual of Pastoral Psychology*; W. L. Northridge,
Psychology and Pastoral Practice; E. Waterhouse, *Psychology and Pastoral Work*.
[2] S. Hiltner, *Preface to Pastoral Theology*, p. 51.
[3] A. T. Boisen, *The Exploration of the Inner World: A Study in Mental Disorder and Religious
Experience*.

time novel approaches to counselling were being introduced, especially through the rapidly spreading influence
of Carl Rogers. All this meant that when, shortly after the
war, chairs in practical theology were established pastoral
theology appeared to have a quality of novelty about it. Four
influential men began their work at this time, namely,
Carroll Wise at Garrett Theological Seminary,[4] Paul Johnson
at Boston University,[5] Wayne Oates at Southern Baptist
Theological Seminary[6] and Seward Hiltner, himself at the
University of Chicago and then later at Princeton Theological
Seminary.

Seward Hiltner has been the most influential of the four in
introducing the new approach to pastoral theology. Hiltner was
ordained as a Presbyterian minister in 1935, having been greatly
influenced in his training by both John McNeill and Anton
Boisen. Immediately he began to influence others through his
formative work as Secretary of the Council for the Clinical
Training of Theological Students. Then through a host of other
societies, a prolific amount of writing, his regular university
teaching and his contributions to the journal *Pastoral Psychology*,
he began to reshape the concept of pastoral theology. His legacy
continues to have effect even though the discipline has now
begun to move beyond him.

His seminal ideas are to be found in *Preface to Pastoral Theology*
which was published in 1958. Pastoral theology was defined as
'the theological theory resulting from study of the operations
of pastor and church approached from the shepherding
perspective'.[7] He rejected the traditional view, as, for example,
it had been seen by John McNeill in his *History of the Cure of
Souls*, that it was to do with the discipline, comfort and edification of the church. Instead, he argued that the primary
content of the discipline had to do with healing, sustaining and
guiding. Closely related were the operation of communicating,
which included evangelism and education, and organizing,
which included ecclesiastical administration, but these were not

[4] C. A. Wise, *Religion in Illness and Health* (1942), *Psychiatry and the Bible* (1956) and *The Meaning of Pastoral Care* (1966).

[5] P. E. Johnson, *Pastoral Ministration* (1955), *Personality and Religion* (1957) and *Psychology of Religion* (1959).

[6] W. Oates, *The Bible in Pastoral Care* (1953), *Protestant Pastoral Counselling* (1962) and *The Christian Pastor* (1964). Oates is the most distinctively theological and sees the minister as a representative of Christ.

[7] Hiltner, *Preface to Pastoral Theology*, p. 69.

the essential elements of pastoral theology as such.[8]

His originality lay not only in the reorganization of the discipline and its relation to other aspects of theology, but in terms of the method which was to be adopted. His training in clinical psychology led him to emphasize the value of the case-study approach through which, after a detailed analysis of the individual cases, general principles could be derived.[9] In itself, that was not new. Several, such as Ichabod Spencer whom he cites extensively, had used case studies before. But what was new was the approach to the case study and reliance on it as the standard technique. Spencer was a pietist who imposed a narrow framework on the interpretation of his cases which excluded certain questions and compartmentalized spiritual issues from the rest of life. Hiltner insisted that the interpretation must take into account that man was an integrated being in a social context. Pietistic compartmentalization was therefore misleading. Whilst finding much to commend in Spencer he rejects him as too superficial in his understanding, too unaware of the dynamics involved in the counselling process and too willing to separate body, soul and culture.[10]

How then does Hiltner approach the healing, sustaining and guiding functions of the pastor? Healing implies a restoration of functional wholeness, a condition which for one reason or another has been lost.[11] It must be seen as a process in the direction of wholeness. The lack of wholeness arises out of a defect such as mental deficiency, an invasion such as bacteriological infection, a distortion such as lack of sufficient vitamins or unwise cultural practices, or from decisions which are not consciously made but may be arrived at as a result of one's heredity and environment. Where does sin fit in? Hiltner argues that it is necessary to see sin not as judicially connected with suffering, since Jesus himself denied such a connection in John 9, but rather as motivationally connected in that sin causes sickness when a decision is wrongly or perversely made. Sin therefore cannot be disconnected from suffering.

To illustrate his argument he discusses a person who is suffering from overweight. Its cause can be traced to a complex

---

[8] The relationship between this and other branches of theology are helpfully spelt out in, *ibid.*, p. 28.

[9] W. B. Oglesby (ed), *The New Shape of Pastoral Theology*, p. 13. For an example see I. F. McIntosh, *Pastoral Care and Pastoral Theology*.

[10] Hiltner, *Preface to Pastoral Theology*, pp. 82–85, 114.   [11] *Ibid.*, pp. 89–115.

set of factors. It may be due to glandular activity, which would be a defect. It may include an element of distortion, in that having been denied affection as a child the person resorted to eating as a psychological compensation. Then again, invasion may be present because of the way in which the food acts on him once the cycle is initiated. But none of these are complete in themselves. The element of decision is also present in that the person may well lack the discipline to maintain the diet he has been prescribed. So it is not right to attribute the illness to sin in the traditional sense that he is being punished by his suffering. And yet sin is present in the wrong decisions which he is making. This, Hiltner argues, is good news; for only when a person deeply recognizes sin for what it is, and his own responsibility for it, can the healing begin. This recognition is the first part of the healing process.

In this process of healing it is essential that the person be treated as a whole and that the soul should not be separated from other dimensions of life. Such a separation will not lead to true healing. What is called for is co-operation with the medical and other services so that the total needs of the person can be met and an integrated approach to healing can be devised.

Hiltner recognizes that not all situations lend themselves to healing, and where total restoration is not possible the pastor is involved in sustaining. Two situations where such a ministry is vital are in the presence of bereavement and in the face of an irreversible illness. The purpose of sustaining is to enable the person to find courage to confront his situation and to put a new heart in him, and this, according to Hiltner, goes beyond traditional methods of comforting which were so unaware of the dynamics of the suffering and crude and short-sighted in their methods and aims. The sustainer need not be strong. His purpose is to enable the sufferer to draw on the resources which are available to him, not to provide them himself. Sustaining is best accomplished when more than sustaining is in view and when there is a desire to head, as far as possible, in the direction of healing. The ministry of sustaining must be set in the context of the Christian view of hope, and here Hiltner warns against two opposite dangers. On the one hand, hope which is set exclusively in this world is no hope at all, and on the other hand, hope which is set exclusively in the next world impairs the process of sustaining and equally leads to a hopelessness now.[12]

It is perhaps in his chapter on guiding that Hiltner displays his greatest unease at traditional approaches to pastoral theology.[13] Guiding is not to be coercive but rather it is to be educative and should proceed through the evoking and leading out of the inner feelings and understanding of the person seeking counsel. He rejects the traditional ideas of discipline, because they are too directional and assume far too much by way of moral foundations. Ideally he accepts that moral theology is important, but practically it has been used to impose duty on people rather than to effect true guidance. He will not accept that moral theology should dictate to pastoral theology. All that is permissible is a negotiation between the two disciplines. Pastoral theology seeks to build on what the person already understands and the resources he already possesses, even if he has temporarily forgotten them. In building on these internal dimensions of life the pastoral theologian must be allowed to be novel in his guidance and cannot be content to work within a restricted framework which is to be externally applied, no matter who the person is or what their circumstances are.

Hiltner had many original and important things to say regarding pastoral theology and the value of his contribution should not be underestimated.[14] His concern for the whole person and his insistence that an individual approach to each person be adopted are laudable. His rejection of superficial, generalized and externally imposed pastoral direction and of general principles which are not based on careful examination of individual cases, together with his openness to other disciplines, including those of social and behavioural sciences, are equally commendable.

There are, however, some fundamental weaknesses in his approach which have subsequently become more and more evident and which have caused not a little reaction in the more recent discussions of pastoral theology. The weakest point of Hiltner's approach lies in the area of his theology. Even his strongest supporters recognize that the early case-study approaches to pastoral counselling were nearly all reductionist and

---

[12] *Ibid.*, pp. 116–144.   [13] *Ibid.*, pp. 145–172.

[14] For an assessment of his contribution see 'Pastoral Theologian of the Year: Seward Hiltner', *Pastoral Psychology* 29 (1980), pp. 5–77.

let the psychological tail wag the theological dog. Hiltner himself was not exempt from that accusation.[15] His own theological orientation was liberal and even exhibits some tendencies towards Unitarianism,[16] and he rejoices that it is among those who reject moralism, legalism, dogmatism and perfectionism that the pastoral care movement is spearheaded. He was greatly attracted by the teaching of Paul Tillich[17] and found there a theology which matched the naturalistic tendencies of his own approach.

In the end we can say that 'Hiltner sought to derive theological insights from the participation in and examination of particular human situations . . . illuminated by whatever disciplines may contribute to their understanding'.[18] But is that a sufficient basis for pastoral *theology*? The anthropological centre and the functional approach mean that secularizing tendencies are inherent from the beginning and all too easily the theological aspects become at best vague and at worst non-existent. It also leads to a narrowing of the perspective of pastoral theology so that, in effect, pastoral theology means pastoral counselling or pastoral psychology.

POST-HILTNER DEVELOPMENTS

In the decade following the publication of Hiltner's *Preface* several scholars adopted his perspective and pastoral theology entered a phase when the correlative approach to theology and psychology was dominant.[19] Daniel Williams wrote *The Minister and the Care of Souls*, in which he discussed the relationship between the Christian account of grace and the psychological account of acceptance. The theological anchorage is very clear in Williams and he avoids reductionism, and yet he is able to use Rogerian psychology to refine his understanding of the atonement and of forgiveness. In similar vein Don Browning wrote *Atonement and Psychotherapy* in an attempt to make explicit the theological assumptions latent in Rogers' client-centred theories of counselling. Subsequently James Lapsley wrote

[15] Oglesby, *New Shape*, p. 14 and J. L. Adams and S. Hiltner (eds), *Pastoral Care in the Liberal Churches*, p. 112.

[16] Adams and Hiltner, *Pastoral Care*, p. 242. Hiltner comments, 'I have never been a Unitarian but I have been close.'

[17] Oglesby, *New Shape*, p. 14.

[18] G. Griffin, 'Pastoral Theology and Pastoral Care Overseas', *ibid.*, p. 18.

[19] For a thorough review of this phase see D. Browning, 'Images of Man in Contemporary Models of Pastoral Care', *Interp.* 33 (1979), pp. 146–156.

Salvation and Health, in which he was critical of the over-identification of the theological concept of salvation with the contemporary psychological view of health.

Another work, published like Browning's in 1966, may be taken as representative of the concerns of this period. Like Browning, Thomas Oden was concerned to discover the theological assumptions in Rogerian psychology. In *Kerygma and Counselling* he set out his view that Carl Rogers makes a number of implicit assumptions which the Christian proclamation makes explicit. He set himself the Herculean task of finding points of identity between the theology of Barth and the psychology of Rogers. He does not equate them in spite of there being many analogies between them since they see themselves as different in their aims and objectives. Justification in Christ is not the same as making a better psychological adjustment to life.[20] Nor does he seek merely to translate the language of psychology into the language of theology, but to expose the theology which is already present in the approach of psychotherapy.[21]

The essence of Oden's argument is that the whole process of psychotherapy makes no sense apart from certain assumptions about the nature of being and that these assumptions are Christian. Underlying the acceptance of the client by the counsellor is the assumption that the client is acceptable and that must mean that he is acceptable by the ground of being itself. There can be no other basis for it.[22] Indeed, although operating at different levels, one can see the connection between the activity of God, the action of the counsellor and the response of the client. Oden spells it out like this,

God's activity	*Therapist's action*	*Client's response*
Incarnation	Empathetic understanding	Self-understanding
Divine congruence	Therapeutic congruence	Self-identity
Forgiveness	Acceptance	Self-acceptance
Grace	Permissiveness	Self-direction
Divine love	Unconditional positive regard	Love for others

[20] T. C. Oden, *Kerygma and Counselling*, pp. 15–18. Thomas Oden remains one of the most influential writers of pastoral theology. His recent works show a desire to explore the 'classic' Christian tradition thoroughly in a way that his earlier more liberal works did not.   [21] *Ibid.*, p. 83.   [22] *Ibid.*, p. 21.

Other points of contact could be identified. The fall is seen by psychologists as incongruence and the bondage of the will as the distortion of awareness, resulting in defensiveness and anxiety.[23] Even so, there are essential points of difference. To Oden, psychology offers a soteriology without a Christology. It wants to offer salvation but is merely humanistic in its frame of reference and fails to see man in his deepest dimension as a created being in need of a relationship with his creator.[24] However, rather than writing off the approach as valueless because of this restriction, Oden instead tries to develop it more fully and to claim it for God.[25] Whatever the psychologist may say, his assumptions suggest that he cannot adequately work within an atheistic framework and he should be invited to explore those assumptions more deeply.

This does not mean that Oden wants to turn all psychotherapists into preachers of the gospel. The value of their therapy lies not so much in what they say as in the accepting relationship which they enter with their client.[26] The pastor, however, must make that proclamation explicit; not simply by words but by the demonstration of the 'therapeutic authority' which Christ gave to his disciples. The church must, if it is true to her Lord, believe that deliverance can be expected and is at hand.[27]

The desire for a correlative approach in the 1960s has given way to a more critical approach in the 1970s. Although the pastoral theologians of the 1960s were not uncritical of the human sciences, they seemed to betray the attitude that they were somewhat overawed by them and credited them with a higher status of truth than they did theology. A growing number of voices, including that of James Lapsley, have begun to question this and to ensure that a genuine two-way dialogue between theology and the human sciences takes place. The most persuasive voice in this regard has been that of Don Browning, who has pleaded for much more serious attention to be given to the moral context and ethical dimensions of pastoral theology and a rejection of the easygoing attitudes of some psychological approaches which appear to condone all behaviour however destructive or sinful it might be.[28] Some

[23] *Ibid.*, p. 87. [24] *Ibid.*, p. 111. [25] *Ibid.*, p. 144. [26] *Ibid.*, pp. 28f.
[27] *Ibid.*, pp. 152–170.
[28] D. S. Browning, *The Moral Context of Pastoral Care* and 'Pastoral Theology in a Pluralistic Age', in D. S. Browning (ed), *Practical Theology*, pp. 187–201. See also W. B. Oglesby, 'Present Status and Future Prospects in Pastoral Theology', *Pastoral Psychology* 29 (1980), p. 41.

would see Browning as over-identifying pastoral theology with Christian ethics, and if that were so it would unnecessarily restrict the field, but it is more accurate to see Browning as mounting a vigorous and healthy corrective to a discipline which was in danger of going awry.

At the same time there has been a desire to see the discipline develop so that it can speak with a voice that is publicly acceptable and academically credible. In order to do this it needs to continue the discussion of the nature of the knowledge with which it deals.[29] But it must also not be ashamed of its historic roots. Its distinctive contribution is to articulate the Christian tradition to which it belongs and which has served the world so well in the past. To forsake that is to sell its birthright.[30] But it also needs to take the offensive and to point out the limits inherent in secular therapies, highlighting their inadequacies and the religious assumptions which are implicit, if openly denied, within them. The call here is to sharpen the focus of the correlative method put forward by Oden and Browning in the previous decade.[31]

A further recent development has been the desire to break out of the 'psychological captivity of pastoral theology'.[32] Although since Hiltner lip-service has been paid to the social context of the person seeking counsel, the healing perspective was almost exclusively psychological. Now there is a call not only to take the social and communal aspects of the individual more seriously[33] but to rediscover the prophetic aspect of pastoral care which was apparent in the Old Testament, and to move towards the politicization of pastoral care. Even if this demand to be involved in social action and public policy lies uneasily with the more personal and priestly elements in pastoral care, Alastair Campbell, one of its chief proponents, believes it will make for a richer theology of pastoral care.[34]

Campbell's request is not only consistent with biblical pastoral theology but hard to reject in the light of our contemporary experiences. The writings of Bishop David Sheppard, which many regard as political or social, are the expression of deep

---

[29] R. J. Hunter, 'The Future of Pastoral Theology', *Pastoral Psychology* 29 (1980), pp. 65–69.

[30] Browning, *Practical Theology*, pp. 191f.   [31] *Ibid.*, pp. 193–195.

[32] A. V. Campbell, 'The Politics of Pastoral Care', *Contact* 62 (1979), p. 4.

[33] J. Lapsley, 'Pastoral Theology Past and Present' in Oglesby, *New Shape*, p. 44 and W. J. Everett and J. J. Backmeyer, *Disciplines in Transformation*.

[34] Campbell, 'Politics of Pastoral Care', pp. 2–14.

struggles with pastoral problems that individual or even family and group counselling would never solve. It cannot be said too strongly that his books are pastorally inspired, not ideologically motivated.[35] Similarly the development of liberation theology comes in part from a desire to have a pastoral theology which speaks to the real-life condition of oppressed and downtrodden people even if in practice it is a theology which is often adulterated with Marxism. If such enterprises were legitimate in the world of the Old Testament, they are now not only legitimate but imperative in view of the heightening of political consciousness, social awareness and increased communication of our contemporary world.

A valiant attempt has recently been made by Everett and Backmeyer[36] to clarify the relationships between theology, psychology and sociology so that there can be a genuine mutual trilateral interchange. Their formulations prove in many ways a bit too neat, but even so they are right to stress the need to allow each of the three disciplines to transform each of the others, whilst maintaining their own integrity. To keep this aim clear they suggest that we must reject less adequate relationships which have often been adopted. They mention five forms of relationship which they consider inadequate – rejection of other disciplines, the addition of parts of a discipline to one's own, the reduction of another discipline to one's own, the corroboration of one's discipline by others and translation of one discipline into the terms of another. For all its limitations, *Disciplines in Transformation* sets out a much more mature pattern for the disciplines which contribute to pastoral theology. It is as if the starry-eyed romance between theology and behavioural sciences is now over. Furthermore the relationship has progressed through the uncritical phase of the honeymoon and the partners are now in a position to criticize each other confidently without fear of rejection, misunderstanding or a betrayal of trust.

---

[35] D. S. Sheppard, *Built as a City* (1974) and *Bias to the Poor* (1983).
[36] Everett and Backmeyer, *Disciplines in Transformation*.

EVANGELICAL PASTORAL THEOLOGY[37]

In assessing the factors which shape the present discussion of pastoral theology, William Oglesby has listed the growth of evangelicalism and the rediscovery of faith which, he writes, 'suggest that the religious resources which are intrusted to us as part of the heritage of faith may now be utilized in a fashion not experienced in recent years'.[38]

One has to look back to Eduard Thurneysen's *A Theology of Pastoral Care*, published in English in 1962, for a major contribution to pastoral theology from an evangelical, if Barthian, perspective.[39] Thurneysen argued that the exclusive ingredient of pastoral care is the word of God. He recognized the weakness of pietist views of Scripture with their tendency to subjectivism and insisted that the word of God must 'retain its self-sufficiency and stands over against all human piety' and that 'man must not cease to be its pupil'.[40] The core of pastoral theology then was the communication of the word of God, which was primarily achieved through preaching. Pastoral care differs in that it is the communication of the word of God on an individual rather than corporate level and is aimed at reducing the distance between the preacher and the hearer. Contrary to common belief Thurneysen stresses that it cannot replace the sermon, nor can it be the exclusive province of the pastor, nor should it be reserved for special occasions alone.

Only one technique of pastoral care is recognized and that is conversation. The two partners in the conversation experience deep fellowship with one another under the word of God. They are aliens to each other brought together by the word of God. It is the manner of the conversation, rather than the subject, which makes it pastoral. Fearlessness and open-mindedness are needed so that both partners can be taken where the word of God wants to lead them. The purity of any pastoral conversation

---

[37] It is not our intention to give a comprehensive treatment of all evangelical pastoral theologies, still less of all evangelical theories of counselling. The work of Thurneysen and Adams is selected for its significance. Other approaches, such as that of Frank Lake in his *Clinical Theology*, could also have been included. On a wider front the work of Paul Tournier and Jack Dominian could easily have merited inclusion. For a wider review see G. R. Collins (ed), *Helping People Grow*.

[38] Oglesby, 'Present Status', pp. 38f.

[39] The general criticisms of Barth's view of Scripture are also relevant to Thurneysen, but should not obscure the positive nature of his work.

[40] E. Thurneysen, *A Theology of Pastoral Care*, p. 31.

is riddled with temptations and Thurneysen recognizes that prayer is essential if it is to be kept pure.[41] One such temptation lies in the area of curiosity and Thurneysen warns,

> This hearing must never be arbitrary. No mere psychological interests, arising out of pleasure in the richness and diversity of human experience, must interfere. It must be controlled, obedient hearing, and this means a hearing which already includes the partner in the realm of the Word. It will be a hearing that comes very close to prayer. . .[42]

A second danger is the danger of judgmental Pharisaism. To give way to this temptation, however, is to deny totally the true nature of pastoral conversation. It puts the counsellor above the counsellee rather than on the same level, with both being under the word of God.[43] And it denies the only message a counsellor has, which is that of forgiveness. 'There was and there is . . . no other content of pastoral speaking within the church than forgiveness of sins.'[44] Thurneysen insists that the counsellor must always take his stand on forgiveness and never resort to law as an alternative strategy. It is true that the command to repent is in some senses a law, but it is joyful good news which announces liberation and it remains forgiveness and nothing but forgiveness even if it is expressed as a command.[45] Pharisaism and forgiveness are as incompatible as fire and water and the pastoral worker must flee even the most disguised form of Pharisaism as he would flee the devil himself.[46]

Thurneysen's stress on the word of God and the good news of forgiveness as the sole message of the pastoral counsellor raises questions as to his understanding of man's problem and the place he gives, if any, to contemporary human sciences. All man's problems, to him, can be traced to sin, and the illnesses and difficulties which other counsellors often tackle are but symptoms of that underlying trouble. At root man lives in conflict, as Paul makes clear in Romans 7, and it is as the basis of that conflict is dealt with through forgiveness and grace that the sick person can find healing. Other approaches to resolving that conflict, although they may be of some value, are ultimately superficial. Until the bolt is withdrawn between God and man

---

[41] *Ibid.*, p. 343. [42] *Ibid.*, p. 128. [43] *Ibid.*, p. 109. [44] *Ibid.*, p. 147.
[45] *Ibid.*, p. 258. [46] *Ibid.*, p. 176.

and the sufferer discovers acceptance by God, he will never find true healing.[47]

This does not mean that Thurneysen dismisses psychology and psychiatry as valueless. Indeed, he sees them as useful auxiliary tools which aid our understanding of human nature and he urges co-operation with medical practitioners.[48] None the less, he does argue that psychology and pastoral care belong to different orders. Pastoral care has to do with the soul – an independent sovereign entity which stands over against the body – the inner aspect of man which was created to relate to man.[49] Psychology and psychiatry start from different presuppositions which are philosophically alien to Christianity and therefore the pastor must exercise critical discernment in using them. They too stand under the judgment of the word of God, whether they recognize it or not.[50] Moreover it is wrong to view them as the same enterprise simply expressed in different vocabularies. They are 'unexchangeably different', for, as Thurneysen comments, 'the barrier of sin cannot be surmounted even by the best analysis'.[51] The net effect of Thurneysen's position then is to create a strong separation between theology and contemporary human sciences.

In two respects Thurneysen may be justly criticized. Firstly he is too grudging about the contribution which the psychological and sociological disciplines might make. Secondly, he is unnecessarily restrictive in confining all pastoral care to the issue of forgiveness.

On both of these counts one can understand, however, why he took the stand he did. He was writing at a time when much pastoral theology had sold out to the infant sciences and had lost its nerve. It seemed to have nothing distinctive to offer and its spiritual perspective was under threat of extinction. The uncritical attitude which many adopted towards contemporary science was both naïve and dangerous and seemed to ignore that man was a spiritual being, and that a spiritual solution to his problems had been made available in Christ. Thurneysen then was concerned to revive confidence in Scripture and prayer and to hold the central citadel of grace intact in spite of all that threatened to undermine it. Despite possible misunderstandings therefore, his stress on God and grace, on Scripture and

[47] *Ibid.*, pp. 226–241. [48] *Ibid.*, pp. 200 and 221. [49] *Ibid.*, pp. 54f.
[50] *Ibid.*, pp. 131 and 200. [51] *Ibid.*, pp. 226 and 245.

prayer, on the distinctive role of the pastor and the spiritual need of the seeker is one for which we must be grateful. It is a deeply moving work which lays the foundations for a true evangelical pastoral theology.

EVANGELICAL ANTI-PSYCHIATRY

A more recent attempt at an evangelical pastoral theology has come from Jay Adams, who is Dean of the Institute of Pastoral Studies and Visiting Professor of Practical Theology at Westminster Theological Seminary. But it is a theology which has proved extremely controversial, having been heartily welcomed by some and heavily criticized by others.[52] The substance of some of his teaching is controversial, but the controversial aspects of his writings have been heightened by their polemical style and by their prolific flow. To date Adams has produced more than thirty books[53] in which his arguments are minutely cross-referenced to his other works, so making it difficult on a number of vital occasions for the reader to get a complete grasp of his teaching on specific topics.

Adams begins with the strong belief that Christian counselling has sold its birthright for a mess of pottage by subjecting biblical truth to contemporary psychology, or even by trying to integrate the two. The psychologies of Freud, Rogers and Skinner are dismissed, not only as psychologies which fail to effect change but as theories which are fundamentally in error. More than this, the whole perspective of present-day psychiatry, which sees problems as if they were diseases needing to be cured and therefore as problems which invade a person's life and for which he is not responsible, is a dangerous fallacy. Cutting loose the ties, therefore, with recent trends Adams seeks to relaunch what he sees as a biblical framework for pastoral care.[54]

In so doing he argues that the root cause of all our problems

---

[52] See J. D. Carter, 'Adams' Theory of Nouthetic Counselling', *JPT* 3 (1975), pp. 143–155; R. Winter, 'Jay Adams – is he really biblical enough?', *Third Way* 5/4 (1982), pp. 9–12; and R. Abraham, 'Yes, Jay Adams is biblical enough', *Third Way* 5/7 (1982), pp. 15–16.

[53] Chief among his books are *The Big Umbrella* (1973), *The Christian Counsellor's Manual* (1973), *Competent to Counsel* (1972), *More Than Redemption* (1979) and *Shepherding God's Flock* (1975).

[54] *Big Umbrella*, pp. 39–61.

is sin. He does not attribute all problems and suffering to the direct sin of the one seeking counsel, as many have claimed.[55] He recognizes that the cause of the misery may be the result of demonic activity, may have an organic basis or that it may lie outside the individual who suffers. None the less, with the vice-like grip of a dog playing with an old slipper, he will not let go of the concept of sin as central to pastoral care. Only as he views the problems as having their origin in sin does the pastor have anything to say and any hope to offer. All suffering and misery can be traced back to the sin of Adam. More immediately, even if a sinful pattern of living has not been the direct cause of suffering and its origin lies elsewhere or with others, there is still the vital question as to how the sufferer reacts to it. His sinful reaction may aggravate it or his Christian reaction may minimize it and cause it to be used for God's glory. The burden of Adams' concern is evident when he writes,

> Even when a child has been tragically sinned against (and Nouthetic Counsellors do not minimise the tremendous influence of parents and others, as some falsely claim), it is possible (and always necessary) for the counsellor to discover the sinful patterns of response to such sin that the counsellee developed (perhaps as a child). Others, though very influential, exert their influence only though such responses. A child, born a sinner (because of his sinful nature), will develop many such wrong habitual responses that may persist into adulthood and cause him much difficulty. But – and this is important – others cannot cause those patterns . . . Others are responsible for their sin against God and the counsellee, but God holds him responsible for his response to it.[56]

The task of the counsellor is to confront the person with his sin and with God's demands and way of effecting change. The emphasis on confrontation as the primary pastoral method derives from Paul's use of the verb *nouthetō* in Colossians 1:28 and elsewhere where it means 'I confront' or 'I set right'. The root of the word means 'I put in mind'. 'Nouthetic counselling is, in short, confrontation with the principles and practices of

---

[55] *Competent to Counsel*, pp. 108f. and *More than Redemption*, pp. 139f.

[56] J. Adams, 'Nouthetic Counselling', in G. Collins (ed), *Helping People Grow*, p. 156. See also *Manual*, pp. 117–140.

scripture.'[57] Its method is to teach the counsellee verbally with the motive of benefiting him.

It stresses that man must face up to his own responsibility for sin and that if he does so there is a greater hope that he can change, since he places himself in line with God's verdict on his life and is able to adopt strategies which lead to change. When the problem has been identified from a biblical perspective and responsibility accepted, then the counsellor can move to drawing up a programme for change. The programme will be designed to enable the counsellee to stop practising his wrong behaviour and to start behaving in a right way. Sin so often has become engrained through sheer habit, so the counsellor seeks to enable dehabituation of the wrong and rehabituation of the right.[58] The problem is not solved simply by putting off wrong behaviour. Adams is right to stress that biblically speaking (Col. 3:5–14 and Eph. 4:17 – 5:2) it is only as wrong behaviour is abandoned and right behaviour adopted that the problem is resolved.[59]

The change which occurs through doing and practising the right thing is not a superficial change. It is one brought about by the Holy Spirit, who is the principal person involved in all counselling situations.[60] It is a change which runs deep, for it changes a person's attitudes and emotions. Adams argues, contrary to popular opinion, that the Bible teaches that it is not our feelings which shape our attitudes and behaviour. Rather it is our behaviour which shapes our attitudes and these in turn shape our feelings. Counselling, then, must start with behaviour and not, as so often, with the emotions or even the attitudes.[61]

Jay Adams has, without doubt, made an enormous contribution to the revival of a biblical pastoral theology. He has restored the confidence of many in their role as pastors, as distinct from being psychologists with a religious hue. He has restored, too, the confidence of many in the Bible as a sufficient and relevant textbook to deal with man's problems. He has restored confidence in the power of the Holy Spirit to bring about changes in people's lives. He has uncovered man's basic problem as being that of sin for which he is responsible, rather

[57] *Competent to Counsel*, p. 51.   [58] *Manual*, pp. 191–216.
[59] *More than Redemption*, pp. 237–248.   [60] *Manual*, pp. 5–8.
[61] *Competent to Counsel*, pp. 93–96 and *Manual*, pp. 112–116.

than being a problem which lies in his environment or heredity. He has put feelings in their right context, which is quite an accomplishment in a culture which has been termed by Christopher Lasch 'the culture of narcissism'. And he has swept through much of the unnecessary and pretentious paraphernalia of the medical perspective which has laden counselling down. He has not been afraid to point out when he thought the emperor had no clothes. What is more, he has shown a concern to relate his counselling to his doctrine[62] and to place it firmly in the context of the church.[63]

In spite of this there remain a number of major weaknesses in his approach which so blemish it as to render it seriously defective as an evangelical pastoral theology. These weaknesses mostly arise from his desire to assert one aspect of truth so strongly that he does so at the expense of others. Four issues in particular might be mentioned.

Firstly, he so wishes to argue against the climate of non-directive counselling in which he finds himself that he almost exclusively sees counselling as directive and confrontational. Indeed, his approach is called 'nouthetic counselling'. Granted that nouthetic counselling needed rehabilitating and that its rejection by others was a serious flaw, we must surely argue that this is not the whole of the biblical teaching on counselling. Whereas the Greek verb *noutheō* is used thirteen times in the New Testament, other relevant words are also used and one in particular, *parakaleō*, which is variously translated 'I comfort', 'I exhort', 'I beseech' and 'I console', etc., is used well over a hundred times. Is there not much more to pastoral care than simply confronting a person with the responsibility for his sins? As David Carlson has pointed out, if we take Jesus as our model we find that he was by no means always confrontational. There were many occasions when he was comforting and supportive, acting as priest rather than as prophet.[64]

Secondly, despite all his protests and qualifications the net effect of his approach is to have a truncated view of sin. One appreciates why he should want to emphasize sin as an act for which individuals are responsible. That too has been denied

---

[62] *More than Redemption* is an explicit attempt to relate counselling to systematic theology.
[63] *Ibid.*, pp. 276–296.
[64] J. D. Carter, 'Adams' Nouthetic Counselling', and D. Carlson, 'Jesus' Style of Relating. The Search for a Biblical View of Counselling', *JPT* 4 (1976), pp. 181–192.

with disastrous consequences. But sin is not merely an external, individual and behavioural act as he implies. Adams seems to have little understanding of the depth and inwardness of sin. And surely the pastoral counsellor needs to give thought to the way in which the consequences of sin are visited upon the children to the third and fourth generation (Dt. 5:9). This is not to exempt the individual from bearing the responsibility for his reaction to the situation. It is, however, to open up the possibility of a more adequate pastoral care being offered. Adams strongly recognizes the need to counsel people in the context of their family. It is curious therefore that he should be so negligent about their wider environment.

Thirdly, his total rejection of contemporary psychology is a sad return to an unhealthy pietism. Not only is it uncalled for but it is also somewhat inconsistent. Although he claims to reject all outside knowledge and to be guided solely by Scripture, his own approach, as he himself admits, owes much to the anti-psychiatry of Thomas Szasz and O. Hobart Mowrer. It also has much in common with the reality therapy of Herbert Munro. What is more, it has recognizable parallels in its teaching about dehabituation and rehabituation with the much-condemned behaviourism of B. F. Skinner, although, of course, Adams would deny this.[65] In addition, one wonders why he is prepared to admit the place of contemporary medicine but totally deny the place of contemporary psychology. One must certainly maintain a radically critical attitude to psychiatry and never blame its errors on God's natural revelation. But is that really to say that the God who could use the heathen king Cyrus to accomplish his will cannot give the contemporary psychologist some insight into truth among the multitude of his own ideas?

Fourthly, and not unrelated, is the fact that he seems to have an inadequate doctrine of creation. He is so concerned to stress the significance of the fall that other aspects of creation seem to be forgotten. One can sympathize with Adams' desire for all men to know God as saviour, but what place does he give to them knowing him as creator? Take, as an example, his attitude to the counselling of non-Christians. He simply sees no point in counselling the unbeliever, because there is no point in coun-

---

[65] R. Winter, 'Adams . . . biblical enough?', p. 12.

selling any man unless it can be done in depth. Depth counselling only makes sense to a person who is regenerate. All that
precedes this therefore is pre-counselling. Once a man is truly
converted there is the possibility of tackling his real problems
and finding real solutions. To settle for first aid when radical
surgery is needed is both futile and dangerous, because it offers
the counsellee a false security.[66] This, says Adams, has always
been the beginning of liberalism. Again one has to say that he
has a point. But is it the whole point? As creator, is not God
interested in man's welfare? Whilst one would most readily
agree that man's welfare is only ultimately secured in salvation,
and whilst one would deprecate all that would side-track the
counsellor from announcing the gospel, surely there are lesser
acts of God's mercy and kindness, and aspects of his natural
revelation, from which the unconverted might rightly benefit.

Jay Adams has provided us with a stimulating and provoca-
tive pastoral theology. But it is one to which we can give only
two cheers, not three. It is a partial pastoral theology. And it is
to be hoped that by engaging in discussion with it, a more
balanced and adequate evangelical pastoral theology may yet
emerge.

CATHOLIC PASTORAL THEOLOGY

Our survey of contemporary pastoral theology would be incomplete without a brief reference to Roman Catholicism. If one
had chosen to dig through the layers of worldliness and hypocrisy, at any period in history, one would have always
discovered in Catholicism a rich layer of genuine spiritual direction. The best pastors of Catholicism, and they are not too
rare, have always taken the task of providing deep individual
spiritual guidance as seriously as a good Puritan divine. The
spiritual director would counsel through conversation and letter
and be concerned about 'fundamental correction and
progressive guidance'. The difference between the Catholic and
the Puritan lies not in their conscientiousness but in the content
of their direction. The Catholic gives a central place to liturgy
and the observance of the sacraments and in particular to the
place of confession and penance.[67]

---

[66] *More than Redemption*, pp. 309–326, especially pp. 318f. and *Big Umbrella*, pp. 95–112.
[67] See McNeill, *Cure of Souls*, pp. 287–307 for a summary.

Convinced of the value of this, traditional Catholics have been very slow to show much interest in the behavioural sciences and, with few exceptions, a more scientific approach to pastoral theology along the lines proposed by Seward Hiltner is almost unknown among them.[68] Prayer was considered of far more importance than psychology. Until recently, therefore, Catholics would have understood pastoral theology as the practical training which a priest was given in order to conduct his craft. If the definition was inclusive it might also have embraced moral theology as an essential component, being the means by which the priest would form his judgments as to the direction he should give.

The Second Vatican Council, however, resulted in much troubling of these tranquil waters and there were signs following it of the same desire for a more adequate approach to pastoral theology as was evident outside Catholicism. Karl Rahner wrote of the need for pastoral theology to assume a higher status than before. He recognized the confusion of understanding as to what pastoral theology was. He rejected the 'practical tips approach' and defined it instead as 'scientific and theological research into the task laid upon the church in the present of achieving the fulness of her own nature as Church'.[69]

Three significant points emerged in Rahner's essay. Firstly, he recognizes that his definition of pastoral theology might be seen as simply a new way of talking about ecclesiology, so he sharply distinguishes between the two. Ecclesiology concerns the doctrine and constitution of the church. Pastoral theology keeps the contemporary situation of the church clearly in focus and filters all its discussion through the appropriate lens. Secondly, Rahner is much more positive about the value of contemporary human sciences than many Catholics had been previously. He insists that they must be examined from a theological point of view, but they are not to be ignored. Thirdly, he argues that pastoral theology should be made a significant branch of study in the theological curriculum and that the teaching of all the other theological disciplines should be given a pastoral orientation. He is even able to provide a tentative

[68] Oglesby, *New Shape*, p. 42.
[69] K. Rahner, 'The New Claims which Pastoral Theology makes upon Theology as a whole', in *Theological Investigations*, vol. 11, p. 118.

example of the radical effect this would have on the syllabus of a Catholic seminary.

Although Rahner is able to point to a few scholars who have made a start in this direction, he admits that it is largely an agenda for the future. Much of his own writing, however, gives some indication of the pastoral orientation which he believes all theology should have. His writings are encyclopaedic but include many essays that tackle a theology of some contemporary problem or other, such as the questions thrown up by technology, pluralism, and other religions.[70] Another recurring theme is the question of guilt and forgiveness, to which we may turn as an illustration.[71]

All Rahner's theology stems from his view of God and it is ultimately on this that the rest of his theology stands or falls.[72] His pastoral concern is seen in his anxiety over modern man's difficulty in believing. He is not interested in the traditional philosophical proofs for the existence of God, but he does want to provide modern man with a ground for believing. This he finds within man himself. God is not an individual existent alongside other existents. Rather God is that infinite and holy mystery which lies at the core of our innermost being. We reach him in our innermost depths and in our furthest aspirations, as man's transcendental experiences show.

To sin is to reject that transcendent presence at the core of our being. By our concrete acts we deny our inmost self and violate others. To say that we are guilty is to stress our own responsibility for the negative act which we have done. Such guilt imprisons a man within disappointment, loneliness and despair, characteristics of human finitude. Rahner, therefore, paints sin and its consequences in the most dire of colours. It is no light matter but deeply offensive.

Yet that same transcendent presence which we have betrayed by sin is also known to man as a God of grace. Man in the depths of his being knows a hope which reaches out beyond the finite, which encompasses the wrong, which leads to a love which is deeper than the rejection of sin and which provides a forgiveness from beyond man himself. God somehow redeems

[70] Many relevant essays will be found in *Theological Investigations*, vols. 10 and 11.

[71] This section is based on J. N. King, *The God of Forgiveness and Healing in the Theology of Karl Rahner*.

[72] For an introduction to his complex theology see K.-H. Weger, *Karl Rahner: An Introduction to his Theology*.

and heals the past. If asked how one knows that such a gift of forgiveness is available, Rahner answers that the very presence of the hope within man's experience is proof of the existence of the gift. If it was not there man would not experience the longing for it.

Man's despair at sin, which gives rise to hope, must lead him to respond in conversion. Conversion involves the distancing of one's self from the sin, the changing of the core decision which gave rise to sin and the opening up of one's self to a process of healing and change, which Rahner stresses may well be a difficult and painful path to take.

Rahner's theology is a sophisticated attempt to address modern secular man about the basic issues of the faith. But its existential foundations lead to a vagueness which in turn leads him to a thoroughgoing relativism. Thus, in all that we have said about forgiveness and redemption, it has not been necessary to refer to Christ. This is not to say that Rahner does not have a Christology. He has a clear place for the person of Jesus as the 'absolute bringer of salvation', even if his anthropological basis once more leads him to some original views about Jesus and the atonement. In the end one has to say that, for all Rahner's sincere attempts to translate biblical ideas into a contemporary vocabulary, one cannot be sure that he ends up talking about the same ideas at all and on some occasions it is very clear that he does not.

Rahner's pastoral orientation is to be envied. But his theological foundations are such as to prevent him from being able to construct a stable superstructure. A pastoral orientation should not be equated with a capitulation to existentialism or to any other theology which exclusively starts with man. There remains a need therefore for a more orthodox pastoral theology among Roman Catholics.

CONTEMPORARY APPLICATION

12

Changing gear . . . an explanation

The reader deserves to be warned that in our final section we change gear quite dramatically. To change gear in a car necessitates driving at a different speed and in a different style. So it is here. So far we have tried to provide a balanced but critical survey of the field of pastoral theology. Now we make no such attempt.

This section introduces five issues which have been selected for their contemporary relevance. Many others could have been chosen, but in the opinion of the author these are among the most important issues facing the church, especially the evangelical wing of the church, at the present time.

The secular or pluralist context in which we live dictates that the problem of believing should be right at the top of our agenda. Although, sadly, it must be admitted that the church rarely appreciates the lethal nature of the contemporary atmosphere and therefore often misses the significance of the problem. Evangelicals pride themselves on a right understanding of the gospel, yet what they preach and how they live are often in contradiction. It is this commonplace tragedy that requires that the pastoral theologian should examine the issue of forgiveness. No age is exempt from the problems of suffering and it is impossible for any pastoral theology to ignore it. Two recent factors, namely a new awareness of suffering brought about by the mass media and the challenge of the theology of healing, mean that the subject needs to be discussed afresh. The sad but pervasive spectacle of divided churches, which are often divided in the name of renewal, forces the subject of unity on to the agenda. Then in the final chapter we take up the problems of the ministry which were outlined in chapter one and assess present claims and counter-claims about the ideal nature of the ministry in the light of what has been written previously in this book.

Just as no attempt has been made to cover every issue, so these chapters make no attempt at being comprehensive guides to the subjects. Each chapter offers an argument. Even so, it is

247

best to regard them as loosely constructed reflections, which illustrate possible approaches, rather than definitive statements which are carefully documented. They offer no rigorous method, since it is doubtful if a systematic method, in the modern academic sense, is appropriate to a theology which is pastoral. As Frank Wright has said, 'Pastoral theology cannot appeal to those who are addicted to neat formulations: it is bound to be untidy and imprecise, an uneasy attempt at integration which must always be changing and shifting in emphasis.'[1] What these chapters do is to illustrate a variety of useful approaches. The strength of the case-study method is recognized, although it is not used in a way which would please Seward Hiltner. The contribution which can be made by history, sociology and psychology is also acknowledged. But the boundaries between pastoral *theology* and other disciplines are carefully observed and within theology the primacy is given to Scripture. True to our definition of pastoral theology, the chapters attempt to keep the relationships between objective truth and subjective experience to the forefront of the argument.

In changing gear I leave it to the reader to decide whether it is a change up or a change down. No doubt his verdict will reflect his own personal needs and whether he reads primarily as a scholar or as a pastor. All that matters is that, whatever the direction of the change, the car is driven to its destination safely and its passengers are able to ride in comfort and security.

---

[1] F. Wright, *The Pastoral Nature of the Ministry*, p. 3.

13

Belief

Sixty-three years before the birth of Christ, the Roman general Pompey breached the walls of Jerusalem and killed 12,000 priests and Jews in order to put down a rebellious high priest. On entering Jerusalem his immediate action was to go into not only the Temple, which was blasphemous enough, but the holy of holies. To his astonishment he found it empty. Like all Romans he found it difficult to envisage a religion without something tangible at its centre.

There are many regular worshippers today who have not been as brave as Pompey. They fear to push through the curtain and expose the core of their faith lest they too should find nothing there. The outward rituals are maintained and in order to conform to family expectations or out of a sense of habit or social convenience they remain involved in church where, since appearances are deceptive, many regard them as convinced believers. But at the heart of their faith they lack reality. The evangelical church is not conspicuous for encouraging honesty and so they suffer in silence, afraid of being rebuked or ostracized if they should air their doubts.

THE QUESTION OF DOUBT

Simply to pigeonhole the issue as one of doubt could lead to our misunderstanding the nature of the problem, with the result that we fail to engage in a true pastoral theology which grapples with the depth of the despair involved. So care needs to be exercised. The issue is not so much one of a specific doubt as a creeping paralysis of unbelief which is imbibed through the atmosphere. Since doubt is a complex phenomenon it is worth clearing the ground by making some preliminary comments on it before tackling the issue before us.

Contrary to popular thinking, doubting is not necessarily wrong. The word is often mistakenly taken as meaning the same as unbelief, whereas it correctly means to be 'in two minds'. Unbelief means a refusal to believe or a rejection of belief, whereas doubt often entails the asking of questions or the voicing of uncertainties from a basic position of faith. Of course, these questions may lead in either direction. They could lead to unbelief and therefore warning signs need to be erected. On the other hand they could lead, if satisfactorily resolved, to the strengthening of faith. What is important is to recognize that it is often the silencing, rather than the voicing, of doubts which sows the seeds of future unbelief.

Robert Davidson has shown how frequently some of the greatest Old Testament believers voiced their doubts and how, too, their often agonizing questionings as to what God was doing or demanding gave rise to some of the most profound spiritual writings of the Old Testament. The roll-call of the heroes of the faith in Hebrews 11 could be matched by a roll-call of doubters, and many names would appear in both lists. Moses voiced questions that sprang 'unasked from the apparent meaninglessness of a crisis situation'.[1] Elijah, after Carmel, vented his feelings about the puzzling absence of God. Jeremiah even feared that he might be the plaything of an angry God. The psalmists voiced the contradiction they felt between the faith they were taught and the experience they had, whilst the prophets had to struggle with the delayed fulfilment of their words. These Old Testament 'unevangelical prayers'[2] and statements of perplexed faith led to a firmer hold on God.

In his brilliant analysis of contemporary doubt Os Guinness has identified seven common 'families of doubt'.[3] The first four, he suggests, have to do with deficiencies in coming to believe and the last three with difficulties in continuing to believe. They are:

Doubt arising from ingratitude
Doubt from a faulty view of God
Doubt from weak foundations
Doubt from a lack of commitment
Doubt from lack of growth
Doubt as a result of unruly emotions
Doubt from fearing to believe.

[1] R. Davidson, *The Courage to Doubt*, p. 69.   [2] *Ibid.*, p. 8.
[3] Os Guinness, *Doubt: Faith in Two Minds*.

In each case Guinness shows how sensitive pastoral care can be offered which avoids both the soft option and the hard response and which can successfully move the doubter to surer faith. Fundamental to his analysis is the idea that it is wrong to think that doubt reflects a lack of faith, since often it has to do with a lack of knowledge. Stable faith and true understanding are intimately connected, and again and again it is due to ignorance or defective knowledge that doubts arise. The answer then is not to encourage the doubter to try harder to believe, as if it is some wish that will be fulfilled if only we wish hard enough for it. Rather it is to treat doubt as a symptom and to deal with the shaky foundations, both of a doctrinal and personal kind, on which the faith is built.

THE WIDER QUESTION OF PLAUSIBILITY

Every pastor recognizes these families of doubt and will have offered help to many who have faced them. But for many today doubt will not be so easily articulated, nor perhaps so easily resolved. These people will not so much argue about the truth-claims of Christianity as doubt whether Christianity is any longer plausible. In other words, for them the battle is not whether Christianity is true but whether it *seems* to be true. In their minds they know the answers, but in their bones they fear lest they be mistaken. This is not to underestimate the importance of truth. It is simply to recognize that much has already been written in that area and to acknowledge that, like a chameleon, the devil is always putting on a new disguise in order to fool God's people into unbelief. The struggle to believe for many today revolves around the problem of plausibility.

Take Jane as an example. She was converted at fourteen through an evangelistic outreach and immediately became an enthusiastic member of a keen young people's fellowship and her school Christian Union. School work suffered a bit and her parents complained that she treated home as if it were a hotel, because she always seemed to be out at church. In spite of this they supported her in her new-found faith, although they did not share it. For two years she made rapid progress as a Christian and was looked up to by many as an example. Then she left school and went to work in a bank where no-one was a Christian and none of her colleagues seemed to give any serious thought to God. He simply did not appear to enter their world. When that was combined with the attractions of their more adult world, it was increasingly difficult for grown-up Jane to identify with the teenage girl who was converted. She never really doubted, nor consciously stopped believing – she just drifted.

Or take Alan. He came from a non-Christian home, but when his local Christian youth club were going off to camp his parents were glad that he had the opportunity to join them. Living in a Christian atmosphere for a fortnight and being surrounded by such fine examples of muscular Christianity, it was almost inevitable that towards the end of camp Alan should have visited the padre's tent and made a commitment. Mind you, together with countless other young people who had made such commitments that summer, it did not last. Soon after returning to home and school, the faith was as distant and unreal a memory as the holiday itself.

These familiar cases are, in a way, straightforward. Countless variations of a more complex kind could be added. There are those who seem firmly committed but then move and never identify actively with another church. There are those who are strong believers in Christianity until knocked sideways by other faiths or until, with seeming inexplicable ease, they become converts to another religion. There are those who are committed to a religious answer to life, only later to forsake it to follow politics, psychology or some other ideology in the belief that the answers they offer are more relevant to the world's questions. The stories could be multiplied. They happen all the time. In our world people are always getting converted and then reconverted; becoming converts and then becoming ex-converts.

It is helpful to remember that this is just what Jesus led his followers to expect in his parable about the sower and it is just what happened in his own ministry, as John 6:60–66 records. Sometimes it is helpful to ask whether such people were ever genuinely converted in the first place. Sometimes we can see that the convert made only a superficial response and genuine spiritual life was never in him. Those who have been genuinely converted have the life of the Spirit within them which should go on growing and empowering the Christian life, in spite of the spiritual malnutrition which results from an absence of fellowship. But the question may equally lead to a sterile academic debate which seeks to penetrate the mystery of who is and who is not regenerate and to judge men and women in a way which belongs only to God. This question, therefore, may not always settle the matter.

AN ALTERNATIVE APPROACH

Another level of analysis is possible, using the insights of sociology, or the branch of it that is called the sociology of knowledge.[4] Like other approaches to sociology, the sociology of knowledge is not concerned about the validity of the views it seeks to describe, and this is a serious weakness in its approach. Its concern is to explain the means by which people come to adopt and maintain their views about life, and to describe the general meaning systems that exist at a given time. On both these counts the discipline can be helpful. On the personal level it can help us to examine how belief can be sustained. On the social level it can help us to understand why belief is difficult.

Sociology of knowledge views man as being constantly involved in a dialectical process. To a young baby it appears as if the world of culture and the various meanings and interpretations of life he or she is given are fixed. They have an objective appearance and seem as factual as the material world. In reality, as one soon learns, this is not so. Man creates his own world of culture and places his own interpretation and meaning on events. He is, in fact, the most creative of all creatures. Having created his world of meaning it then takes on an objective status and acts back on the individual, so much so that all his future understanding and interpretation of the world is shaped by it.

All cultural activity, science no less than art or religion, is constructed in this way. Language is a good example. The child is taught how to speak properly and is given the rules of pronunciation, grammar, prose and poetry as if they were fixed. As a child one would not have been surprised to have been taken to a glass case in some museum and shown 'the Queen's English', as if it actually existed. But two things eventually persuade the child that language is not as 'out there' as he had

---

[4] The best introduction remains the works of Peter Berger, *A Rumour of Angels* (1971); *The Social Construction of Reality* (with Thomas Luckmann) (1972) and *The Social Reality of Religion* (1973).

been led to believe. Firstly, some people speak other languages and have their own vocabulary, rules and even script. Secondly, he discovers that his own language has changed greatly over the centuries and that some of the most admired writers and poets of his own day break all the rules! Paradoxically, they are often acclaimed just because of their creativity. Note that in saying this the sociologist is not concerned with what is right and wrong – only to describe how things come about.

Not every individual is going to be drastically creative. For the most part, although he has the potential to be creative, he will receive his interpretations from others and accept them into the structures of his consciousness. It will be as if he will put on a pair of spectacles through which he sees the world and not even be aware that he has got them on. He will believe he sees what is there with his naked eye rather than realizing that he is interpreting what he sees through a filter.

How does this process come about? It comes about through socialization. Each human being belongs to a network of relationships from the start. The first and primary example of this is the family where significant others, people like mum and dad, feed us with a world-view. This world-view is maintained by conversation which both explicitly and implictly serves to underline the reality of the world as they see it. There will also be rituals which keep their version of reality going. For example, the Christian family will have a world-view which says that we are dependent on God for our food and should be grateful to him for it. The saying of grace before a meal will be a ritual which underlines that and it may come as a shock to the Christian child when he eventually goes home to tea with a friend, to a family where they do not share that world-view and do not say grace. It is not just that he does not know when to begin eating his tea; it is that they see the world differently – it cannot therefore be as fixed as he thought. The world-view will also be maintained by 'legitimations'; that is, explanations which justify and explain it. So at the elementary level a boy is told, 'Boy's don't play with dolls; it's cissy.' There will also be sanctions so that the creative deviant will be brought back into line and techniques will be employed to persuade him to go on shoring up the world-view he has begun to question; 'If you don't eat your cabbage which is good for you, you can't have any pudding!'

Life is fine while this single world-view is imposed upon it. The views will be firmly held and unquestioned. But problems arise because the world in which we live offers a multiplicity of world-views and indeed, as we shall see later, is committed to the belief that such a variety is important. When one begins to encounter other world-views the reality of one's own begins to be weakened. So the child goes off to school and finds that teachers, who are also 'significant others', see things differently from his parents and may even ridicule certain views which parents hold. Then come friends and the influence of their families. Shortly after the child gets involved in clubs and leisure pursuits where other interpretations and values are given; over-laying all of these is the influence of the media which propagates a different, often very 'unreal' world-view as well. This plurality of choice often means that the child, even if he does not reject his parents' world-view, at least does not remain as firmly committed to it as they are. This holds true over the complete range of cultural activity, including religion.

To summarize, the vital element in this process of socialization is what the sociologists call 'plausibility structures'. They are networks of relationships inhabited by 'significant others' who help to give and maintain a person in the belief that his interpretation of the world is plausible. They do so by explicit and implicit conversation, by rituals, by offering legitimations and by applying sanctions.

Now let us apply this kind of analysis to the sad cases of Jane and Alan which we mentioned earlier. Jane was a bright girl capable of pursuing higher education, an opportunity which never came the way of her parents. Her whole school career had weakened their world-view and their encouragement to her to do well and get involved in all that was offered further served to undermine it. At the time when she was particularly open to receiving new interpretations she became a Christian. Her interest can be attributed not least to the attractiveness and liveliness of those she knew to be Christians and to a particular teacher, whom she much admired, who was well-known for his Christian views. She entered, therefore, a new plausibility structure where 'significant others' confirmed her world-view. This world-view was maintained by regular conversation with fellow Christians and the almost daily rituals of Christian Union meetings, youth fellowship meetings and prayer meetings. It was also maintained by the habit she quickly adopted of private prayer and Bible study. When problems cropped up there were always those much wiser, and much admired, like the teacher at school and the youth leader at church, who could answer them. So the legitimations were given. If at any time she seemed to deviate, by, for example, not attending a meeting, sanctions were soon applied and she was 'talked to' by some of her seniors. Her failure to observe the 'quiet time' was frowned upon and she was made to feel disapproval if her neglect was found out.

So far so good. But then Jane left school and entered a totally different plausibility structure where 'significant others' seemed to have no place for God (or if they did privately they certainly did not show it in the business world), and where there were no conversations which put God into the picture of their lives. Rather, the conversations, rituals, legitimations and sanctions all served a different end and God was forgotten. Jane wanted to do well in that world and so it meant studying in the evenings for her professional exams. She was no longer able to attend Christian events quite so often, and even if she were they were no longer quite so appropriate to her, as they were chiefly geared either for those still at school or for her parents' generation. The Christian plausibility structure was gradually supplanted by a different one which told her that it was no longer plausible to believe seriously in God. So she drifted from faith.

The case of Alan is even more acute. For two weeks at camp he lived in a totally Christian plausibility structure, where everyone who mattered, certainly every officer whom he viewed as a hero, was a Christian. They both implicitly and explicitly talked all the time of a Christian view of the world. Rituals, legitimations and sanctions ('if you do not attend the meetings you will have to be sent home') were all present in glorious technicolour. In a sense it was easy for him to accept their views. They had warned him of difficulties when he returned home, but they had not told him the half. He could have coped with the ridicule but he did not meet any. His new-found faith was not persecuted; it was just suffocated, for no-one in Alan's family saw the world through Christian eyes and nor did anyone who was significant to him at school. His contact with the youth club at church was not great and the hour or so he spent in the Christian plausibility structure each week was insufficient to weight the Christian world-view successfully against the world-view that omitted God.

The practical implications of this for our evangelism and pastoral care are enormous. It should lead us to question whether evangelism to children, as if they were individuals isolated from their family units, is the best way forward. It may lead us to re-examine the wisdom of 'away' conversions at camps and houseparties unless we can make sure they are part of an on-going plausibility structure. It should make us more sensitive to the great anticlimax many will feel when moving from the spiritual hot-house of a school or college Christian Union to the spiritual deep-freeze of the working world. Plausibility structures can be unhealthily strong as well as unhealthily weak. But the stories point, too, to the deeper question of the spiritual barrenness which every believer meets.

ANATOMY OF THE CONTEMPORARY WORLD-VIEW

An examination of the nature of the western world has led Peter Berger[5] to argue that there are three dominant factors which consciously or unconsciously shape our world-view. They form an overarching plausibility structure which the believer must believe in or believe against. The first is the commitment to technology which induces a problem-solving attitude to the world and the deep belief that life is capable of infinite improvement. Whatever the problem, the solution lies in our own hands and will eventually be discovered by rational means. More knowledge, more research and more money will lead to Utopia. True, there are many who are concerned about where technology is taking us, as is seen most clearly in the anti-nuclear lobby. But mainline society is totally geared to moving at the behest of technology. The critics are not taken too seriously. In fact, many of them are regarded as embarrassing eccentrics.

Technology therefore inculcates an attitude which is hostile to belief in the supernatural. It was neatly summed up by an advert for BP Chemicals in 1979 which, under a picture of five loaves and two fish, read: 'The world grows at a rate of 175,000

[5] For a complete exposition see P. Berger, *The Homeless Mind* (with B. Berger & H. Kellner).

extra mouths to feed every day. To keep them fed can't depend on miracles but on skill and technology.'[6] The concept of mystery has been exiled. Everything is capable of investigation, understanding and resolution. As Os Guinness has said, solving the problems of the world is now a matter of working Rubik's cube rather than unlocking the riddle of the universe.[7]

The second factor is bureaucracy. At first sight it may not seem as detrimental to faith in a living God as technology and yet a closer examination of its implications show it to be so. Bureaucracy believes that any problem, or rather its solution, is capable of organization. But such organization demands that it be conducted on the basis of competence. The only people who can administer the solution must have the right paper qualification to do so and people must be pigeon-holed. For example, in once giving a statement to the police about a neighbour, whose dead body I had discovered after we had failed to persuade her to answer the door, I found that I was not permitted to say 'on entering the room I found her dead', because that was a medical judgment and I was not a medical doctor, although I clearly knew a corpse when I saw one! More than this, bureaucracy works on an impersonal level and is committed to the concept of justice or fairness. Thus the social security officer is not meant to favour his relative who makes a claim, but must authorize only what is his due with strict impartiality. All this means that the personal dimension of life has been squeezed out and that our understanding of grace is therefore minimal.

The third, and perhaps crucial, factor is the commitment, already mentioned, to pluralism. Pluralism means that individuals face unlimited choice in which world-view to adopt. It is a value which is deeply embedded in the structure of our society. Schools hope to broaden a pupil's horizons and train him to argue from diverse viewpoints, weighing all the factors involved rather than trotting out unquestioned beliefs. The media in its continuous flow of noise constantly puts forward all the views on a subject. A documentary which will convince a viewer of the evil of apartheid one day will be contradicted by an inter-

[6] *The Daily Telegraph*, 21 September 1979.
[7] Os Guinness, *The Gravedigger File*, p. 62. This is the best popular exposition of the issues raised here.

view setting out the reasonableness of the system the next day and cause the viewer to be confused or to change his mind. The epitome of viewing at the present time is the open-ended chat show, where no conclusions are drawn and no winners or losers are nominated. Mobility, both physically and in the job market, means that we no longer have a geographical or vocational home, but that our futures are peculiarly open.

The psychological effects of this have been to create a condition of homelessness in our minds. Most people are no longer settled, convinced and unchanging in their world-view. What is true generally has specific implications for religion. The influx of immigrants and the shrinking of the world through television has meant that the diverse faiths of other people have deposited themselves on the Christian believer's doorstep. Add this to the lack of religious commitment to be found among those who by their cultural tradition are Christian and it is easy to see why faith in the living God has become difficult. It is hard to stand against the world and be sure that your interpretation is right. It is not unknown therefore for Christians to drift or to be converted, for a time, to something else, until they are converted to something different again.

There probably never was a time when there was only ever one version of reality passed down from generation to generation. But the degree and commitment to choice has never been so mind-boggling. It has left many punch-drunk to the extent that they never choose at all. It is also true that there was a time when the public acknowledgment of religion was greater and that its importance in our society was more socially agreed. For all its faults it meant that a believer inhabited a general plausibility structure which was favourable to faith. Now it has become a private affair which is not allowed to intrude in the real public world. Faith is no more allowed to affect one's business decisions than is one's membership of the budgerigar owners' club. The believer lives on a small island surrounded by a sea of secularism.

This will sound to some like a depressing reductionism. Is faith no more than an individual choice which we make as a result of various social forces at work? To see it in this light would be a misunderstanding. Remember that the sociology of knowledge is not concerned to evaluate the *truth* of the views

259

held, which must be accepted or dismissed on other grounds, but only to describe the means by which we come to adopt and maintain them. To say that faith needs a plausibility structure to sustain it is not to cast doubt on its truth, any more than saying that for a person to need food to sustain him casts doubt on whether he is God's creation. Man was created by God as a physical, spiritual and social being and the sociology of knowledge looks at the social dimension, examining the normal principles by which God works. In itself, therefore, it is incomplete but not necessarily wrong. In fact its analysis can be illuminating and can enable the pastor to offer more effective pastoral care as he attends not only to the question of objective revelation but to the way in which humans experience faith. It enables him to pay attention to plausibility structures which are there, whether he sees them or not.

A BIBLICAL PERSPECTIVE

The problems of which we have spoken are not new, although we encounter them in a distinctively modern form. The true people of God have always been in a minority and the plausibility of their belief has always been under threat. Granted that it may have been easier to believe in a supernatural dimension to the world in times gone by, none the less, technology and bureaucracy are only the modern counterparts of the world of idolatry and politics in which the Old Testament believers lived. And pluralism has always been a fact of life to one degree or another. The experience of the Jews during the exile is particularly fertile in this connection. The later chapters of Isaiah, as we have seen,[8] and the story of Daniel speak to these very issues. How is it possible to believe in a world where faith in the living God seems implausible and faith in the gods of Babylon seems a lot easier? How can faith be maintained when the plausibility structures of that faith have been shattered and one is forced to live in an alien plausibility structure? All the conversation, rituals, legitimations and sanctions of Babylon were contrary to those of the Jews. These are issues which need to be addressed seriously in our counselling and teaching, now as then. The way in which the Old Testament handles these

[8] See pp. 49–53.

issues gives us a way forward.

But the concern is just as evident in the New Testament, so much of which was written to maintain true faith in the face of competing plausibility structures. It too, therefore, points to possible ways forward.

We saw how Luke-Acts was concerned to deal with the accumulating doubts of Theophilus so that he might know certainty in his faith and have the evidence of many infallible proofs to support him.[9] Part of Luke's answer was to record the way in which the supernatural world, in terms of the activity of the Spirit and the progress of the word of God, could be traced in the natural world. Paul Minear, whilst longing for modern pastors like Luke, doubts whether his solution is any longer viable.[10] With men no longer predisposed to believe in the supernatural, he believes that a different route will have to be followed. But is Luke's solution so irrelevant? In Luke's own day too there were many who found it hard to accept a supernatural world-view. On the other hand, in our day, for all the atmosphere of secularism which we have described, it is quickly prone to evaporate – supernaturalism seems to be very resilient. Man finds it curiously unsatisfying, as many are now learning.[11]

Secularism is sometimes no more than a thin veneer, maintained in public out of fear of admitting anything else, but gladly cast off with the work-clothes on returning home. It is incapable of coping with the deeper questions of life and is frequently punctured by a family crisis or the onset of suffering. Thousands show, by their fascination with the occult, that belief in the supernatural is not dead. The growth of new religious movements demonstrates man's hunger for the eternal. And whilst the intellectuals may be able to hold the possibility of supernatural intervention consistently at arm's length, countless others are not. It was interesting, following the burning of York Minster in July 1984 after the consecration of the controversial Bishop of Durham, to see both archbishops rush headlong to deny that it was divine intervention, as if God were not capable of such intervention. Ordinary men and women,

---

[9] See pp. 69–73   [10] P. S. Minear, 'Dear Theo', p. 150.

[11] A whole body of sociological literature now recognizes the enduring religious nature of man, including D. Bell, *Sociological Journeys*; R. Bellah, *Beyond Belief*; P. Berger, *Facing up to Modernity*; and even B. Wilson, *Religion in Sociological Perspective*.

however, whilst not necessarily claiming that the act was divine judgment, were more willing to believe in the possibility that God would do such a thing. The irony of the situation exposed the raw nerve of secularism and showed how deep down, as one would expect if they are God's creatures, many still had some hankering after him.

The apostle John, too, is concerned about the question of plausibility. His Gospel is concerned to provide eye-witness grounds for believing but recognizes that not all will have such proof available to them. Its climax is to pronounce a special blessing on those who have not seen and yet still believe. In the book of Revelation he explains the apparent contradiction between faith and experience caused by the activity of Rome. The tension there is between a seen and temporal power, for which there was a massive plausibility structure, and an unseen and eternal power for which there was not.

Of the variety of approaches to the problem of plausibility in the Bible perhaps Hebrews is outstanding. Although often regarded as obscure because it speaks to Jewish believers about apparently in-house concerns, no book speaks more clearly about the threat of unbelief in the church, and it is a superb demonstration of pastoral theology confronting pluralism. The readers were in danger of drifting away from the Christian faith, probably back to Judaism. They were certainly struggling against the odds, surrounded by other religious world-views which seemed more plausible. How does the author handle the problem?

Firstly, he recognizes it as a problem. He knows that he is going to encourage a faith in things which could not be seen (11:1). It was easier to believe in Judaism with its Temple, its rituals, its tradition and its law. Before Christianity it may have been the least tangible of the faiths, but it was still more tangible than the Christian faith was. He does not dismiss his readers' problem and snap back a simple command that they should just believe. He sympathetically demonstrates that true faith has always faced the same predicament of being unable to prove, despite all the firm evidence which supports it, that its object is there (11:3–40).

Secondly, he carefully explains the object and nature of true faith. It is faith in Jesus Christ by whom God has spoken in ultimate terms to the world (1:1 – 3:6). God's revelation is the basis of their faith.[12] Belief in God is more than a mere attempt on man's part to make sense of his world. It is a response to what God has done to make himself known within the dimensions of human history and human experience, supremely through Jesus Christ.

And wherever pluralism threatens faith it is crucial that the historic foundations of the incarnation, death and resurrection of Christ are carefully laid. These foundations lead to the inescapable conclusion of the uniqueness of Christ. It is not only that he provides a better way to know God, but that he provides the only way. Although courtesy should always be extended to those of other views, the glad embrace offered by many to pluralism is not an option for the Christian. It cuts at the very roots of our teaching and causes the Christian flower to wither.

Thirdly, he exposes the shortcomings of other world-views and so undermines their plausibility. His main attention is naturally reserved for Judaism, which was the chief rival to Christianity for the faith of his readers. Throughout the letter he carefully takes one aspect of the teaching of Judaism after another and shows how inadequate it is. Rather than being desperately wrong, he shows how Judaism is incomplete, since it anticipates the coming of Jesus. It becomes dangerous if faith rests there and mistakes it as God's final word.

Others, however, faced different world-views which, for them, were just as persuasive. Moses in the court of Pharaoh (11:24–25) could have easily remained there to enjoy it. It must have seemed so much more real than serving 'the one who is invisible'. Yet he chose to leave it, realizing that the pleasures of sin could be enjoyed only for a short time. To Rahab the walls of Jericho and all they symbolized must have been a very strong plausibility structure. What could possibly make them fall? Yet, for whatever reason, she chose a world-view which in Jericho would have put her in a minority of one! The only thing is that the walls did fall down and she was eventually proved right. Much greater attention needs to be paid today to

[12] The concept of revelation should not be taken as the opposite of the social construction of reality and they should not be made to conflict with each other. The social construction of reality describes the mechanism by which revelation is received and interpreted. Thus, for example, in the teaching and miraculous works of Jesus the revelation of God was evident, but not all saw it as such. The revelation of God is an essential ingredient in Christian theology in view of man's fallen nature and his intrinsic inability, without divine intervention, to come to a true picture of God.

the debunking of contemporary world-views which exclude God. Like the Old Testament prophets we ought to be willing to mock at idols and expose their folly rather than being ourselves sucked in to worship, uncritically, at their altars.

Fourthly, the author shows an understanding of the importance of plausibility structures, even though he would never have heard of the term! He constantly encourages his readers to take their cue from significant others. The most important significant other is Jesus (12:2–3). His own life of suffering and endurance is to be their pattern. If they really have understood him they will be able to withstand the lure of other world-views. But he does not stand alone. A host of other witnesses serve to remind them of the rightness of their path (12:1), as do their own leaders who meant so much to them (13:7).

He stresses how essential conversation is to the maintenance of their faith. The believer needs others to speak to about his world-view (3:13 and 10:25). To go it alone is to court spiritual disaster. The Jews themselves knew the importance of temple worship and of reminding themselves of the great acts of God. Christians were in no way exempt from the same need. Fellowship which is strong, honest and relevant is vital.

The same is true of rituals, using the term in its broadest sense. It is important to meet together so that conversations can take place, but these must also be supported by right behaviour patterns. 13:1–5, with its encouragement to love, morality and contentment, is an example of that.

Most of Hebrews takes the form of a legitimation. The author carefully explains the difference, in passages too numerous to mention, between what they believed and what the Jews believed, and gives reasons as to why their belief was right and that of the Jews wrong. As a further example of a legitimation, note how the author confronts the problem as to why, if their world-view was right, they were struggling and suffering so much. His answer examines the discipline of the Lord (12:4–13) and underlines once more the message that the seen and the immediate are never the complete picture.

The sanctions are also there. Interspersed throughout the letter are warnings about the consequences of drifting away. Here, in some of the most vivid terms employed in the New Testament, the judgment of God is threatened (3:7–19; 6:4–6; 10:26–31 and 12:14–29) and Israel's historical experience of judgment is used as a justification for this interpretation of God.

CONCLUSION

Any world-view, natural or supernatural, is a matter of faith. We commit ourselves to it without being finally able to prove that it is right or wrong. Some may commit themselves mindlessly to a world-view. But the Christian need not do so, since there is a mass of evidence to support his world-view which reaches its climax in Jesus Christ. But in the end belief remains a matter of trust and the Christian cannot avoid the challenge to commit himself. 'Without faith it is impossible to please God, because anyone who comes to him must believe that he exists and that he rewards those who earnestly seek him' (11:6). Hebrews abounds in exhortations to faith (*e.g.* 4:1–2), but they occur only in the context of a realization that faith is not easy and the believer needs to belong to a plausibility structure which will inhibit the slide into unfaith.

As with many other parts of Scripture, Hebrews sets out a pattern for the pastor who tries to aid the believer struggling with the problem of plausibility. It puts forward a theology for the drifter and seeks to bring him back to a hardy faith. Sociology complements this and offers some insight into how vital this theology is for the contemporary Christian. The particular concerns of believers may no longer be Jewish ritual or temple worship, but the principles remain the same and, if anything, the tension between the visible and the invisible has become even stronger.

The believer may well enter the holy of holies and find it empty. He may well find the more tangible altars to other gods more in evidence. But the most real is not always the most visible and he need not be intimidated into unbelief.

14

Forgiveness

THE NEED FOR FORGIVENESS

David came from a lovely, supportive Christian family and he himself was a keen evangelical Christian. He was always ready to throw himself into the needs of his church and the first to volunteer his already scarce time for the latest evangelistic outreach. He was a spiritual activist to an extreme degree who worked simply in order to earn enough money to live, so that he could spend his time in Christian service. His spirituality was intense. God always seemed to be demanding more of him and he was always reaching out, never satisfied, after more of God. His doctrine could not be faulted, but though he believed in a God of love, and spoke frequently to others about him, there seemed little evidence in his life that he knew him. It was the holiness and judgment of God of which he spoke most frequently.

It was not surprising that with David's taut personality he should suffer from disabling headaches, which became increasingly more crippling and for which there was no obvious physical explanation. The headaches caused David the further frustration of putting him out of spiritual action from time to time, with the resulting fear that he was letting God down.

Prolonged pastoral care eventually took us to the heart of the problem. His unbalanced view of God had been subtly encouraged by his family. They had certainly loved him and wanted the best for him, but their love had always been tinged with the need for David to live up to their expectations, which were really very modest but none the less always present. The expectations seemed determined by the need to live up to a certain image in the church and to maintain a certain respectability before the neighbours.

That would have been bad enough and might have led, as so often, to a defective view of God and a general spiritual insecurity. But in David's case it was compounded. Several years before, as a respected member of his youth fellowship, he had slept on a few occasions with his girl-friend. She seemed, long since, to have forgotten the issue and was happily married to someone else. But he was riddled with guilt and lived in daily terror that he would be found out. Above all, he feared the pain which such exposure would bring to his parents and the rejection which would come his way.

Unable to confess his guilt and to experience forgiveness, David had been driven to prove to himself that he was acceptable to God by his ceaseless activity and, since this buried the problem rather than dealt with it, the guilt found expression through the physical channel of the headaches.

It was a stunning rebuke that one who had been a member of an evangelical church all his life knew nothing of the gospel in his experience. Whilst believing in a gospel based on faith he was living a gospel based on works. All his upbringing and the preaching for commitment which he heard Sunday after Sunday conspired to make it so.

Once David was led to an understanding of the true gospel he faced up to his sin and confessed it. In doing so he exchanged a worldly grief, which was preoccupied with himself and others and which leads to destruction, for a godly grief which leads to true repentance and salvation (2 Cor. 7:10). Then he was absolved in the name of Christ and his whole psychology began to change. The relief was visible and the headaches left him and have not returned for many years.

David represents thousands of evangelicals who theoretically believe the good news of Jesus but never actually experience the forgiveness he brings. Rather than knowing freedom from guilt and sins forgiven, they bury the guilt and hope it will never be discovered whilst they busy themselves in the right activities, hoping subconsciously that these will be enough to justify them in God's sight. Some will give expression to these turmoils by the development of neurotic symptoms, as David did. Others will appear relatively healthy and function normally whilst, in Paul Tournier's words, remaining 'unwitting invalids'.[1]

The ministry of forgiveness lies at the very core of the Christian ministry and must not be supplanted by another message. In a case like David's and in that of the many others who,

[1] P. Tournier, *Guilt and Grace*, p. 137.

resulting from our disturbed society, display some emotional or psychological imbalance, the temptation is to resort to offering them psychological or psychiatric therapy of one form or another. Doubtless something of value would have been achieved if this had happened in David's case. His guilt feelings could have been reduced and his faulty view of God, which was little more than a projection of his parents' demanding personalities, could have been improved. But it would not have fundamentally altered the problem, since his guilt was real and moral, not simply the result of faulty learning. It was only after the real problem had been uncovered and faced that dealing with the bad psychology made much sense and, in this, as in other cases, having discovered forgiveness, many of the psychological difficulties resolved themselves.

THE DISTINCTIVENESS OF THE GOSPEL

The pastor, then, must not forsake his distinctive role. He is a minister of God's grace, not a purveyor of psychological acceptance.[2] This is not to deny a genuine role for good psychotherapy or to pretend that the pastor has nothing to learn from the psychologist regarding his counselling technique. But it is to say that the pastor must not sell his birthright. His acquaintance with contemporary psychology is often superficial and brings him into contact only with the pop psychology cult of self-acceptance. This cult in itself is tantamount to a religion[3] and to devote oneself to it leads to the danger of preaching another gospel.

Five aspects of the Christian gospel may be highlighted to show the distinction between the gospel and pop psychology. The first difference is that the gospel deals with man's relationship with God, whereas psychology deals with man's relationship to himself or to his fellow men.

Secondly, the basis of acceptance according to the gospel is the forgiveness which is to be found through the historic work of Jesus Christ (1 Cor. 15:3–4). Psychology seems to rely on

---

[2] D. D. Williams, *The Minister and the Care of Souls*, pp. 78f. and 117f. For a detailed critique of the relationship between the thinking of the psychologist Melanie Klein and the theology of forgiveness see D. Atkinson, 'The Freedom of Forgiveness', *Third Way* 5/10 (1982), pp. 4–7 and 'Forgiveness and Personality Development', *Third Way* 5/11 (1982), pp. 18–21.

[3] See P. Vitz, *Psychology as Religion*.

some deep anthropological principle about the value of self-acceptance, or of reaching out beyond yourself for help in times of desperation without being able to be sure that the right kind of help is there. But the gospel says that, whilst men were in no position to help themselves, God took the initiative and came to the rescue (Rom. 5:6–8). Salvation is to be found, not in some vague hope, but in the definite historical expression of God's grace in the life, death and resurrection of Jesus Christ. Without that revelation and activity man might hope but he could not be sure that salvation was available.[4]

The third difference is that the Christian gospel takes sin more seriously than any contemporary psychology. It is true that some psychologies are concerned to face man with his responsibility for his wrong deeds and the moral consequences of his actions. But none goes as deep as the gospel. Sin is not only an offence against man but against a personal God (Ps. 51:4 and Lk. 15:18). It is not just a list of wrong actions but, since the fall, it has marred our complex personalities,[5] including our ability to be honest with ourselves. It may therefore be possible by therapy to remove certain guilt feelings but not to provide forgiveness between a man and his creator. And only such forgiveness can deal with man as a sinner through and through.

A fourth contrast lies in the fact that, whilst the therapist seeks to identify with his client's pain and failure, and his entering into it is even spoken of occasionally in terms of incarnation, the cross of Jesus is much more than God merely identifying with the sinner. It does speak of God's identification with sinful man. The one who was perfectly righteous became unrighteous for man. God's identification with our sin could not be greater (2 Cor. 5:21 and Heb. 4:15). But it is more than that. The cross went beyond identification and achieved a solution. The solution demanded that the offence against God be paid for.[6] Here is not an acceptance of man which papers over the cracks but an acceptance which is made possible because the fundamental issues have been resolved.

Fifthly, the place man occupies in therapy and in the process of salvation is different. In psychology the answer lies within him or in the action he takes to resolve his own problems. In

---

[4] Francis Schaeffer, *True Spirituality, passim.*
[5] Tournier, *Guilt and Grace*, pp. 128–133.
[6] On the deep feeling that everything must be paid for see *ibid.*, pp. 174–180.

the gospel man has nothing to offer. He has only to believe the promise of God. George Bernard Shaw wrote, 'Forgiveness is a beggar's refuge; we must pay our debts.'[7] His objection to the offer of free pardon in Christ strikes a chord within most of us. But that is the way it is. If there is anything we could do to commend ourselves to God then, to put it as starkly as Paul does, Christ's death was a waste (Gal. 5:2).

But, it will be objected, man must repent, confess and believe. True, but these are not merits which earn man his salvation, although it is all too easy to think of them as such. Luther was so aware of this danger that he advised that people should go occasionally to communion without having confessed, 'so that man learns to trust God's mercy more than his own confession or effort. For not enough can be done against that accursed trust in our own works'.[8] What shocking advice! But Luther was a wise pastor and knew that shock is sometimes a necessary pastoral strategy if people are truly to lay hold of the gospel. Repentance, confession and faith are not conditions of forgiveness so much as the route through which grace comes or 'the receiving surface of divine pardon'.[9] In Augustus Toplady's familiar words, our only way of approach is to say,

> Nothing in my hand I bring;
> Simply to Thy cross I cling;
> Naked, come to Thee for dress;
> Helpless, look to Thee for grace;
> Foul, I to the fountain fly;
> Wash me, Saviour, or I die.

WHY FORGIVENESS IS DIFFICULT TO EXPERIENCE

David could probably have said all this. Why then did he not experience forgiveness? The answer, quite simply, is that he did not believe it. He had not become desperate enough to believe it, and his whole Christian training militated against him accepting it. He did not see sin as an offence against God. He was more concerned about the damage to his reputation than the offence he had caused God. Neither did he accept that

---

[7] Quoted by H. R. Mackintosh, *The Christian Experience of Forgiveness*, p. 184.
[8] 'A Discussion on how Confession should be made', *LW*, vol. 39, p. 40.
[9] Mackintosh, *Forgiveness*, p. 211.

the work of Christ was enough. Even if he had once believed it at his conversion he was now, like the foolish Galatians, 'trying to attain (his) goal by human effort' (Gal. 3:3). He did not believe he had nothing to offer God. Indeed, everything he did cried out that he had a lot to offer God.

The doctrine changed from the level of theory and rose to the level of experience when his headaches became so severe that he was driven to share it with someone else and that counselling faced him up with the need for honest confession. In these pastoral conversations the truth which he had heard, or rather misheard, a thousand times in church was clarified and personally applied. He then began to exercise faith, that is, to inform his subjective experience with the objective truths of the gospel. His story demonstrates the truth of Paul Tournier's assertion that the private word is far more effective than any general absolution,[10] and stresses the need for every pastor to devote time to such private conversations.

Protestantism has been uneasy about confession and wary of the pastor acting as a confessor, and rightly so. Ritual confession too readily degenerates into a meaningless act. And there is nothing in Scripture which limits the right of absolution to the ordained ministry. Any Christian brother acting in the name of Christ, and conscious of being on a level with his Christian brother, is able to assure another of his forgiveness in Christ where true repentance is evident (Gal. 6:1 and Jas. 5:16). But our fears of 'confession' have resulted in our isolating the individual before God and cutting him off from his fellow believers at the very point where he needs their help. Contemporary psychology combines with pastoral experience to show how vital it is that men do confess their sins to one another. Though psychological and pastoral conversations are not the same, as we have observed,[11] similar psychological dynamics are at work.

The personal verbal confession of sin assists a person to accept his moral guilt and view it in the same light as God does. It is too easy to fool oneself and only pretend confession is accomplished simply by mulling it over in the mind. The confessional conversation means the sinner cannot escape. The psalmists knew how easy it was to run away and demonstrated

[10] Tournier, *Guilt and Grace*, p. 204.
[11] Tournier overstresses the relationship, giving the impression that the two forms of conversation are identical, *ibid.*, pp. 149f. and 204.

the value of this cathartic method (Pss. 32 and 51). Furthermore, it is so often in confession that the forgiveness which is known about theoretically seizes the penitent and becomes real.[12] God's forgiveness is assured and the one who has been broken is no longer left to flounder in his sins.

Once David saw what Christ had done for him, took God at his word, gave up trying to justify himself, and really believed, then the experience of forgiveness became alive for him. Let us make no mistake here. Forgiveness is to be experienced and is not just a fact to be accepted irrespective of experience. According to H. R. Mackintosh it was the later Reformers who separated the aspect of God's judicial acquittal of our sin from our inward experience, so that the one had no necessary effect on the other.[13] Certainly no biblical writer writes of forgiveness as a distant academic fact. The biblical expectation is that a man should 'taste and see that the Lord is good' (Ps. 34:8). But it is important to understand what we experience and what we do not.

Mackintosh defined forgiveness as 'an active process in the mind and temper of a wronged person, by means of which he abolishes a moral hindrance to fellowship with the wrong-doer and re-establishes the freedom and happiness of friendship'.[14] Forgiveness is about the reconciliation of relationships and the restoration of communion. This enables us to see what we cannot claim for it and follow through what we can.

The quest for forgiveness is the theme of Morris West's explicit but moving novel entitled *The World is Made of Glass*. It is the story of a European brothel-keeper called Magda who seeks to deal with the scars her life has inflicted. She undertakes a course of psychoanalytic therapy with Carl Jung, during which the deep turmoils within her, and him, are stirred and unloosed but never resolved. The real hero of the story is a Roman Catholic doctor who, on the surface, has the least to offer but who leads Magda nearer to the experience of forgiveness than anyone. In the course of explaining to her what forgiveness means he says,

> You've got it wrong my dear. It isn't innocence which is restored, but the relationship between the Creator and the

---

[12] Thurneysen, *A Theology of Pastoral Care*, p. 290.

[13] Mackintosh, *Forgiveness*, p. 137. Schaeffer agrees, *True Spirituality*, p. 102.

[14] Mackintosh, *Forgiveness*, p. 33.

creature. The child says, 'I'm sorry'. The Father embraces him back into the family. But we carry the scars of our follies until we die.[15]

Yet, as he had already said to her, the doctrine of forgiveness means that new beginnings are possible and that instead of seeing oneself as a freak and oddity, or a failure, one can see oneself as chosen and loved.[16]

THE EFFECTS OF FORGIVENESS

Forgiveness does not necessarily exempt us from the consequences of our wrong actions, nor from the psychological scars they inflicted, any more than conversion would automatically heal a broken leg. The prodigal son on returning home, though freely forgiven by his father, had still spent a tremendous amount of money which would not suddenly and mysteriously reappear in his bank account and he still had the broken relationship with his brother to face. Dr Martyn Lloyd-Jones put it as strongly as to say that 'the fundamental elements in our personality and temperament are not changed by conversion and rebirth. The new man means the new disposition, the new understanding, the new orientation, but the man himself, psychologically, is essentially what he was before'.[17] Whatever progress we may make on earth, physical and psychological perfection are going to have to wait for heaven or the Lord's return.

So does forgiveness have any effect in the area of our personalities? The answer must be an emphatic yes. It did in David's case. The headaches left him and he began to relax as a person. The taut spring began to unwind. He became more accepting of other people and less harsh in his judgments. Such changes frequently result from a true experience of forgiveness and to expect them is consistent with the teaching of Scripture. The Old Testament recognizes the close connection between receiving forgiveness and healing (*e.g.* Pss. 41:4; 103:3 and Is. 57:17–21). And it acknowledges that the healing which forgiveness brings is both of a physical and a psychological kind (see,

---

[15] M. West, *The World is Made of Glass*, p. 89.   [16] *Ibid.*, p. 75.
[17] Quoted in I. H. Murray, *D. Martyn Lloyd-Jones: The First Forty Years 1899–1939*, facing p. 1.

for example, Ps. 147:3). This understanding is reinforced in the ministry of Jesus where physical healing is sometimes spoken of in terms of salvation as, for example, in Mark 5:34 or 10:52, and where wholeness of person and forgiveness through Christ is explicitly connected as, for example, in Mark 2:1–12.

So Francis Schaeffer rightly asserts that, though forgiveness will not bring complete healing, it does make a real and substantial difference.[18] If people know that God has forgiven them and accepted them in Christ, no matter what they are or what they have done, then conscience can no longer condemn. Schaeffer describes his conscience as a big black dog straining at the leash and threatening to devour him. But because of the completed work of Christ, he is able to say 'Down, be still!' and the dog has no leg to stand on and no option but to obey! That in itself may lead to a release of tensions and anxieties, which thus frees a Christian who suffers from a wrong sense of psychological guilt.

Knowing that God has accepted a person in Christ may well remove other fears – of failure, of not living up to expectations, of being thought odd or of rejection, of being found out, of letting God down. Release from these fears will enable a person to function in a healthier way and, paradoxically, to reach the goals he or she strove for but previously found blocked by their anxieties. The acceptance of God may well lead a person to accept himself or herself and so be less defensive. The understanding of God's forgiveness, so freely given to them, should certainly lead them to forgive others as the teaching of Jesus makes abundantly clear (Mt. 6:12 and 18:23–35). When apologies are made, resentments released and hatchets buried, there can be substantial healing of relationships.

What forgiveness does is to give a perspective in which the whole of life can be seen. It would be a delusion to claim that it removes every problem and every scar. Many will still struggle with self-condemnation and others will continue to wrestle with psychological difficulties.

It sometimes seems easier to believe that God has forgiven us than it is to forgive ourselves. The objective truth is that God has blotted out our transgressions and remembers our sins no more (Is. 43:25). But we somehow keep managing to resurrect

---

[18] Schaeffer, *True Spirituality*, pp. 93–147.

them. It reminds me of the word processor which I am using at the moment. On it there is a key labelled 'break' and, if pressed, all that has been typed into the computer's memory disappears and seems irretrievably lost. The carefully composed words are a thing of the past, gone for ever. Such is the quality of God's forgiveness. But then one learns that there is a way of getting them back, if you do it quickly. A swift operation with other keys will make the apparently irretrievable accessible once more. God has pressed the 'break' key on our sins and we persist in dragging them back!

Forgiveness does not restore our innocence and the memory of past sins continues, but the self-condemnation which accompanies it needs putting in its place. If God, the sovereign of the universe, has decreed the matter finished, who are we to keep putting the item back on the agenda of our minds? This self-condemning memory can be disabling and lead to a sense of inferiority which prevents us from being the true sons of God and keeps us as slaves in his house (Gal. 3:26 – 4:7). It is important, therefore, to transform specific guilt into a genuine sense of unworthiness. When this is done, far from being disabling, our memory will lead to a true sense of liberty and a profound sense of gratitude. How is this possible? To quote Martyn Lloyd-Jones' comments in reference to depression,

> The main art in the matter of spiritual living is to know how to handle yourself. You have to take yourself in hand, you have to address yourself, preach to yourself, question yourself. You must say to your soul 'Why are you cast down' – what business have you to be disquieted? You must turn on yourself, and say to yourself, 'Hope thou in God' – instead of muttering in this depressed unhappy way. And then you must go on to remind yourself of God, Who God is and what God is and what God has done, and what God has pledged himself to do. Then having done that, end on this great note: defy yourself, and defy other people, and defy the devil, and the whole world . . .[19]

As he never tired of saying, our trouble is that we listen to ourselves too much but we do not talk to ourselves enough.

[19] D. M. Lloyd-Jones, *Spiritual Depression: Its Causes and Cure*, p. 21.

Not all of a person's psychological difficulties will be cured by his experience of forgiveness. They may be relieved, but more often what forgiveness will do is provide the sufferer with courage to face his difficulties and seek help to resolve them. The Christian is not immune from mental illness, and it is both foolish and dangerous to pretend that he is. Nor is moral guilt before God the only form of guilt which is real. Some, for example, who suffer from depression may find that an experience of the forgiveness of God cures it. But depression is a multi-headed monster and other remedies may be needed as well. For some it is a deep personality trait, for others a reaction to their situation and for still others it is endogenous.[20] The pastor needs to encourage each sufferer to seek appropriate medical attention, unless he wishes to be guilty, by his negligence, of causing worse suffering. Therapy, drugs and electroconvulsive therapy all have their part to play according to the needs of the patient and the cause of his depression.[21]

Pastoral care, then, will need to be comprehensive and the skilful pastor will recognize the need for a person to be ministered to at all levels at once. Practical, social, medical and psychiatric help are not in competition with each other. Rather they complement each other in enabling people to move to greater wholeness. An either/or mentality can be damaging to the very people we seek to help. But the pastor's central role must not be forgotten and he must not allow himself to be forced into the role of a social worker or other caring professional. He must hold to the centre, to the message of grace and announce it in the sure and certain belief that it is the most radical and relevant answer that he can provide to the problems of those he meets.

---

[20] In simple terms, depression may be either reactive, that is caused by a reaction to circumstances external to the individual, or endogenous, that is an illness, often associated with old age, that develops from within the individual. See further J. White, *The Masks of Melancholy*.

[21] Depression is an immense problem and has rightly been called 'the common cold of psychological illnesses'. Were this a textbook on pastoral counselling it would be right to devote much space to the issue. But the reader is referred to J. White's book, *The Masks of Melancholy*, as a highly recommended guide to the subject and one which contains valuable insight for the pastor.

THE RECURRING THREAT TO EVANGELICALISM

Eduard Thurneysen, who has done so much to expound this theme, gently chides us for our timidity.[22] We are not nearly audacious enough in our preaching of the message of grace. We fear a lack of response, forgetting the ministry of the Holy Spirit, who moves those to whom we talk to respond. We fear too to take the risk which is inherent in the gospel itself. Our zeal for the honour of the Lord leads us to fend off the threat of antinomianism with the result that we seem to qualify God's unconditional grace. Like the critics whom Paul answers in Romans, we cannot believe it is that simple.

Perhaps the greatest recurring threat to evangelicalism is that it so easily degenerates into Pharisaism and therefore its greatest pastoral need is to be true to the doctrine of grace. Whilst no longer tempted to demand circumcision of our members, countless other demands are made on them – the demand for respectability, for the achievement of certain moral standards, for certain spiritual experiences and for the punctilious observance of certain rituals. Our preaching often seems so laced with demands that it is heard as sheer moralism and not as good news. Romans and Galatians need to be addressed all over again to the contemporary church.

Not only do we need to believe and communicate the gospel of grace, but we need to create accepting fellowships where we demonstrate our commitment to it. The fashion in some churches is to emphasize the need to share and to be totally honest and intimate with all in the fellowship, even with strangers. Such a demand too easily slips into a new legalism and is unhealthy. It creates fellowships which are introspective and man-centred. Wearing one's heart on one's sleeve is not always good for the individual or for the person who is forced to see it. We have a need to relate to different sizes of groups with different degrees of intimacy and only with a very few can we be healthily intimate. Yet, the desire which has motivated this reaction, perhaps overreaction, to the impersonal formalism of many churches, is understandable. The atmosphere in so many churches encourages hypocrisy because no-one ever gets close enough to others to know whether they are genuine or merely

---

[22] E. Thurneysen, *A Theology of Pastoral Care*, p. 188.

acting. But it also means that many with deep personal problems, imprisoning them in the most terrible guilt, leave without ever having had their needs met.

Every congregation has within it those who are burdened with sin and guilt. There are those who have engaged in dishonest acts, those who have committed adultery, those struggling with homosexuality, those who feel deserted because of a marriage failure or who are angry or violent, those who feel worthless and depressed. The agonies come in all shapes and sizes. For them, the Davids of our churches, it is vital not only that we preach a message of grace but that they experience relationships of grace within the fellowship of the church. Non-threatening, non-judgmental honesty must be the prevailing atmosphere. At the same time discipline must not be forsaken and a concern for holiness must be maintained, for only as it is will many have the courage to face the sin and the failure instead of trying to hide from it. Only as they do not feel they have to be something or live up to certain standards will they feel able to unburden themselves to others who will help them in accordance with the law of Christ (Gal. 6:2). Only so will they really grasp the dimensions of God's grace which will free them from guilt and enable them to begin to effect changes in all aspects of their life.

CONCLUSION

In a broken world, such as ours, there is no greater need than that we rediscover our confidence in the gospel. Too often we have been like restless sheep looking at the apparently greener pastures in other fields. The fields of politics, psychology and sociology, in which Christians should be involved, have their place. But the gospel deals with a more fundamental issue than they will ever touch. Whilst they essentially deal with man's relationship to himself or to his fellow men, the gospel deals with man's relationship to God. To bring about reconciliation in that relationship by leading people into an experience of forgiveness is not only to bring about the most profound change a man can know, but also the most relevant change, for it affects him at the very core of his being and has implications for every other dimension of his life.

Our confidence in the gospel needs restoring not only in

relation to other fields which would seek to alleviate man's problems but in relation to contemporary evangelical practice. We have too often been guilty of adding to the gospel our own social and cultural demands and in doing so have qualified the love of God. We need to learn to take the risk of ministering justification by faith alone, without spoken or unspoken qualification.

15

Suffering

There is a staggering amount of suffering around. One of the surprising features of life for most young men entering the ministry is that they are immediately confronted on every hand with grief and suffering of immense depth. The pastor dare not trot out glib answers. They only increase the suffering and betray his lack of understanding. Yet he must have answers which lift the sufferer out of subjectivism. They must be answers which are both realistic and feeling and, at the same time, demonstrate an awareness of Scripture.

THE PROBLEM OF PAIN: DISCUSSED AND EXPERIENCED

When C. S. Lewis lost his wife he expressed his anguish on paper and argued aloud through his bereavement. At one point he wrote, 'Talk to me about the truth of religion and I'll listen gladly. Talk to me about the duty of religion and I'll listen submissively. But don't come talking to me about the consolations of religion or I shall suspect that you don't understand.'[1] It is interesting to compare this subjective expression of pain in *A Grief Observed* with his earlier objective discussion of *The Problem of Pain*.

At its simplest the problem of pain is that God either lacks goodness or power or both. How is man to reconcile belief in an omnipotent and good God with suffering? Lewis advances numerous arguments to show that they are reconcilable. Omnipotence must be defined carefully. An all-powerful God has power to do all that is intrinsically possible. But it is no limitation on omnipotence to say that he cannot do nonsense or that which is intrinsically impossible. The truth of this can be seen in creation. God created free self-conscious souls, but that entailed creating an environment over against which the soul could become self-conscious. An environment which varied at every whim would rule out all possibility of freedom

[1] C. S. Lewis, *A Grief Observed*, p. 23.

and choice and so God at the same time had to create a relatively independent and inexorable world of nature. But such nature, being fixed and obeying constant laws, is not going to be equally beneficial to all. Lewis concludes, 'Try to exclude the possibility of suffering which the order of nature and the existence of free-wills involve and you find that you have excluded life itself.'[2]

The second main feature of Lewis' argument is to examine what it means to claim that God is good. His basic premise is that we confuse goodness with kindness. God is love, and true love which genuinely cares is bound to be exacting in its relationships. A parent who truly cares for his child will not permit the child to do what he pleases, however destructive or sinful that action might be. True love cares to the extent that it shapes and disciplines and punishes.

> You asked for a loving God: you have one. The great spirit you so lightly invoked, the 'lord of terrible aspect', is present: not a senile benevolence that drowsily wishes you to be happy in your own way, not the cold philanthropy of a conscientious magistrate, nor the care of a host who feels responsible for the comfort of his guests, but the consuming fire Himself, the love that made the worlds, persistent as an artist's love for his work and despotic as a man's love for a dog, provident and venerable as a father's love for a child, jealous, inexorable, exacting as love between the sexes.[3]

Next, Lewis turns his attention to sin and suggests that many of our problems with suffering arise because we fail to appreciate the badness of our sin. We view sin superficially, thinking that time will cancel it out or that, because everyone does it, it cannot be so bad. But in the fall we turned from God to self and rejected our true and creaturely position. Sin cannot be minimized and once we arrive at a true perception of it we see what a horror we must be to God. Once we have arrived there we must see that God's wrath against sin is an inevitable corollary of his goodness.

But what of pain? Admitting that pain is present in the world, Lewis lays the blame for four-fifths of it at man's own door. Simply because it exists man inflicts it on others and, in so doing,

---

[2] C. S. Lewis, *The Problem of Pain*, p. 22.   [3] *Ibid.*, pp. 34f.

multiplies it. Pain itself is not good and yet God uses it for good and often speaks most clearly to man through it. Suffering shatters the illusion that all is well and shatters the illusion of man's self-sufficiency. Suffering challenges man to surrender himself to God and does so in a way which means that self-surrender arises from pure motives rather than because of the pleasure it will derive. If life were all joy, pleasure and happiness we would be content with it, and with this world as it is, and we would leave God out. With relentless logic, Lewis pursues his argument into the realms of hell and confutes the sentimental objections which are raised against the doctrine. Although the doctrine of hell can never be tolerable, in his view, it can at least be shown to be moral. Many of our objections to it stem from false medieval pictures of it. In the long run. God must draw the line somewhere. Then, as Lewis cogently argues,

> In the long run the answer to all those who object to the doctrine of Hell, is itself a question: 'What are you asking God to do?' To wipe out their past sins and, at all costs, to give them a fresh start, soothing every difficulty and offering every miraculous help? But He has done so, on Calvary. To forgive them? But they will not be forgiven. To leave them alone? Alas, I am afraid that is what He does.[4]

Would Lewis have altered any of his argument had he written *The Problem of Pain* after his bereavement rather than before? The answer must be no. *A Grief Observed* is written with a new depth of feeling and the protest against the evil of suffering is more intense. Yet the book is clearly written by the same man arguing on the same ground and willing to turn his arguments on himself. As before, Lewis has a healthy sense that we must be God-centred not man-centred in our thinking. What may appear to us to make no sense whatsoever may look very different to God. Conversely the very questions which we most want to ask may really be irrelevant or just plain nonsense and therefore unanswerable, even by God.

Lewis recognizes that, however unendurable it may be, suffering is an inescapable fact of life. If God is good, the sufferings must be necessary or he would not inflict them. If

---

[4] *Ibid.*, p. 116.

he is not good, just a cosmic sadist, he would inflict them in any case. Either way man cannot win. But Lewis is not content to leave it in the balance. His own conviction is clearly seen to be what it was before. Suffering is not good in itself but God uses it for good. The dentist may well inflict pain or induce fear, but his purposes in so doing are good. So it is with God.[5]

Similarly, as before, he argues that the suffering is needed to shatter our illusions and drive us to surrender to God.

> Bridge-players tell me that there must be some money on the game 'or else people won't take it seriously'. Apparently it's like that. Your bid – for God or no God, for a good God or the Cosmic Sadist, for eternal life or nonentity – will not be serious if nothing much is staked on it. And you will never discover how serious it was until the stakes are raised horribly high; until you find that you are playing not for counters or for sixpences but for every penny you have in the world. Nothing less will shake a man – or at any rate a man like me – out of his merely verbal thinking and his merely notional beliefs. He has to be knocked silly before he comes to his senses. Only torture will bring out the truth. Only under torture does he discover it himself.[6]

The same uncompromising logic which rejects sentimentalism is evident in both works. In neither is there easy consolation. And yet there is in both of them a strong consolation. It seems that *The Problem of Pain* stood Lewis in good stead when the pain became personal. Of course, he shouted and kicked and screamed. But he did not reject his previous position. Rather he advanced it in one important respect: that which was before a sound but academic argument now became a sound and personal experience. His rigorous but sympathetic approach to the problem of suffering provides a classic illustration of pastoral theology.

TRADITIONAL CONSOLATION

C. S. Lewis may well have protested against the idea that religion had any consolation to offer to those who suffered, but

---

[5] *Grief Observed*, p. 36. [6] *Ibid.*, p.34.

the task of providing consolation has always been a major aspect of the work of the pastor. The task is among the most difficult the pastor has to perform. It is difficult because ultimately suffering remains a mystery. Something can be said, however, to put it in perspective and perhaps alleviate it or enable the sufferer to gain from his experiences. For example, we might reduce the anxiety which arises when the sufferer feels that God is directly punishing him for his sin. In view of Paul's words to the Corinthians (1 Cor. 11:30) it cannot be denied that there may be some connection between suffering and sin. But the book of Job should put paid to the idea that there is an automatic connection between sin and suffering, and Jesus explicitly taught that suffering is not necessarily caused by individual sin (Lk. 13:1–3; Jn. 9:1–3). None the less all our attempts at explanation fall short of what we would like to know, and hear. Our understanding remains acutely limited and in the end we are called, like Job, to submit to God and to accept our creatureliness with humility.

What, then, can be said by way of consolation? Firstly, God is not indifferent to our suffering but has himself experienced, in Christ, the depth and anguish of it. Hebrews 2:9 speaks of Christ tasting death in solidarity with all men and thereby providing man with a way of defeating his worst enemy. 1 Peter 4:1 stresses that Christ actually experienced suffering in his body and the whole of Peter's first letter provides an assurance that God sympathizes with us in suffering. As Christ entered the darkness of man's suffering through his incarnation, so we too are often called to share the burden and anguish of another's suffering. We are often to do so silently (Is. 53:7; 1 Pet. 2:21–23), without rushing to easy explanations or justifications of God.

Secondly, God is 'the Father of compassion and the God of all comfort' (2 Cor. 1:3). Our instinctive reaction to suffering is often to hit out at God. Fortunately the Bible is realistic about human emotions and often identifies with these reactions in the Psalms and Jeremiah. But God never willingly inflicts pain (La. 3:32–33), and man's desire to apportion blame – less still to blame God – is often the least important thing to do in the circumstances. God has revealed himself as a God who can be discovered through pain. It often brings people to the end of their own resources and so encourages them to draw on God.

284

Even if the sufferer knows God well, pain frequently brings a new dimension to his or her relationship, and God's love is experienced in hitherto undreamt of depths. It was like that for David Watson. He commented that his cancer had led him to enjoy God more than ever before and that the reality of worship had never meant so much to him as it did then. He wrote, 'we need to find God's love and stay resting in it. Nothing is more important than that'.[7] In addition, it must not be forgotten that discipline is an expression of God's commitment to us (Heb. 12:4–13) and, far from causing us to question God, it should make us more convinced of his love.

Thirdly, God uses suffering for our good. God is not engaged in an evenly matched struggle with evil (Is. 45:7), but reigns over it. The affirmation that God brings good out of evil is to be heard on the lips of God's people from Joseph (Gn. 50:20) to Paul (Rom. 8:28). And the claim has been vindicated by countless Christians since who have, even if only with the benefit of hindsight, been able to trace God's goodness in their seeming disasters. Paul spoke of the value for our characters of suffering (Rom. 5:3–5), indicating that there are some things which can be learnt only through pain. Peter emphasizes its value in our battle against sin (1 Pet. 4:1). And Jesus spoke of the way in which it could glorify God (Jn. 9:1–3). So an effective ministry of consolation will not merely lend support to the sufferer, but will encourage him to learn and grow through suffering. True consolation will prevent the sufferer from gradually slipping downhill in his attitude towards God, himself and others. It will want to challenge self-centred attitudes and promote spiritual development through the experience.

Fourthly, suffering unites us to Christ. A Christian cannot have fellowship with his Lord fully unless he identifies with the suffering his Lord endured (Phil. 3:10). For the Christian suffering is not something to be avoided at all costs but is, when it comes, something to be welcomed as a means of furthering our union with Christ. After the suffering will come the glory; but just as in Christ's life suffering was a necessary prelude to his glory, so it is in ours. 'Do not be surprised at the painful trial you are suffering, as though something strange were happening to you. But rejoice that you participate in the suffer-

---

[7] D. Watson, *Fear No Evil*, p. 63.

ings of Christ, so that you may be overjoyed when his glory is revealed' (1 Pet. 4:12–13).

Fifthly, suffering will not endure for ever. The resurrection of Jesus gives us the confident hope that man's enemies have been defeated and it is only a matter of time before our experience of pain is over. Suffering will probably not be interminable in this life (1 Pet. 5:10), but even if it is we can be sure of the time when God will finally terminate it, when he puts an end to the frustration which the whole of creation experiences (Rom. 8:18–25). In the mean time we are called to patient hope.

These consolations may well need to be supplemented with an attempt to grapple with the hard and persistent question as to how a good God could allow suffering. People will rarely permit us to avoid that issue. So the focus of our pastoral care will need to broaden, along the lines set out by C. S. Lewis, but not at the expense of our primary responsibility of putting sufferers into personal touch with God. This broader focus can degenerate into a philosophical argument which titillates the mind but does not change the person. But it need not do so and it may well inject a note of objectivity into what might otherwise be a very introspective and subjective episode.

Thomas Oden[8] has reviewed the teaching of the church through the ages on this subject and has set out twelve arguments which have been frequently employed. Each separate answer has its limitations. Yet when combined they are powerful and can still prove useful if adapted and handled with care. In short, they are:

1. God does not directly will suffering, although it occurs by his permission as a result of our finitude and sin.

2. God gave us the extraordinary gift of finite freedom, but that carried with it the possibility of abuse.

3. God would not have permitted evil at all unless he could draw good out of evil.

4. God's power is not limited by the existence of evil. Rather it enhances God's power that he takes the risk of creating men with a measure of freedom and is not threatened by the opposition which might result.

5. In the same way in which a medication is sometimes needed to purge the body, or a harsh regime is needed to

---

[8] T. C. Oden, *Pastoral Theology, Essentials of Ministry*, pp. 226–244.

produce physical fitness, so affliction may be needed to produce personal health and growth.

6. Chastisement serves a purifying and educative purpose.

7. Christians do not despair over evil, though it is deeply ingrained in society as well as in individuals. They trust in a God who is beyond comprehension and yet one who has made himself sufficiently known in history, culminating in the coming of Christ, to encourage them to trust him for what they cannot see or understand.

8. Suffering puts goodness into bold relief and in so doing increases our capacity to enjoy life.

9. Opposition, tension and struggle are necessary to growth, development and healthy formation.

10. Our finitude means we are not capable of receiving God's complete and incomparable goodness.

11. Evil is a deprivation of good. So the existence of evil can bring about good. For example, the existence of disease can call forth human effort and love in combating it which would not otherwise exist.

12. God, being infinitely good, would create a world which was the best possible world. It may not seem to be the best possible world from my personal viewpoint, but that is because God has created what is best for the whole rather than what is best for me. (This point neglects the effect of the fall upon creation which means that our world is not now God's best creation; it remains an interesting philosophical comment none the less.)

THE CHALLENGE OF HEALING

The traditional ministry of consolation has been under fire in recent years because of the re-emergence of the ministry of healing. In this, many claim to have rediscovered a gift of the Holy Spirit and to have righted an imbalance in Christian teaching. Scripture, it is said, not only has much to teach about the value of suffering but also about the possibility of healing. Francis MacNutt, a respected spokesman in this area, justifiably complains that the church instils an attitude towards suffering which completely undercuts any desire for healing. The dominant attitude is that suffering is sent by God and therefore to ask for healing is to oppose his will. Whilst it may be permissible to ask for some relief, it is better for the sick person to endure the suffering. He complains of an 'undue emphasis on the cross and the benefits of suffering'[9] and speaks of the conditioning that most Christians undergo which leaves them with a pagan view of God in which suffering is equated with punishment for sin. In contrast, MacNutt argues that the healing of Jesus is central to the gospel and integral to the revelation of God as a God of love.[10] This he argues is where the accent of biblical teaching falls.

Those who minister in this area do not all display the wisdom of MacNutt. As with any rediscovered emphasis there are always those who go to extremes and it would be well to detail a number of disturbing features of this ministry which must be disowned.

It must be recognized that whenever signs and wonders are performed there is always the danger that people will see the signs as an end in themselves rather than as a pointer to God, and seek the miracle for its own sake rather than for the sake of the God who works it. In the ministry of Jesus it was evident that the working of mighty deeds was a stumbling-block for some rather than a stepping-stone to faith. For this reason it is not unreasonably asserted that Jesus' own attitude to the working of miracles was one of some reticence (Mt. 11:21–22; 16:4; Mk. 1:32–38; Jn. 4:48; 12:37). Jesus worked miracles in the context of the word of the gospel and the two were not divorced.

There is a danger of reducing God and making him less than sovereign. Some speak as if he is a sort of personal, portable chemist so that, instead of resorting to medicines, God is expected, at the least ache and pain, to step in and remove it. If every hair on our heads is numbered (Mt. 10:30), it is fair to believe that God is interested in the smallest details of our lives. But to use him constantly to increase our personal comfort and to believe that he is constantly at our beck and call is to exchange the living God for an idol.

Then some make impetuous and bold claims which make God out to look a fool when they are not fulfilled. The strong assertion that it is God's will to heal a person who subsequently dies, and the raising of people's faith to believe in the miracu-

---

[9] F. MacNutt, *Healing*, p. 41.   [10] *Ibid.*, pp. 98–108.

lous, only subsequently to have it disappointed, has recently become a major pastoral problem. The problem of unanswered prayer has taken on a whole new dimension of urgency as a result. It has to be said, too, that the answers some have given to this problem have been less than honest.

To say that the sick person died because the church lacked faith or did not pray sufficiently is, in some cases, blatantly untrue. The claim that prayer was answered and God has healed when a sick person dies, even though it is clear to all that physical restoration to this life was expected, is a delusion. Similarly, to pray about a distressing medical problem expecting God to heal it, and then to rejoice that God has lengthened the sick person's leg, which has nothing to do with his condition, is to turn God into a laughing-stock. To claim that healings have taken place even though we have not yet experienced them is totally out of tune with Scripture. Our dishonesty does not glorify God. Sad pastoral experiences should motivate us to humble caution in the claims we make with our mouths (Ec. 5:2–3, 7). Our desire to be 'in' on God's action has sometimes led us to risk other people's spiritual well-being. Scripture simply does not allow us to indulge in the glib pretence that healing is always intended or available.

A further pastoral problem has arisen over the connection between faith and the working of a miracle. In some cases in the Gospels the connection between them is clear. On the one hand Jesus attributes his working of some miracles to the faith of the sick person or of others (Mk. 2:5; 5:34; 9:23–24; 10:52). On the other hand he was prevented from working miracles in his own area because of their lack of faith (Mt. 13:58). Yet the connection is not always explicit (*e.g.* Jn. 5:1–9). Some today act as if there is an iron law connecting the faith of the one seeking healing and God's working of a miracle. Not only does this limit God's power in an illegitimate way, but it easily gets transformed into an instrument of spiritual tyranny. It slides from a gospel of grace, where God acts in his sovereign love and power for a person's good, into a gospel of works, where God's love is merited by the act of believing and the miracle is sustained only as long as one keeps believing.

Then again, we might point to people's attitudes to death as a further problem. To listen to some Christians talk one would not think that death had been defeated and that man's last

enemy had lost its sting (1 Cor. 15:54–56). They still speak as
if death is a defeat, to be avoided at all costs. How different
was the attitude of Paul in 2 Corinthians 5:1–10 and Philippians
1:20–23! It is surely the unbeliever who should desire to hold
on to this life with the sort of grim determination revealed in
the way some people pray for the healing of others.

The fresh emphasis which has recently been given to the
ministry of healing has caused the number of pastoral problems
to mushroom. But excellent goods are not to be rejected simply
because they have poor salesmen. The evangelical pastor will
seek to conform his practice, in this area as in others, to the
revelation of Scripture and not form his views on the basis of
personal reactions to unfortunate pastoral experiences.

There can be no disagreement that healing and the working
of other miracles was integral to the ministry of Jesus. Even a
cursory reading of Mark's Gospel would impress that fact on
the reader. Who could dissent from Tom Smail's conclusion
when he writes,

> Jesus' ministry has often been expounded in terms of the
> truth he taught and the compassion he showed. But inextri-
> cably bound up with these is the specifically charismatic
> dimension. He taught and he loved, with power and with
> authority to change people and things, and to do for them
> and to make happen in them, what his word declared and
> what his love desired. There is no need to set up any oppo-
> sition between the gospel as declaration of truth, service of
> love and act of power.[11]

It is evident too that during his lifetime Jesus committed his
authority to his disciples and that in their ministry they not
only preached but worked miracles (Mk. 6:7–13; Lk. 9:1–6). This
authority was not limited to the twelve, since the seventy-two
came back from their tour rejoicing that 'even the demons
submit to us in your name' (Lk. 10:17). The rest of the New
Testament bears witness to the fact that the early church
expected to continue this marriage between the preaching of
truth and the act of power after the death of Jesus (Acts; 1 Cor.
2:4). But that was no more than Jesus himself had led them to

[11] T. Smail, *Reflected Glory*, p. 101.

expect (Mk. 16:15–18; Jn. 14:12).

There is an impressive body of theological teaching which insists that such miracles were signs of the initial inbreaking of God's kingdom and were not to be expected after the time of Christ and his apostles. We readily grant that they are signs of the inbreaking of the kingdom, but there seems to be nothing in Scripture to justify the conclusion that they were to be phased out after the New Testament period. History would certainly seem to contradict that verdict, since miracles and healing have always been a fact of the church's life even if they have not always been prominent.

It is surely not so odd to expect our ministry to include this dimension of the supernatural when we claim to believe in the living God who raised Jesus from the dead. Indeed, faithfulness to the teaching of Jesus about ministry would seem to demand it. Such acts of power still glorify God by demonstrating his authority over evil and his invasion of the kingdom of darkness. They still glorify God by demonstrating his love in a dramatic way in the lives of those who are imprisoned by powers which are stronger than they are but not stronger than Christ. For all our advances in science and technology, men are still gripped by forces and fears which are greater than them and from which they need to be delivered. The forces have changed little since the days of Christ. They are still the forces of oppressive human structures, nature, disease, demons, sin and death.[12]

Part of the value of a healing ministry is that it is a constant challenge to our faith. On numerous occasions, Jesus confronted his followers with their lack of faith and he did so, not in an abstract way, but by confronting them with definite situations where a miracle was required (Mk. 4:40; 5:36; 9:23). It is too easy to have a vague or academic faith; one which believes in God's power in theory but never actually sees it at work in practice. The faith of traditional mainstream evangelicalism has frequently erred on the side of the cerebral. It is noteworthy that when, in past history, it has encountered the miraculous, the typical evangelical reaction has been to say that God could intervene in such a way if he chose to do so but that, in this particular instance, he had not done so. Doubtless on many occasions that was a wise reaction, but on other

---

[12] See above, p. 65.

occasions it smacks of hedging your bets both ways. The challenge of healing is a challenge to lay our faith on the line. Faith demands not just a general openness to the possibility of miracle but on occasions a specific commitment to the intervention of God.

In our present context the ministry of healing might be said to have added significance. Although some people are credulous, the majority are rationalists. The working of miracles challenges their secularism and 'matter of fact' view of the world. This is not to say that miracles are compelling proofs for the unbeliever. They are not. Faith is required to interpret what happens as an act of God. Without faith unbelievers remain sceptical, mere curiosity seekers or rank atheists. Even so, healing through unexpected means does at least raise strong question marks about a secular world-view. Such a ministry is likely to be more effective in penetrating the armour of rationalism which so many wear as a protection against God than a ministry which is merely verbal.

James 5:14–16 speaks of the ministry of healing as it might be conducted in an on-going pastoral context. It takes its stand firmly on the possibility of healing. It also stresses the need for faith. The faith of the sick person, although not explicitly mentioned, is presumably demonstrated by the action of calling for the church leaders. However, the need for faith in praying for the one who is sick is the point around which the whole passage revolves.

But James has more to say. In James, as in the Gospels, the word of the gospel and the act of power are not separated. The topic of healing is no sooner introduced than James apparently changes the subject to talk about sin and the need for forgiveness. In doing so he reminds us of the close, but not inevitable, connection between the two. It suggests that an effective ministry of healing is possible only in a broader pastoral context. Since man is a complex but unified being, ministry to the whole person, and not simply to the body, is essential. It is often only after a process of ministry to a person's spiritual, moral and emotional dimensions that healing in the physical dimension takes place or is even appropriate.

The mention of anointing 'in the name of the Lord' and of praying 'in faith' points to another important issue. Before praying for healing, the mind of Christ needs to be discerned or else it cannot be done in his name or in faith. To rush in and pray for healing, without so much as considering whether it is the will of the Lord for this individual, may well lead to much heartache and confusion subsequently, if the healing does not occur. It is clearly not within the purposes of God to heal all. Paul sought healing for his 'thorn in the flesh', but God's grace was made known to him through it rather than in relieving him of it. Timothy, Trophimus and Epaphroditus were apparently all ill without healing taking place. Discernment, then, is crucial in ministry to the suffering. Without discerning God's will we have no right to use the authority of the name of the Lord and without discernment it is impossible to pray in true faith.

Another vital aspect of James' teaching is the need for the work of healing to be conducted by the leadership of the church as representatives of the whole church. It matters not whether they are called elders or whether their label has another name on it. It is their role and function which is important. They are the pastoral leaders of the fellowship. Some may have a special gift of the Spirit to heal and in a regular pastoral ministry it is wise to seek to identify who they are so that an integrated ministry to the suffering might be conducted. But it is certainly unwise to permit those who consider themselves to have this gift to exercise it uninvited by the sufferer and uncoordinated with their pastoral leaders. For one who has the gift of healing to act in an independent manner in a local church is a denial of the basic principles which Paul sets out regarding spiritual gifts in 1 Corinthians 12 and often results in more pastoral problems than it solves. It is precisely this lack of discipline which has resulted in many of the problems mentioned above.

The ministry of healing should never be divorced from the theology of suffering. Because we live in a fallen world the experience of pain is redeemable, useful and even sometimes necessary. Paul Brand tells the moving story of painstakingly reconstructing the fingers and tendons of one of his leprosy patients, only to have them all quickly eaten away by rats while the man slept, just because he lacked the advantage of feeling pain which would have alerted him to the unwelcome attention of the rats. The man knew he could not be free without pain.[13] Not all suffering can or should be alleviated whilst we remain

13 P. Brand and P. Yancey, 'Putting pain to work', *Leadership* 5/4 (1984), pp. 121f.

members of this fallen world. In spite of that, a balance must be kept. It is equally important to ensure that the theology of suffering is not divorced from a theology of healing. Whenever suffering is encountered the mind of the Lord must be sought and we must seek to discern, often imperfectly, what his intentions are. We dare not approach it with our minds already made up as to whether healing or continued suffering is the inevitable course to be followed in this individual case.

A WIDER PERSPECTIVE

Our concern with suffering is often too parochial. If we show the nature of our concern for those who suffer only by the way we pray for them then, it has to be said, our concern is very limited. Most of the time our prayer meetings sound like the ritual recitation of a hospital waiting-list. Of course it is right for us to be concerned about our friends who are about to enter hospital, but have we an equal concern for those who have no hospital to go to? Moreover, do we realize that suffering is far wider than an absence of physical health?

In Britain, suffering still abounds despite the momentous contribution made to the nation's welfare by state agencies and schemes. There are still 'communities of the left-behind'[14] where deprivation of education, housing, employment and health is severe. But these communities live in relative luxury when compared with those who suffer elsewhere in the world. Some years ago a United Nations report detailed a little of the suffering of Latin America:

Two-thirds of the population were physically undernourished.
Three-fourths were illiterate.
One-half were suffering from infectious and deficiency diseases.
The overwhelming majority of the population were landless.
Living conditions were unstable, mainly because of their dependence on market forces controlled by those in other

[14] D. S. Sheppard, 'The poverty that imprisons the spirit', The 1984 Richard Dimbleby Lecture, *The Listener*, 19 April 1984, p. 9. Sheppard argued that there were two Britains, the one 'Comfortable Britain' and a second which he terms 'the Other Britain' where deprivation was rife.

countries who owned their industries and protected their own profits.[15]

Even the fortunes of Latin America are not drastic in comparison with the acute famines and droughts of some areas of the world. And in addition there is the widespread threat to human rights through political tyranny and military oppression.

The indifference which the church of the comfortable West has shown to such suffering and the absence of a theology which deals with it have given rise to a whole new movement in theology. Under various titles, political theology or liberation theology has risen in response to a crying need. But since Marxism often appeared to speak to the issues more than Christianity, these theologies have often had an unhealthy dependence on that atheistic philosophy. Yet the Bible is not silent on these matters.

It reveals God's concern for people who suffer. The concern is evident throughout the Old Testament, but reaches its highest points in the deliverance which God offers his people through the exodus from Egypt and the hope he offers them during their experience of the exile. Beyond this, the regular teaching of the law and the prophets demonstrates God's desire to restrain evil, limit greed and condemn oppression. His concern is not limited to his own people but embraces all those who are unjustly oppressed (Ps. 33:13–15, 18–19; Am. 9:7).

The Bible teaches that God is a righteous God who will judge men for their evil and unjust oppression of others (Am. 1:3 – 2:16). Their actions are not unnoticed and they will be called to account for their behaviour. This judgment is seen to be working out already in the ups and downs of international relationships and within the normal categories of human history (Dn. 4:32).

It speaks of the inauguration of a kingdom whose success is assured and which stands over against the way in which men conduct their affairs under the control of Satan, even if they do not realize it. The kingdom of God has the most radical of natures (Lk. 1:46–55) and takes full account of the needs of the underdogs (Lk. 4:17–21).

It points forward to the time when the kingdom will be

---

[15] Quoted by J. M. Bonino, *Revolutionary Theology Comes of Age*, pp. 22f.

fully realized in a way which is not yet possible (Mt. 25). It therefore calls forth hope for the future in spite of all in our present experience that would suggest that such hope is foolish.

It faces realistically the complexity and intricacy of evil and the way in which man cannot defeat it without divine help. As David Sheppard confesses, 'The more I face these great human issues in our cities, the more I know that solutions are beyond our own human resources. These apparently secular concerns force me back repeatedly on to my spiritual resources.'[16] There is only one who has overcome the world's organized system of evil (Jn. 16:33).

It insists too that the person who knows God should be involved in bearing the hurts of his neighbours and in seeking to right the wrongs which have caused them (Lk. 10:25–37). A foremost exponent of liberation theology, Gustavo Gutierrez, agrees that evangelical conversion is 'the touchstone of all spirituality' but warns that 'Our conversion to the Lord implies this conversion to the neighbour'. Conversion is a radical transformation of our thinking and feeling; it means living as Christ did and therefore reorientating our lives to the oppressed person, the exploited social class, the despised race and the dominated country.[17]

This overview is not intended as an exhaustive pastoral theology of suffering.[18] It is merely intended to encourage us to broaden our perspective and realize that dealing with suffering, other than that of physical illness, is a quite legitimate biblical concern. Not only so, but in our world where the mass media intrude the suffering of the world into our living-rooms through the television news day after day, a theology that addresses suffering of that global dimension is imperative. It may be that many of the answers are the same as those we would wish to address to sick individuals, writ large. But not all our answers will fall into this category. It may be that we shall never be able to eliminate the element of mystery which is involved. But it will surely be that unless we can testify to a God who is as concerned about the starving millions of our world and its

---

[16] D. S. Sheppard, 'The poverty that imprisons', p. 9.

[17] G. Gutierrez, *A Theology of Liberation*, pp. 204f. For an evangelical exposition of Christian social involvement see J. R. W. Stott, *Issues Facing Christians Today*, pp. 2–28.

[18] See J. A. Kirk, *Liberation Theology*, pp. 95–135, for an excellent exposition of the relevant biblical passages by an evangelical scholar.

oppressed peoples as he is about the back pain that individual members of our churches suffer, we shall not have a God who is credible.

CONCLUSION

The task of a pastoral theology for the suffering is to take man's most difficult experience, which gives rise to a welter of human emotions, and try to place it in a more objective perspective. In so doing the pastor will seek, to the limits of his finite human understanding, to explain the ways of God to men. He will seek to show that God's power, holiness and love are not irreconcilable in the face of suffering. In addition, he will want to exploit the episode of suffering for good, using it to enable the sufferer to grow in the grace of God. He will keep before him the power of God to heal and, in the context of a ministry to the whole man, he may pray in faith for grace to be given in suffering or in death or for healing. Any of these courses will bring honour to God's name, even among unbelievers. But he will not suffer from tunnel vision. He will be aware of the immense problem of suffering in our world and will not ignore the need to speak in a relevant way to that as well.

The pastor will stand as a constant reminder that God does not readily grieve or afflict; that even when he does, God remains sovereign over it and is not engaged in an open-ended contest with evil but is a deliverer and a saviour. Isaiah records the situation exactly,

For this is what the high and lofty One says – he who lives for ever, whose name is holy: 'I live in a high and holy place, but also with him who is contrite and lowly in spirit, to revive the spirit of the lowly and to revive the heart of the contrite. I will not accuse for ever, nor will I always be angry, for then the spirit of man would grow faint before me – the breath of man that I have created. I was enraged by his sinful greed; I punished him, and hid my face in anger, yet he kept on in his wilful ways. I have seen his ways, but I will heal him; I will guide him and restore comfort to him, creating praise on the lips of the mourners in Israel. Peace, peace, to those far and near,' says the Lord. 'And I will heal them.' But the wicked are like the tossing sea, which cannot rest, whose waves cast up mire and mud. 'There is no peace,' says my God, 'for the wicked.' (57:15–21)

16
Unity

One of the sharpest issues facing any congregation at the present time is the question of unity. To be more exact it is a question of how to resolve the tension produced by a commitment to unity at the same time as a commitment to progress and purity. The new wind of God's Spirit, and the human counterfeits which have accompanied it, have forced many to face this question, often in the most painful way. The reactions have been varied. For some the threat of division has been enough to reject anything to do with the charismatic movement out of hand. They have tried to preserve their unity at all costs. Others have been open to the winds of change but, whilst the more traditional among them have lamented the insecurities and confusion caused by the new ways of worship and the new forms of leadership, the more radical have been frustrated by the slow progress which the reforms have made. Still others have felt that the present-day church is so infiltrated by nominal Christianity that the only way to be true to the Spirit is to leave the old structures and all that they represent and to form new structures which do not inhibit their progress or taint their purity.[1]

Whilst the national ecumenical juggernaut has been grinding to a halt, the question of unity has been put on the agenda of every local church. It is at that level, the level of face-to-face relationships, that the real ecumenical problems have to be unravelled. Among the array of attempts which have been made to solve the issue, many have been unworthy appeals to human tradition, selfish interests or party concerns, and a lack of doctrinal or biblical understanding has often been evident. The Bible is not to blame, since it addresses the issues on numerous occasions and shows how subtle the threat of division is. Indeed the matter is even mentioned in a letter to the happiest church of the New Testament, that of Philippi who faced the threat of

---

[1] A. Wallis, *The Radical Christian*, pp. 122–136.

division (4:2 and 2:1–11). The problem has not been too much, but too little, doctrine.

IS DIVISION ALWAYS WRONG?

The threat of division has always been present in history and some of the worst divisions of the past are today celebrated as some of the greatest watersheds in the formation of our evangelical tradition. Evangelicals by constitution would be among the first to argue that there was need for separation when the truth of the gospel was at stake (Jn. 17:17–21). They, of all people, do not see unity as an end in itself and insist that it can be pursued only from the starting-point of truth.[2]

Regretfully, it seems as if in every generation God has needed to remind the church of a neglected aspect of truth or to bring new life to a moribund body by raising up a group of men to do so who were met with opposition and rejection. Often this resulted in new groups being formed. Luther, Smyth, Wesley, Darby, Booth, to name but a few, are among the chief representatives of this trend. They were far from perfect and the movements which have followed them have, with time, become even less perfect still, but who would deny that their radical departures were not of God? It would be surprising if this tendency, which has been evident through history,[3] were not at work in our own day. This historical perspective must give us sympathy for the perplexity some feel when condemned by the leaders of existing church structures for starting new ones when those leaders themselves glory in what, in an earlier day, was a breakaway movement.[4]

This does not mean that to be faithful to God the only option open to us is to leave our traditional churches for the new ones. History also shows that the new movements can have a dramatic reforming and reviving effect on the older structures which then equally bring glory to God. The Wesleyan Revival of the eighteenth century, for example, had a most beneficial effect on both the Anglican and Free churches by the end of that century and gave rise to a whole new emphasis on the

---

[2] D. M. Lloyd-Jones, *The Basis of Unity*.
[3] E. Troeltsch, *The Social Teachings of the Christian Churches*, vol. 2, p. 993.
[4] A vivid expression of that perplexity can be found in G. Coates, *What on Earth is this Kingdom?* p. 136. In the book Coates lurches between sympathy for those who wish to stay in traditional denominations and proposals for scrapping those denominations altogether!

preaching of the true gospel at home and overseas.

It must be also be remembered that division is not always destructive. There is ample evidence that the church can grow healthily by division just as biological cells do. History confirms the teaching of church growth scholars that the division of a local church should be actively considered as a major strategy in growing the church.[5] This may happen even when, as in some divisions which have taken place in recent years, division has occurred for less than the purest of motives. In a way, when growth takes place through painful division, it is only a variation on the theme of Acts 8:1, where God had to send persecution to shake the church out of its cosy fellowship in order to spur a new advance. Persecution, like division, may be evil, but God can use it for good.

However, in spite of these justifications for division, it cannot be said too strongly that division is always potentially destructive. Jesus warned that 'every kingdom divided against itself will be ruined, and every city or household divided against itself will not stand' (Mt. 12:25). We need to bear in mind that for every occasion when division is of God there are ten occasions when it is not. For all our claims about pursuing new life in the Spirit or doctrinal purity, the cause most often lies in our sinful personalities and our unwillingness to seek the elusive biblical pattern of holiness with its emphasis on love and unity.

A LESSON FROM HISTORY

One man who understood that most clearly was Richard Baxter. He wrote a lengthy work on *The Cure of Church Divisions* which contains an amazing amount of relevant pastoral advice for today. In Baxter's day the church was in turmoil and many were leaving the Church of England for purer churches elsewhere. With astute insight and spiritual depth he addresses sixty propositions to those who would cause division and a further twenty-two to the pastors who had to handle the situation. Though Baxter is no friend of the separatists, it is evident that he understands their desire and it is clear that he would not lay all the blame at their feet. In fact, he is prepared to

---

[5] D. McGavran, *Understanding Church Growth*, p. 13.

concede that there are times when it is permissible to leave one company of Christians to worship with another. But the spirit and attitude is all-important. Space prohibits the inclusion of all Baxter's propositions, but a number of the more important ones may be paraphrased.[6] Those most likely to cause division were, in his view, the younger and less mature Christians who were a bit spiritually hot-headed. He begs to remind them:

1. Not to forget the legitimate differences between being a younger and older Christian.

2. To be wary of the deep-rooted temptation to spiritual pride.

4. Not to desire to be superior in holiness through distancing themselves from their fellow Christians.

5. Of the doctrine of the visible and invisible church.

6. Of the need to recognize the difference between the visible and invisible church, so that they do not demand more of the church on earth than God does.

7. Of the important place Scripture gives to unity and concord.

8. That the best Christian, when he sees something in the church in need of amendment, seeks to reform it and does not use it as an excuse for division.

9. That for a church to excommunicate the impenitent is a duty, but for the godly to separate themselves from the church is usually a sin.

10. That excommunicating a person is not to be done glibly but in accordance with Matthew 18:15–18.

12. That Christ graciously received the weakest that came to him and that church discipline must conform to this gospel.

13. That even so they must not be indifferent to sin, since Christ came to destroy it and sanctify men. Holiness and peace must go together.

16. That when talking about the credibility of a Christian's profession it must be understood that there are various degrees of credibility.

19. That it is wrong to be so committed to a divided sect that harm is brought to the universal church and Christian cause.

20. Of the need to be very suspicious of religious passions, and to distinguish carefully between a sound and sinful zeal;

[6] R. Baxter, *The Cure of Church Divisions* (1670).

lest the Holy Spirit is blamed for giving birth to sin and we are deluded into thinking that we are pleasing God when we are actually offending him deeply.

21. That religious people who speak evil of others should not be believed or even given a hearing.

22. That the state and actions of others should not be judged.

26. That it is unwise to spend more time in the company of zealous Christians who criticize their more sober brothers than in the company of more charitable Christians who show that principles that kill love are a sin and mischief.

27. That it is possible to misinterpret the answers to our prayers, believing that God has approved of them when we are really only seeing the effects of our own prejudices, passions and ignorances.

28. Of the need to test all revelations and opinions by the word of God, however much we are impressed by the person who voices them.

29. That care needs to be exercised when uncertain in case, in a desire to find a solution to our troubled minds, we follow a path that becomes a snare.

30. That one must be a learner until fit and called to teach.

32. That it is wrong to lay greater stress on different ways of praying than Christ did. Sincerity, not form, is the test.

33. That errors in the way others worship should not be made out to be greater than they are.

35. Of the impossibility of separating oneself from all faulty worship.

38. That truth must not be neglected but neither should one insist on every detail of it at the expense of peace in the church.

41. That one should not be taken in by a preacher just because he is enthusiastic.

43. That causes should not be judged by their followers. Some bad men support good causes and some good men reject them.

45. To aim for the highest degree of holiness but not for superiority. Aim to be the best, not the first.

46. That deliberate sinners who scandalize the church should be given a wide berth, but that weak Christians should be brought as close into the fellowship as possible.

47. Of the danger, in opposing error, of swinging the pendulum to the opposite extreme, which is just as bad.

48. That there is need to talk more about our own faults than the faults of others.

49. Of the need to talk about the good in others rather than their faults.

50. It is a wiser course to instruct and exhort than to reprove and find fault.

52. That revenge of heart and tongue is as bad as physical revenge.

59. That if for any reason it is impossible to go on meeting together, it is still necessary to keep unity in faith and love. Spiritual condescension, let alone worse, is not permitted.

To the pastors he gave additional instructions. They were to be spurred on by the threat of division to examine themselves and their teaching and to reform it wherever it was deficient (1–3).[7] Whatever the weaknesses of others they were not to react with impatience or self-justification (4). It was essential that pastors discerned the causes of the divisions (5, 6, 7, 9 and 11). In separating were people rejecting the validity of the church universal or just expressing a preference for the ministry or worship of another? Were such people lacking in understanding about the church and its structures but, even so, strong in grace? It was the latter that really mattered. Discernment was necessary too in deciding the difference between a tolerable and an intolerable error in the church.

Baxter's realism led him to stress the disparity between what men understand now and what they will understand afterwards. 'The church here', he wrote, 'is a hospital of diseased souls; of whom none are perfectly healed in this life' (10). His pastoral skill is seen in his sensitivity towards the weakest of Christ's servants (8, 10 and 18) and his awareness that older Christians are liable to be disconcerted by the enthusiasts among them (19). His advice on handling those who were divisive urges the pastor to work at teaching them truth (16) and warns him against defensively imposing restrictions on them in the hope of cramping their style (15). Pastoral care must be carefully balanced. To neglect the divisive would mean that the pastor could no longer do them good. Yet to give in to them in order to keep them constantly happy would be to create a

---

[7] The numbers in brackets refer to the paragraph numbers in Baxter. These clauses were reproduced in *The Banner of Truth* 259 (1985), pp. 19–20.

rod for his own back. 'Make them not your rulers nor follow them into their exorbitancies, to get their love or to escape their censors' (20).

In his final two pieces of advice Baxter encourages pastors to set a good example. If they show themselves to be envious of the more popular preachers among them and resort to peevish backbiting and quarrelsomeness, how can they hope to maintain unity in their congregations (21)? Then he urges them to study the Scripture on 'love and tenderness, meekness and patience' until these qualities become a part of their nature and flow naturally from themselves.

The advice Baxter gives to pastors has never been more needed than at the present time. It is sad to reflect that many divisions have been precipitated by the pastors themselves, either because they are impatient for change and force the pace in a particular direction, or because they use their strong authority to resist change, or because they are prepared to minister to a section of their flock who relate more easily to them and to neglect others (see Acts 20:28). It is readily acknowledged that such pastors are often motivated by the highest ideals and are subject to much frustration. None the less, what kind of a shepherd is it who divides and scatters the flock? Baxter saw that in addition to knowledge, utterance, holiness and heavenly-mindedness the pastor needed to excel in prudence (2). And so it is. A little more patience and a lot more prudence would have saved much heartache caused by the divisions of recent years.

The contemporary application of all that Baxter wrote is apparent and it is worth studying as the wise and perceptive advice of an experienced pastor. But we can go further, for Baxter's concerns beat with the same tempo as those of Scripture and it is there that the source for our pastoral theology is to be found.

A BIBLICAL PERSPECTIVE

No part of the Bible speaks more directly to our situation than Ephesians. Many have turned to Ephesians 4 in recent days for help in understanding the rediscovery of spiritual gifts which have become more widely operative in the churches. But the very same passage sets out the basic principles of unity in the church. Ephesians can be only fully understood once it is realized how serious the threat of division was in the Ephesian church. It was no more an academic issue to them than it is to us. What obstacles to unity they faced! Ephesus was such a cosmopolitan city that it was known as 'the landing stage'. To live there was like living permanently at Heathrow airport. Underlying the racial and cultural divisions was the grand canyon between Jew and Gentile. It was this very division which Christ died to overcome (2:14–18).

Even more, without reading much between the lines, other causes of division can be discerned behind chapters 4 and 5. There were the divisions caused by personality clashes (4:1–6); those due to tensions over spiritual gifts (vv. 7–13) and those caused by spiritual immaturity (vv. 14–15). More disastrously still there was the unchristian behaviour of many who claimed to be Christians but who still felt the powerful attraction of their unregenerate way of life (vv. 16–32). There must have been a disappointingly low level of spiritual life in Ephesus for Paul to write as he did. What hope of unity was there in a church where lying, anger, dishonesty, impure speech and even immorality and drunkenness (5:3–18) were never far from the surface? All this was in addition to the normal relationship tensions faced by any church as a result of sexual, generational and social class differences (5:21 – 6:9) And this is to say nothing of the designs which Satan had on the church and the spiritual hostilities in which they were engaged (6:10–18).

How does Paul tackle the issue? The whole letter sets out a complete pastoral theology for a church facing division. And, although we shall focus on only one part of it, it is wise to set this in its broader context. The letter begins with a discussion of the nature of the church and lays down three major foundations as the basis for our corporate behaviour. Firstly Paul shows how valuable a possession the church is to God (1:1–23), with the clear implication that no-one can live unthinkingly or carelessly as a member of this church. Secondly, he sets out the basis for membership in the church. In the church, status, racial background and man-made goodness count for nothing. The only basis for membership is grace through faith (2:1–10). From this Paul draws the self-evident conclusion that it cuts at the very heart of the gospel if the church is to be divided into first- and second-class citizens for any reason whatever (2:11–22).

Thirdly, Paul demonstrates how the group of Christians meeting in Ephesus fit into God's eternal and cosmic plan (3:1–21). They have a significance which far outweighs how they perceived themselves when they were squabbling, and Paul is sure that a greater understanding of who they really were would make them behave differently.

Having set the scene Paul now tackles the issue of disunity head-on. Four powerful arguments are advanced to persuade them to live in harmony. They are first to consider *the nature of their calling* (4:1–3). This will lead them to realize that certain attitudes will inevitably need cultivating. They are not qualities which come naturally. In fact, these same qualities are often condemned outright by the world as evidence of weakness. But this is the stuff of which the church is to be made.

Humility must force out pride. Pride is so subtle and all-pervasive that a rigorous campaign needs to be waged to root it out. Pride of race, tradition, family, Christian experience and knowledge all form a trap which, once it is sprung, leads to division in the church. It always needs to be remembered that the pattern Christ set before the church was that of a little child, not that of an adolescent sixth-former who knows it all. Gentleness is a strong quality. We mistake it too easily for spinelessness. The word is used of a horse which has been broken in. It describes the need for our characters to be sensitive to the control of God's touch on the reins so that all the drive, energy and zeal we have can be channelled to good effect. Without that control our zeal can be as useless and destructive as an untamed horse. We may bolt all over the place, knocking over fences and knocking down people, but we shall be of no use to our Master.

Patience means, in Chrysostom's words, 'to have a wide and big soul'. It is a 'spirit which has the power to take revenge but never does so'. It means that we will not give in to anger or resentment. It also means we will not give up too easily on others with whom we disagree. Love is the overarching quality which never carries with it, when used in such contexts in Scripture, the idea that it is an emotion you feel. It is rather the down-to-earth quality of giving oneself in service to another by an act of will.

Peacefulness likewise is an active quality. Some people seem to suffer from a permanent conflict mentality and view the whole of life from a hostile perspective. The mature Christian is not always seeking battles or starting skirmishes. Nor is he always putting himself forward in a game of one-upmanship. Rather he works to overcome conflict and create a climate of acceptance and harmony. Peace is fragile and so easily broken by our self-assertiveness and self-centredness. It must be treated with great care.

It is just at this point that many Christians duck the issue. We are not sufficiently prepared to work at the cultivation of these elusive personal qualities and we give up too easily. Divisions and tensions are produced precisely because we are not humble, gentle, patient, loving and peaceful. We ride roughshod over these qualities claiming to want a fuller experience of God's Spirit. But it is impossible to obtain more of God if the way we go about it contradicts his calling so fundamentally. It is important to grasp that Paul is not just giving human advice to make life more comfortable. He is explaining the meaning of our Christian calling.

But then Paul goes deeper. The Ephesians are, secondly, to consider *the nature of their God* (vv. 4–6). He says to them, in effect, that in asking them to be united he is not asking them to achieve something which is impossible. All he is asking is that they preserve a unity which the Holy Spirit has already given and one which is built into the heart of their God and their gospel. Their unity is no more than a by-product of the unity of the Godhead. Their task therefore is not to manufacture unity, still less to invent it. They are merely to 'make every effort to keep the unity of the Spirit'. As Markus Barth has observed,[8] there would be no great point in mentioning the oneness of God if that oneness was absolute. What possible connection would that have for such manifold creatures as the members of the church? But the point Paul makes is that God is three in one and yet unity is the very essence of the Godhead.

The one Spirit is the one who creates the one body and gives believers one common hope. Unless, then, there were several Spirits it is nonsense to divide. The Lord is the one subject of our faith and the one with whom we are united in baptism. There are not several Lords on whom we have come to believe

[8] Barth, *Ephesians 4 – 6*, p. 467.

and baptism (whatever its mode) does not symbolize union with several different Lords. Again, therefore, it makes nonsense to divide. Pushing further, Paul shows how there is above all 'one God and Father *of all*'. He creates one family. The unity of God and his work means, in John Stott's words, that 'the unity of the church is as industructible as the unity of God himself. It is no more possible to split the church than it is to split the Godhead.'[9] What then is the use of trying?

The unity of the Godhead and of our gospel means that the very constitution of our faith is a unity. In practice it may not always seem so, but that is the truth of the matter and we need to adjust our practice to come into line. God is not going to adjust his truth to come into line with our practice. Rivalry in the church therefore strikes at the very root of the church.

Thirdly the Christians are invited to consider *the nature of their exalted Saviour* (vv. 7–13). It is interesting to note how contemporary the sensitivities of this chapter are. Paul has already spoken of the way in which the Spirit and baptism point to unity – two issues over which the church has fallen out more than most. Now he comes to the matter of spiritual gifts, another issue over which there has been much division. He recognizes the diversity of the gifts (v. 11) and the way in which they will be widely distributed within the church so that not all its members will be able to claim to possess them all. He emphasizes too that the purpose of these particular gifts, which are leadership gifts for the church as distinct from others he mentions elsewhere, are to equip the church for its task whilst it proceeds on the path towards maturity, an aspect of which is unity. They are neither for private enjoyment nor to be the justification for getting a factional group around an individual who exercises one gift as opposed to another. Such a course of action is a denial of the teaching of verses 12 and 13. Indeed they are the sinews of the church, given both to provide for its growth and to hold the body together.

Moreover, the basic point that Paul makes about spiritual gifts is that they are the gifts of the ascended and exalted Christ. Subtly changing Psalm 68:18, where the victorious king is seen receiving tribute gifts from those he has conquered, Paul highlights the generosity of our Saviour. He is a true liberator and

---

[9] J. R. W. Stott, *The Message of Ephesians. God's New Society*, p. 151.

having conquered our enemies he does not take gifts from us but gives gifts to us. His secure victory and his supremacy in the universe mean that he need not be calculating and miserly in his distribution of gifts. He will give as he sees fit and as there is need. He will not keep his subjects short. Why then fight over spiritual gifts? To some he will give one gift and to others another. There is no room for envy or jealousy. Nor is there room for superiority and condescension. To relate to fellow Christians with differing gifts in that way is to cast a slur on the exalted Christ. To summarize, the gifts are given to enable growth towards the goal of maturity under the government of the risen Christ.

Fourthly, the Christians are invited to consider *the nature of their gospel*. To behave divisively suggests that they have not fully grasped the gospel. To argue that they cannot change is just not true. The good news which they had learnt in Christ meant that a fundamental change had taken place in the motivating centre of their lives, which would enable them to put off old ways of behaviour and adopt new ones. To say that this is not possible is to question whether they ever did escape the ignorance from which the unregenerate world suffers.

From this basic premise (vv. 17–24) Paul hammers home the message by a series of applied examples as to where the changes should be taking place. Each of the issues mentioned, as Dr Martyn Lloyd-Jones perceptively noted,[10] are issues which would destroy fellowship unless dealt with in the power of Christ. True fellowship cannot survive, let alone thrive, where members lie to each other, are angry with each other, steal from each other or are unforgiving in their relationships. The section on applied ethics, then, in the second half of the chapter is not a new subject but rather a further unfolding of the doctrine and unity of the church which Paul had expounded. Each individual point is clearly related to doctrine. Within the space of a few short verses (vv. 25–32) there are references to the doctrine of the church, of Satan, of the Holy Spirit, of the second coming and of salvation. Paul brings the injunctions to a climax by taking his readers back to the gospel. The simple yet demanding rule is that we are to treat each other as God in Christ treated

---

[10] D. M. Lloyd-Jones, *Darkness and Light*, p. 222.

us (v. 32). That means that we cannot possibly engage in unforgiving, resentful, destructive behaviour and claim that we are going on with God. If we have understood the gospel we shall be forgiving to others.

CONCLUSION

Paul does not give a pragmatic answer to the threat of division, but a basic theological critique which demands attention and calls the whole church back to central issues. We so often claim that the causes of our division are spiritual when they are frequently matters of personality or culture. To claim that one particular form of worship is more biblical than another is hard to justify and the desire for structure or spontaneity, one vocabulary or another, is often a reflection of how we are interpreting our Bibles through cultural spectacles rather than anything else.

What is *not* cultural is the biblical demand for unity. Those who divide the church in a desire to go on with God must ask how they can do so if they are flying in the face of God's obvious command to be united. It is easy to erect tests whereby we measure the spirituality of another. We do it in terms of whether they like a certain type of church music, whether they raise their arms in worship, whether they have a particular gift of the Spirit or whether they can endure a certain length of sermon. But these are not biblical tests. Yet time and again Scripture lays down its own tests – the tests of humility, gentleness, patience, love and peace. We must keep these clearly in focus and allow them to govern our relationships with each other.

The only biblical grounds for separation would appear to be when the central truth of the gospel is denied (Gal. 1:6–10 and 1 Jn. 2:18–19). To divide on lesser grounds will mean that we exempt ourselves from submitting to God's proving school in the church and sign ourselves out from the very place where we might grow in holiness. It also means that we fail to live according to biblical truth and we cannot be surprised therefore if complications follow.

Many would want to respond that it is not that easy and only a ivory tower academic would pretend that it is. Denominations are a fact of our history and we cannot wipe the slate clean and pretend that they do not exist. That forces on us the choice to worship with one group of Christians or another. Practical reasons, such as the current needs of our family, may lead us to separate from one group and join another from time to time. Our different temperaments may also indicate that different styles of worship are called for, some enjoying a more exuberant or spontaneous style whilst others preferring a quieter and more structured style of worship. The call for unity is not a call for uniformity and there is evidence that the early church, despite massive unity in Christ, did not enjoy uniformity in their style of worship.

But where such separation does take place we must work hard to preserve the unity which we have in the Spirit. Imperialist claims that one group is where it is really happening rather than another are not permitted. The feeling that one is the true church whilst the other has not yet begun, assuming they are both faithful to the central truth of the work of Christ, is not allowed.

Division can be of God, for the truth is divisive (Mt. 10:34 and Lk. 12:51). But we need to be sure that it is God's truth which is causing the division and not our own preference. The weight of God's truth would indicate the need to remain in patient fellowship with those who, though belonging to Christ, do not see eye-to-eye with us about a thousand and one little things in the church. This is not to accept the lowest common denominator mentality for our churches. On all sides there needs to be that serious commitment to press on towards maturity – but let us remember that unity is an aspect of that maturity. It is to resist the temptation to be impatient with that which is less than ideal. Some time ago Derek Prince spoke these prophetic words,

> There are two things, the actual and the ideal. To be mature is to see the ideal and live in the actual. To fail is to accept the actual and reject the ideal. To accept only that which is ideal and refuse the actual is to be immature. Do not criticise the actual because you have seen the ideal, do not reject the ideal because you have seen the actual. Maturity is to live with the actual but hold on to the ideal.[11]

[11] The documentary source is now untraceable, but it is a message which Derek Prince has spoken on a number of occasions and which has appeared in various magazines.

That seems to express the character of apostolic balance. Many of the New Testament epistles were written because the actual church was far from ideal. The answer was not to divide and think that it was ever possible in this fallen world to create the ideal. It is still no answer. It was to go on living with the actual whilst keeping before you the ideal and working strenuously towards it. That was why Paul wrote Ephesians.

17

Ministry

A cacophony of voices today competes to proclaim the funeral rites of the traditional ministry. Sociologists say that the profession is dying.[1] Ecclesiastical bureaucrats say that it is breaking up under the strain of new patterns of church and community life and cannot survive.[2] Charismatics fear that it is lingering too long and are doing their level best to switch off the life-support machine.[3] Meanwhile a number of ministers themselves confirm its terminal state. Some remain to bewail their aches and pains, whilst others opt for a more defined ancillary job or drop out altogether.

The reality is of course much more complex. Geographers, striving to express something of the reality of a land mass, do so by abstracting one dimension of that reality and representing it on a map and by repeating the exercise until they have a series of maps which begin to express the complexity they see. In this final chapter we shall attempt to do the same regarding the ministry.

THE SATISFACTION MAP

The announcement that the funeral of the traditional ministry will take place shortly is grossly exaggerated. To exchange the metaphor for a simile, it is like looking at oneself in a fairground hall of mirrors only to meet a reflection of reality, but one in which certain parts of one's anatomy are out of proportion. What critics forget is that, for all the problems, there are thousands of ministers today who continue to function more or less in a traditional way and who gain much job satisfaction in doing so. They find ministry rich, rewarding and fulfilling as they grow ever closer to their people and see lives changed by the power of God. They believe that God has called them to the

---

[1] A. Russell, *The Clerical Profession* and R. Towler and A. Coxon, *The Fate of the Anglican Clergy*.
[2] J. Tiller, *A Strategy for the Church's Ministry*, pp. 11–44.
[3] G. Coates, *What on Earth is this Kingdom?* and P. Greenslade, *Leadership*.

ministry and they would not exchange places with anyone. They are content with the routine of pastoral duties and find a multitude of opportunities for service through the extended family of the church. They are happy in the leading of worship and in regular preaching and they rejoice when modest growth occurs. Many ministers, far from being restless, are content.

Maybe some of that contentment is due to the fact that they do not have very great ambitions. For even the most satisfied must surely be aware of the inhospitable climate in which they minister. Secular beliefs, morality determined by the statistical average and a fragmented society mean that their flocks are, for the most part, shrinking. Those outside are resorting to their services less and less. Some of the satisfied try to ignore these uncomfortable facts by burying themselves in the frantic life of the flock. And since they are adored by their flocks they derive warmth from them and a degree of insulation which protects them from the harsh winds of the outside world. In this way they actually cease to be shepherds. Instead of leading the flock to richer pastures, they become caretakers, befriended and pastored themselves by the flock.

In spite of the many who genuinely find ministry satisfying, the truth has to be faced that many do not. They complain of being isolated and frustrated. They feel uncared for by those above them in the ecclesiastical hierarchy and unloved by those below them in the church. They recognize that the church authorities are doing their best. But bishops, moderators and superintendents, or whatever, are just too busy keeping the essential bureaucratic machinery running to pastor the pastors adequately. Of course there are worthy exceptions, but that is the general picture. And pastors do not wish to present themselves to their superiors as inadequate malcontents in case it hinders their career prospects, such as they are. Some pastors may look for support elsewhere, in groups beyond the church and denomination, but this sometimes causes suspicion and further undermines relationships.

The members of the church meanwhile think that ordination has made the pastor spiritually and emotionally self-sufficient and they never get close enough to him to discover otherwise. The pastor struggles to live up to the image his members have of him and tries to conform to their expectations, which is probably the root of his problem. Consequently he often gets trapped and becomes defensive and resists help when it is offered, because he would regard himself as a failure if he accepted it. And depression, which is internalized anger, anger which cannot be expressed and so turns in upon itself and attributes all blame to the one who already feels worthless, is often the downward path he begins to tread. He struggles on, undernourished himself and inevitably giving less and less satisfying food to the flock. Whatever spiritual authority he once had then meets resistance and he too ceases to function as a true pastor.

It is no answer to say that he should derive his support from his colleague group. There is often a lack of theological harmony among ministers and so the fraternal, presbytery or chapter-meeting as the case might be, rather than being a spiritually supportive body, retreats to deal with business matters or inoffensive topics on which they can all agree. Even where there is more theological coherence pastors often fail to let down their defences and admit to real needs. Equally they feel unable to share real joys. They are acutely aware that pride, superiority, envy and jealousy are always lurking in the wings of their conversations and they do not want to give opportunity to those unspiritual emotions. So they mistakenly think that it is better to avoid any relationship in depth, lest temptation be encouraged. Spiritually and emotionally, therefore, they are starved.

The ministry is a lonely and stressful occupation chiefly because of the enormous demands and expectations which the pastor faces. If he is to lead, which is why he is there, he must take risks. But many fear doing so, not least because they are dependent on those they might offend for their bread-and-butter support. However skilful the pastor might be, he is almost bound to offend some, whilst pleasing others. There are other fears, like the fear of failure, of intimacy and of the unknown, which restrain the pastor from taking risks. John C. Harris' detailed study of *Stress, Power and Ministry* demonstrates how crucial the pastor's reaction to this dilemma is. It can make the difference between functioning freely and with spiritual authority or of suffering stress and being pastorally incapacitated.

Harris points out that while tension is healthy, in that it produces renewal and rebirth, fear has the opposite effect. He suggests that a failure to express one's own personal views and values in ministry, for fear that people will disagree, is harmful and results in stress and discouragement. Rather, he recommends that the pastor should learn to act with autonomy. He writes,

> In our day it is popular to define autonomy as freedom to do your own thing, free of the claims of others, usually others like bosses, parents, organizations, neighbors who we fear will take control over us, if they haven't already, and block our way to self-fulfillment. That view of autonomy distorts its essential meaning in the service of a type of spiritual isolation, that if successful, completely demoralizes a person's capacity to be autonomous.
>
> The root meaning of autonomy is to be self-governing. To be autonomous is to stand on one's own feet in authentic relationship with other persons.[4]

Such an autonomy is evident in the life of Jesus (Mk. 1:35–39) and in the life of Paul (especially in his relationship with Corinth as recorded in 2 Corinthians). Such autonomy frees a person to be more open and honest in his relationships with others and less manipulative in his discussion. The strategy which Harris recommends for leadership is to use his influence in an integrative fashion. That is to say that the pastor should not seek to hide from the congregation or his fellow leaders, but seek to share power, to act together, to be open and mutually to influence each other. This exploits the tensions most creatively, minimizes the damage caused by differences and uses the potential of the members to the full. The risk is that in more fully sharing things, the pastor may not get all the answers he had hoped for. But he is likely to get more this way than by resorting to other strategies and he is also likely to survive the stress of the task more easily.

Harris argues that pastors more usually adopt other strategies to maintain their power and in doing so actually work themselves into a corner. Many resort to 'reactive influence', where they try to gain power through compliance with congregational values and expectations. Such a strategy, though having some obvious advantages in seeking to maintain stability, denies the

---

[4] J. C. Harris, *Stress, Power and Ministry*, p. 75.

real struggles which exist and often leads to the pastor being depressed. Another strategy he might adopt is that of 'proactive influence', where the pastor asserts his power over others and tries to shape the congregation unilaterally. It imposes on the pastor 'anxious burdens of self assertion' and may threaten the congregation's stability. The third strategy, which is commonly found, is that of 'inactive influence', where the pastor fails to confront any of the real issues, becomes preoccupied with irrelevancies and rapidly gets absorbed by the trivia of parish life. This strategy enables the pastor to retreat from the tensions of exercising power but, equally, causes him to accomplish nothing.[5]

In discussions with ministers, Harris was able to identify a list of experiences which they considered stifled them. The list supports his view that a strategy of 'integrative influence' would give greater freedom for pastors to exercise their ministry and reduce the stress involved. The discussions identified:

> having to say yes to every demand
> fear of strong opposing viewpoints
> appeasing aggressive women leaders
> fear of feedback – finding out how I come across
> not voicing needs for more money
> the need to appear busy
> inability to challenge parish values effectively
> inability to state my own job wishes clearly
> lack of feedback – never knowing how I come across
> need to be liked by everyone
> sitting on my values and convictions
> unable to change any of these frustrations.[6]

Clearly the recommendation that pastors should seek greater personal autonomy is dangerous unless the definition Harris gives to it is carefully observed. He distinguishes it radically from autocracy and is in no way advocating a greater authoritarianism which rides roughshod over the values and feelings of the congregation. That only results, as much recent experience shows, in damaged and divided congregations and bewildered or arrogant ministers. None of that is glorifying to God. But if

---

[5] *Ibid.*, pp. 95–114.   [6] *Ibid.*, pp. 134f.

autonomy means to be self-governing in authentic relationships with others then it should be pursued. In Harris' words,

> In today's church, the pastor's ability to lead with authority is, above all, an act of personal autonomy. In particular, it involves his capacity to face fear in himself, to share influence, to lead the membership into reflections upon the meaning of life together, to build an atmosphere where the irrational forces of church life are taken seriously, to have the courage to reveal his own needs and judgments and to be accessible to influence in return. To be sure, religious authenticity requires not only autonomous people, but autonomous relationships. Yet the pastor cannot wait for someone else to begin; he must have Abraham's vision and courage – to start alone the journey with its unforseen ending.[7]

THE STYLE MAP

A second map which has similarities to the first has been drawn by Dr Montagu Barker.[8] Dr Barker is a consultant psychiatrist and lecturer in psychiatry, who has great experience in dealing with the stresses imposed by the ministry, not only on the ministers themselves but on their families. He comments that, while there is much talk in the secular world about the support structure needed for the caring professions, there is little similar talk in the church. What is more, the various patterns of ministry recommended and willingly undertaken by ministers serve to enhance the stress of the job. He has identified three patterns of ministry.

The minister who is a leader. This minister has the style of a business executive. He runs his church in a highly efficient manner like a well-managed organization. Leadership meetings in the church become like company board meetings and the only support structure the pastor has consists of his fellow professionals. Throughout the church there are good management structures and good information-flow and all services and campaigns are conducted with professionalism and expertise. The church is looked upon as an example of excellence and a model for others to imitate.

---

[7] *Ibid.*, p. 94.
[8] M. Barker. This unpublished material is included with Dr Barker's permission.

The minister himself is sustained by his success and derives enormous fulfilment from his work. But the price of his success is paid elsewhere. This style of ministry takes its toll on the minister's wife and family. The minister's wife married a pastor, not a tycoon. Some wives will adopt the role of a prima donna and enjoy it. But more often the wife will retreat into an independent life, become isolated from her husband's ministry and suffer depression. The unavoidable stress factor implicit in this style of ministry is the lack of finance. The minister may wish to behave as if he is an executive and may want his wife to live like one, but he is not paid like one. So he cannot live up to his self-imposed expectations.

The price for this style of ministry is also met by the church which becomes clerically dependent. The members depend on going from one successful event or project to another. All the time this happens they have little real relationship with each other and the heart of fellowship is missing. The real growth of the church is limited. In reality this type of church is neither self-sufficient nor mutually supportive.

The minister who is a servant. This minister is person-centred. He is always available and much loved. He has a profound influence on the community, since in his frequent visiting nothing ever seems too much trouble for him and his interests and patience seem to know no bounds. Some aspects of his ministry may suffer. For example, he may not devote sufficient attention to sermon preparation and therefore deliver half-baked ideas from the pulpit from time to time. But his people are willing to overlook that deficiency in the light of his excellent pastoral skills. His sustenance comes from being wanted and his support comes from fellow ministers.

This style of ministry also takes its toll. The minister himself may pay the price of being too available and occasionally burns his fingers by not being able to deliver his promises or live up to people's high expectations. When this happens the minister sometimes retreats into a new kind of professionalism and takes up counselling in a big way, acquiring skill and techniques at a considerable cost.

His family will certainly pay the cost of his over-availability. They will find that outings and special celebrations are cancelled and they are neglected in the service of others. But the church too pays a cost. This pastor wet-nurses them through every issue, so in their own way they become clerically-dependent. They never reach maturity because they never bear responsibility. Perhaps the one to pay the biggest price is this poor man's successor, since he can never hope to measure up to the standards which have been set.

The minister who is a member. This, Dr Barker maintains, is the biblical pattern. Casualties of the pastoral ministry abound because they themselves refuse to have pastors and put themselves into a special category which exempts them from the needs of ordinary mortals. When crises occur they find they have no pastor and their fellow ministers or fraternals are ill-equipped to cope. Only as the unbiblical elevation of the clergyman is rejected and the biblical incorporation of the minister into the body takes place can the minister and his family receive the care they need. The minister like everyone else will need to have close and committed friendships within his congregation. These will not only provide for the ordinary support that every family needs, but will provide the few with whom the minister can relate in depth, thrashing out his own doubts and problems. The minister needs these few, just as Jesus did the inner circle of his disciples. The policy that the minister should have no friends in his congregation but should find his support elsewhere is destructive and isolating.

Dr Barker's analysis simplifies reality, since most pastors do not conform exactly to one or other of his categories. Furthermore, it is an overstatement to claim that the minister as member is *the* biblical pattern. The Bible does place the pastor as a member of the congregation. Yet it also speaks of the leader and servant role of the pastor, although it means something slightly different by these than Dr Barker does. Nonetheless, he has outlined something of increasing significance as the impersonal trends of our society affect ministers as much as everyone else. Dr Barker argues that the rot sets in when we isolate a ministerial candidate in theological college since, from then on, he is distanced from the rest of the church. Whilst that pattern of training is unlikely to be abolished overnight, even if it were right to do so, surely much could be done to correct expectations and attitudes both among ministers and their congregations so that unbiblical and costly styles of ministry can be abandoned.

THE STRUCTURAL MAP

This map is dominated by two basic categories, although many ministries will not fit exactly in one or the other and many have attempted to combine the two. Broadly speaking, there is the institutional ministry and the charismatic ministry. Some may argue that these are pejorative terms. Certainly the labels are inexact. Institutional ministry includes a great deal of charisma and charismatic ministry rapidly becomes institutionalized. The New Testament pattern for ministry involves both. None the less, these rough labels will serve as a guide.

Institutional ministry is how we might describe the traditional understanding of ministry. It emphasizes the distinction between the clergy and the laity. It takes men out of the laity and sets them apart for training in a theological college which usually concentrates on academic matters. Once these fairly rigorous academic standards have been reached it sets them apart further by conferring on them the status of ordination and appointing them to tasks which the laity do not usually legitimately perform.

Such a practice has not arisen without reason. Before theological colleges emerged in the nineteenth century many clergy were set apart by their social status rather than their theological knowledge and they remained fairly ignorant of basic spiritual or theological issues. No wonder the church of that time was spiritually powerless. The emphasis on the need to train ministers is at least better than that! Training in a college setting has the advantage of providing students with the opportunity to learn widely and rapidly and to break free from the parochialism which would be imposed on them if training was restricted to on-the-job training done in their own church. Institutional ministry takes seriously the need for skill and learning if the task of ministry is to be performed well.

Institutional ministry also ensures that people are able to devote themselves fully to the work of the ministry and to do so free from the energy-sapping need to earn one's income at the same time as trying to cope with the pressing pastoral needs of others. Ministry therefore becomes a priority rather than a leisure activity undertaken only if any hours remain once work is done. The freedom to be available is a plus factor for institutional ministry.

Another plus factor which is often claimed is that an institutional approach to ministry preserves order in the church. It prevents anyone from setting up as a leader or teacher, no matter how misguided or ignorant he may be, and it inhibits the church from following such people merely on the basis of their subjective response. Institutional ministry erects a set of objective standards which measure a candidate's suitability for the ministry. By demanding examination and subscription to articles or statements of faith it can guard the truth.

A further argument in favour of institutional ministry is that, in theory, it does create a structure and a colleague group which is mutually supportive for those in it.

Closer examination, however, shows that not only do these advantages fail to work but that they create disadvantages which outweigh the advantages. The belief that institutional ministry preserves good order is a fiction. With so many leading ecclesiastics denying the basic teachings of the Christian church, in spite of having passed all necessary tests and subscribed to all necessary articles, it shows that the claim is patent nonsense.

Similarly the claim that it takes training seriously is correct in theory but needs reviewing in practice. The establishment of theological colleges and faculties separated from the churches inevitably meant that in time they would substitute their own goals for those of the churches. Academic theology, which is unrelated to the churches, therefore begins to predominate and may, apparently, be taught even by unbelievers without anyone thinking it odd. But what sort of training is that? It is a training which educates the pastor out of step with God and out of touch with the people he will serve and to a level beyond which he can effectively communicate with them. Academic training is necessary, but not at the expense of the spiritual and personal training which in the end makes the minister.

Such a ministry leads also to a caste distinction which is unbiblical. The divorce between clergy and laity is nowhere to be found in the pages of the New Testament. True, there is the recognition of leaders and of leadership gifts, but always firmly in the context of the body of Christ and their gifts are always for the development of ministry in others (Eph. 4:11–12). The boundaries are never sharply defined and no caste system is envisaged. This divorce leads to the myth of the omnicompetent ministry – the illusion that one man can and should do it all.

323

The laity say, 'It's his job, that's what we pay him for.' And the clergy say, 'That's my job; why are you interfering?' It creates clerically-dependent congregations and inhibits the spiritual development of members of the church. The divorce also contributes to the feeling of isolation to which we have referred and from which so many suffer. So it both stunts the growth of the body and restricts the growth of the minister.

Further complications follow in the wake of this unbiblical distinction. Many of these complications are of a legal kind, such as who has the right to administer the sacraments,[9] or which ordinations should be recognized as valid,[10] or whether it is right to ordain women or not. Too few seem to recognize that the real problem is not the ordination of women but ordination itself.[11] Much of the prolonged, painful and introverted discussion which has taken place over that issue in recent years would have been rendered irrelevant if the church had not adopted a civil service approach to ministry.

The problems of the institutional ministry have led some to swing violently in the opposite direction in favour of a ministry which is charismatic. This form of ministry too can claim to have a number of advantages.

It recognizes that the prime qualification needed for ministry is not the attainment of certain academic standards but the ability to exercise one or more spiritual gifts. That being so, rather than isolating potential leaders in theological colleges, it marks them out for training within the local fellowship. Ministers arise from and minister to the congregations of which they are a part. So the authority they have is dependent on spiritual recognition and on the quality of the relationships they maintain. This concept of ministry takes seriously the concept of the church as a body and the training, if there is any, is in-service and practical.

Charismatic ministry nearly always endorses plural leadership and reacts strongly against one-man-ministry. The team serves as a natural structure for mutual support and is less isolating. Free from the legal restrictions of the institution the pattern of ministry can be flexible and can adapt to a changing situation quickly and be responsive to new needs. It can expand

[9] Tiller, *Strategy*, p. 67.   [10] *Baptism, Eucharist and Ministry*, 51–55, p. 32.
[11] John Stott does recognize this as the root problem in *Issues Facing Christians Today*, p. 253.

more rapidly and include many more people in it, so allowing people to grow in stature rather than remain dependent.

Paradoxically, such a style of ministry has often brought a new emphasis on authority. There has been a stress that leaders should be allowed to lead and they must be followed if spiritual progress is to be made. Institutional authority is often regarded as vacuous. In an institutional system people want to have a leader so that they can boast of his status, but do not always want him to lead them anywhere. In a charismatic context people are anxious to follow the direction in which the leader is taking them and so much more progress is possible.

But this approach to ministry, too, is not exempt from problems. The absence of control has given rise to people of all kinds setting themselves up as leaders, which they can easily do as long as they can get a small group, sometimes of gullible people, around them. It gives rise to as much bad leadership as good leadership. What it tends to avoid, since it is so dependent on a voluntary following, is indifferent leadership which can so easily claim sanctuary within institutional structures. But it must be admitted that, whilst the good charismatic leader may be good, the bad charismatic leader may be very bad.

This form of leadership is liable also to degenerate into leadership by the ignorant. When this happens leaders cease to be shepherds and become more like sheep-dogs. They do not love and nourish their sheep. They simply snap at their heels and exhort them forcefully to move in the desired direction. The absence of theological training and of wider perspectives can be disastrous. If those who have no knowledge of history are condemned to repeat its mistakes, those with no knowledge of theology are condemned to repeat its heresies. And they do. The lack of the broader biblical and historical understanding often leads to a misreading of the situation they are in which, in turn, sometimes produces tragic pastoral consequences. The emphasis on experience needs to be tempered by attention to truth. The Spirit and the word are only ever separated at our peril.

Furthermore, in spite of the boast that the clergy/laity distinction is abolished in a charismatic form of ministry, often all that has happened is that the division has put on a new suit of clothes and simply appears in a new guise. The rediscovery of authority is both a great asset and a great liability, for many ride roughshod over the carefully qualified use of authority outlined by Paul[12] and abuse it for their own ends. Then the clergy/laity distinction, far from being abolished, takes on a new force.

One of the things that history teaches is that all such charismatic movements fulfil their objectives of growth, flexibility and spontaneity well to start with, but that they have difficulty maintaining that achievement. The absence of foundations and tradition often leads to the movement fragmenting or disintegrating. Alternatively it fairly quickly hardens into a new structure and begins to suffer from all the problems that they had condemned in the institutional form of ministry.

The revival of a charismatic form of ministry has been a recurring pattern in history and it ought not to come as an unwelcome surprise in our own day.[13] Rather its revival should be welcomed as a vigorous challenge to the quality of the institutional ministry and as an incentive to reform and revitalize it. Institutions are always suffering from hardening of the arteries and so are in need of rejuvenation. It should lead to repentance for the status distinctions which have served as the foundation of the institutional ministry and for the way in which ministry has so often been measured by the wrong standards. It should stimulate a re-examination of patterns of ministry to ensure that spiritual leadership is exercised in such a way that the body of Christ, and the members of it, grow. It should lead to a desire to put the pulpit back into touch with the pew. It should give us a concern to overcome the isolation of the pastor and see him as no more than a gifted member of the congregation.

But the revival of a charismatic form of ministry is not to be welcomed uncritically. Some of the triumphalist claims need to be treated with scepticism. History cannot be ignored and its lessons must be heeded. The worship of anti-intellectualism honours God no more than the worship of intellectualism. The vitality and life which have been discovered need to be channelled in such away that it will achieve lasting results. It is too easy to build an exciting but trivial movement which succeeds in the end only in scattering its casualties once more across the pages of history. Authority needs to be used within its biblical

[12] See pp. 114–118.
[13] See further, D. J. Tidball, *An Introduction to the Sociology of the New Testament*, pp. 123–136.

limitations or else it can be a dangerous and destructive weapon.

Our earlier examination of Pauline ministry rejected the idea that there was a divorce between charismatic gifts and institutional ministry and we do well to remember the need for both these aspects to complement each other if ministry is to be mature. The charismatic form of ministry should pay as much attention to the questions raised by institutional forms of ministry as the institutional should to the charismatic. If either side neglects the other the issues ignored will sooner or later forcefully present themselves for attention. But by then it will be too late to benefit from them and the chance of a more wholesome style of ministry will have been missed.

THE FUNCTIONAL MAP

A further map is needed to guide us in our understanding of the task performed by the minister today. Much of the pressure a minister faces, as we have seen, derives from the multitude of functions he is expected to perform and multitude of roles he is expected to assume. The pressure exerted by this variety is aggravated further by the lack of an agreed agenda. Faced with so many demands, the minister himself frequently lists his priorities in one order whilst the congregation often silently assume that he is working to another.

Among the tasks expected are those of preacher, teacher, trainer, pastor, visitor, counsellor, celebrant of worship, performer of religious ceremonies, leader of the congregation, administrator, denominational servant, ecumenical pioneer, community representative and prophet. It is a useful exercise for any minister to list these and invite at least his church leaders, if not his whole congregation, to discuss the order of priorities in which they would place them. Such discussion leads to a greater understanding and agreement between them as to what the pastor should do and how they can complement him.

From this list four tasks stand out as primary, although other tasks naturally gather around them. The resulting constellations shape one's basic definition of ministry. They are teacher, pastor, priest and prophet. It has been argued that denominational socialization is very significant in forming which of these functions the minister puts first.[14] Denominations are still influential and cannot be discounted, even in these days when they are less imposing than they were. Even so, the basic orientation to ministry is also determined by one's theological understanding of ministry.

Teacher. John Stott speaks for many in saying that 'The chief function of the pastor is teaching and to feed and pastor his sheep'.[15] It is an emphasis derived from the Reformation and it remains the principal evangelical orientation to ministry. It has dictated our church architecture by ensuring that the pulpit is central and that our sanctuaries resemble lecture theatres. It has also governed our style in that it has justified the restriction of ministry to one man, at the front, teaching through the medium of a monologue. Other methods of learning, *e.g.* through groups or self-discovery, are viewed with some suspicion. At its worst it degenerates into the cerebral and sterile imparting of information and it exalts the minister so much that an unhealthy gulf is fixed between him and the pew.[16] But it need not fall into either of these traps.

The essential features of this orientation to ministry are its commitment to truth, its belief in the authority and sufficiency of Scripture and its conviction that the word of God will effect change in people's lives and produce conversions and growth in the church. Where this emphasis is to be found, it is believed that the need for personal counselling will lessen. William Still, who has provided one of the clearest recent expositions of this style of ministry, has said,

> My pastoral work of personal dealing, considerable though it is, has been greatly reduced through the years, because the building up of men's faith by the ministry of the Word of God solves so much in their lives, and enables those who receive it and seek to live by it to understand and solve so much in other lives that instead of becoming a liability on my time and energy, they become pastors themselves.[17]

---

[14] S. Ransom, A. Bryman and R. Hinings, *Clergy, Ministers and Priests*, pp. 164f.
[15] J. R. W. Stott, *One People*, p. 45.
[16] D. M. Lloyd–Jones, *Preaching and Preachers*, pp. 83, 121–142.
[17] W. Still, *The Work of the Pastor*, pp. 15f.

Furthermore, he shows that the pitfalls of this orientation to ministry can and must be avoided. This ministry demands the highest calibre of spiritual man to engage in it effectively:

> To be true pastors, your whole life must be spent in knowing the truth of this Word, not only verbally, propositionally, theologically, but religiously, that is, devotionally, morally, in worshipping Him whose commands it contains, in all the promised grace and threat of those commands. To be pastors you must be fed men, not only on knowledge, but in wisdom, grace, humility, courage, fear of God and fearlessness of men.[18]

Priest. Whilst Evangelicals shy away from a priestly orientation to ministry, the truth is that many of the essential features of a priestly ministry accord exactly with their central concerns. The fear of Evangelicals is that the priest usurps the mediatorial role of Christ himself and that men look to the minister for absolution from sin rather than to Christ. Furthermore, a priestly orientation so often brings with it the baggage of the Old Testament, from which the New Testament Christian should be gloriously free. So there are elements of salvation by ritual and sacrament and through the repeated offering of the sacrifice of Christ, in contrast to his completed work, which must be rejected. A further liability is that it makes the celebration of religious ceremonies almost exclusively the province of the priest. So if worship, communion, baptism, a marriage or a funeral is to be conducted, the priest has to do it. At its worst it turns him into a religious performer and keeps him so busy with public rites that he is prevented from exercising real pastoral care.

Michael Ramsey, a former Archbishop of Canterbury, has expounded the work of the priest in a way that would command general commendation. He affirms the role of the priest in contemporary society even though he is aware of the growth of secularism, the reaction against piety and the widespread questioning of authority and of institutions. The priest, he argues, continues to have representative significance as displaying, enabling and involving the church.[19]

---

[18] *Ibid.*, p. 10.   [19] M. Ramsey, *The Christian Priest Today*, p. 6.

Ramsey's chief concern is that the priest should act as an agent of reconciliation (2 Cor. 5:20) between God and men. The central thrust of ministry, therefore, has to do with the forgiveness of sins. Whilst recognizing that the priest no longer has a monopoly on trying to improve the lot of man, Ramsey comments,

> Yet amidst all the activities for the putting right of human ills there is so often a whole dimension missing, the dimension of sin and forgiveness. It not seldom happens that psychiatry, instead of liberating the patient into the realm of moral responsibility and the issues of conscious sin and forgiveness, can substitute medicine for moral responsibility. It is this dimension of sin and forgiveness which the priest keeps alive by an office which represents the forgiving church and the forgiving Lord Jesus.[20]

In order that the priest should be the channel of God's grace Ramsey stresses that he must be a man of theology, not in order that he might be erudite but in order that he may be simple.[21] He must be a man of prayer, for it is through prayer that the authentic knowledge of God comes and that theology comes alive.[22] More controversially, Ramsey states that he must be a man of the eucharist. It is here that absolution for sins can be found, but only as the person seeking forgiveness comes in repentance.[23] Ramsey has no wish to restrict the priest to a narrow pietism but insists that this message of sin and forgiveness, of repentance and conversion, is one which deeply affects man in society. Whilst declining to advocate particular political programmes he insists that the priestly role, if effective, will affect man in all his relationships and therefore shape his political attitudes and values.[24]

The most succint summary of the work of the priest is to be found, appropriately, in the Exhortation in the Order of Holy Communion in the *Book of Common Prayer*:

> And because it is requisite, that no man should come to the holy Communion, but with a full trust in God's mercy, and with a quiet conscience; therefore if there be any of you, who

[20] *Ibid.*, p. 8. See also p. 52. [21] *Ibid.*, p. 7. [22] *Ibid.*, p. 9.
[23] *Ibid.*, p. 50. [24] *Ibid.*, pp. 34–42.

by this means cannot quiet his own conscience herein, but requireth further comfort or counsel, let him come to me, or to some other discreet and learned Minister of God's Word, and open his grief; that by the ministry of God's holy Word he may receive the benefit of absolution, together with ghostly counsel and advice, to the quieting of his conscience, and avoiding of all scruple and doubtfulness.

Pastor. Although pastor is a comprehensive term for the work of the ministry, we have something more particular in mind in distinguishing it as a separate orientation to ministry. Traditionally, the pastor has been a spiritual guide, not just in providing moral direction or by steering a person towards the forgiveness of God, but also by walking with people through the crises and sufferings of life. The pastor's aim is to lead his sheep to green pastures, but the road thither may lie through cold and dark valleys and the pastor must be present then as well. This view of the ministry sees the function of the pastor as primarily a helper and counsellor.

Although much in this role sounds traditional, the way in which it has recently been expounded puts it in a different light.[25] The problems and pressures of life seem to be treated with a new seriousness. No attempt is made to minimize the fullest dimensions of suffering, doubt and despair and trite answers are shunned. The answers sought do not lie in directive counselling but rather in the sharing of oneself. The pastor is not above the person seeking help but is one with him and is most effective when able to share his own weaknesses and fears and to open himself up to the person in need of help. So in what sense does the pastor help? Frank Wright, struggling to express this style of ministry, writes:

Perhaps *absorb* is the one word which catches best the attitude I seek to describe: to be able to absorb other people's feelings without reflecting them is a great pastoral gift . . . Pastors need to be able to absorb other people's depressions, and today, especially, they may have to absorb a lot from people who feel they have been abandoned by the church. Absorption is at the heart of so much pastoral method, and certainly

[25] See, for example, A. V. Campbell, *Rediscovering Pastoral Care*; H. J. M. Nouwen, *The Wounded Healer*; and F. Wright, *The Pastoral Nature of the Ministry*.

of forgiveness. Jesus on the cross absorbed all the feelings of hatred which were loosed upon him, and his response, 'Father, forgive them, for they do not know what they are doing', stopped the power of evil to produce more evil.[26]

Alastair Campbell points out that such a ministry may deepen the experience of pain rather than permit people to take quick but unwise escape routes. He sets out the purpose of this ministry in these terms,

By remaining with people but at the same time refusing to take the escape from pain they seek, we can restore their courage to voice their deepest fears and to express the anguish they find so threatening. Our main task is to wait and watch with them, that simple service which Jesus asked for (in vain) from his friends.[27]

A number of biblical themes support this view of ministry. In the incarnation Jesus Christ did enter fully into man's existence, yet without sinning, and is therefore able to sympathize with us in our weaknesses. It is through his wounds that we are healed. Pastors, therefore, who seek to be 'wounded healers' are only imitating Christ. This style of ministry, too, takes seriously Christ's description of the good shepherd as one who knows his sheep intimately and lays down his own life for them. Furthermore the image of the Holy Spirit as the paraclete lends credence to the need to stand alongside the sufferer to offer comfort, in the fullest sense of the word, to him.

Yet there is need for caution about this orientation to ministry. The unease arises from the apologetic approach to having answers. It must be confessed that too often Evangelicals have unfeelingly proclaimed Christ as the answer before they have ever stopped to ask what the question is. Yet, surely, what distinguishes the Christian pastor from a multitude of other carers who enter into the existential despair of man's existence is that he does have answers in Christ. Jesus must be proclaimed to be the light of the world to those who sit in darkness and the resurrection to those who face death.

It would be wrong to give the impression that Evangelicals

---

[26] Wright, *Pastoral Nature of the Ministry*, p. 64.
[27] Campbell, *Rediscovering*, p. 44.

have not been affected in their own way by these trends. Their answers may be more directive, but many have felt the despair of man's condition more deeply than previous generations would have done and have found that the traditional way of preaching and pastoring cuts little ice in the face of these complex problems. So they have adopted a pastoral approach which gives priority not to the pulpit but to the counselling room. Counselling is seen by some as the primary role of the pastor. This approach often reveals its practitioners to be children of their age, not only by the attention they have given to existential questions, but also because they often link their theology to a particular, and inevitably temporary, psychological approach. The pastor has exchanged the coat of the spiritual general practitioner for the specialist psychologist.[28]

It would be wrong to trivialize the problems of our age. The church must both enter fully into the depth of suffering that is experienced and provide specialist help to enable people to work through their tangled problems. The pastor, by his availability and care for the individual sheep, plays a crucial role in this. But to interpret pastoral ministry exclusively, or even predominantly, in this way is unbalanced. The pastoral ministry has wider concerns. There are many who need a pastor who do not face particular problems as such. They need to be built up and strengthened in Christ even when life is relatively problem-free. Moreover, the pastor must resist the temptation to forsake the spiritual resources available to him for the apparently more attractive psychological approaches which are in fashion. Helpful though their insight into human nature may be, he remains first and foremost a man of God.

Prophet. Still others would wish to stress a fourth function of the ministry. The teacher, priest and pastor are largely in-house concerns. Pastors who adopt those orientations to ministry are largely concerned with the interests of their members. Their primary focus is the health and development of their own organization. Some would view that as a cosy and inadequate conception of ministry. If, in William Temple's famous dictum, 'the church is the only organisation on earth which exists for

---

[28] On the difference of role see M. Barker, 'Models of pastoral care: medical, psychological and biblical', in M. A. Jeeves (ed), *Behavioural Sciences: A Christian Perspective*, pp. 230–245.

those who are not yet its members', pastoral ministry must be orientated towards those outside. This may take the form of evangelism, although those who argue this case are usually more concerned with the ministry's prophetic role than its evangelistic mission.

The motivation for this orientation to ministry comes from two quarters. Firstly, it is theological.[29] It arises from an understanding of God as creator and not just as redeemer. It sees that God's concern still lies with the world he has made and is not confined to the church he has saved. Moreover it stresses that the coming of Jesus inaugurated the kingdom of God and that God's kingdom is not identical with the church but is much wider, even if principally manifested through it. It sees, too, the church as a showcase of a renewed humanity. It is precisely because the church belongs to a kingdom of justice and righteousness that will one day be fully inherited that its members live now in right relationship with their fellow men and fight for justice here on earth.

Secondly, the motivation is sociological. Towler and Coxon,[30] in predicting the future of the ministry, admit that its survival and success, in the short term, lie with the pastor who sees his function in terms of serving and building up the church. But they argue that, with the rampant march of secularization and the ravages of institutionalization, success can be only short-term. In the long term, the only hope of success is for religious professionals to break free from the walls of their religious clubs and escape into the world. There they must set about Christianizing society once more 'so that godliness may be saved from being the hobby of a few'.

At first sight their argument seems convincing. But Alan Gilbert has justifiably erected a big question mark over it by arguing that such preoccupation with the world may prove fatal to the church. He sees another way forward:

> even if history does prove accommodation to have been a strategy of extinction for mainstream Protestantism, a small, intense, resolute, essentially intolerant religious culture will

---

[29] The arguments can be found, from an evangelical standpoint, in J. Gladwin, *God's People in God's World*; D. S. Sheppard, *Built as a City*; and J. R. W. Stott, *Issues Facing Christians Today*. Another important forum and thorough discussion of prophetic ministry can be found in R. Gill, *Prophecy and Praxis*.

[30] Towler and Coxon, *Fate of the Anglican Clergy*, p. 205.

continue to resist the secular 'world', striving to change it. For the new sectarianism to succeed in effecting any general re-conversion of post-Christian Britain would, of course, involve a reversal of profound movements of secularization and modernization – a transformation of the very essence of modern industrial society – and that is a possibility about as likely as the prospect 2,000 years ago, that an insignificant Jewish cult might succeed in turning the great classical world upside down![31]

The theological argument for a prophetic form of ministry is sounder than the sociological argument. The sociological argument, moreover, freed from the discipline of theological prescription, has the danger of politicizing the church rather than Christianizing the nation. The theological argument, however, provides the essential discipline necessary to ensure that the pastor who exercises his ministry outside of the church does so as a representative of God, aware that he is fighting a spiritual battle. He does not therefore submerge himself in human tactics or arguments.

The four approaches to the function of ministry presented in this map are not as sharply defined in reality as they have been drawn. It is true that the teaching orientation has been associated with evangelicalism, the priestly function with high churchmanship, the pastoral orientation owes much to contemporary psychology and philosophy and the prophetic stance has been associated with broad churchmanship. Whilst wishing to maintain strongly the value of the traditional evangelical conception of ministry, it is good that the other orientations to ministry have recently been more highly appreciated. An understanding of their perspectives provides a more balanced approach and ultimately a more effective approach to ministry.

CONCLUSION

A recent article complained that the average ministerial experience of preaching to a small congregation week in and week out was a far cry from the high ideals about preaching which

---

[31] A. D. Gilbert, *The Making of Post-Christian Britain*, p. 153.

had been set before the writer at theological college. 'I sometimes think it is easy for great and famous men to write exciting
books about preaching and pastoral work, because they have
ministered in big churches. Would they have been so
enamoured with the role if less gifted and with small
congregations?' [32] It will be tempting for some to dismiss the
high ideals set out earlier in this book as unrelated to their
own experience of pastoral ministry. Ideals can be hard and
discouraging taskmasters. But most of the ideals here were
forged through the struggles of ordinary church life. It is just
that fact which provides a Chrysostom or a Baxter with an
authority to command a hearing. But even if that were not the
case, it would still be wise to consider the ideals set before us
in Scripture and history. Ideals are needed to lift our heads out
of the quagmire of our own experiences, to lift us out of our
subjectivism, to widen our vision, to challenge our negligence
and to stretch our abilities. Whilst we must remain careful to
ensure that we are not condemned and enslaved by them, we
must equally be careful to learn humbly that we are not the
skilful shepherds we ought to be.

Many are inclined to predict radical changes ahead for the
ministry. In my view, although new patterns will be introduced,
it is unlikely that a cataclysmic revolution in ministry is about to
dawn. Churches remain conservative institutions and changes
are likely to creep upon them only gradually. The developments
outside the main denominations will have a useful role to play
in disturbing the comfort of the traditional ministry. But they
themselves are likely to begin to encounter the same insti-
tutionalizing forces which will sap their vitality before too long.
There will, then, remain for some time to come a role for the
pastor who, rather than being a specialist or consultant, can be
more exactly compared to a general practitioner in the church.

Such an argument is not intended to be complacent or
defeatist. It is because this is the likely scenario that the more
important lessons of Scripture and history must be learnt. What
are these lessons?

Skilful shepherds must reject the bureaucratic concept of
ministry, derived from the Roman empire, which has tied the
ministry in academic, legal and prestigious knots from which

[32] G. Neal, 'The call to the ministry – some mid-point reflections', *The Fraternal* (October 1984), pp. 10f.

even Houdini would find it hard to escape.

Skilful shepherds will base their ministry on their spiritual calling, spiritual character and spiritual gifts.

Skilful shepherds will be sensitive to the wind of the Spirit. This will lead to a flexibility of operation and to an all-round ministry where there is no divorce between the spoken word of God and the miraculous work of the Spirit.

Skilful shepherds will place their ministry firmly within the body of Christ. They will remember that even while they are shepherds they are also sheep. In this way their isolation will be overcome, pastoral support will be mutually given and cultural distinctions between leadership and led will be reduced.

Skilful shepherds will see ministry as a plural exercise on the part of the body of Christ rather than as one man's job. A diversity of skills and roles will then emerge and team-ministry will be sought after.

Skilful shepherds will not seek training until the gifts of ministry are evident and tested. They will not put themselves forward on the basis of wishful thinking about hoped-for but untried potential.

Skilful shepherds will see the ministry as a task which demands training. The complexity of people's problems and the eternal significance of the pastor's work will cause them to reject a casual or self-confident attitude towards ministry. They will recognize that skill is demanded of shepherds who are to nourish the sheep. The skill will consist of a deep knowledge of the word of God and a deep knowledge of people infused into a personality which has been trained in godliness.

Skilful shepherds will realize that the most essential food on which to nourish the sheep is the word of God. They will not be overwhelmed by people's experiences nor overawed by their arguments. With gentleness and patience they will seek to submit the subjective experiences and perceptions of men to the objective and revealed truth of God.

Skilful shepherds will lead the sheep. They will not be content for the flock to remain as they are, nor even to manage them more efficiently. They will seek the growth of the flock numerically. They will also seek their progress, individually and corporately, towards maturity. They will not be managers, for managers deal in seen realities, but leaders, for leaders deal in unseen potentials.

Skilful shepherds 'prepare God's people for works of service, so that the body of Christ may be built up until we all reach unity in the faith and in the knowledge of the Son of God and become mature, attaining to the whole measure of the fulness of Christ' (Eph. 4:12–13).

Bibliography

R. Abraham, 'Yes, Jay Adams is biblical enough', *Third Way* 5/7 (1982), pp. 15–16.

J. E. Adams, *The Big Umbrella* (Nutley, N.J.: Presbyterian and Reformed Publishing Company, 1973).

J. E. Adams, *The Christian Counsellor's Manual* (Nutley, N.J.: Presbyterian and Reformed Publishing Company, 1973).

J. E. Adams, *Competent to Counsel* (Nutley, N.J.: Presbyterian and Reformed Publishing Company, 1972).

J. E. Adams, *More than Redemption* (Grand Rapids: Baker, 1979).

J. E. Adams, 'Nouthetic Counselling', in G. R. Collins (ed), *Helping People Grow* (Santa Ana: Vision House, 1980), pp. 151–164.

J. E. Adams, *Shepherding God's Flock* (Nutley, N.J.: Presbyterian and Reformed Publishing Company, 1975).

J. L. Adams and S. Hiltner, *Pastoral Care in the Liberal Churches* (Nashville: Abingdon Press, 1970).

J. Adamson, *The Epistle of James. NICNT* (Grand Rapids: Eerdmans, 1976).

Ambrose of Milan, *On the Duty of Clergy. NP-NF* Second Series, vol. 10 (Grand Rapids: Eerdmans).

R. S. Anderson (ed), *Theological Foundations for Ministry* (Edinburgh and Grand Rapids: T. & T. Clark and Eerdmans, 1979).

Apostolical Constitutions. A-NCL, vol. 17 (Edinburgh: T. & T. Clark, 1870).

D. Atkinson, 'Forgiveness and personality', *Third Way* 5/11 (1982), pp. 18–21.

D. Atkinson, 'The Freedom of Forgiveness', *Third Way* 5/10 (1982), pp. 4–7.

J. Atkinson, *Martin Luther and the Birth of Protestantism* (Harmondsworth: Pelican, 1968).

Augustine, *On Christian Doctrine. NP-NF* First Series, vol. 2 (Grand Rapids: Eerdmans).

Augustine, *On the Catechising of the Uninstructed. NP-NF* First Series, vol. 3 (Grand Rapids: Eerdmans).

P. D. L. Avis, *The Church in the Theology of the Reformers* (London: Marshall, Morgan & Scott, 1981).

R. H. Bainton, 'The Ministry in the Middle Ages', in H. R. Niebuhr and D. D. Williams (eds), *The Ministry in Historical Perspective* (New York: Harper & Row, 1983).

J. G. Baldwin, *Haggai, Zechariah, Malachi. TOTC* (London: Tyndale Press, 1972).

R. Banks, *Paul's Idea of Community* (Exeter: Paternoster Press, 1980).

Baptism, Eucharist and Ministry (Geneva: WCC, 1982).

G. W. Barker, W. L. Lane and R. Michaels, *The New Testament Speaks* (New York: Harper and Row, 1969).

M. Barker, 'Models of pastoral care: medical, psychological and biblical', in M. A. Jeeves (ed), *Behavioural Sciences: A Christian Perspective* (Leicester: IVP, 1984), pp. 230–245.

C. K. Barrett, *The First Epistle to the Corinthians*. Black's *NTC* (London: A. & C. Black, 1968).

C. K. Barrett, *The Gospel according to St John* (London: SPCK, 1955).

G. Barth, 'Matthew's Understanding of the Law', in G. Bornkamm, G. Barth and H. J. Held (eds), *Tradition and Interpretation in Matthew* (London: SCM, 1963), pp. 58–164.

K. Barth, *Church Dogmatics*, iv, Part 2 (Edinburgh: T. & T. Clark, 1958).

K. Barth, *The Theology of Schleiermacher* (Edinburgh: T. & T. Clark, 1982).

M. Barth, *Ephesians 4 – 6. AB* (New York: Doubleday and Cox, 1974).

Basil of Caesarea, *Letters. NP-NF* Second Series, vol. 8 (Grand Rapids: Eerdmans).

R. J. Bauckham, *Jude, 2 Peter. WBC* (Waco, Texas: Word Books, 1983).

R. Baxter, *The Cure of Church Divisions* (London: Nevil Symmons, 1670).

R. Baxter, *The Reformed Pastor*, with an Introduction by James I. Packer (Edinburgh: Banner of Truth, abridged edition, 1974. First published 1656).

F. W. Beare, *The First Epistle of Peter* (Oxford: Blackwell, 1958).

G. R. Beasley-Murray, *The Book of Revelation. NCB* (London: Oliphants, 1974).

D. M. Beegle, *Moses, the Servant of Yahweh* (Grand Rapids: Eerdmans, 1972).

D. Bell, *Sociological Journeys* (London: Heinemann, 1980).

R. Bellah, *Beyond Belief* (New York: Harper & Row, 1970).

E. W. Benson, *Cyprian: His Life, His Times, His Work* (London: Macmillan, 1897).

P. L. Berger, *Facing up to Modernity* (Harmondsworth: Penguin, 1979).

P. L. Berger, *A Rumour of Angels* (Harmondsworth: Penguin, 1971).

P. L. Berger, *The Social Reality of Religion* (Harmondsworth: Penguin, 1973).

P. L. Berger, B. Berger and H. Kellner, *The Homeless Mind* (Harmondsworth: Penguin, 1974).

P. L. Berger and T. Luckmann, *The Social Construction of Reality* (Harmondsworth: Penguin, 1972).

E. Best, *Mark: The Gospel as Story* (Edinburgh: T. & T. Clark, 1983).

H. Bettenson (ed), *Documents of the Christian Church* (London: OUP, 1963).

H. W. Beyer, '*Kubernesis*', *TDNT*, vol. 3 (Grand Rapids: Eerdmans, 1965), pp. 1035–1037.

E. Beyreuther, 'Shepherd', *NIDNTT*, vol. 3 (Exeter: Paternoster Press, 1978), pp. 564–569.

W. P. de Boer, *The Imitation of Paul* (Kampen: J. H. Kok, 1962).

J. M. Boice, *Witness and Revelation in the Gospel of John* (Exeter: Paternoster Press, 1970).

A. T. Boisen, *The Exploration of the Inner World: A Study in Mental Disorder and Religious Experience* (New York: Willett, Clark & Co, 1937).

J. M. Bonino, *Revolutionary Theology Comes of Age* (London: SPCK, 1975).

G. Bornkamm, G. Barth and H. J. Held (eds), *Tradition and Interpretation in Matthew* (London: SCM, 1963).

P. Brand and P. Yancey, 'Putting Pain to Work', *Leadership* 5/4 (1984), pp. 121f.

W. Bridge, *Lifting Up of the Downcast* (Edinburgh: Banner of Truth, 1979).

C. Bridges, *The Christian Ministry* (London: Banner of Truth, 1958. First published 1849).

A. E. Brooke, *The Johannine Epistles. ICC* (Edinburgh: T. & T.

Clark, 1912).

P. N. Brooks (ed), *Seven-Headed Luther* (Oxford: OUP, 1983).

T. Brooks, *Heaven on Earth* (London: Banner of Truth, 1961. First published 1654).

C. Brown and H. Seebuss, 'Moses', *NIDNTT*, vol. 2 (Exeter: Paternoster Press, 1976), pp. 635–643.

R. Brown, 'An Early Christian Conception of the Pastoral Office', *The Fraternal* (July 1978), pp. 3–11.

R. Brown, 'Luther as a Pastoral Counsellor', unpublished lecture.

R. Brown, *The Message of Hebrews. Christ Above All. BST* (Leicester: IVP, 1982).

R. Brown, *Pastoral Care: An Early Christian Perspective.* Annual Laing Lecture (Northwood: London Bible College, 1977).

R. E. Brown, *The Gospel According to John.* 2 vols *AB* (London: Geoffrey Chapman, 1971).

D. S. Browning, *Atonement and Psychotherapy* (Philadelphia: Westminster Press, 1966).

D. S. Browning, 'Images of Man in Contemporary Models of Pastoral Care', *Interp.* 33 (1979), pp. 146–156.

D. S. Browning, *The Moral Context of Pastoral Care* (Philadelphia: Westminster Press, 1976).

D. S. Browning (ed), *Practical Theology* (San Francisco: Harper & Row, 1983).

F. F. Bruce, *The Epistle to the Hebrews. NICNT* (London: Marshall, Morgan and Scott, 1965).

F. F. Bruce, 'The Revelation of John', in G. C. D. Howley (ed), *A New Testament Commentary* (London: Pickering and Inglis, 1969), pp. 629–666.

W. Brueggemann, 'Covenanting as Human Vocation', *Interp.* 33 (1979), pp. 115–129.

M. Bucer, 'Visitation of the Sick', in D. F. Wright (trans and ed), *Common Places of Martin Bucer.* Courtney Library of Reformation Classics, vol. 4 (Appleford: Sutton Courtenay Press, 1972), pp. 429–451.

M. Bucer, 'Von der Waren Seelsorge . . .', in *Martini Bucer Opera Omnia Series I: Deutsche Schriften*, vol. 7 (Gutersloh and Paris, 1964), pp. 67–245.

T. C. Butler, *Joshua. WBC* (Waco, Texas: Word Books, 1983).

G. B. Caird, *A Commentary on the Revelation of St John the Divine.* Black's *NTC* (London: A. & C. Black, 1966).

J. Calvin, 'Draft Ecclesiastical Ordinances', in *Theological Treatises*, translated by J. K. S. Reid. *LCC*, vol. 22 (London: SCM, 1954).

J. Calvin, *The Epistles of Paul to the Romans and to the Thessalonians*, edited by D. W. & T. F. Torrance. *CC* (Edinburgh: St Andrew Press, 1961).

J. Calvin, *Institutes of the Christian Religion*. 2 vols (London: James Clarke, 1962).

J. Calvin, *St John 1–10*, edited by D. W. & T. F. Torrance. *CC* (Edinburgh: St Andrews Press, 1959).

J. Calvin, *St John 11–21 and First John*, edited by D. W. & T. F. Torrance. *CC* (Edinburgh: St Andrews Press, 1961).

J. Calvin, *The Second Epistle of Paul to the Corinthians and the Epistles to Timothy, Titus and Philemon*, edited by D. W. & T. F. Torrance. *CC* (Edinburgh: Oliver & Boyd, 1964).

A. V. Campbell, 'The Politics of Pastoral Care', *Contact* 62 (1979), pp. 2–14.

A. V. Campbell, *Rediscovering Pastoral Care* (London: Darton Longman & Todd, 1981).

H. von Campenhausen, *Ecclesiastical Authority and Spiritual Power in the Church of the First Three Centuries* (London: A. & C. Black, 1969).

D. Carlson, 'Jesus' Style of Relating. The Search for a Biblical View of Counselling', *JPT* 4 (1976), pp. 181–192.

D. A. Carson, 'Recent literature on the fourth gospel: some reflections', *Themelios* 9 (1983), pp. 8–18.

D. A. Carson and J. D. Woodbridge (eds), *Scripture and Truth* (Leicester: IVP, 1983).

J. D. Carter, 'Adams' Theory of Nouthetic Counselling', *JPT* 3 (1975), pp. 143–155.

W. E. Chadwick, *The Pastoral Teaching of St Paul. His Ministerial Ideals* (Edinburgh: T. & T. Clark, 1907).

B. S. Childs, *Exodus*. *OTL* (London: SCM, 1974).

John Chrysostom, *On the Priesthood*. *NP-NF* First Series, vol. 9 (Grand Rapids: Eerdmans).

J. Clayton, *St Hugh of Lincoln* (London: Burns, Oates & Washbourne, 1931).

W. A. Clebsch and C. R. Jackee, *Pastoral Care in Historical Perspective* (New York: Harper and Row, 1967).

G. Coates, *What on Earth is this Kingdom?* (Eastbourne: Kingsway Publications, 1983).

G. R. Collins (ed), *Helping People Grow* (Santa Ana: Vision House, 1980).

H. Conzelmann, *The Theology of Luke* (London: Faber and Faber, 1960).

P. Cotterell, *The Eleventh Commandment* (Leicester: IVP, 1981).

G. G. Coulton, *Ten Medieval Studies* (Cambridge: CUP, 1930).

P. C. Craigie, *The Book of Deuteronomy*. NICOT (London: Hodder & Stoughton, 1976).

C. E. B. Cranfield, *The Epistle to the Romans*. ICC, vol. 2 (Edinburgh: T. & T. Clark, 1979).

C. E. B. Cranfield, *The Gospel According to Mark*. CGTC (Cambridge: CUP, 1963).

O. Cullmann, *Early Christian Worship* (London: SCM, 1953).

O. Cullmann, *Peter: Disciple, Apostle, Martyr* (London: SCM, 1953).

Cyprian, *Epistles*. A-NCL, vol. 8 (Edinburgh: T. & T. Clark, 1868).

Cyprian, *On the Immortality*. A-NCL, vol. 8 (Edinburgh: T. & T. Clark, 1868).

R. W. Dale, *The Evangelical Revival* (London: Hodder & Stoughton, 1880).

R. W. Dale (ed), *The Life and Letters of John Angell James* (London: Nisbet, 1849).

P. Davids, *The Epistle of James*. NIGTC (Exeter: Paternoster Press, 1982).

R. Davidson, *The Courage to Doubt* (London: SCM, 1983).

R. Davies and G. Rupp (eds), *A History of the Methodist Church in Great Britain*, vol. 1 (London: Epworth Press, 1965).

W. Dean, 'Successful House Groups – Lessons from History', *Church Growth Digest* (Autumn–Spring 1983–1984).

V. A. Demant, *The Responsibility and Scope of Pastoral Theology Today* (Oxford: OUP, 1950).

L. Dewar and C. E. Hudson, *A Manual of Pastoral Psychology* (London: Philip Allen, 1932).

D. L. Douie, *Archbishop Pecham* (Oxford: OUP, 1952).

J. D. G. Dunn, *Jesus and the Spirit* (London: SCM, 1975).

J. D. G. Dunn, *Unity and Diversity in the New Testament* (London: SCM, 1977).

W. Eichrodt, *Ezekiel*. OTL (London: SCM, 1970).

W. Eichrodt, *Theology of the Old Testament*, vol. 1 (London: SCM, 1961).

J. H. Elliott, *A Home for the Homeless. A Sociological Exegesis of 1 Peter and its Situation and Strategy* (London: SCM, 1981).

E. E. Ellis, *The Gospel of Luke. NCB* (London: Oliphants, 1974).

E. E. Ellis, 'The Role of the Christian Prophet in Acts', in W. W. Gasque and R. P. Martin (eds), *Apostolic History and the Gospel* (Exeter: Paternoster Press, 1970).

T. W. Engstrom and E. R. Dayton, *The Art of Management for Christian Leaders* (Waco, Texas: Word Books, 1976).

W. J. Everett and J. J. Backmeyer, *Disciplines in Transformation* (Washington: University of America Press, 1979).

P. Fairbairn, *Pastoral Theology* (Edinburgh: T. & T. Clark, 1875).

G. G. Findlay, *Fellowship in Life Eternal* (London: Hodder & Stoughton, 1909).

P. T. Forsyth, *Positive Preaching and the Modern Mind* (London: Hodder & Stoughton, 1907).

R. Y. K. Fung, 'Charismatic Versus Organised Ministry', *EQ* 52 (1980), pp. 195–214.

V. P. Furnish, *Theology and Ethics in Paul* (Nashville: Abingdon Press, 1968).

V. P. Furnish, 'Theology and Ministry in the Pauline Letters', in E. E. Shelp and R. Sunderland (eds), *A Biblical Basis for Ministry* (Philadelphia: Westminster Press, 1981), pp. 101–144.

E. Gibbs, *I Believe in Church Growth* (London: Hodder & Stoughton, 1981).

A. D. Gilbert, *The Making of Post-Christian Britain* (London and New York: Longman, 1980).

R. Gill, *Prophecy and Praxis* (Basingstoke: Marshalls, 1981).

S. M. Gilmour, 'Pastoral Care in the New Testament Church', *NTS* 10 (1964), pp. 393–398.

W. Gladden, *The Christian Pastor and the Working Church* (Edinburgh: T. & T. Clark, 1901).

J. Gladwin, *God's People in God's World* (Leicester: IVP, 1979).

M. Green, *2 Peter and Jude. TNTC* (London: Tyndale Press, 1968).

P. Greenslade, *Leadership* (Basingstoke: Marshalls, 1984).

F. Greeves, *Theology and the Cure of Souls* (London: Epworth Press, 1960).

Gregory of Nazianzus, *In the defence of his flight to Pontus. Oration II. NP-NF* Second Series, vol. 7 (Grand Rapids: Eerdmans).

Gregory the Great, *The Book of Pastoral Rule. NP-NF* Second Series, vol. 12 (Grand Rapids: Eerdmans).

G. Griffin, 'Pastoral Care and Pastoral Theology Overseas', in W. B. Oglesby (ed), *The New Shape of Pastoral Theology* (Nashville: Abingdon Press, 1969).

M. Griffiths, *Cinderella with Amnesia* (London: IVP, 1975).

L. Grollenberg, J. Kerkhofs, A. Houtepen, J. J. A. Vollebergh and E. Schillebeeckx, *Minister? Pastor? Prophet?* (London: SCM, 1980).

O. Guinness, *Doubt: Faith in Two Minds* (Berkhamsted: Lion, 1976).

O. Guinness, *The Gravedigger File* (London: Hodder & Stoughton, 1983).

R. H. Gundry, *Matthew. A Commentary on his Literary and Theological Art* (Grand Rapids: Eerdmans, 1982).

D. Guthrie, *Hebrews. TNTC* (Leicester: IVP, 1983).

D. Guthrie, *New Testament Introduction* (London: IVP, 1970).

D. Guthrie, *New Testament Theology* (Leicester: IVP, 1981).

G. Gutierrez, *A Theology of Liberation* (London: SCM, 1974).

G. Haendler, *Luther on Ministerial Office and Congregational Function* (Philadelphia: Fortress Press, 1981).

D. R. Hall, 'Pauline Church Discipline', *Tyndale Bulletin* 20 (1969), pp. 3–26.

J. C. Harris, *Stress, Power and Ministry* (Mount St. Alban: The Alban Institute, 1977).

H. J. Held, 'Matthew as Interpreter of the Miracle Stories', in G. Bornkamm, G. Barth and H. J. Held (eds), *Tradition and Interpretation in Matthew* (London: SCM, 1963), pp. 165–299.

G. Herbert, *The Country Parson* and *The Temple*, edited by J. N. Wall (London: SPCK, 1981).

K. Hess, 'Serve', *NIDNTT*, vol. 3 (Exeter: Paternoster Press, 1978), pp. 544–549.

D. Hill, *The Gospel of Matthew. NCB* (London: Oliphants, 1972).

S. Hiltner, *Preface to Pastoral Theology* (Nashville: Abingdon Press, 1958).

H. T. Hoekstra, *Evangelism in Eclipse* (Exeter: Paternoster Press, 1979).

B. Holmberg, *Paul and Power* (Lund: C. W. K. Gleerup, 1978).

H. E. Hopkins, *Charles Simeon of Cambridge* (London: Hodder & Stoughton, 1977).

C. W. Horland, 'Anfectung in Luther's Biblical Exegesis', in F. H. Littell (ed), *Reformation Studies, Essays in Honour of Roland H. Bainton* (Richmond, Virginia: John Knox Press, 1962).

P. E. Hughes, *A Commentary on the Epistle to the Hebrews* (Grand Rapids: Eerdmans, 1977).

E. Hulse, 'The Puritans and Counselling Troubled Souls', *Foundations* 8 (1982), pp. 6–28.

R. J. Hunter, 'The Future of Pastoral Theology', *Pastoral Psychology* 29 (1980), pp. 58–69.

J. A. James, *An Earnest Ministry the Want of the Times* (London: Hamilton Adams, 1848).

M. A. Jeeves (ed), *Behavioural Sciences: A Christian Perspective* (Leicester: IVP, 1984).

J. Jeremias, *'poimēn'*, *TDNT*, vol. 6 (Grand Rapids: Eerdmans, 1967), pp. 485–502.

M. Jeschke, *Discipling the Brother* (Scottdale: Herald Press, 1972).

P. E. Johnson, *Pastoral Ministration* (London: James Nisbet, 1955).

P. E. Johnson, *Personality and Religion* (Nashville: Abingdon Press, 1957).

P. E. Johnson, *Psychology of Religion* (Nashville: Abingdon Press, 1959).

Justin Martyr, *First Apology. A-NCL*, vol. 2 (Edinburgh: T. & T. Clark, 1867).

E. Käsemann, *Essays on New Testament Themes* (London: SCM, 1964).

H. C. Kee, *Community of the New Age* (London: SCM, 1977).

J. N. D. Kelly, *The Epistles of Peter and Jude. Black's NTC* (London: A. & C. Black, 1969).

J. Kent, *Jabez Bunting: The Last Wesleyan. Wesley Historical Lecture* (London: Epworth Press, 1955).

D. Kidner, *Wisdom to live by* (Leicester: IVP, 1985).

J. N. King, *The God of Forgiveness and Healing in the Theology of Karl Rahner* (Washington: University of America Press, 1982).

R. M. Kingdon, *Geneva and the Coming of the Wars of Religion in France, 1555–1563* (Geneva: 1956).

J. A. Kirk, *Liberation Theology* (Basingstoke: Marshalls, 1979).

K. E. Kirk, *The Apostolic Ministry* (London: Hodder & Stoughton, 1946).

C. Kruse, *New Testament Foundations of Ministry* (London: Marshall, Morgan & Scott, 1983).

H. Küng, *The Church* (London: Search Press, 1968).

G. E. Ladd, *A Theology of the New Testament* (Grand Rapids: Eerdmans, 1974).

W. L. Lane, *The Gospel of Mark. NICNT* (London: Marshall, Morgan & Scott, 1974).

J. Lapsley, 'Pastoral Theology Past and Present', in W. B. Oglesby Jnr (ed), *The New Shape of Pastoral Theology* (Nashville: Abingdon Press, 1979), pp. 31–48.

J. Lapsley, *Salvation and Health* (Philadelphia: Westminster Press, 1972).

W. S. LaSor, D. A. Hubbard and F. W. Bush (eds), *Old Testament Survey* (Grand Rapids: Eerdmans, 1982).

A. B. Lawson, *John Wesley and the Christian Ministry* (London: SPCK, 1963).

G. Leonard, *God Alive: Priorities in Pastoral Theology* (London: Darton, Longman & Todd, 1981).

C. S. Lewis, *A Grief Observed* (London: Faber and Faber, 1961).

C. S. Lewis, *The Problem of Pain* (London: Fontana, 1957).

P. Lewis, *The Genius of Puritanism* (Haywards Heath: Carey Publications, 1975).

B. Lindars, *The Gospel of John. NCB* (London: Oliphants, 1972).

T. M. Lindsay, *The Church and the Ministry in the Early Centuries* (London: Hodder & Stoughton, 1902).

D. M. Lloyd-Jones, *The Basis of Unity* (London: IVF, 1962).

D. M. Lloyd-Jones, *Darkness and Light. An Exposition of Ephesians 4:17 – 5:17* (Edinburgh: Banner of Truth, 1982).

D. M. Lloyd-Jones, *Preaching and Preachers* (London: Hodder & Stoughton, 1971).

D. M. Lloyd-Jones, *Spiritual Depression: Its Causes and Cure* (London: Pickering and Inglis, 1965).

R. Longenecker, *The Ministry and Message of Paul* (Grand Rapids: Zondervan, 1971).

R. Lovelace, *Dynamics of Spiritual Life. An Evangelical Theology of Renewal* (Exeter: Paternoster Press, 1979).

M. Luther, *Luther's Works* (Philadelphia: Fortress Press, 1955–).

M. Luther, *Luther: Letters of Spiritual Counsel*, translated and edited by T. Tappert. *LCC*, vol. 18 (London: SCM, 1955).

U. Luz, 'The Disciples in the Gospel according to Matthew', in G. N. Stanton (ed), *The Interpretation of Matthew* (London: SPCK, 1983), pp. 98–128.

R. Macaulay and J. Barrs, *Christianity with a Human Face* (Leicester: IVP, 1978).

E. McCracken (trans and ed), *Early Medieval Theology. LCC*, vol. 9 (London: SCM, 1957).

D. McGavran, *Understanding Church Growth* (Grand Rapids: Eerdmans, 1970).

H. R. Mackintosh, *The Christian Experience of Forgiveness* (London: Collins, 1961).

H. R. Mackintosh, *Types of Modern Theology* (London: Fontana, 1964).

I. F. McIntosh, *Pastoral Care and Pastoral Theology* (Edinburgh: St Andrew Press, 1972).

J. T. McNeill, *A History of the Cure of Souls* (New York: Harper & Row, 1977).

F. MacNutt, *Healing* (Notre Dame, Indiana: Ave Maria Press, 1974).

R. Maddox, *The Purpose of Luke-Acts* (Edinburgh: T. & T. Clark, 1982).

A. J. Malherbe, 'Gentle as a Nurse. The Gnostic Background to 1 Thessalonians ii', *Nov. T* 12 (1970), pp. 203–217.

I. H. Marshall, *The Epistles of John. NICNT* (Grand Rapids: Eerdmans, 1978).

I. H. Marshall, *Luke – Historian and Theologian* (Exeter: Paternoster Press, 1979).

I. H. Marshall (ed), *New Testament Interpretation* (Exeter: Paternoster Press, 1977).

I. H. Marshall, 'Pauline Theology in the Thessalonian Correspondence', in M. D. Hooker and S. G. Wilson (eds), *Paul and Paulinism* (London: SPCK, 1982), pp. 173–183.

I. H. Marshall, *1 and 2 Thessalonians. NCB* (Grand Rapids: Eerdmans, 1983).

R. P. Martin, *Mark – Evangelist and Theologian* (Exeter: Paternoster Press, 1979).

R. P. Martin, *New Testament Foundations*, 2 vols (Grand Rapids: Eerdmans, 1975, 1978).

E. Massaux, *Influence de l'évangile de Saint Matthieu sur la Litera-ture Chrétienne avant Saint Irenée* (Louvain: Publications Univ-ersitaires, 1950).

H. T. Mayer, *Pastoral Care, Its Roots and Renewal* (Philadelphia: John Knox Press, 1979).

W. A. Meeks, 'The Man from Heaven in Johannine Sectarianism', *JBL* 91 (1972), pp. 44–72.

F. van der Meer, *Augustine the Bishop* (London and New York: Sheed & Ward, 1961).

P. S. Minear, 'Dear Theo (The Kerygmatic Intention and Claim of the Book of Acts)', *Interp.* 27 (1973), pp. 131–150.

C. L. Mitton, *The Epistle of James* (London and Edinburgh: Marshall, Morgan & Scott, 1966).

L. Morris, *Commentary on the Gospel of John. NICNT* (Grand Rapids: Eerdmans, 1971).

L. Morris, *Luke. TNTC* (London: IVP, 1974).

C. F. D. Moule, 'The Individualism of the Fourth Gospel', in *Essays in New Testament Interpretation* (Cambridge: CUP, 1982), pp. 91–109.

R. H. Mounce, *The Book of Revelation. NICNT* (Grand Rapids: Eerdmans, 1977).

W. Munro, *Authority in Paul and Peter. SNTS Monograph 45* (Cambridge: CUP, 1983).

I. H. Murray, *D. Martyn Lloyd-Jones: The First Forty Years 1899–1939* (Edinburgh: Banner of Truth Trust, 1982).

J. Myrc, *Instructions for Parish Priests* (London: Early English Text Society, 1868).

G. Neal, 'The Call to the Ministry – Some Midpoint Reflections', *The Fraternal* (October 1984), pp. 9–16.

H. R. Niebuhr and D. D. Williams (eds), *The Ministry in Historical Perspective* (New York: Harper & Row, 1983).

C. R. North, *The Second Isaiah* (Oxford: OUP, 1964).

W. L. Northridge, *Psychology and Pastoral Practice* (London: Epworth Press, 1938).

The Nottingham Statement. The Official Statement of the Second National Evangelical Anglican Congress (London: Falcon, 1977).

H. J. M. Nouwen, *Creative Ministry* (New York: Image, 1978).

H. J. M. Nouwen, *The Wounded Healer* (New York: Doubleday, 1972).

G. F. Nuttall, *Richard Baxter* (London: Nelson, 1965).

W. Oates, *The Bible in Pastoral Care* (Philadelphia: Westminster Press, 1953).

W. Oates, *The Christian Pastor* (Philadelphia: Westminster Press, 1964).

W. Oates, *Protestant Pastoral Counselling* (Philadelphia: Westminster Press, 1962).

T. C. Oden, *Kerygma and Counselling* (Philadelphia: Westminster Press, 1966).

T. C. Oden, *Pastoral Theology: Essentials of Ministry* (San Francisco: Harper & Row, 1983).

W. B. Oglesby Jnr (ed), *The New Shape of Pastoral Theology. Essays in Honour of Seward Hiltner* (Nashville: Abingdon Press, 1969).

W. B. Oglesby Jnr, 'Pastoral Care and Counselling in Biblical Perspective' *Interp.* 26 (1973), pp. 307–326.

W. B. Oglesby Jnr, 'Present Status and Future Prospects in Pastoral Theology', *Pastoral Psychology* 29 (1980), pp. 36–45.

J. J. van Oosterzee, *Practical Theology* (London: Hodder & Stoughton, 1889).

T. H. L. Parker, *John Calvin* (London: Dent & Sons, 1975).

L. Paul, *A Church by Daylight* (London: Geoffrey Chapman, 1973).

L. Paul, *The Deployment and Payment of the Clergy* (London: CIO Publishing, 1964).

G. L. Phillips, 'Faith and Vision in the Fourth Gospel', in F. L. Cross (ed), *Studies in the Fourth Gospel* (London: Mowbray, 1957), pp. 83–96.

H. D. Rack, 'The Decline of the Class Meeting and the Problem of Church Membership in Nineteenth-century Wesleyanism', *Proceedings of the Wesleyan Historical Society* 39 (1973), pp. 12–21.

G. von Rad, *Old Testament Theology* (Edinburgh and London: Oliver & Boyd, 1962).

G. von Rad, *Wisdom in Israel* (London: SCM, 1972).

K. Rahner, *Theological Investigations*, vols. 10 and 11 (London: Darton, Longman & Todd, 1973, 1974).

A. M. Ramsey, *The Christian Priest Today* (London: SPCK, 1972).

S. Ransom, A. Bryman and R. Hinings, *Clergy, Ministers and Priests* (London: Routledge & Kegan Paul, 1983).

K. H. Rengstorf, *'Huperetēs'*, *TDNT*, vol. 8 (Grand Rapids: Eerdmans, 1972), pp. 530–544.

H. Ridderbos, *Paul. An Outline of His Theology*, (Grand Rapids: Eerdmans, 1975).

T. Rowe, *St Augustine, Pastoral Theologian* (London: Epworth Press, 1974).

P. F. Rudge, *Management in the Church* (London: McGraw Hill, 1976).

A. Russell, *The Clerical Profession* (London: SPCK, 1980).

J. O. Sanders, *Men from God's School* (London: Lakeland, 1974).

F. A. Schaeffer, *True Spirituality* (Wheaton: Tyndale House, 1971).

L. Schaller, *The Change Agent* (Nashville: Abingdon Press, 1972).

E. Schillebeeckx, *Ministry* (London: SCM, 1981).

F. D. Schleiermacher, *Brief Outline of the Study of Theology*, translated by T. N. Tice (Atlanta: John Knox Press, 1966).

J. H. Schütz, *Paul and the Anatomy of Apostolic Authority*. SNTS Monograph 26 (Cambridge: CUP, 1975).

E. G. Selwyn, *The First Epistle of Peter* (London: Macmillan, 1946).

G. Shaw, *The Cost of Authority. Manipulation and Freedom in the New Testament* (Philadelphia: Fortress Press, 1982).

W. G. T. Shedd, *Homiletics and Pastoral Theology* (London: Banner of Truth, 1965).

E. E. Shelp and R. Sunderland (eds), *A Biblical Basis for Ministry* (Philadelphia: Westminster Press, 1981).

D. S. Sheppard, *Bias to the Poor* (London: Hodder & Stoughton, 1983).

D. S. Sheppard, *Built as a City* (London: Hodder & Stoughton, 1974).

D. S. Sheppard, 'The poverty that imprisons the spirit', *The Listener*, 19 April 1984, pp. 8–12.

T. Smail, *Reflected Glory* (London: Hodder & Stoughton, 1975).

S. Smalley, *John: Evangelist and Interpreter* (Exeter: Paternoster Press, 1978).

C. E. Smith, *Innocent III: Church Defender* (Louisiana: Louisiana State University, 1951).

D. M. Smith, 'Theology and Ministry in John', in E. E. Shelp and R. Sunderland (eds), *A Biblical Basis for Ministry* (Philadelphia: Westminster Press, 1981).

G. A. Smith, *The Book of Isaiah*, vol. 2 (London: Hodder & Stoughton, 1897).

R. W. Southern, *Western Society and the Church in the Middle Ages* (Harmondsworth: Penguin, 1970).

C. H. Spurgeon, *An All-Round Ministry* (London: Passmore & Alibaster, 1900).

C. H. Spurgeon, *The Early Years* (London: Banner of Truth, 1962).

C. H. Spurgeon, *Lectures to my Students* (London: Marshall, Morgan & Scott, 1962).

M. Staniforth (trans), *Early Christian Writings* (Harmondsworth: Penguin, 1968).

G. N. Stanton, 'Introduction: Matthew's Gospel: A New Storm Centre', in G. N. Stanton (ed), *The Interpretation of Matthew* (London: SPCK, 1983), pp. 1–19.

A. M. Stibbs, *The First Epistle General of Peter. TNTC* (London: Tyndale Press, 1959).

W. Still, *The Work of the Pastor* (Aberdeen: Didasko Press, 1976).

J. R. W. Stott, *The Epistles of John. TNTC* (London: Tyndale Press, 1964).

J. R. W. Stott, *Issues Facing Christians Today* (Basingstoke: Marshalls, 1984).

J. R. W. Stott, *The Message of Ephesians. God's New Society. BST* (Leicester: IVP, 1979).

J. R. W. Stott, *The Message of 2 Timothy. Guard the Gospel. BST* (London: IVP, 1973).

J. R. W. Stott, *One People* (London: Falcon, 1969).

B. H. Streeter, *The Primitive Church: studied with special reference to the origins of the Christian Ministry* (London: Macmillan, 1929).

J. Sweet, *Revelation. SCM Pelican Commentaries* (London: SCM, 1979).

S. Sykes, *Friedrich Schleiermacher* (London: Lutterworth Press, 1971).

J. B. Taylor, *Ezekiel. TOTC* (London: Tyndale Press, 1969).

M. H. Taylor, *Learning to Care, Christian Reflection on Pastoral Practice* (London: SPCK, 1983).

W. Temple, *Readings in St John's Gospel* (London: Macmillan, 1968).

Tertullian, *On Baptism. A-NCL*, vol. 11 (Edinburgh: T. & T.

Clark, 1869).

G. Theissen, *The Social Setting of Pauline Christianity* (Edinburgh: T. & T. Clark, 1982).

J. A. Thompson, *Deuteronomy. TOTC* (London: IVP, 1974).

W. G. Thompson, *Matthew's Advice to a Divided Community* (Rome: Biblical Institute Press, 1970).

M. Thornton, *The Function of Theology* (London: Hodder & Stoughton, 1968).

M. Thornton, *Pastoral Theology: A Reorientation* (London: SPCK, 1956).

E. Thurneysen, *A Theology of Pastoral Care* (Richmond: John Knox Press, 1962).

D. J. Tidball, *An Introduction to the Sociology of the New Testament* (Exeter: Paternoster Press, 1983).

J. Tiller, *A Strategy for the Church's Ministry* (London: CIO Publishing, 1983).

R. B. Tollinton, *Clement of Alexandria*, vol. 1 (London: Williams & Norgate, 1914).

P. Tournier, *Guilt and Grace* (London: Hodder & Stoughton, 1974).

R. Towler and A. P. M. Coxon, *The Fate of the Anglican Clergy* (London: Macmillan, 1979).

E. Troeltsch, *The Social Teachings of the Christian Churches*, vol. 2 (London: George Allen & Unwin, 1931).

A. Vinet, *Pastoral Theology* (Edinburgh: T. & T. Clark, 1853).

P. Vitz, *Psychology as Religion* (Grand Rapids: Eerdmans, 1977).

S. Volbeda, *The Pastoral Genius of Preaching* (Grand Rapids: Zondervan, 1960).

G. S. M. Walker, *The Churchmanship of St Cyprian* (London: Lutterworth Press, 1968).

G. S. M. Walker, *The Growing Storm. Sketches of Church History from AD 600 to AD 1350* (London: Paternoster Press, 1961).

A. Wallis, *The Radical Christian* (Eastbourne: Kingsway Publications, 1981).

A. F. Walls, 'Introduction' to A. M. Stibbs, *The First Epistle General of Peter. TNTC* (London: Tyndale Press, 1959).

E. Waterhouse, *Psychology and Pastoral Work* (London: Hodder & Stoughton, 1939).

D. Watson, *Fear No Evil* (London: Hodder & Stoughton, 1984).

D. Watson, *In Search of God* (London: Falcon, 1974).

D. Webster, 'Simeon's Pastoral Theology', in A. Pollard and M. Hennell (eds), *Charles Simeon 1759–1836* (London: SPCK, 1959), pp. 73–119.

K.-H. Weger, *Karl Rahner: An Introduction to His Theology* (London: Burns & Oates, 1980).

J. Wesley, *Letters*. Standard Edition, edited by J. Telford. 8 vols (London: Epworth Press, 1931).

J. Wesley, *Sermons on Several Occasions*, edited by J. Beecham, vol. 3 (London: Wesleyan Conference Office, 1876).

M. West, *The World is Made of Glass* (London: Hodder & Stoughton, 1983).

C. Westermann, *Isaiah 40–66. OTL* (London: SCM, 1969).

J. A. Wharton, 'Theology of Ministry of the Hebrew Scriptures', in E. E. Shelp and R. Sunderland (eds), *A Biblical Basis for Ministry* (Philadelphia: Westminster Press, 1981).

J. White, *The Masks of Melancholy* (Leicester: IVP, 1982).

R. E. O. White, *An Open Letter to Evangelicals* (Exeter: Paternoster Press, 1964).

J. A. Whyte, 'New Directions in Practical Theology', *Theology* 76 (1973), p. 235.

D. D. Williams, *The Minister and the Care of Souls* (New York: Harper & Row, 1977. First published 1971).

G. H. Williams, 'The Ministry in the Ante-Nicene Church' and 'The Ministry in the Later Patristic Period', in H. R. Niebuhr and D. D. Williams (eds), *The Ministry in Historical Perspective* (New York: Harper & Row, 1983).

B. Wilson, *Religion in Sociological Perspective* (Oxford: OUP, 1982).

S. G. Wilson, *The Gentiles and the Gentile Mission in Luke-Acts* SNTS Monograph 23 (Cambridge: CUP 1973).

R. Winter, 'Jay Adams – is he really biblical enough?', *Third Way* 5/4 (1982), pp. 9–12.

C. A. Wise, *The Meaning of Pastoral Care* (New York: Harper & Row, 1966).

C. A. Wise, *Psychiatry and the Bible* (New York: Harper & Row, 1956).

C. A. Wise, *Religion in Illness and Health* (New York: Harper & Row, 1942).

H. W. Wolff, *Anthropology of the Old Testament* (London: SCM, 1974).

A. S. Wood, *The Inextinguishable Blaze* (Exeter: Paternoster Press, 1967).

F. Wright, *The Pastoral Nature of the Ministry* (London: SCM, 1980).

W. Zimmerli, *Man and his Hope in the Old Testament* (London: SCM, 1971).

W. Zimmerli, *Old Testament Theology in Outline* (Edinburgh: T. & T. Clark, 1978).

J. van Zyl, 'John Calvin the Pastor', in *The Way Ahead*. Papers read to the Carey Conference 1975 (Haywards Heath: Carey Publications, 1975), pp. 69–78.

Index of biblical references

General index